T0332895

# Digital Transformation for Promoting Inclusiveness in Marginalized Communities

Munyaradzi Zhou
*Midlands State University, Zimbabwe*

Gilbert Mahlangu
*Midlands State University, Zimbabwe*

Cyncia Matsika
*Midlands State University, Zimbabwe*

A volume in the Advances in IT
Standards and Standardization
Research (AITSSR) Book Series

Published in the United States of America by
    IGI Global
    Engineering Science Reference (an imprint of IGI Global)
    701 E. Chocolate Avenue
    Hershey PA, USA 17033
    Tel: 717-533-8845
    Fax:  717-533-8661
    E-mail: cust@igi-global.com
    Web site: http://www.igi-global.com

Library of Congress Cataloging-in-Publication Data

Names: Zhou, Munyaradzi, 1983- editor. | Mahlangu, Gilbert, 1978- editor. |
    Matsika, Cyncia, 1985- editor.
Title: Digital transformation for promoting inclusiveness in marginalized
    communities / Munyaradzi Zhou, Gilbert Mahlangu, and Cyncia Matsika,
    editors.
Description: Hershey, PA : Engineering Science Reference, [2022] | Includes
    bibliographical references and index. | Summary: "This book harnesses
    digital transformation in promoting inclusiveness in marginalized
    communities through exploring opportunities and challenges for digital
    inclusion in marginalized communities and determining change mechanisms
    required to enhance digital transformation so those communities have the
    opportunity to participate in all sectors of the economy"-- Provided by
    publisher.
Identifiers: LCCN 2022970054 (print) | LCCN 2022970055 (ebook) | ISBN
    9781668439012 (hardcover) | ISBN 9781668439029 (paperback) | ISBN
    9781668439036 (ebook)
Subjects: LCSH: Digital divide. | Information society. | Equality.
Classification: LCC HM851 .D545228 2022  (print) | LCC HM851  (ebook) | DDC
    302.2/31--dc23/eng/20220302
LC record available at https://lccn.loc.gov/2022970054
LC ebook record available at https://lccn.loc.gov/2022970055

This book is published in the IGI Global book series Advances in IT Standards and Standardization Research (AITSSR) (ISSN: 1935-3391; eISSN: 1935-3405)

British Cataloguing in Publication Data
A Cataloguing in Publication record for this book is available from the British Library.

All work contributed to this book is new, previously-unpublished material.
The views expressed in this book are those of the authors, but not necessarily of the publisher.

For electronic access to this publication, please contact: eresources@igi-global.com.

# Advances in IT Standards and Standardization Research (AITSSR) Book Series

ISSN:1935-3391
EISSN:1935-3405

Editor-in-Chief: Kai Jakobs RWTH Aachen University, Germany

## MISSION

IT standards and standardization are a necessary part of effectively delivering IT and IT services to organizations and individuals, as well as streamlining IT processes and minimizing organizational cost. In implementing IT standards, it is necessary to take into account not only the technical aspects, but also the characteristics of the specific environment where these standards will have to function.

The **Advances in IT Standards and Standardization Research (AITSSR) Book Series** seeks to advance the available literature on the use and value of IT standards and standardization. This research provides insight into the use of standards for the improvement of organizational processes and development in both private and public sectors.

## COVERAGE

- Standards for information infrastructures
- Standards Research and Education Activities
- Descriptive Theory of Standardization
- Conformity assessment
- Open source and standardization
- Intellectual Property Rights
- Economics of Standardization
- Emerging roles of formal standards Organizations and consortia
- Management of Standards
- Prescriptive Theory of Standardization

IGI Global is currently accepting manuscripts for publication within this series. To submit a proposal for a volume in this series, please contact our Acquisition Editors at Acquisitions@igi-global.com or visit: http://www.igi-global.com/publish/.

# Titles in this Series

For a list of additional titles in this series, please visit:
www.igi-global.com/book-series/advances-standards-standardization-research/37142

*Handbook of Research on Evolving Designs and Innovation in ICT and Intelligent Systems for Real-World Applications*
Kandarpa Kumar Sarma (Gauhati University, India) Navajit Saikia (Assam Engineering College, India) and Mridusmita Sharma (Gauhati University, India)
Engineering Science Reference • © 2022 • 430pp • H/C (ISBN: 9781799897958) • US $380.00

*The Strategies of Informing Technology in the 21st Century*
Andrew Targowski (Independent Researcher, USA)
Engineering Science Reference • © 2022 • 557pp • H/C (ISBN: 9781799880363) • US $240.00

*Developing Countries and Technology Inclusion in the 21st Century Information Society*
Alice S. Etim (Winston Salem State University, USA)
Information Science Reference • © 2021 • 318pp • H/C (ISBN: 9781799834687) • US $205.00

*IT Auditing Using a System Perspective*
Robert Elliot Davis (Walden University, USA)
Information Science Reference • © 2020 • 260pp • H/C (ISBN: 9781799841982) • US $215.00

*Handbook of Research on the Evolution of IT and the Rise of E-Society*
Maki Habib (The American University in Cairo, Egypt)
Information Science Reference • © 2019 • 602pp • H/C (ISBN: 9781522572145) • US $245.00

*Global Implications of Emerging Technology Trends*
Francisco José García-Peñalvo (University of Salamanca, Spain)
Information Science Reference • © 2018 • 323pp • H/C (ISBN: 9781522549444) • US $185.00

IGI Global
PUBLISHER of TIMELY KNOWLEDGE

701 East Chocolate Avenue, Hershey, PA 17033, USA
Tel: 717-533-8845 x100 • Fax: 717-533-8661
E-Mail: cust@igi-global.com • www.igi-global.com

# List of Reviewers

Jooste Carlien, *Sefako Makgatho Health Sciences University, South Africa*
Gombiro Cross, *Bindura University of Science Education, Zimbabwe*
Kuranga Cry, *University of Pretoria, South Africa*
Denga Edna, *American University of Nigeria, Nigeria*
Chengetanai Gibson, *Botswana Accountancy College, Botswana*
Motjolopane Ignitia, *North-West University, South Africa*
Zvarevashe Kudakwashe, *University Zimbabwe, Zimbabwe*
Chitanana Lockias, *Midlands State University, Zimbabwe*
Sambo Paul, *Great Zimbabwe University, Zimbabwe*
Musungwini Samuel, *Midlands State University, Zimbabwe*
Marambi Sheltar, *Midlands State University, Zimbabwe*
Furusa Samuel Simbarashe, *Midlands State University, Zimbabwe*
Chitata Tavengwa, *Midlands State University, Zimbabwe*

# Table of Contents

# Detailed Table of Contents

**Chapter 1**
*Gilbert Mahlangu, Midlands State University, Zimbabwe*
*Munyaradzi Zhou, Midlands State University, Zimbabwe*
*Cyncia Matsika, Midlands State University, Zimbabwe*

Fully participating in the digital economy involves understanding enabling factors for digital inclusion. The chapter analyzed and synthesized existing knowledge on factors that could enhance digital inclusion in marginalized communities. The factors that enable digital inclusion for marginalized communities in developing economies were extracted and mapped into a taxonomy table using thematic analysis and constant comparative analysis, and they were clustered into five multidimensional constructs: digital access, attitude, digital skills, actual usage, and impact of digital inclusion. These factors act as enablers in speeding up digital inclusion—they form a vigorous model for driving digital inclusion and evaluating digital initiatives in marginalized communities. A model to ensure digital inclusion initiatives to address the realities faced by those who have been marginalized from the digital economy by moving away from an inclusive digital approach that is grounded on a technological perspective is developed.

**Chapter 2**
*Cyncia Matsika, Midlands State University, Zimbabwe*
*Munyaradzi Zhou, Midlands State University, Zimbabwe*
*Gilbert Mahlangu, Midlands State University, Zimbabwe*

Information communication technologies (ICTs) to support teaching and learning in marginalized communities is a major drawback that alienates developing countries from the digital space. This chapter proffers digital inclusion in education for marginalized communities by using and merging cloud computing, augmented, and virtual reality (AVR) technologies. A systematic review of the literature was conducted. Diana Laurilliard's six learning types in the conversational framework was used to establish how digital technology is utilized and widely adopted in education in the context of marginalized communities. AVR technology embedded in the cloud supports all the six learning types and promote digital inclusion in education. A model that marginalized communities can utilize was developed. Future research can develop a model that captures the university-wide curriculum needs of higher institutions of learning in marginalized communities and the training of the educators to use ICTs to reduce the digital divide and improve digital literacy.

**Chapter 3**

    *Njodzi Ranganai, Manicaland State University of Applied Sciences, Zimbabwe*
    *Tendai Shelton Muwani, Manicaland State University of Applied Sciences, Zimbabwe*
    *Nyasha Sakadzo, Manicaland State University of Applied Sciences, Zimbabwe*
    *Andrew Tapiwa Kugedera, Zimbabwe Open University, Zimbabwe*
    *Florence Chimbwanda, Zimbabwe Open University, Zimbabwe*
    *Lemias Zivanai, Midlands State University, Zimbabwe*
    *Briget Munyoro, Midlands State University, Zimbabwe*

Digitalization is an important agriculture tool for achieving the Sustainable Development Goals (SDGs) in marginalized and remote communities. There is a scarcity of data linking digitalization, sustainable agriculture production, marginalized and remote communities in Sub-Saharan Africa. This study reviews digitalization for sustainable agriculture production in marginalized and remote communities of Sub-Saharan Africa. A total of 150 published papers from 2000-2022 were retrieved, and all those outside Africa were removed to leave a total of 125 papers. Results obtained indicate that digital technology transforms agriculture by promoting precision agriculture in marginalized rural communities in a more efficient approach by integrating different processes. Econet Wireless Zimbabwe is offering various bundle options which come through small messages (SMS) and call centers such as Eco-Farmer. Governments should invest in and make policies to improve digitalization in marginalized communities as it ultimately solves challenges such as nutrition, food insecurity, and climate change.

## Chapter 4

*Njodzi Ranganai, Manicaland State University of Applied Sciences,*
*Zimbabwe*
*Tendai Shelton Muwani, Manicaland State University of Applied*
*Sciences, Zimbabwe*
*Lemias Zivanai, Midlands State University, Zimbabwe*
*Briget Munyoro, Midlands State University, Zimbabwe*
*Nyasha Sakadzo, Manicaland State University of Applied Sciences,*
*Zimbabwe*

The amalgamation of modern innovation, technological skills, and processes used to establish business models and satisfy customers in different societies is referred to as digital transformation. Digital transformation facilitates the development of economies, ways of doing business, and social constructs among marginalized communities. Digital inclusiveness has significantly been applied in a number of areas in communities and resource-constrained environments such as health, education, and agriculture. A systematic literature review was carried out. The authors find out that inclusiveness has great opportunities and challenges in digitally transforming marginalized communities. The implementation of interconnected digital innovation technologies provides new challenges and opportunities spanning the whole of Africa. This chapter explores the key drivers of digital technologies, the contribution of technology, gender imbalances, and challenges and opportunities for digital inclusiveness in remote areas.

## Chapter 5

*Samuel Musungwini, Midlands State University, Zimbabwe*
*Petros Venganayi Gavai, Midlands State University, Zimbabwe*
*Samuel Simbarashe Furusa, Midlands State University, Zimbabwe*
*Raviro Gumbo, Midlands State University, Zimbabwe*

This chapter looks at Zimbabwe, a developing country in Sub-Saharan Africa that aspires to reach an upper-middle-income economy by 2030 through digital inclusiveness. Digital transformation (DT) and digital innovation (DI) may be the fundamental foundation to attain economic growth and productivity. To transit to Society 5.0, nations should develop robust technological systems, powerful, knowledgeable human resources, and a strategic direction policy by harnessing (DT) and (DI). A qualitative stance is applied using in-depth interviews and focus group discussions. Digital innovation identifies issues characterizing marginal communities in Zimbabwe that must be addressed to ensure that digital transformation targets rural areas, border posts, the informal sector, smallholder farmers, artisanal miners, vendors, and women (rural). The chapter then climaxes with a framework that if implemented may usher in Society 5.0, which may ensure that people, things, and technologies are all interconnected and intersect in the cyber and physical spaces.

# Chapter 6

This chapter approached the national digital policy as a target for bridging the digital divide to gain digital dividends that will help in socio-economic development. The chapter argues that digital dividends are key to developing countries as they have helped break the digital divide that has been there for so long. Nevertheless, the findings reveal that some marginalized communities exist in developing countries like Zimbabwe, especially semi-urban and rural communities. Zimbabwe is yet to strengthen the pillars of digital transformation. The chapter recommends that the government and regulators consider taking the outside-in strategy to narrow the digital divide in the country.

# Chapter 7

Digital transformation is happening at a considerable rate in the developing world; however, its adoption seems higher in the developed world. Therefore, this chapter aims to present the key drivers or pillars that make up digital transformation in developing countries. The chapter argued that strategy, technology, and innovation are the broad categories that influence digital transformation in any country, whether developing or developed. Also, the chapter articulates what has been happening in the developing world, focusing on Southern Africa to achieve digital transformation. A framework for digital transformation that consists of three broad pillars strategy, technology, and innovation was proposed. Lastly, the chapter proposed that future researchers on digital transformation can focus on the broad pillars of digital transformation.

## Chapter 8

*Briget Munyoro, Midlands State University, Zimbabwe*
*Lemias Zivanai, Midlands State University, Zimbabwe*
*Ranganai Njodzi, Manicaland State University of Applied Sciences, Zimbabwe*
*Tendai Shelton Muwani, Manicaland State University of Applied Sciences, Zimbabwe*

Many technologies are referenced in the case of digital transformations, but internet technologies, emerging technologies, internet of things (IoT), analytical technologies, and mobile technologies are the most relevant in this chapter. Internet technologies, a collection of internet-based communication tools, can be used in the digital transformation of marginalized populations. Internet of things help marginalized communities seek opportunities, meet new targets, and minimize threats as people can have physical objects or self-reporting devices that improve productivity and rapidly bring vital information to the surface. When all this information has been collected, there is a need to identify the patterns and trends and produce meaningful insights using the analytical tools. Mobile technologies are technologies that go where a user goes, so communication, buying and selling, and making payments are possible with mobile phones. Governments and corporates should facilitate the adoption of digital technologies to promote digital inclusion in marginalized communities.

## Chapter 9

*Tendai Shelton Muwani, Manicaland State University of Applied Sciences, Zimbabwe*
*Lemias Zivanai, Midlands State University, Zimbabwe*
*Briget Munyoro, Midlands State University, Zimbabwe*
*Njodzi Ranganai, Manicaland State University of Applied Sciences, Zimbabwe*
*Nyasha Chipunza, Manicaland State University of Applied Sciences, Zimbabwe*

Most societies have been in abject poverty owing to a lack of proper education, gender alienation, and socio-economic and political factors. Localized external economies, particularly economies of scale and scope, as small firms specialize and engage in a division of labor, are among the benefits of clustering. Clusters are important because geographical agglomeration has the potential to help small businesses overcome size constraints, advance technologically, and improve competence in local and global markets. The adoption of technologies has the effect of replacing the old way of doing things with manual and mechanical methods. The study examined the potential of clustering to help marginalized communities to become integrated and improve their quality of life in a digital society and concluded that ICTs can, if adopted and used properly, shift and destroy social boundaries between the elite and the segregated. Future research can look at the adoption of digital technologies in marginalized areas.

**Chapter 10**

*Wilfreda Indira Chawarura, Midlands State University, Zimbabwe*
*Rukudzo Alyson Mawere, Midlands State University, Zimbabwe*

The developments in digital technology and information communication technology (ICT) have increased over the past 20 years and improved livelihoods, especially in developed countries with 97% access level to the internet and digital technology. However, those in African countries have had challenges accessing the internet, and the advent of the COVID-19 pandemic exacerbated the situation. The remote areas in Zimbabwe have not been spared as they experience challenges in the adoption of digital technology. Globally people are increasingly using information and communication technology (ICT) as a way of life to communicate, study, and access healthcare and entertainment, amongst other things. Investigating the causes of digital exclusion in general and also in the context of social exclusion in Zimbabwe is pertinent. This chapter seeks to fill a gap in the existing literature by exploring the opportunities and challenges that digital inclusion and exclusion bring to the marginalized societies in Zimbabwe.

**Chapter 11**

*Tendai Shelton Muwani, Manicaland State University of Applied Sciences, Zimbabwe*
*Njodzi Ranganai, Manicaland State University of Applied Sciences, Zimbabwe*
*Lemias Zivanai, Midlands State University, Zimbabwe*
*Briget Munyoro, Midlands State University, Zimbabwe*

The use of digital gadgets and services is pervasive. Digitalization in data, information, and technologies is driving the Fourth Industrial Revolution (also known as 4IR or Industry 4.0), resulting in a global digital divide. The chapter proposes a strategy in collaboration with a variety of service sector partners that would allow governments to capitalize on the possibility of closing the technology gap between nations in a manner that benefits inclusive and sustainable growth in middle and low countries. Emerging revolution and internet access can strengthen socio-economic development and improve people's way of living, but they also have the potential to widen political divides, undermine democracy, and increase inequality. In response to COVID-19, the chapter also proposes digital technologies as tools for achieving sustainable development goals and digitalization response measures in marginalized societies.

## Chapter 12

*Samuel Simbarashe Furusa, Midlands State University, Zimbabwe*
*Samuel Musungwini, Midlands State University, Zimbabwe*
*Petros Venganayi Gavai, Midlands State University, Zimbabwe*
*Melody Maseko, Midlands State University, Zimbabwe*

The chapter explores the concept of digitalization and digital technology and its importance. The research is based on a systematic literature review, which analyzed articles on digitalization and digital technologies. However, primacy was given to articles on the digitalization of organizations in a marginalized context. The chapter identified the critical success factors and formulation of a digitalization strategy formulation for the transformation of marginalized communities in Zimbabwe. Therefore, the authors highlight the need to explore human-centered digital transformation capabilities and dynamic capabilities in developing countries. The chapter then formulated a strategy for the digitalization of marginalized communities in a developing context.

# Preface

Globally, digital transformation has become the pinnacle of any community as most societies are seemingly becoming digital. Digital technology has significantly impacted how societies function in developed and developing countries alike. In the discourse of digital transformation, Information Communication Technologies (ICTs) are the key infrastructures enabling various marginalized communities to join and participate in the digital economy. The developments in digital technology and Information Communication Technology (ICT) have increased over the past twenty years and improved livelihoods, especially in developed countries with 97% access level to the internet and digital technology. People are increasingly using ICTs as a way of life to communicate, study, and access health care and entertainment, amongst other uses. The landscape underlying digital transformation for marginalized community clusters reflects larger transitions and expansion of the rural economy, healthcare services, agriculture, and education.

One of the realities characterizing the globe (Global South and North) is the exclusion of marginalized communities in digital transformation. Marginalized communities are severely left behind in the digital transformation drive because of remoteness and economic marginalization. People living in marginalized communities are rarely considered in the digital transformation process. Often marginalized communities suffer from severe material deprivation, which leads to more challenging living conditions because of accentuated migration, school abandonment, disabilities, very few workplaces, subsistence agriculture, low life expectancy, and absence of consumer goods, among other factors. Consequently, their exclusion has resulted in a lack of participation in the digital space and bigger economy, and living in this reality has catastrophic consequences for the digital economy. This is because digitally excluded communities cannot access various digital services that impact health, commerce, agriculture, and education, to mention a few. To promote digital inclusiveness in marginalized communities in the Global South, there is a need to deconstruct the illusion that digital transformation is an urban phenomenon.

Digital inclusion is still a long way, especially in marginalized communities. The deployment of ICTs in rural areas has not fully transformed the lives of those living in marginalized communities. Rural communities in developing economies are still battling marginalization due to a lack of digital inclusion. Economic marginalization makes it difficult for marginalized people to access the internet and computing devices constantly. They usually find themselves in the peripherals of digital inclusion because there is low penetration of internet and broadband infrastructures. Developing economies have not developed comprehensive digital inclusion initiatives to promote inclusivity in the digital economy. The current practice, which focuses on deploying ICT infrastructure, village halls, telecentres, and community information centres (CICs) in rural areas to promote universal access, has not significantly enhanced digital inclusion.

The digital transformation offers a prospect to invigorate efforts to attain the Sustainable Development Goals (SDGs) by 2030 and reconsider methods toward rural development. According to the United Nations Development Programme (UNDP) standpoint, inclusive digital transformation involves enhancing the availability, accessibility, and adoption of digital technologies for everyone. However, the advancement in technology, though welcoming and improving the livelihood of the society and economies, had varying opportunities and outcomes for different population subgroups. Technology has put the world many steps ahead even though, in some instances, its emergence unearthed a separation and exclusion of communities in the digital universe.

Inclusive digital transformation ensures that digital technologies are collectively available, accessible, and embraced and allow profound use of the Internet and digital services for all. This involves a meticulously constructed and executed transformation procedure aimed at maximizing the advantages of the digitalization of societies and alleviating the propensity of digital transformation to aggravate current digital inequalities. Information systems research has made visible contributions to dissecting issues related to digital inclusion. Globally, several studies have reported ICT access and usage as the key factors driving digital inclusion. Contemporary debates on digital inclusion argue that there is a need to recognize digital inclusion as a multifaceted phenomenon comprising dimensions rooted in socio-economic structures such as skills, engagement, attitude, and participation rather than understanding it (digital inclusion) solely in terms of access. Useful attempts to an inclusive digital transformation look beyond ICTs to ensure that other digital transformation mechanisms accentuate inclusion. Thus, digital inclusion is more than just the penetration of ICTs.

Therefore, fully participating in the digital economy involves understanding enabling factors for digital inclusion, which can be classified as follows: Digital Access, Attitude, Digital Skills, Actual Usage, and Impact of digital inclusion. Rapid technological change without a systematic approach to inclusive and sustainable development risks entrenching existing inequities with respect to who can access, use, and benefit from these interventions while creating new ones. Governments in developing economies should engage in public-private initiatives to ensure that all areas have access to telecommunication infrastructure and ensure marginalized communities are digitally included. These synergistic partnerships can lead to establishing basic and relevant infrastructure to ensure affordable and robust broadband and access in rural communities and other communities that do not have access. The involvement of the government in enacting laws and regulations to promote digital transformation is a critical component of achieving digitalization. Thus, developing a clear vision for digital collaboration and the future must become a top priority of governments in developing economies. As a result, the book aims to promote digital inclusion in marginalized communities by discovering digital technologies, digital inclusion factors, and approaches that can help marginalized communities become inclusive.

## TARGET AUDIENCE

Since digital transformation is perceived as an ecosystem comprising various activities, this book will be of particular interest to governments, non-governmental organizations, academia, research, industry, marginalized communities, and technopreneurs.

## ORGANIZATION OF THE BOOK

The book is organized into 12 chapters. A brief description of each of the chapters follows:

Chapter 1 analyzed and synthesized existing knowledge to find factors that could enhance digital inclusion in marginalized communities. The chapter argues that digital inclusion is a precondition for participating in the digital economy; therefore, fully participating in the digital economy involves understanding enabling factors for digital inclusion. The findings from this study revealed the underlying mechanisms shaping digital inclusion in the discourse of digital transformation for developing economies and act as an instrument for driving digital inclusion for marginalized communities.

Chapter 2 proffers digital inclusion in education for marginalized communities by using and merging Cloud Computing, Augmented and Virtual Reality (AVR) technologies. Diana Laurilliard's Six Learning types in the Conversational Framework was used to establish how digital technology is utilized and widely adopted in education in the context of marginalized communities. A model which marginalized communities can utilize was developed. The authors argued that future research could develop a model that captures the university-wide curriculum needs of higher institutions of learning in marginalized communities and the training of the educators to use ICTs to reduce the digital divide and improve digital literacy.

Chapter 3 explored digitalization for sustainable agriculture production in marginalized and remote communities of Sub-Saharan Africa. The chapter reveals that digital technology transforms agriculture by promoting precision agriculture in marginalized rural communities. The authors argued that digitalization is one of the recipes for sustainable agriculture in achieving United Nations (UN) sustainable development goals (SDGs) in marginalized and remote communities. Since digital innovation technologies in farming activities have altered agricultural practice, the chapter concludes that digital innovation technologies and digital inclusion of sustainable agriculture should become the center of an attraction throughout the farming cycle.

Chapter 4 investigated the challenges and opportunities for digital inclusion in marginalized communities. The chapter argues that the implementation of interconnected digital innovation technologies provides new challenges and opportunities spanning the whole of Africa. The chapter found that digital inclusiveness offers a variety of challenges and opportunities to marginalized communities. Access, affordability, and lack of digital skills were the major challenges confronting marginalized communities. The chapter concludes that digital transformation in marginalized communities can be achieved by addressing the factors promoting marginalization in rural communities.

Chapter 5 alludes that digital transformation (DT) and digital innovation (DI) may be the fundamental foundation to attain economic growth, and productivity. A framework was developed and its implementation may usher in Society 5.0, which may ensure that people, things, and technologies are all interconnected and intersect in the cyber and physical spaces.

Chapter 6 approached the national digital policy as a target for bridging the digital divide to gain digital dividends that will help in socio-economic development. The chapter argues that digital dividends are key to developing countries as they have helped break the digital divide that has been there for so long. Nevertheless, the findings reveal that some marginalized communities exist in developing countries like Zimbabwe, especially semi-urban and rural communities. Zimbabwe is yet to strengthen the pillars of digital transformation. The chapter recommends that the government and regulators consider taking the 'outside-in' strategy to narrow the digital divide in the country.

Chapter 7 presented the key drivers or pillars that make up digital transformation. The chapter argued that strategy, technology, and innovation are the broad categories that influence digital transformation in any country, whether developing or developed.

Also, the chapter articulates what has been happening in the developing world, focusing on Southern Africa to achieve digital transformation. A framework for digital transformation that consists of three broad pillars strategy, technology, and innovation was proposed. Lastly, the chapter proposed that future researchers on digital transformation can focus on the broad pillars of digital transformation.

Chapter 8 identified technologies such as internet, Internet of Things (IoT), analytical, and mobile technologies as the most relevant in digitally transforming marginalized communities. The authors revealed that many social movements had been made feasible by technological advancements such as the Internet, which have allowed previously marginalized groups to express themselves and coordinate campaigns to effect change. The chapter highlighted that digital technologies provide solutions for the marginalized through e-health, e-governance, poverty alleviation, and the inclusion of people with special needs. The authors strongly recommend that governments, corporates, and individuals should use some or all mentioned technologies to reduce marginalization in communities.

Chapter 9 sought to determine the clusters for digital transformation that can help marginalized communities become more integrated and improve their quality of life in a digital society. Clusters are geographically concentrated groups of intertwined producers, corporate entities, suppliers, and related institutions that generate direct and indirect collaborations, culminating in market integration. In the context of this research, clusters of transformation were based on three pillars: education, health, and agriculture.

Chapter 10 investigates the causes of digital exclusion in general and in the context of social exclusion in Zimbabwe. This chapter seeks to fill a gap in the existing literature by exploring the opportunities and challenges that digital inclusion and exclusion bring to the marginalized societies in Zimbabwe. The chapter reports that most developing countries are in the first level of the digital divide, primarily about access to digital devices and the internet. The chapter recommends that the government should engage in public-private initiatives to ensure all areas have access to telecommunication infrastructure and ensure that marginalized communities are digitally included.

Chapter 11 proposes a strategy that would allow governments to seize the opportunity to close the digital divide between nations and people to promote inclusive economic growth in low- and middle-income countries in collaboration with a diverse range of public and private sector partners. In response to COVID-19, the chapter also proposes digital technologies as tools for achieving sustainable development goals and digitalization response measures in marginalized societies.

Chapter 12 explores the concept of digitalization and digital technology and its importance. The chapter identified the critical success factors and formulation of a digitalization strategy formulation for the transformation of marginalized communities in Zimbabwe. Therefore, we highlight the need to explore human-cantered digital transformation capabilities and dynamic capabilities in developing countries. The chapter then formulated a strategy for the digitalization of marginalized communities in a developing context.

*Munyaradzi Zhou*
*Midlands State University, Zimbabwe*

*Gilbert Mahlangu*
*Midlands State University, Zimbabwe*

*Cyncia Matsika*
*Midlands State University, Zimbabwe*

Chapter 1

# Multidimensional Factors Enabling Digital Inclusion in Marginalised Communities of a Developing Economy

**Gilbert Mahlangu**
*Midlands State University, Zimbabwe*

**Cyncia Matsika**
iD https://orcid.org/0000-0003-3764-2413
*Midlands State University, Zimbabwe*

**Munyaradzi Zhou**
iD https://orcid.org/0000-0002-2184-0290
*Midlands State University, Zimbabwe*

## ABSTRACT

*Fully participating in the digital economy involves understanding enabling factors for digital inclusion. The chapter analyzed and synthesized existing knowledge on factors that could enhance digital inclusion in marginalized communities. The factors that enable digital inclusion for marginalized communities in developing economies were extracted and mapped into a taxonomy table using thematic analysis and constant comparative analysis, and they were clustered into five multidimensional constructs: digital access, attitude, digital skills, actual usage, and impact of digital inclusion. These factors act as enablers in speeding up digital inclusion—they form a vigorous model for driving digital inclusion and evaluating digital initiatives in marginalized communities. A model to ensure digital inclusion initiatives to address the realities faced by those who have been marginalized from the digital economy by moving away from an inclusive digital approach that is grounded on a technological perspective is developed.*

DOI: 10.4018/978-1-6684-3901-2.ch001

## INTRODUCTION

The rapid diffusion of technology has resulted in digital transformation and the digital economy through digital inclusion. Digital inclusion is a critical principle in the digital economy and digital transformation. In principle, digital inclusion is at the heart of digital transformation and is fundamental to promoting sustainable rural development, economic prosperity, social equality, quality of service, and quality of life (Adam & Alhassan, 2021; Gibreel & Hong, 2017; Haenssgen, 2018; Low et al., 2021; Ye & Yang, 2020). Globally, many regions have invested heavily in technology to ensure that they promote digital inclusiveness and participation in the digital economy. According to Adam and Alhassan (2021), digital inclusion is a conception in which populations from marginalized communities can access and use information communication technologies (ICTs) — enabling them to participate in the digital economy and benefit from digitization initiatives. Thus, ICTs enable various marginalized communities to connect to an inclusive society.

Simply put, digital inclusion is concerned with addressing the phenomenon of digital exclusion faced by marginalized communities. Even though the meaning of digital inclusion has evolved, generally, it implies that digital inclusion is largely dependent on access to ICTs and the capacity to utilize them for everyday life. Adam and Alhassan (2021) declared that communities that cannot access and use ICTs are at the peril of digital exclusion as they lack access to various electronic services and opportunities in the digital economy.

Although digital transformation has made some positive contributions to promoting digital inclusion in developing countries, there are still challenges, including access, affordability, digital skills, and usage (Aruleba & Jere, 2022). Rural communities usually find themselves in the peripherals of digital inclusion because there is low internet and broadband infrastructures penetration. In addition, most people in rural communities are living in deep poverty; internet services and computing devices are not affordable (Aruleba & Jere, 2022). The lack of digital skills to use computing devices leads to negative effects on social and economic activities. According to Molala and Sebatana (2021, p.2), "The disparities in internet connectivity between well-developed and least developed countries have socio-economic implications. The digital divide is likely to plunge least developed countries into poverty and exacerbate social exclusion in those countries". This implies that digital exclusion impedes societies to socio-economic development; digitally excluded communities cannot access various digital services that impact health, commerce, agriculture, and education, just to mention a few. Thus, the significance of this study was to ensure that digital inclusion initiatives address the realities faced by those who have been marginalized from the digital economy by moving away from a digital inclusive approach that is grounded on a technological perspective.

## OBJECTIVES OF THE CHAPTER

The objectives of the chapter focuses on making contributions in the field of digital inclusion.

1.  The objective of this chapter was to examine dimensions that enable digital inclusion in marginalized communities in the context of a developing economy.
2.  Develop a multidimensional model for enabling digital inclusion in marginalized communities.

## BACKGROUND

Marginalized communities are severely left behind in the digital transformation drive. They are viewed by Sevelius et al. (2020) as communities left out of conventional social, economic, educational, and/or cultural life, making them more susceptible to digital exclusion. This implies that digital inclusion caches several dimensions. Globally, rural communities in developing economies are still battling the phenomenon of marginalization due to a lack of digital inclusion (Aziz & Aziz, 2020; Correa & Pavez, 2016; Helsper, 2017; Park et al., 2019; Quimba et al., 2020). Developing economies have not developed comprehensive digital inclusion initiatives to promote inclusivity in the digital economy. The current practice which focuses on deploying ICT infrastructure, village halls, telecentres, and community information centres (CICs) in rural areas to promote universal access (Ndinde & Kadodo, 2014; Willis, 2019), has not provided significant impetus in enhancing digital inclusion (Gounopoulos et al., 2020). As a result, digital inclusion for marginalized communities remains a persistent issue that is yet to be solved regardless of numerous mediation programs targeted at enhancing the deployment of ICT infrastructure and inspiring participation in the digital economy (Avgerou & Madon, 2009; Aziz & Aziz, 2020; Correa & Pavez, 2016; Ekbia, 2016; Helsper, 2017; Nemer, 2016; Park et al., 2019; Ye & Yang, 2020). There is no doubt that these policies are inadequate in driving digital inclusion.

## MAIN FOCUS OF THE CHAPTER

This chapter examines the factors that contribute to more digitally inclusive communities in developing economies. This research is one of the early studies to examine the factors enabling digital inclusion using a multidimensional model in emerging economies.

## The Discourse of Digital Inclusion

Digital inclusion emerged as a response to the growing concern of digital exclusion and lack of participation in the digital economy by the population of marginalized communities. In the discourse of digital inclusion, ICTs are the key infrastructures enabling various marginalized communities to join and participate in the digital economy (Islam & Inan, 2021; Nemer, 2016; Ye & Yang, 2020). Digital access has assumed an important role in promoting connected communities. Access to ICTs has remained one essential method to surmount the challenges of the marginalization practice in rural areas. Contrary to this position, while the adoption of ICTs in emerging economies has been renowned for having an effect on the transformation of economies and societies, a substantial number of the populace is still excluded from the digital economy (Adam & Alhassan, 2021; Kalenda & Kowaliková, 2020; Park et al., 2019; Uy-Tioco, 2019). Digital disparities have been observed in digital government, digital health, digital education, and digital business. There are gaps between people and populations in accessing and using various digital technologies to access the services listed above, and the underlying mechanisms shaping digital inclusion are not yet clear. The question *of how digital inclusion can be enabled in marginalized communities* persists in the discourse of digital transformation for developing economies.

The deployment of ICTs in rural areas has not fully transformed those living in marginalized communities (Avgerou & Madon, 2009; Haenssgen, 2018; Nyika, 2020). Several studies have challenged the use of a techno-centric approach toward digital inclusion since it is reductionist and deterministic (Correa & Pavez, 2016; Gibreel & Hong, 2017; Rangaswamy, 2008; Seale, 2009; Servaes, 2015; Sipior & Ward, 2005). Although the literature provides evidence that marginalized communities in developing economies are excluded from digital transformation, there is little research that explains the factors that enable digital inclusion. Most studies have been preoccupied with digital exclusion factors and/or challenges of digital inclusion (Al-Muwil et al., 2019; Correa & Pavez, 2016; Islam & Inan, 2021; Smidt, 2021; Yu et al., 2018), digital divide as well as developing scales for measuring digital access (Al-Muwil et al., 2019) without considering how digital inclusion can be enabled. Yet, digital inclusion should enrich the lives of people living in marginalized communities rather than merely providing access. This study argues that "access-by-default" does not infer digital engagement. Consequently, this has made it difficult to operationalize digital inclusion initiatives.

While developed countries aspire to wider digital inclusion, Aziz and Aziz (2020) argued that developing economies only desire physical access. Whereas providing access is a progressive step towards digitization, Islam and Inan (2021) argued that the focus of digital inclusion should be on access and connectivity and promoting inclusion to meet the social and economic needs of marginalized communities. A more inclusive community requires the creation of linkages between technological infrastructure, social infrastructure, and the economic infrastructure in a rural village. Contemporary debates on digital inclusion argue that there is a need to recognize digital inclusion as a multifaceted phenomenon comprising dimensions that are rooted in socio-economic structures such as skills, engagement, attitude and participation (Helsper, 2017; Sevelius et al., 2020) rather than understanding it (digital inclusion) solely in terms of access. In the same vein, Servaes (2015) mentioned that access to technology only is not adequate to strengthen digital inclusion and represent an integrated view of the real world of marginalized communities; hence, the question to be answered in this chapter is defined as follows:

- *What factors contribute to more digitally inclusive communities in developing economies?*

## Factors Driving Digital Inclusion

Information systems research has made visible contributions to dissecting issues related to digital inclusion. Globally, several studies have reported ICT access and usage as the key factors driving digital inclusion (Adam & Alhassan, 2021; Castillo et al., 2019; Chohan & Hu, 2020; Kalenda & Kowaliková, 2020; Nielsen et al., 2019; Nyika, 2020; Park et al., 2019; Ye & Yang, 2020). For instance, Kalenda and Kowaliková (2020) highlighted that many populations in most developing economies are excluded from digital transformation due to lack of internet access and low digital-savvy. In the same vein, Nyika (2020) revealed that several communities remain digitally excluded because they lack digital skills and have limited or no access to digital technologies. Chohan and Hu (2020) conceptualized digital access and digital competency as the highly substantial factors for digital inclusion and further argued that citizens from marginalized communities are likely to have limited access to digital technologies, resulting in a lack of digital competencies to use digital technologies. In their study on *"Intersections between connectivity and digital inclusion in rural communities"*, Park et al. (2019) reported that lack of access to the internet and appropriate digital abilities are the central cause of digital exclusion. As a result, most research on digital inclusion has focused on digital access and digital literacy as the key enablers— thus viewing digital inclusion from a technological perspective. This evidence highlights the importance and the existential relationship between ICT access and uses for digital inclusion.

Practically, if digital inclusion is construed as complex, multifaceted, and multi-layered, its implementation should reflect this to be successful. Nevertheless, this research and other scholars (Al-Muwil et al., 2019; Correa & Pavez, 2016; Sevelius et al., 2020) maintain that digital inclusion is both complex and multifaceted and cannot be fully enabled by focusing only on access and usage. Likewise, Correa and Pavez (2016) advised that "it is necessary to address digital inclusion as a multidimensional issue by including the sociocultural angle" (p.50). Specifically, this study argues that digital inclusion has multidimensional constructs; therefore, it cannot be considered merely in dual conditions of having access and skills to use digital tools or not. Also, while access and usage are key enablers for participating in the digital economy, this techno-centric focus on digital inclusion does not cover a broad spectrum of digital transformation factors. Arguably, focusing excessively on digital technologies and digital skills as enablers to digital inclusion overlooks other important enablers that are 'non-digital'.

Similarly, Adam and Alhassan (2021) claimed that digital inclusion should be seen in ways further than access and usage since these constructs have varying degrees — rural communities do not experience uniformity in digital exclusion. According to Correa and Pavez (2016), isolated rural communities are confronted with particular contextual challenges that should be considered when developing digital inclusion initiatives. Also, Hernandez and Roberts (2018) argued that digital inclusion hinges on inclusive policies developed in consultation with marginalized communities who are often excluded from digital transformation. Besides, Correa and Pavez (2016, p. 250) recounted that: "Digital inclusion in rural communities persists to be a great concern for policymakers". Park et al. (2019) suggested that marginalized communities require a customized policy framework for digital inclusion; thus, it can be argued that digital inclusion begins with policies that promote digital engagement. Most importantly, these policies should be guided by the premise that digital inclusion in marginalized people is generally useful when co-formed with communities to ensure fruitful engagement (Robinson et al., 2020).

## Theoretical Framework

The study of the adoption and usage of information technology employs various models and frameworks (Alotaibi & Wald, 2012; Lou & Li, 2017; Zabadi, 2016). These include, but are not limited to, Theory of Planned Behaviour (Samuel et al., 2020), Technology Acceptance Model (Olumide, 2016), Technology Organisation and Environment framework (Alves Nascimento et al., 2016), Unified Theory of Acceptance and Use of Technology model (Witarsyah et al., 2017). However, according to Al-Muwil et al. (2019, p. 638), "the lack of theoretical models for e-inclusion has prevented the identification of specific factors that impact digital inclusion". Thus, the study hinges on the diffusion of innovation theory to position rural communities in developing economies within the continuum of digital inclusion. The diffusion of innovations theory proposes how new interventions spread through social systems over time. According to Rogers (2003), there are five categories of adopting innovation: innovators, early adopters, early majority, late majority and laggards.

Literature reports that urban communities belong to the first three categories due to their proximity to the state of the art ICT infrastructure (Rashid, 2016; Rice, 2017; Scott & Mcguire, 2017). In addition, these communities have better material access, cognitive access and social access for early innovations (Yu et al., 2018). On the other hand, rural communities belong to the last two categories due to ICT poor environment and digital exclusion (Gounopoulos et al., 2020; Park et al., 2019; Rice, 2017). Rural communities have limited access to and ability to use ICTs. Marginalized communities lack access and proficiency to participate in the digital economy (Carmi & Yates, 2020; Lai & Widmar, 2020; Park et al., 2019) since they are usually the last to access high-speed broadband and the latest technologies. Therefore, there can be no doubt that rural communities are always left behind in the diffusion of innovation model.

## Frameworks and Models for Digital Inclusion

Literature review shows that few models and frameworks focus on digital inclusion. Therefore, this chapter draws on the extensive literature on digital exclusion, e-inclusion, digital divide, and digital transformation to model factors enabling digital inclusion in marginalized communities of a developing economy. The review process used keywords, backward search, and forward search. Keyword search signifies the querying of value academic archives using a particular word or expression identified as the keyword (Levy & Ellis, 2006). This technique formed the initial stage of literature search and subsequent identification of relevant studies. Using the keywords digital exclusion, digital inclusion, e-inclusion, e-exclusion, digital divide, marginalized communities, rural areas, and digital transformation, the study located *"Balancing Digital-By-Default with Inclusion: A Study of the Factors Influencing E-Inclusion in the UK"* by Al-Muwil et al. (2019) as the first article. Afterwards, the study used a backwards search to understand the origin of digital inclusion, while the forward search was employed to recognize the development of the phenomenon (Levy & Ellis, 2006). Table 1 presents a summary of studies adapted for digital inclusion.

## Defining Constructs

A total of 18 constructs were extracted from studies adapted for digital inclusion. Researchers ordered the constructs in a tabular form and defined them to create textual data that would facilitate thematic analysis and constant comparative analysis.

*Table 1. A summary of studies adapted for digital inclusion*

| Study | Dimensions | Reference |
|---|---|---|
| Balancing Digital-By-Default with Inclusion: A Study of the Factors Influencing E-Inclusion in the UK | • Availability<br>• Accessibility<br>• Satisfaction<br>• Capability<br>• Influence<br>• Intention<br>• Attitude<br>• Continuity | Al-Muwil et al. (2019) |
| The new digital divide: the confluence of broadband penetration, sustainable development, technology adoption and community participation | • Technology<br>• Socio-economic factors<br>• Community involvement<br>• Digital convergence | Armenta et al. (2012) |
| The effects of digital inclusion and ICT access on the quality of life: A global perspective | • ICT access<br>• ICT usage<br>• Quality of life | Dzang & Osman (2021) |
| Going Beyond Telecenters to Foster the Digital Inclusion of Older People in Brazil | • Access<br>• Peer support<br>• Control<br>• Interaction | Ferreira et al. (2016) |
| Digital Inclusion in Rural Areas: A Qualitative Exploration of Challenges Faced by People From Isolated Communities | • Motivation<br>• Attitude<br>• Engagement | Correa (2019) |
| A framework for digital divide Research | • Material access<br>• Mental access<br>• Skills access<br>• Usage access | Dijk (2002) |
| Digital Inclusion: An Analysis of Social Disadvantage and the Information Society | • Basic digital engagement<br>• Social digital engagement<br>• Economic digital engagement | Helsper (2013) |
| Roland Berger's Digital Inclusion Index | • Accessibility<br>• Affordability<br>• Ability<br>• Attitude | Low et al. (2021) |
| The 'relative utility' approach for stimulating ICT acceptance: profiling the non-user | • Access<br>• Skills<br>• Attitude | Verdegem & Verhoest (2008) |
| A multidimensional model of e-inclusion and Its implications | • Access<br>• Usage<br>• Quality of life<br>• Empowerment | Prosser & Zajdela, (2018) |
| Digital inclusion - a conceptual framework | • Internet access<br>• Internet usage<br>• Internet impact | Alamelu (2013) |

Table 2 shows the definitions of digital inclusion constructs extracted from Table 1. Definitions were provided based on either scholarly work or contextual understanding of the construct. Contextual definitions were necessary since digital inclusion is an emerging phenomenon in developing economies and, in some cases, literature defined constructs out of the context of digital inclusion. Thus, context definition carries incredible significance in the elucidation of connotations and understanding of the real meaning of the construct (Dash, 2014).

## Mapping Constructs and Dimensions

The factors that enhance digital inclusion in the context of a developing economy were extracted from Table 1 and mapped into a table of taxonomy using thematic analysis and constant comparative analysis. Taxonomy is the practice and science of the classification of objects (Bradley et al., 2007; Pediatr et al., 2021); hence, it was used in this study to classify digital inclusion factors. Table 3 shows the mapping of constructs and dimensions for digital inclusions. Thematic analysis is a flexible systematic method that allows the researcher to derive themes from textual data to report their interpretation of qualitative data (Ibrahim, 2012). This method provided researchers with a mechanism for coding dimensions into constructs (themes). In addition, thematic analysis ensured that researchers were consistent in the identification of themes. The constant-comparative analysis is an analytical process used in qualitative research for coding and category development (Tie et al., 2019). The constant-comparative technique was used to find consistencies and differences in dimensions and continually refine constructs and theoretically relevant categories. The definition of each dimension was compared with all other related dimensions. Thus, this continual comparative iterative process ensured that dimensions belonged to a single construct, thereby avoiding overlapping dimensions among the constructs.

# SOLUTIONS AND RECOMMENDATIONS

This section proposes a multidimensional model for operationalizing, monitoring, and guiding digital inclusion initiatives for marginalized communities.

## Mapping Digital Inclusion Factors Into a Multidimensional Model

Factors for digital inclusion were mapped into a multidimensional model using an affinity diagram. An affinity diagram is a tool that organizes and groups concepts

*Table 2. Definition of digital inclusion constructs extracted from table 1*

| Construct | Definition or Description |
|---|---|
| Access | The ability of the community to obtain computing devices and connect to the internet and other e-services. |
| Actual Usage | Actual usage shows the true extent of the usage of information technology, given that the use of technology is characterized as voluntary (Amelia, 2016). |
| Attitude | Individuals' temperament to respond with a certain level of favourableness or unfavourableness to an intention or behaviour (Ajzen, 2014). |
| Availability | The quality of ICTs to be used or accessed by a given population. |
| Motivation | This mechanism eventually inspires people to act in the preferred manner (Haque & Haque, 2014). |
| Digital Engagement | This is largely described as users' interactions with e-services to reinforce uninterrupted use (Rodgers et al., 2018). |
| Capability | A person's self-confidence in his/her capacity to act upon a behaviour (Al-Muwil et al., 2019). |
| Digital interaction | The ability of people to interact with each other and various service providers, including the government using digital technologies (Adam & Alhassan, 2021). |
| Intention | The degree to which an individual has devised conscious plans to act or not accomplish some specified potential behaviour (Al-Muwil et al., 2019). |
| Quality of life | This is defined as a distinct purpose-aligned social and value method by which an individual lives, comparative to their aspirations, desires, and living standards (Ruzevicius, 2016). |
| Ability | Ability is defined as the state of being able to do something or one's level of skill at doing something. |
| Satisfaction | This is users' global emotional response to the cognitive appraisal of the value of information technology services (Sun et al., 2012). |
| Digital empowerment | Describe the approach in which marginalized communities have the autonomy to use information technology to realize their potential. |
| Internet impact | This is the marked effect (positive or negative) of using the internet by a certain population. |
| Continuity | This is the notion of making the internet and computing devices part of everyday life such that there is a very thin line or no line between the 'digital world' and 'real world' (Chadwick & Wesson; Helsper, 2017). |
| Digital skills | This is a variety of capabilities to make use of information communication technologies. |
| Affordability | The availability of financial resources is needed to engage in behaviour. |
| Digital convergence | This is the ability of the population to participate collectively in the digital space from different locations. |

into their natural relationships based on predefined categories (Harboe, 2020). Generally, afðnity diagramming is used to analyze contextual inquiry data, and cluster attributes into categories or requirements, problem framing and idea generation. This study used the technique to cluster attributes into categories; thus, the affinity diagram ensured that dimensions for digital inclusion factors were categorized based on their affinity—their similarity or relevance to the construct. Figure 1 shows the multidimensional factors for enabling digital inclusion.

*Table 3. Constructs and dimension mapping*

| Construct (Latent Variables) | Dimension (Observed Variables) |
|---|---|
| Digital Access | Access to internet |
| | Access to computing devices |
| | Access to e-services |
| | Affordability |
| Attitude | Satisfaction |
| | Motivation |
| | Intention |
| Digital Skills | Digital empowerment |
| | Ability |
| | Capability |
| Actual usage | Nature of engagement |
| | Extent of engagement |
| | Continuity |
| | Digital convergence |
| Impact of digital inclusion | Quality of life |

## DISCUSSION

This section discusses the themes (factors) in Figure 1 and their appropriateness to contribute to more digitally inclusive communities in developing economies. Since these factors complement digital inclusion, the researchers could not discuss them in isolation.

### Digital Access, Affordability, Digital Skills, and Actual Usage

Digital access is the capacity to copiously take part in the digital society through access to the internet and digital devices. However, not all communities have comprehensive access to digital tools and digital skills to use digital tools (Adam & Alhassan, 2021); consequently, they are not capable of completely participating in the digital economy. Digital access is one of the underlying mechanisms shaping digital

*Figure 1. Multidimensional factors for enabling digital inclusion*
Source: (Authors)

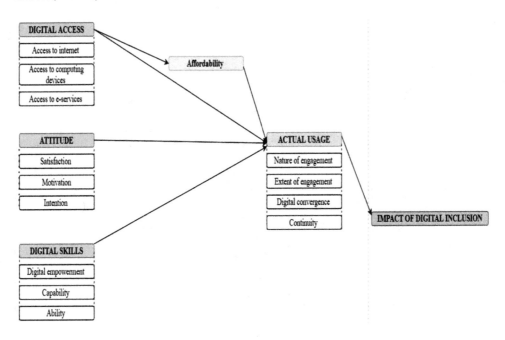

inclusion. Access to ICTs has been understood as one essential way to surmount the challenges of the marginalization practice in rural communities. According to Reisdorf and Rhinesmith (2020, p. 133), "This includes reliable access to the internet at adequate speeds, access to digital devices that meet the users' needs, access to digital skills training". Nevertheless, communities should have affordable access to increase the usage of ICTs. Thus, to enhance digital inclusion, communities should have access to the internet, computing devices and e-services. This implies that digital access, affordability, digital skills, and actual usage are necessary conditions for digital inclusion. Park et al. (2019) reported that lack of internet access and appropriate digital skills are the central cause of digital exclusion. Kalenda and Kowaliková (2020) highlighted that, in most developing economies, a significant number of populations are excluded from digital transformation due to a lack of internet access and digital literacy. As a result, most research on digital inclusion has focused on digital access and digital literacy as the key enablers. Relying on previous studies (for example, Dzang & Osman, 2021; Islam & Inan, 2021; Rangaswamy, 2008; Robinson et al., 2020), this study argues that, to ensure actual usage of digital tools, attempts ought to be made to enhance the digital skills of people, particularly in developing countries where the level of digital literacy is minimal. Therefore, governments and other development partners should endeavour to improve digital access and the digital skills of people together with entirely recognizing the gains of digital transformation.

## RECOMMENDATIONS

Fully participating in the digital economy involves understanding enabling factors for digital inclusion. As a practical contribution, practitioners in developing economies can use the proposed model to monitor and evaluate the implementation of digital inclusion initiatives. In addition, the model will ensure that digital inclusion initiatives address the realities faced by those who have been marginalized from the digital economy by moving away from a digital inclusive approach that is grounded on a technological perspective. Eventually, developing economies can use this model to augment their digital inclusion strategies and policies.

## FUTURE RESEARCH DIRECTIONS

The chapter analyzed and synthesized existing knowledge to find factors that could enhance digital inclusion in marginalized communities. This study is part of the ongoing research on digital transformation in the global South in which a significant number of populations are digitally excluded. The findings from this study revealed the underlying mechanisms shaping digital inclusion in the discourse of digital transformation for developing economies and act as an instrument for driving digital inclusion for marginalized communities. Further inquiry is needed to establish whether digital engagement, particularly in developing economies, is primarily driven by the underlying mechanisms identified in this study so that governments and other stakeholders involved in digital transformation may attend to the 'lagging' dimension of digital inclusion. Future research should empirically test if these dimensions lead to greater digital engagement in marginalized communities.

## CONCLUSION

Digital inclusion is a precondition for participating in the digital economy. It is now necessary for developing economies to realize the benefits of digital transformation. Digital inclusion initiatives for developed economies focus on wider participation in the digital economy, while efforts from developing economies are constricted to access and usage. The study concludes that digital inclusion for marginalized communities should be treated as urgent to ensure that these communities can benefit from digital transformation initiatives. It should not be wholly preoccupied with access to and usage of ICTs thus simply providing access and usage is not enough. Research on digital inclusion should be conceptualized beyond access and usage to provide actionable findings. Low et al. (2021) assert that digital inclusion is enabled by a surfeit of technological, economic, social, and legislative factors that are directly or indirectly linked to digital transformation. Therefore, to address digital marginalization in developing economies, there is a need to investigate and understand multidimensional factors that enable digital inclusion. Understanding these factors will enhance digital inclusion, where digitally marginalized communities are part of the digital transformation process (Kumar et al., 2021). Studies that promote digital inclusion are important in the context of digital transformation for developing economies.

## REFERENCES

Adam, I. O., & Dzang Alhassan, M. (2021). *Bridging the global digital divide through digital inclusion: the role of ICT access and ICT use. Transforming Government: People, Process and Policy*. doi:10.1108/TG-06-2020-0114

Ajzen, I. (2014). *Attitude theory and the attitude-behavior relation*. Academic Press.

Al-Muwil, A., Weerakkody, V., El-haddadeh, R., & Dwivedi, Y. (2019). Balancing Digital-By-Default with Inclusion: A Study of the Factors Influencing E-Inclusion in the UK. *Information Systems Frontiers*, *21*(3), 635–659. doi:10.100710796-019-09914-0

Alamelu, K. (2013). Digital inclusion - a conceptual framework. *International Journal of Advanced Research in Management and Social Sciences*, *2*(12), 228–248.

Alotaibi, S. J., & Wald, M. (2012). Towards a UTAUT-based model for studying the integrating physical and virtual identity access management systems in e-government domain. *2012 International Conference for Internet Technology and Secured Transactions, ICITST 2012*, 453–458.

Alves Nascimento, L., Bouzada, M., Gonçalves, A., & Pitassi, C. (2016). *Factors that influence the adoption and implementation of public digital accounting according to the evaluation by managers of brazilian companies*. doi:10.4301/S1807-17752016000200003

Amelia, R. (2016). *Determinacy of actual usage through behavioral intention CIMB NIAGA*. Academic Press.

Armenta, A., Serrano, A., & Cabrera, M. (2012). *Information Technology for Development The new digital divide : the confluence of broadband penetration, sustainable development, technology adoption and community participation.* doi:1 0.1080/02681102.2011.625925

Aruleba, K., & Jere, N. (2022). Exploring digital transforming challenges in rural areas of South Africa through a systematic review of empirical studies. *Scientific American, 16*, e01190. doi:10.1016/j.sciaf.2022.e01190

Avgerou, C., & Madon, S. (2009). Information society and the digital divide problem in developing countries Book section. *Perspectives and Policies on ICT in Society*, 205–218.

Aziz, A., & Aziz, A. (2020). Digital inclusion challenges in Bangladesh : The case of the National ICT Policy ICT Policy. *Contemporary South Asia, 0*(0), 1–16. doi: 10.1080/09584935.2020.1793912

Bradley, E. H., Curry, L. A., & Devers, K. J. (2007). *Qualitative Data Analysis for Health Services Research : Developing Taxonomy, Themes, and Theory.* doi:10.1111/j.1475-6773.2006.00684.x

Carmi, E., & Yates, S. J. (2020). *What do digital inclusion and data literacy mean today?* doi:10.14763/2020.2.1474

Castillo, J. G. D., Cohenour, E. J. C., Escalante, M. A. S., & Del Socorro Vázquez Carrillo, I. (2019). Reducing the digital divide in vulnerable communities in southeastern Mexico. *Publicaciones de La Facultad de Educacion y Humanidades Del Campus de Melilla, 49*(2), 133–149. doi:10.30827/publicaciones.v49i2.9305

Chadwick, D., & Wesson, C. (2016). *Digital Inclusion and Disability.* Springer Science and Business Media LLC.

Chohan, S. R., & Hu, G. (2020). Strengthening digital inclusion through e-government: Cohesive ICT training programs to intensify digital competency. *Information Technology for Development, 0*(0), 1–23. doi:10.1080/02681102.2020.1841713

Correa, T. (2019). *Digital Inclusion in Rural Areas : A Qualitative Exploration of Challenges Faced by People From Isolated Communities Digital Inclusion in Rural Areas : A Qualitative Exploration of Challenges Faced by People.* doi:10.1111/jcc4.12154

Correa, T., & Pavez, I. (2016). Digital Inclusion in Rural Areas: A Qualitative Exploration of Challenges Faced by People From Isolated Communities. *Journal of Computer-Mediated Communication, 21*(3), 247–263. doi:10.1111/jcc4.12154

Dash, N. S. (2014). *Context and Contextual Word Meaning*. Academic Press.

Dijk, J. Van. (2002). *A framework for digital divide The Pitfalls of a Metaphor*. Academic Press.

Dzang, M., & Osman, I. (2021). Technology in society The effects of digital inclusion and ICT access on the quality of life : A global perspective. *Technology in Society, 64*(September). doi:10.1016/j.techsoc.2020.101511

Ekbia, H. R. (2016). *Digital inclusion and social exclusion : The political economy of value in a networked world*. doi:10.1080/01972243.2016.1153009

Ferreira, S. M., Sayago, S., & Blat, J. (2016). Information Technology for Development Going Beyond Telecenters to Foster the Digital Inclusion of Older People in Brazil. *Lessons Learned from a Rapid Ethnographical Study., 1102*. Advance online publication. doi:10.1080/02681102.2015.1091974

Gibreel, O., & Hong, A. (2017). *A Holistic Analysis Approach to Social*. Technical, and Socio-Technical Aspect of E-Government Development. doi:10.3390u9122181

Gounopoulos, E., Kontogiannis, S., Kazanidis, I., & Valsamidis, S. (2020). The Impact of the Digital Divide on the adoption of e-Government in Greece. *KnE Social Sciences, 2019*, 401–411. doi:10.18502/kss.v4i1.6002

Haenssgen, M. J. (2018). The struggle for digital inclusion: Phones, healthcare, and marginalization in rural India. *World Development, 104*, 358–374. doi:10.1016/j.worlddev.2017.12.023

Haque, M. F., & Haque, M. A. (2014). *Motivational Theories – A Critical Analysis Motivational Theories – A Critical Analysis*. Academic Press.

Harboe, G. (2020). *Real-World Affinity Diagramming Practices : Bridging the Paper – Digital Gap*. doi:10.1145/2702123.2702561

Helsper, E. (2017). *The social relativity of digital exclusion : Applying relative deprivation theory to digital inequalities*. doi:10.1111/comt.12110

Helsper, E. J. (2013). *Digital inclusion : An analysis of social disadvantage and the information society*. Academic Press.

Hernandez, K., & Roberts, T. (2018). Leaving No One Behind in a Digital World. *Ids K4D*, 1–34. https://assets.publishing.service.gov.uk/media/5c178371ed915d0b8a31a404/Emerging_Issues_LNOBDW_final.pdf%0Ahttps://www.ids.ac.uk/publications/leaving-no-one-behind-in-a-digital-world/

Ibrahim, M. (2012). *Thematic analysis : A critical review of its process and evaluation.* Academic Press.

Islam, M. N., & Inan, T. T. (2021). *Exploring the Fundamental Factors of Digital Inequality in Bangladesh.* doi:10.1177/21582440211021407

Kalenda, S., & Kowaliková, I. (2020). The digital exclusion of vulnerable children: Challenge for sustainability issues in czech social work practice. *Sustainability (Switzerland), 12*(23), 1–24. doi:10.3390u12239961

Kumar, R., Subramaniam, C., & Zhao, K. (2021). Special issue on digital inclusion. *Information Systems and e-Business Management,* 1–4. doi:10.100710257-021-00531-6

Lai, J., & Widmar, N. O. (2020). *Featured Article Revisiting the Digital Divide in the COVID-19 Era.* doi:10.1002/aepp.13104

Levy, Y., & Ellis, T. J. (2006). *A Systems Approach to Conduct an Effective Literature Review in Support of Information Systems Research.* Academic Press.

Lou, A. T. F., & Li, E. Y. (2017). *Integrating Innovation Diffusion Theory and the Technology Acceptance Model : The Adoption of blockchain technology from business managers' perspective (Work in Progress).* Academic Press.

Low, J., Dujacquier, D., & Kaur, S. (2021). *Bridging the digital divide, improving digital inclusion in Southeast Asia.* Academic Press.

Molala, T. S. (2021). *The connection between digital divide and social exclusion : Implications for social work.* Academic Press.

Ndinde, S., & Kadodo, W. (2014). The Role of Community-Based Information Centers in Development: Lessons for Rural Zimbabwe. *International Journal of Learning, Teaching and Educational Research, 2*(1), 44–53.

Nemer, D. (2016). *From Digital Divide to Digital Inclusion and Beyond : A Positional Review Is Access Enough ?* doi:10.15353/joci.v11i1.2857

Nielsen, M. M., Carvalho, J., Backhouse, J., & Makpor, M. (2019). *A global framework for digital inclusion.* Academic Press.

Nyika, G. T. (2020). Use of ICTS for socio-economic development of marginalized communities in rural areas: Proposals for establishment of sectoral Rural Entrepreneurial Networks. *Journal of Development and Communication Studies, 7*(1–2), 71–91. doi:10.4314/jdcs.v7i1-2.5

Olumide, O. D. (2016). Technology Acceptance Model as a predictor of using information system' to acquire information literacy skills. *Library Philosophy and Practice (e-Journal), 1*–27. doi:10.1016/j.ygyno.2014.12.020

Park, S., Freeman, J., & Middleton, C. (2019). Intersections between connectivity and digital inclusion in rural communities. *Communication Research and Practice, 5*(2), 139–155. doi:10.1080/22041451.2019.1601493

Pediatr, A., Dis, I., & Yazdani, S. (2021). *A Model for the Taxonomy of Research Studies : A Practical Guide to Knowledge Production and Knowledge Management.* doi:10.5812/pedinfect.112456.Review

Prosser, A., & Zajdela, N. (2018). *A multidimensional model of e-inclusion and its implications.* Academic Press.

Quimba, F. M. A., Rosellon, M. A. D., Quimba, F. M. A., & Rosellon, M. A. D. (2020). *Digital Divide and the Platform Economy : Looking for the Connection from the Asian Experience.* Academic Press.

Rangaswamy, N. (2008). Telecenters and Internet cafe's: The case of ICTs in small businesses. *Asian Journal of Communication, 18*(4), 365–378. doi:10.1080/01292980802344208

Rashid, A. T. (2016). Digital Inclusion and Social Inequality: Gender Differences in ICT Access and Use in Five Developing Countries. *Gender, Technology and Development, 20*(3), 306–332. doi:10.1177/0971852416660651

Reisdorf, B., & Rhinesmith, C. (2020). *Digital Inclusion as a Core Component of Social Inclusion.* doi:10.17645/si.v8i2.3184

Rice, R. E. (2017). *Divide and diffuse : Comparing digital divide and diffusion of innovations perspectives on mobile phone adoption.* doi:10.1177/2050157915590469

Robinson, L., Schulz, J., Dodel, M., Correa, T., Villanueva-mansilla, E., Leal, S., Magallanes-blanco, C., Rodriguez-medina, L., Dunn, H. S., Levine, L., McMahon, R., & Khilnani, A. (2020). Digital Inclusion Across the Americas and Caribbean. *Digital Inclusion Across the Americas and the Caribbean., 8*(2), 244–259. doi:10.17645i. v8i2.2632

Rodgers, S., Thorson, E., & Rodgers, S. (2018). Special Issue Introduction. *Digital Engagement with Advertising, 3367*(1), 1–3. Advance online publication. doi:10.1 080/00913367.2017.1414003

Rogers, E. M. (2003). Elements of diffusion. *Diffusion of Innovations, 5,* 1–38.

Ruzevicius, J. (2016). *Quality of Life and of Working Life : Conceptions and Research.* Academic Press.

Samuel, M., Doctor, G., Christian, P., & Baradi, M. (2020). Drivers and barriers to e-government adoption in Indian cities. *Journal of Urban Management, 9*(4), 408–417. doi:10.1016/j.jum.2020.05.002

Scott, S., & Mcguire, J. (2017). *Using Diffusion of Innovation Theory to Promote Universally Designed College Instruction.* Academic Press.

Seale, J. (2009). *Digital Inclusion.* Academic Press.

Servaes, J. (2015). *The tools of social change : A critique of techno-centric development and activism.* doi:10.1177/1461444815604419

Sevelius, J. M., Gutierrez, L., Sophia, M., Haas, Z., Mccree, B., Ngo, A., Jackson, A., Clynes, C., Venegas, L., Salinas, A., Herrera, C., Stein, E., Operario, D., & Gamarel, K. (2020). Research with Marginalized Communities : Challenges to Continuity During the COVID - 19 Pandemic. *AIDS and Behavior,* (7), 1–4. doi:10.100710461-020-02920-3 PMID:32415617

Sipior, J. C., & Ward, B. T. (2005). Bridging the Digital Divide for e-Government inclusion: A United States Case Study. *Electronic Journal of E-Government, 3*(3), 137–146. doi:10.1108/02640470510631308

Smidt, H. J., & Jokonya, O. (2021). Information Technology for Development Factors affecting digital technology adoption by small-scale farmers in agriculture value chains (AVCs) in South Africa. *Information Technology for Development, 0*(0), 1–27. doi:10.1080/02681102.2021.1975256

Sun, Y., Fang, Y., & Lim, K. H. (2012). *User Satisfaction with Information Technology Service Delivery : A Social Capital Perspective.* doi:10.1287/isre.1120.0421

Tie, Y. C., Birks, M., & Francis, K. (2019). *Grounded theory research : A design framework for novice researchers.* doi:10.1177/2050312118822927

Uy-Tioco, C. S. (2019). 'Good enough' access: Digital inclusion, social stratification, and the reinforcement of class in the Philippines. *Communication Research and Practice, 5*(2), 156–171. doi:10.1080/22041451.2019.1601492

Verdegem, P., & Verhoest. (2008). The 'relative utility' approach for stimulating ICT acceptance : profiling the non-user. *European Journal of EPractice,* 1–11.

Willis, K. S. (2019). *Making a 'Place' for ICTs in Rural Communities.* Academic Press.

Witarsyah, D., Sjafrizal, T., Fudzee, M. F. M., & Salamat, M. A. (2017). The critical factors affecting e-government adoption in indonesia: A conceptual framework. *International Journal on Advanced Science, Engineering and Information Technology*, *7*(1), 160–167. doi:10.18517/ijaseit.7.1.1614

Ye, L., & Yang, H. (2020). From digital divide to social inclusion: A tale of mobile platform empowerment in rural areas. *Sustainability (Switzerland)*, *12*(6), 2424. Advance online publication. doi:10.3390u12062424

Yu, B., Ndumu, A., Mon, L. M., Fan, Z., Yu, B., Ndumu, A., & Mon, L. M. (2018). *E-inclusion or digital divide : An integrated model of digital inequality digital divide*. doi:10.1108/JD-10-2017-0148

Zabadi, A. M. (2016). Adoption of Information Systems (IS): The Factors that Influencing IS Usage and Its Effect on Employee in Jordan Telecom Sector (JTS): A Conceptual Integrated Model. *International Journal of Business and Management*, *11*(3), 25. doi:10.5539/ijbm.v11n3p25

## KEY TERMS AND DEFINITIONS

**Digital Convergence:** The ability of the population to participate collectively in the digital space from different locations.

**Digital Engagement:** Users' interactions with e-services to strengthen continuous use ICTs in everyday life.

**Digital Exclusion:** The lack of access to technology and digital skills to participate in the digital economy.

**Digital Transformation:** The integration of digital technology into social and economic activities of the population.

**Digitization:** The use of digital technologies to transform the socio-economic conditions of rural communities.

**Empowerment:** The approach in which marginalized communities have the autonomy to use information technology to realize their potential.

**Rural Communities:** Sparsely populated lands lying outside urban areas with low-density cells.

# Chapter 2
# Digital Inclusion in Education Using Cloud Computing and Augmented and Virtual Reality

**Cyncia Matsika**
https://orcid.org/0000-0003-3764-2413
*Midlands State University, Zimbabwe*

**Munyaradzi Zhou**
https://orcid.org/0000-0002-2184-0290
*Midlands State University, Zimbabwe*

**Gilbert Mahlangu**
*Midlands State University, Zimbabwe*

## ABSTRACT

*Information communication technologies (ICTs) to support teaching and learning in marginalized communities is a major drawback that alienates developing countries from the digital space. This chapter proffers digital inclusion in education for marginalized communities by using and merging cloud computing, augmented, and virtual reality (AVR) technologies. A systematic review of the literature was conducted. Diana Laurilliard's six learning types in the conversational framework was used to establish how digital technology is utilized and widely adopted in education in the context of marginalized communities. AVR technology embedded in the cloud supports all the six learning types and promote digital inclusion in education. A model that marginalized communities can utilize was developed. Future research can develop a model that captures the university-wide curriculum needs of higher institutions of learning in marginalized communities and the training of the educators to use ICTs to reduce the digital divide and improve digital literacy.*

DOI: 10.4018/978-1-6684-3901-2.ch002

## INTRODUCTION

Teaching and learning are evolving with advancements in technology and the inclusion of digital technologies, especially throughout the unprecedented COVID-19 pandemic era. Digital technologies influence the what, how, where, and why students are learning, and who they are learning from worldwide. Digital technology brings about an arsenal of benefits in the educational sector. Classes and programs are now available online, and physical textbooks are gradually being substituted by various digital devices connected to online media and offer personalized online teaching and learning. The virtual lectures, lessons, projects, and instructions offer each student access to diverse facilitators, collaboration, communication, critical thinking, creativity, and an increase in data-driven instruction and results (Cabero-Almenara, 2019; Pranoto & Panggabean, 2019; Valverde-Berrocoso, 2020). Many educational institutions are using digital technologies to easily, quickly, and cost-effectively connect students with a huge range of resources and digital services during teaching and learning. However, the many benefits of learning with Cloud Computing and AVR technologies are not being realized by marginalized communities because of lack of access.

Marginalized communities allude to areas that are excluded from the prevalent profitable, academic, cultural, and social life. Instances of marginalized communities include excluded areas due to their immigration status, sexual preference, race, personal identity, dialect, age group, and physical aptitude. Marginalization, therefore, transpires as a result of an unequal balance of power among sects (Sevelius et al., 2020). Indicators that categorize marginalized groups include education, housing, and occupancy. Often marginalized communities suffer from severe material deprivation, which leads to harder living conditions because of accentuated migration, school abandonment, disabilities, very few workplaces, subsistence agriculture, low life expectancy, and absence of consumer goods, among other factors (Niţă & Pârvu, 2020). Marginalization is positioned by classism and institutional racism and the magnitude to which the communities are deep-rooted into an array of oppression (Calabrese Barton & Tan, 2018). Poverty is considered among the major causes of vulnerabilities that result in marginalization (Michael et al., 2016). Technology, therefore, promotes the digital inclusion of marginalized communities by introducing accessibility and inclusion (Kempin Reuter, 2019). Marginalized areas are defined by economic distress, environmental debasement, and social decay, which leads to unsustainability (Adams et al., 2020). The research study contends that the twin technologies will promote digital inclusion in education.

In the 21st century, transformations regarding how students are assessed and evaluated on their performances inside and outside the classroom are witnessed. Technological advancement is not only enhancing or advancing education, but it is also altering the way educators assess their students and how fast formative and summative assessments and evaluations can be completed fairly. Students can now be assessed by creating and displaying their work on online platforms like Moodle and Google Classroom learning management systems or through social media and other digital platforms. AVR technology is becoming a critical part of university learning as well as student performance enhancement and should be incorporated into teaching and learning (Matsika & Zhou, 2021). In addition, AVR allows online teaching and learning to continue even during educational disruptions (Bao, 2020; Bloom et al., 2020). Online platforms encourage students to continue dialogues outside standard face to face classrooms. Lecturers can observe chat boards so that they understand the concepts that need to be reviewed or refined.

Teaching and learning can be greatly enhanced by introducing digital technologies across all the learning styles (Laurillard, 2007b). There is need to adopt Cloud Computing and AVR technologies to alleviate the resource constraints encountered by the education sector in developing communities. The illusion that digital transformation belongs to developed countries should be re-oriented. Against this backdrop, the Conversational Framework is used to establish how digital learning provides an improved, enhanced, integrated, and motivating learning environment and how AVR and Cloud Computing technologies can be merged to achieve digital inclusiveness in education throughout the marginalized communities.

The utilization of ICTs and disruptive technologies such as AVR and Cloud Computing in teaching and learning can help students obtain the cognitive and affective domains and the digital literacy and psychomotor skills that the 21st-century industry requires. AVR technology, when embedded with Cloud Computing can eliminate infrastructural, software and platform needs which marginalized communities suffer from. Many advantages will be realized from the fusion of the two technologies, which include deepening the understanding of complex educational concepts and accelerating the teaching and learning engagement, problem solving skills, self-exploration and motivation, easy access to information and fun opportunities to practice what they learn (Akçayır & Akçayır, 2017; Bellalouna, 2021; Garzón & Acevedo, 2019; Georgiou & Kyza, 2020; Huuskonen & Oksanen, 2019).

## Objectives of the Chapter

The objectives of the chapter hinges on the application of Dianna Laurillard's Conversational model, augmented virtual reality, and cloud computing.

1.    To explore the six learning types according to Dianna Laurillard's Conversational model.

2. To inform the deployment of digital technologies in resource-constrained environments
3. To integrate Cloud Computing and AVR technologies to promote digital inclusion in marginalized communities

## BACKGROUND

AVR technologies and Cloud Computing, "the twin technologies", through their power and ability to replicate aspects of the real world online possess great potential to significantly transform education and promote digital inclusion. AVR technology alludes to applied science automation that aids users to completely engaging themselves in a computerized simulation by merging the virtual environment with the real environment (Tan & Lim, 2018). Cloud Computing sidesteps the requirement for capital investments in expensive hardware, software, and expensive information technology infrastructure. Therefore, AVR and Cloud Computing technologies offer active learning as all the five senses are engaged during teaching and learning through an affordable digital platform. The utilization of the Cloud to share educational content is still an emerging concern (Sandu et al., 2019). Educators can create content, extract data and engage in online classroom management utilizing cloud services like SaaS, PaaS, and IaaS. As such, AVR technology can be merged with Cloud Computing to enhance teaching and learning as well as support inclusiveness in education. The philosophy of inclusive education aims at helping all students to learn, digital technology fosters inclusiveness in education and should therefore be promoted. Cloud services bridge the infrastructural and ICT equipment gap which marginalized communities encounter (Valverde-Berrocoso, 2020).

Abad-Segura (2020), confirmed that AVR technology has an expanding and dynamic interest in scientific activities, and they also confirmed the technology's link to the Sustainable Development Goals (SDGs). As such, AVR technology should be utilized in education to achieve digital inclusion in marginalized communities (Malungu & Moturi, 2015) AR technology possesses great possibilities in the education sector as it enables the amalgamation of physical information together with digital information through various high-tech configurations to create a new reality (Cabero-Almenara, 2019; Dehghani, 2020; Ferrati, 2019; Flavián, 2019;).

The education sector transforms alongside technological development, the pedagogical and andragogic models should adapt to digitalization in order to achieve the productive adaptation of contents, means, and objectives (Abad-Segura, González-Zamar, Luque-de la Rosa, & Cevallos, 2020). According to the Conversational Framework, talk and chalk are not enough to produce graduates with the 21st-century skills that the industry needs. It is essential to engross students in all the learning types of the teaching and learning activities (Laurillard, 2007b). AVR technology offers effective visualizations that emphasize concepts, which is not possible in a traditional face-to-face lecture as it enables students to explore different realities and alternate their experiences. It creates interest, and students would rather watch concepts unfold rather than read about them; AVR technology increases engagement as it stimulates the interest to learn; makes learning fun, and greatly improves the quality of education (Gargrish et al., 2020; Garzón & Acevedo, 2019; Georgiou & Kyza, 2020; Herpich et al., 2017; Hon, 2019). AVR technology should be integrated with Cloud Computing to endow 21st-century skills to students and bridge the digital divide that the marginalized communities experience.

## MAIN FOCUS OF THE CHAPTER

The chapter focuses on dovetailing the elements of the conversational framework, cloud computing, virtual reality, augmented reality, and digital inclusion in andragogy. The systematic overview of literature focused on the aforementioned terms. The databases targeted were Google Scholar and Web of Science. Literature content was mainly within five years. The measure of internet skills is an important factor for digital inclusion, and educators should equip students as they will inhabit a technology-driven, multitasking, versatile, vibrant, and divergent planet. Diffusion of technology reports indicates elevated levels of technological adoption among students in Nigeria to promote digital inclusion (Iji & Abah, 2019). Digital domains include scholarly search engines, e-learning platforms, social networking media, gamification applications, and websites. The digitally native generation considers digital technology to be the primary source of information for every aspect of life, especially education. Digital inclusion is necessary to attain the Sustainable Development Goals (SDGs). Cloud computing focuses on three main domains, IaaS, SaaS, and PaaS. AVR will explore Virtual and Augmented Reality elements and how all the aforementioned elements can be integrated into a model which marginalized communities can utilize to promote digital inclusion in education.

Internet connectivity continues to be critical in the technological age, as with the skills to navigate the internet. Internet connectivity is more prevalent in the Australian urban setups and less available in the traditionally rural and farming communities. Digital inclusion seeks to address such gaps by training, supporting, and promoting people to acquire the necessary internet connection and skills (Campbell-meier et al., 2020; Marshall et al., 2020). Together with Cloud Computing technologies, AVR aims to resolve akin disparities and drawbacks by encouraging the academic community to utilize technology to revamp education, economics, and social welfare.

Uy-tioco (2019) also argues that digital inclusion is more than just the penetration of ICTs. They postulate in their research study that technological infiltration in the Philippines is mere access to digital technologies defined by unequal, restricted, and strained access (Uy-tioco, 2019). Digital inclusion in education fosters inclusion, especially the twin technologies, as they bridge the digital divide.

A model that promotes artists in marginalized communities, including Russian Kola Peninsula, South Australia, Namibia, and Finnish Lapland was developed to guide virtual arts-based projects. There is a need to develop a model that promotes more than just arts-based research project, but an all-encompassing teaching and learning model that promote digital inclusion at the Higher and tertiary level (Sarantou & Akimenko, 2018).

Cloud Computing and AVR technologies bridge the digital divide and promote digital inclusion in education in resource-constrained communities. Digital under-participation exists within segments of the community that have no access to resources, telecommunications infrastructure, or digital technologies. Digital fringe is mostly witnessed among refugee communities, and they need an internet connection to sustain continuous education (Hespanhol & Farmer, 2018).

The digital fringe is also witnessed in Bangladesh as it is argued that the ICT policy fails to comprehensively solve the issues associated with digital inclusion (Aziz & Aziz, 2020). The twin technologies promote digital inclusion in education and should be adopted to promote digital inclusion.

Digital inequalities also exist in disadvantaged American communities, resulting in prevalent digital skill inequalities (Chen et al., 2021). Cloud and AVR technologies mitigate the digital divide gap in education as they promote digital inclusion.

Rural India and the rural United Kingdom are among the marginalized communities that suffer from digital division, and it is generally agreed that the diffusion of ICTs is essential for development (Haenssgen, 2018; Willis, 2019). A model that universities can adopt to promote digital inclusion in education is of paramount importance.

## FRAMEWORK FOR THE INTEGRATION OF TECHNOLOGY

Integration models help to interpret the responsibilities played by technology in aiding the education process and how it affects the learning experiences and learning outcomes. The TPACK framework discusses three types of knowledge that should be considered when implementing integrated educational technologies. Individually, the types of knowledge under discussion are technology knowledge (TK), pedagogy knowledge (PK), and content knowledge (CK). The TPACK framework integrates knowledge types to offer the best approach to implementing educational technology (ed-tech) during teaching and learning. It profiles how teaching content and how

*Figure 1. The TPACK Framework for the integration of technology*
Source: (Koehler et al., 2013)

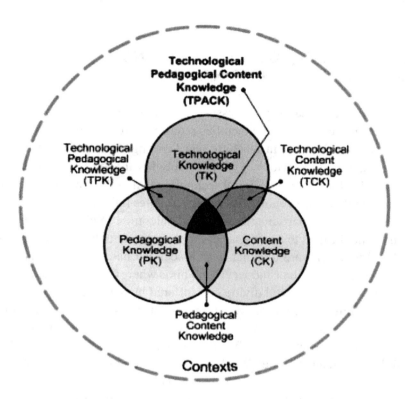

the teacher transmits what is being taught (pedagogy) should shape the foundation for successful ed-tech integration. The sequence of precedence is crucial as the technology being administered must interface with the content and bolster pedagogy to improve the learning experiences (Koehler et al., 2013).

Technological pedagogical knowledge (TPK) delineates connections and interactions that exist amidst the technology and specific andragogic practices, whilst pedagogical content knowledge (PCK) delineates between learning objectives and andragogic practices; lastly, technological content knowledge (TCK) delineates the connections and convergences among the learning objectives alongside the technologies. The triangulation constitutes the TPACK, which accounts for the relationships among the three acknowledged areas. Diagrammatically it is represented as shown:

Similar to the TPACK framework, the Cloud computing, AVR model considers how educators could integrate educational technology in the context of marginalized communities to promote digital inclusion. The framework explicates the requisite knowledge types to successfully integrate technology into education (Koehler et al., 2013).

## DIGITAL INCLUSION, CLOUD COMPUTING, VIRTUAL AND AUGMENTED REALITY

Digital inclusion articulates policy issues, research, and practical efforts to look into the expertise, content, and, amenities required to reinforce education to adopt computers and the internet in teaching and learning Rhinesmith (2016). It goes beyond access issues. Previous research highlights the skills that are necessary prerequisites for one to utilize digital technology. Attention to digital technology skills is highlighted in the report with major variables linking to success in the 21$^{st}$-century workplace and participation in social outcomes. Digital opportunities and inclusion are not limited to girding access to the internet only but extend to girding the availability of software together with associated hardware, plus the pertinent teaching and learning content and services. This is where Cloud computing and AVR technologies bridge the digital divide gap suffered by marginalized communities.

Cloud computing alludes to an emerging computer-based model which empowers timely, on-request network accessibility for a cooperative pool of computing assets, servers, systems, repositories, software, services and applications (Dahunsi & Owoseni, 2014; Namani & Gonen, 2020). Cloud computing services like Infrastructure as a service (IaaS), software as a service (SaaS), and Platform as a service (PaaS) can be merged with AVR technology to achieve digital inclusion in marginalized communities.

Rhinesmith (2016), presented a model that promotes digital inclusion. Metrics that help understand meaningful broadband adoption, which presents an integrated picture of effectiveness and comfort with digital tools, their availability, and the effect of support and training resources was designed. Infrastructure is coined as one of the necessary metrics to achieve digital inclusion. IaaS alludes to the infrastructural services provided by Cloud Service providers relating to networking and traffic redirecting plus virtual machines, among others, that marginalized communities can utilize to bridge infrastructural costs (Rhinesmith, 2016). Instead of an institution purchasing their own hardware and servers' custom made scalable infrastructural resources can be merged with AVR technology to promote teaching and learning through data usage and data sharing (Namani & Gonen, 2020). Educators in marginalized communities do not have the appropriate infrastructure that provides flawless connection across heterogeneous platforms, thus making the development of a methodological paradigm that accommodates IaaS obligatory. According to Aryati (2017), the network platform and the absorptive capacity of various sectors, such as education, should be synchronized. IaaS facilitates synchronization without having to incur infrastructural-related costs. Cloud computing provides infrastructural services without the need to buy physical components like servers which are usually expensive.

Various software and programs which cost money to purchase and maintain are needed to support teaching and learning activities. SaaS is a cloud-based software model that allows students to access their learning materials from any mobile device, provided that there is an internet connection to improve efficiency on the go. SaaS creates an adaptable, versatile, and conducive teaching and learning environment by leveraging cutting-edge digital technologies for both the lecturer and the student through strategic outsourcing and convenient data storage. By its very nature, SaaS provides an economical and scalable way to adopt and or upgrade to digital learning for the marginalized learner as they do not have to buy and install software on individual computers (Marcu et al., 2019). Combined with AVR technology, SaaS can provide a powerful way to reduce the digital division prevalent in marginalized societies. AVR technology is supported by different 3D content. Positioning virtual objects accurately in a place is a demanding task in handheld augmented reality (HAR). The future of the educational curriculum in the 21st century champions the significance of practical modules like technology, science, mathematics and engineering with contemporary European Union (EU) programs deliberating on the common counterattacks to adapting modern instructional methods and invigorating future epochs of scientists. Fresh forecasts on VR alongside AR technologies suggest prospective growth projections equal to $182 billion in profit by the year 2025. AVR has the prospective to turn out to be a measuring tool in education and might revolutionize the academic process by virtue of interacting with educational objects in a 3D environment. Previous research discussed major 3D components of the learning objects which merge into the VR/AR educational ecosystem. The implementation of interactive educational content using AR and 3D visualization technologies in secondary education was explored. Methods, algorithms, architecture, and technological aspects were reviewed (Fuvattanasilp et al., 2021; Mangina, 2018; Sannikov et al., 2015). This particular chapter merges cloud attributes like SaaS that won't require the content to be run on individual devices, SaaS will store the necessary programs and content in the cloud, eliminating any software requirement needs. Interactive educational content will be ubiquitously available through the integration of AVR technology and Cloud Computing to promote digital inclusion in particular and teaching and learning in general.

AVR technology and PaaS can be integrated to bridge platform-related costs and promote digital inclusion in education. PaaS model refers to a computing platform like the operating system (i.e., Windows, Linux, for example), the database (i.e., Oracle, MariaDB, MySQL, etc.), the execution environment, the programming language (i.e., Python, Java, Html, C++, etc.) and web servers which are made accessible to the education sector so that individual costs on the platforms are not incurred. In-house Information Technology (I.T) services may deploy the software and support. Therefore, educators can organize and run the collective software and applications (Ray, 2017).

A research study conducted in Latin America and Europe by nine academic centers: (Brazil, Bolivia, the Dominican Republic, Cuba, Finland, Ecuador, Turkey Poland, and Uruguay) outlined innovative educational issues like digital storytelling, blockchain, flipped learning, or sharing pedagogy or personalized learning. They also alluded to the need to conduct teacher training to prepare educators to use ICTs. This was an attempt to promote digital inclusion, improve digital media literacy, and mitigate digital gaps (Study et al., 2019). AVR technology is very handy even during training and supports remote collaboration. Every Cloud computing model mitigates costs associated with implementation requirements like hardware, platform, and software resources hence there is a need to merge Cloud computing technology with AVR technology in the educational domain to promote digital inclusion in marginalized communities and reap the full benefits of digital technology in education.

Existing research on AR and VR technologies is not yet merged with cloud computing services to reap the full benefits of the twin technologies in marginalized communities. They capture a certain topic like spinal anatomy, cardiothoracic surgery, human anatomy or liver surgery. The 3D content is also available for that particular university or module content (Chen, 2021; Fonseca, 2013; Hansen, 2010; Karambakhsh, 2019; Kurniawan, 2018; Mangina, 2018) There is a need to develop an all-encompassing AVR and Cloud Computing model to capture the holistic needs of a curriculum and to promote digital inclusion in marginalized communities and not just one component of a module or topic.

The proposed AVR architecture constitutes the education creator, virtual trainer for education; knowledge injector in education; cloud computing services and various AVR technology devices. The architecture is discussed in detail in the ensuing paragraphs under the model section.

# DIGITAL INCLUSION AND THE LEARNING TYPES USING LAURILLARD'S CONVERSATIONAL FRAMEWORK

## Learning Through Acquisition

Students acquire knowledge through watching materials, listening, and reading materials provided by the lecturer that the lecturer wants the students to know. The acquisition learning style helps students to learn by giving them information that they should remember and form the basis for complex learning. According to Diana Laurillard, acquisition learning encourages students to develop the learning concept (Laurillard, 2007a). Digital technology through acquisition tools like AVR technology, games, podcasting, screen casting, websites, flipped classrooms, YouTube, Media Hoper, Google Scholar, and journals help students to engage in complex learning and acquire knowledge. Digital tools facilitate the acquisition of learning styles and should be promoted through the integration of AVR technology and Cloud Computing in teaching and learning.

## Learning Through Investigation/Inquiry

Learning through **investigation/inquiry** promotes student-centred learning (andragogy) as it mentors students to become better in comparison and explorative exercises as well as critiquing resources that reflect on the ideas, theories and concepts being inculcated (Laurillard, 2007b). The student is in control of their own learning and developing the 21$^{st}$ century skills that the industry needs. Learning through inquiry is a more active learning process which further develops the learning concept. The students navigate through the resources on their own at their own pace. The essence of investigation learning is to promote synchronous learning, in which the student develops their own knowledge and understanding through investigation digital tools like AVR technology, games, Google Scholar, BBC news and open books. Investigation tools support investigation learning and should be utilized during teaching and learning. AVR and Cloud Computing technologies can bridge the digital divide and should be integrated to achieve digital inclusion.

## Learning Through Collaboration

**Collaboration** learning involves the working together of students to supplement each other's learning through collective production and practice in addition to discussions and feedback (Laurillard, 2007a, 2007b). This type of learning embraces mainly discussions, practice, and production. By sharing the learning processes, students hold up their ideas for scrutiny by their peers and receive feedback from a new perspective. Collaboration enables students to produce a shared output like a project or programming code. Negotiation and persuasion, which require confidence in the students' knowledge are needed for their contribution to receive group approval and to produce the best output they can. Synthesizing their different perspectives may lead to knowledge discovery. Support discovery learning is knowledge structured and sequenced from the simple to the complex (Williams, 2017). Collaboration learning aids students in learning by making them understand and evaluate various perspectives to formulate a joint outcome that all the students have ownership of. Collaboration is much more challenging than discussion because of the requirement to produce something together. Collaboration learning is about taking part in the process of building knowledge itself through participation activities and not acquisition. The fact that the students have to reach a consensus drives iteration through participation and negotiation. Digital technologies that can be used as collaboration tools to engage in active learning include AVR technology, games, mind maps, storyboards, Google docs, padlet, discussion forums and blogs. Collaboration tools support collaborative learning and should be utilized to promote digital inclusion in education. Integrating AVR technology with Cloud Computing becomes an important necessity in solving digital division.

## Learning Through Discussion

**Discussion** learning involves sharing knowledge among students; they consider each other's points of view and attempt to defend their own. It demands the student to communicate their individual beliefs and queries and contest and address their peers or lecturers' ideas and queries (Laurillard, 2007b, 2007a). Discussions further develop the concept. The pedagogic focus of learning through discussion has the advantage of exposing the mutual critique of thoughts and how this steers the growth of a more hypothetical understanding. Discussion benefits students as they are required to learn by remembering and understanding the information they put forward and assess. Digital tools that can be used as discussion tools include AVR technology, games, Google Hangouts, Google Meet, Zoom, Microsoft Teams, blogs and the padlet. Discussion tools enhance the teaching and learning experience and should be taken advantage of to bridge the digital divide in teaching and learning. AVR technology facilitates the discussion learning type and should be merged with Cloud computing to promote digital inclusion in education.

## Learning Through Practice

Learning through **practice** entails producing something for the lecturer to evaluate, which helps students improve their cognitive, psychomotor, and affectional skills through a loop of experimenting with what they learnt, obtaining responses, reviewing approaches, and retrying (Laurillard, 2007b, 2007a). This may be done through manual actions, performing calculations, soft skills, and cognitive processes, among others. Feedback may come from the lecturers, self-reflection or peers, or from the activity itself. Feedback is essential as the student can make meaningful transformations to their practice and improve ensuing actions. Practice permits the student to tailor their activities to the objective of the task if it shows them how to improve the result of their action in relation to the objective. Digital tools that promote learning through practice include AVR technology, text editors like Atom, games, Word Press, quizzes, padlet, polls, and Jamboard. Practice tools aid in the administration of practice learning style and should be adopted in teaching and learning. Integrating AVR and Cloud computing becomes a rhetorical question.

## Learning Through Production

Learning through **production** entails the application of knowledge to create a tangible outcome that can be evaluated (Laurillard, 2007a), for example designing a website or answering an online multiple-choice test. Production encourages students to learn by allowing them to practically create something by applying the knowledge they have acquired. It propels students to consolidate what they have learnt by articulating their conceptual understanding and how they applied it in practice. Digital production tools that can be used include AVR technology, Atom text editor, games, google forms, blended space, and WordPress.

Conclusively, digital technologies like AVR not merely cover all the learning types proposed by (Laurillard, 2007b, 2007a) but enable quick attainment of educational tasks; enhance teaching and learning performance and process; increases productivity; and, most importantly, will produce graduates who possess the 21st-century skills needed by the 21st-industry (Sorko & Brunnhofer, 2019; Turkan et al., 2017; Yilmaz & Batdi, 2016; 2020).

Diana Laurillard's Conversational Framework presents a learner-centered strategy for education. The best learning experiences combine all six learning types which were discussed in the preceding section.

Learning is an educational endeavor that develops both practice and theory. Theories are developed, then they generate actions, and the response to the action then adjusts the theory to generate better actions. Theory and practice each assist the other. The Conversational Framework positions the learner at the center. The student can obtain assistance from the lecturer on one hand and from peers as an alternative.

Leaners and lecturers form and distribute their practice through activities, reviews, and feedback in an educational environment. The interactions pose a window of opportunities for practice to prevail. A challenging learning environment calls for the integration of theory and practice to obtain the best meaningful feedback. The Conversational Framework identifies recognizable learning activities which together cover all the six learning types (Production, Acquisition, Collaboration, Discussion, Inquiry, and Practice).

AVR technology should therefore be adopted in teaching and learning in marginalized communities to bridge the digital divide between the bountiful and the poverty-stricken to reap the full benefits that digital inclusion brings to the table

*Figure 2. The conversational framework for supporting the formal learning process.*
*Source: (Laurillard, 2008)*

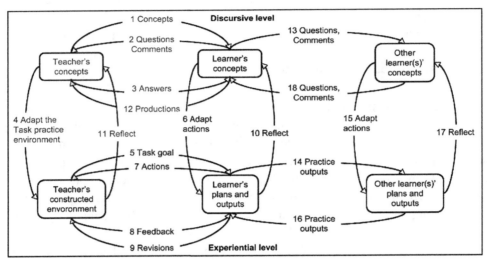

in education, especially during disruptions, as it enhances all the six learning types (Luz Yolanda Toro Suarez, 2015; Ornstein & Hunkins, 2018; Ra et al., 2019).

## CLOUD COMPUTING, AVR MODEL

Pursuant to the merged Cloud Computing and AVR technologies, below is a diagrammatical representation of the model.

The model has various components which have to work together for digital inclusion to be achieved. The first layer comprises three components: the AVR, the education creator, the virtual trainer, and the knowledge injection. The education creator is responsible for generating the teaching and learning materials that will utilize the advantages of the twin technology. The education creator needs support from both the government as a policy maker and the institutions of higher learning as the developer and implementer of the curriculum to support digital inclusion in marginalized communities. The virtual trainer promotes transformative education, learning through experience, autonomous learning, problem-based learning, action learning, and other andragogic learning types to enhance the teaching and learning experience while promoting digital inclusion concurrently. The knowledge injection functionality alludes to a repository that stores the knowledge on the AVR platform. The merged platform (Cloud computing and AVR technologies) consists of the VR component, AR element, library content, branding component, and cloud. The AVR

*Figure 3. Cloud computing, AVR model*
Source: (authors)

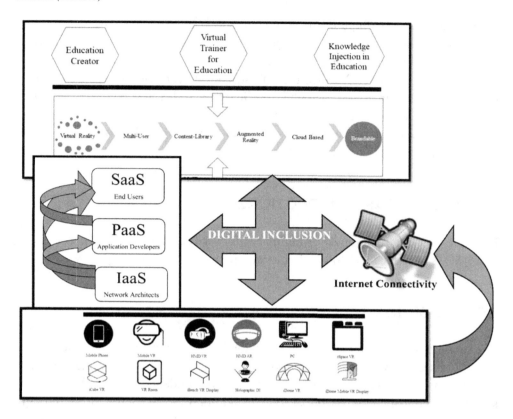

deck provides support throughout assorted devices and diverse patrons (learners and educators alike) foster collaborative training, teaching, and learning practices. The deck also consists of the content library, which supports the AVR lectures and objects to transfer knowledge. Institutions can customize the platform through the utilization of the brandable component. Content is accessible ubiquitously, thereby promoting digital inclusion in marginalized communities.

Cloud computing services like SaaS, PaaS, and IaaS are provided to cut software, platform, and infrastructural costs. Internet connectivity alludes to the way learners and educators will be hooked up to the internet. This may include satellite connections, broadband connections, dial-up telephone lines, and various other wireless devices. Stakeholders will connect to the cloud using various digital devices to access the teaching and learning materials via the internet. The last layer comprises various AVR devices that can be used to promote teaching and learning andragogic theories.

## SOLUTIONS AND RECOMMENDATIONS

An AVR and Cloud Computing technology model was developed to promote digital inclusion in marginalized communities. AVR, VR, and AR technologies bring unimaginable benefits to the education sector, while Cloud computing services like IaaS, SaaS, and PaaS bridge the infrastructural needs of the technology. The Conversational Framework explained the learning styles and how digital media can be utilized to promote, support, and enhance all the learning types. A holistic view of the entire curriculum is possible with these twin technologies instead of just developing 3D content for a particular topic.

## FUTURE RESEARCH DIRECTIONS

Future research can examine the training needs of the educators and learners on how to use ICTs to reduce the digital divide and improve digital literacy.

## CONCLUSION

The research study promotes digital inclusion in marginalized communities in the education sector by integrating AVR technology and Cloud computing services. The fusion of the twin technologies will empower students with the 21st-century skill sets to contribute to the global society and improve the quality of life through innovation and industrialization. The training needs of educators can also be fulfilled through the AVR and Cloud Computing model.

## REFERENCES

Abad-Segura, E., González-Zamar, M. D., Luque-de la Rosa, A., & Cevallos, M. B. M. (2020). Sustainability of educational technologies: An approach to augmented reality research. *Sustainability (Switzerland)*, *12*(10), 4091. Advance online publication. doi:10.3390u12104091

Abad-Segura, E., González-Zamar, M. D., Luque-de la Rosa, A., Cevallos, M. B. M., & Bao, W., Luz Yolanda Toro Suarez, Bloom, D. A., Reid, J. R., Cassady, C. I., Murphy, M. P. A., Osman, M. E. T., Papanastasiou, G., Drigas, A., Skianis, C., Lytras, M., Papanastasiou, E., Quintero, J., Baldiris, S., Rubira, R., ... Jové, T. (2020). Global impact of COVID-19 on education systems: The emergency remote teaching at Sultan Qaboos University. *Contemporary Security Policy*, *10*(3), 425–436. doi:10.100700247-020-04728-8

Adams, M., Klinsky, S., & Chhetri, N. (2020). Barriers to sustainability in poor marginalized communities in the United States: The criminal justice, the prison-industrial complex and foster care systems. *Sustainability (Switzerland)*, *12*(1), 220. Advance online publication. doi:10.3390u12010220

Akçayır, M., & Akçayır, G. (2017). Advantages and challenges associated with augmented reality for education: A systematic review of the literature. *Educational Research Review*, *20*, 1–11. doi:10.1016/j.edurev.2016.11.002

Aryati, A. (2017). Mastering Digital Transformation Transforming Government. *The Electronic Library*, *34*(1), 1–5.

Aziz, A., & Aziz, A. (2020). Digital inclusion challenges in Bangladesh : The case of the National ICT Policy ICT Policy. *Contemporary South Asia*, *0*(0), 1–16. doi:10.1080/09584935.2020.1793912

Bao, W. (2020). COVID -19 and online teaching in higher education: A case study of Peking University. *Human Behavior and Emerging Technologies*, *2*(2), 113–115. doi:10.1002/hbe2.191 PMID:32510042

Bellalouna, F. (2021). The Augmented Reality Technology as Enabler for the Digitization of Industrial Business Processes: Case Studies. *Procedia CIRP*, *98*, 400–405. doi:10.1016/j.procir.2021.01.124

Bloom, D. A., Reid, J. R., & Cassady, C. I. (2020). Education in the time of COVID-19. *Pediatric Radiology*, *50*(8), 1055–1058. doi:10.100700247-020-04728-8 PMID:32468286

Cabero-Almenara, J., Fernández-Batanero, J. M., & Barroso-Osuna, J. (2019). Adoption of augmented reality technology by university students. *Heliyon*, *5*(5), e01597. Advance online publication. doi:10.1016/j.heliyon.2019.e01597 PMID:31193247

Calabrese Barton, A., & Tan, E. (2018). A Longitudinal Study of Equity-Oriented STEM-Rich Making Among Youth From Historically Marginalized Communities. *American Educational Research Journal, 55*(4), 761–800. doi:10.3102/0002831218758668

Campbell-meier, J., Sylvester, A., & Goulding, A. (2020). *Indigenous Digital Inclusion : Interconnections and Comparisons.* Academic Press.

Chen, T., Zhang, Y., Ding, C., Ting, K., Yoon, S., Sahak, H., Hope, A., McLachlin, S., Crawford, E., Hardisty, M., Larouche, J., & Finkelstein, J. (2021). Virtual reality as a learning tool in spinal anatomy and surgical techniques. *North American Spine Society Journal, 6*(January), 100063. doi:10.1016/j.xnsj.2021.100063 PMID:35141628

Chen, W., Li, X., & Chen, W. (2021). Digital inequalities in American disadvantaged urban communities : Access, skills, and expectations for digital inclusion programs inclusion programs. *Information Communication and Society, 0*(0), 1–18. doi:10.1080/1369118X.2021.1907434

Dahunsi, F., & Owoseni, T. (2014). Cloud Computing in Nigeria: The Cloud Ecosystem Perspective. *Nigerian Journal of Technology, 34*(1), 209. doi:10.4314/njt.v34i1.26

Dehghani, M., Lee, S. H., & Mashatan, A. (2020). Touching holograms with windows mixed reality: Renovating the consumer retailing services. *Technology in Society, 63*(August), 101394. doi:10.1016/j.techsoc.2020.101394

Ferrati, F., Erkoyuncu, J. A., & Court, S. (2019). Developing an augmented reality based training demonstrator for manufacturing cherry pickers. *Procedia CIRP, 81*, 803–808. doi:10.1016/j.procir.2019.03.203

Flavián, C., Ibáñez-sánchez, S., & Orús, C. (2019). The impact of virtual, augmented and mixed reality technologies on the customer experience. *Journal of Business Research, 100*(November), 547–560. doi:10.1016/j.jbusres.2018.10.050

Fonseca, D., Villagrasa, S., Martí, N., Redondo, E., & Sánchez, A. (2013). Visualization Methods in Architecture Education Using 3D Virtual Models and Augmented Reality in Mobile and Social Networks. *Procedia: Social and Behavioral Sciences, 93*, 1337–1343. doi:10.1016/j.sbspro.2013.10.040

Fuvattanasilp, V., Fujimoto, Y., Plopski, A., Taketomi, T., Sandor, C., Kanbara, M., & Kato, H. (2021). SlidAR+: Gravity-aware 3D object manipulation for handheld augmented reality. *Computers and Graphics (Pergamon), 95*, 23–35. doi:10.1016/j.cag.2021.01.005

Gargrish, S., Mantri, A., & Kaur, D. P. (2020). Augmented reality-based learning environment to enhance teaching-learning experience in geometry education. *Procedia Computer Science, 172*(2019), 1039–1046. doi:10.1016/j.procs.2020.05.152

Garzón, J., & Acevedo, J. (2019). Meta-analysis of the impact of Augmented Reality on students' learning gains. *Educational Research Review, 27*(March), 244–260. doi:10.1016/j.edurev.2019.04.001

Georgiou, Y., & Kyza, E. A. (2020). Bridging narrative and locality in mobile-based augmented reality educational activities: Effects of semantic coupling on students' immersion and learning gains. *International Journal of Human-Computer Studies, 102546*. Advance online publication. doi:10.1016/j.ijhcs.2020.102546

Haenssgen, M. J. (2018). The struggle for digital inclusion : Phones, healthcare, and marginalization in rural India. *World Development, 104*, 358–374. doi:10.1016/j.worlddev.2017.12.023

Hansen, C., Wieferich, J., Ritter, F., Rieder, C., & Peitgen, H. O. (2010). Illustrative visualization of 3D planning models for augmented reality in liver surgery. *International Journal of Computer Assisted Radiology and Surgery, 5*(2), 133–141. doi:10.100711548-009-0365-3 PMID:20033519

Herpich, F., Guarese, R. L. M., & Tarouco, L. M. R. (2017). A Comparative Analysis of Augmented Reality Frameworks Aimed at the Development of Educational Applications. *Creative Education, 08*(09), 1433–1451. doi:10.4236/ce.2017.89101

Hespanhol, L., & Farmer, J. (2018). *The Digital Fringe and Social Participation through Interaction Design*. Academic Press.

Hon, D. (2019). Medical reality and virtual reality. In Studies in Health Technology and Informatics (Vol. 29). doi:10.3233/978-1-60750-873-1-327

Huuskonen, J., & Oksanen, T. (2019). Augmented Reality for Supervising Multirobot System in Agricultural Field Operation. *IFAC-PapersOnLine, 52*(30), 367–372. doi:10.1016/j.ifacol.2019.12.568

Iji, C. O., & Abah, J. A. (2019). Internet Skills as a Measure of Digital Inclusion among Mathematics Education Students: Implications for Sustainable Human Capital Development in Nigeria. *International Journal of Education and Knowledge Management*. https://rpajournals.com/ijekm

Karambakhsh, A., Kamel, A., Sheng, B., Li, P., Yang, P., & Feng, D. D. (2019). Deep gesture interaction for augmented anatomy learning. *International Journal of Information Management, 45*(October), 328–336. doi:10.1016/j. ijinfomgt.2018.03.004

Kempin Reuter, T. (2019). Human rights and the city: Including marginalized communities in urban development and smart cities. *Journal of Human Rights, 18*(4), 382–402. doi:10.1080/14754835.2019.1629887

Koehler, M. J., Mishra, P., Akcaoglu, M., & Rosenberg, J. M. (2013). The Technological Pedagogical Content Knowledge Framework for Teachers and Teacher Educators. *ICT Integrated Teacher Mducation Models*, 1–8. http://cemca. org.in/ckfinder/userfiles/files/ICT teacher education Module 1 Final_May 20.pdf

Kurniawan, M. H., Suharjito, Diana, & Witjaksono, G. (2018). Human Anatomy Learning Systems Using Augmented Reality on Mobile Application. *Procedia Computer Science, 135*, 80–88. doi:10.1016/j.procs.2018.08.152

Laurillard, D. (2007a). *Laurillard's six learning types Inquiry/Investigation Practice Students work together to build on each other's learning through joint practice and*. http://eprints.ioe.ac.uk/627/1/Mobile_C6_Laurillard.pdf

Laurillard, D. (2007b). Pedagogical forms of mobile learning: framing research questions. *Mobile Learning: Towards a Research Agenda*, 153–175. http://eprints. ioe.ac.uk/627/1/Mobile_C6_Laurillard.pdf

Laurillard, D. (2008). The teacher as action researcher: Using technology to capture pedagogic form. *Studies in Higher Education, 33*(2), 139–154. doi:10.1080/03075070801915908

Malungu, C., & Moturi, C. (2015). ICT Infrastructure Sharing Framework for Developing Countries: Case of Mobile Operators in Kenya. *International Journal of Applied Information Systems, 9*(4), 17–24. doi:10.5120/ijais15-451392

Mangina, E. (2018). 3D learning objects for augmented/virtual reality educational ecosystems. *Proceedings of the 2017 23rd International Conference on Virtual Systems and Multimedia, VSMM 2017,* 1–6. 10.1109/VSMM.2017.8346266

Marcu, I. M., Suciu, G., Balaceanu, C. M., & Banaru, A. (2019). IoT based System for Smart Agriculture. *Proceedings of the 11th International Conference on Electronics, Computers and Artificial Intelligence, ECAI 2019*. 10.1109/ ECAI46879.2019.9041952

Marshall, A., Dezuanni, M., Burgess, J., Thomas, J., & Wilson, C. K. (2020). Australian farmers left behind in the digital economy – Insights from the Australian Digital Inclusion Index. *Journal of Rural Studies, 80*(September), 195–210. doi:10.1016/j. jrurstud.2020.09.001

Matsika, C., & Zhou, M. (2021). Factors affecting the adoption and use of AVR technology in higher and tertiary education. *Technology in Society, 67*(July), 101694. doi:10.1016/j.techsoc.2021.101694

Michael, A., Ndaghu, A. A., & Mshelia, S. I. (2016). Assessment of Social Inclusiveness of Vulnerable and Marginalized Groups in Fadama Ii Project in Yola North Local Government Area of Adamawa State, Nigeria. *Scientific Papers. Series Management, Economic, Engineering in Agriculture and Rural Development, 16*(April).

Namani, S., & Gonen, B. (2020). Smart agriculture based on IoT and cloud computing. *Proceedings - 3rd International Conference on Information and Computer Technologies, ICICT 2020*, 553–556. 10.1109/ICICT50521.2020.00094

Niţă, A.-M., & Pârvu, M. C. (2020). Vulnerability and resilience in marginalized rural communities. Case study: projects for reduction of risk exclusion in Dolj County. *Revista de Stiinte Politice, 67*, 103–117. https:// www.proquest.com/scholarly-journals/vulnerability-resilience-marginalized-rural/docview/2447285558/se-2?accountid=14166%0Ahttps://suny-alb.primo. exlibrisgroup.com/openurl/01SUNY_ALB/01SUNY_ALB:01SUNY_ALB?genr e=article&atitle=Vulnerability+and+resi

Ornstein, A. C., & Hunkins, F. P. (2018). Social Foundations of Curriculum. In *Curriculum* (7th ed.). Foundation, Principles and Issues.

Pranoto, H., & Panggabean, F. M. (2019). ScienceDirect ScienceDirect. *Procedia Computer Science, 157*, 506–513. doi:10.1016/j.procs.2019.09.007

Quintero, J., Baldiris, S., Rubira, R., Cerón, J., & Velez, G. (2019). Augmented reality in educational inclusion. A systematic review on the last decade. *Frontiers in Psychology, 10*(AUG), 1–14. doi:10.3389/fpsyg.2019.01835 PMID:31456716

Ra, S., Shrestha, U., Khatiwada, S., Yoon, S. W., & Kwon, K. (2019). The rise of technology and impact on skills. *International Journal of Training Research, 17*(sup1), 26–40. doi:10.1080/14480220.2019.1629727

Ray, P. P. (2017). Internet of things for smart agriculture: Technologies, practices and future direction. *Journal of Ambient Intelligence and Smart Environments, 9*(4), 395–420. doi:10.3233/AIS-170440

Rhinesmith, C. (2016). *Digital Inclusion and Meaningful Broadband Adoption Initiatives Digital Inclusion and Meaningful Broadband Adoption Initiatives.* Academic Press.

Sandu, N., Gide, E., & Karim, S. (2019). Improving learning through cloud-based mobile technologies and virtual and augmented reality for australian higher education. *ACM International Conference Proceeding Series*, 1–5. 10.1145/3348400.3348413

Sannikov, S., Zhdanov, F., Chebotarev, P., & Rabinovich, P. (2015). Interactive Educational Content Based on Augmented Reality and 3D Visualization. In Procedia Computer Science (Vol. 66). Elsevier Masson SAS. doi:10.1016/j.procs.2015.11.082

Sarantou, M., & Akimenko, D. (2018). Margin to Margin. *Arts-Based Research for Digital Outreach to Marginalized Communities.*, *14*, 139–159.

Sevelius, J. M., Gutierrez-Mock, L., Zamudio-Haas, S., McCree, B., Ngo, A., Jackson, A., Clynes, C., Venegas, L., Salinas, A., Herrera, C., Stein, E., Operario, D., & Gamarel, K. (2020). Research with Marginalized Communities: Challenges to Continuity During the COVID-19 Pandemic. *AIDS and Behavior*, *24*(7), 2009–2012. doi:10.100710461-020-02920-3 PMID:32415617

Sorko, S. R., & Brunnhofer, M. (2019). Potentials of Augmented Reality in Training. *Procedia Manufacturing*, *31*, 85–90. doi:10.1016/j.promfg.2019.03.014

Study, C., Countries, F., & Republic, D. (2019). ICT for Learning and Inclusion in Latin America and Europe Case Study From Countries: Bolivia, Brazil, Cuba, Dominican Republic, Ecuador, Finland, Poland, Turkey, Uruguay. doi:10.24917/9788395373732

Tan, K. L., & Lim, C. K. (2018). Development of traditional musical instruments using augmented reality (AR) through mobile learning. *AIP Conference Proceedings*, *2016*(September), 1–7. doi:10.1063/1.5055542

Turkan, Y., Radkowski, R., Karabulut-Ilgu, A., Behzadan, A. H., & Chen, A. (2017). Mobile augmented reality for teaching structural analysis. *Advanced Engineering Informatics*, *34*(October), 90–100. doi:10.1016/j.aei.2017.09.005

Uy-tioco, C. S. (2019). 'Good enough' access : Digital inclusion, social stratification, and the reinforcement of class in the Philippines. *Communication Research and Practice*, *5*(2), 156–171. doi:10.1080/22041451.2019.1601492

Valverde-Berrocoso, J., del Carmen Garrido-Arroyo, M., Burgos-Videla, C., & Morales-Cevallos, M. B. (2020). Trends in educational research about e-Learning: A systematic literature review (2009-2018). *Sustainability (Switzerland)*, *12*(12), 5153. Advance online publication. doi:10.3390u12125153

Williams, M. (2017). John Dewey in the 21st century. *Journal of Inquiry and Action in Education, 9*(1), 91–102.

Willis, K. S. (2019). *Making a 'Place' for ICTs in Rural Communities.* Academic Press.

Yilmaz, Z. A., & Batdi, V. (2016). A meta-analytic and thematic comparative analysis of the integration of augmented reality applications into education. *Egitim ve Bilim, 41*(188), 273–289. doi:10.15390/EB.2016.6707

## ADDITIONAL READING

Bacca, J., Baldiris, S., Fabregat, R., Kinshuk, & Graf, S. (2015). Mobile Augmented Reality in Vocational Education and Training. *Procedia Computer Science, 75*(Vare), 49–58. doi:10.1016/j.procs.2015.12.203

Bernacki, M. L., Greene, J. A., & Crompton, H. (2020). Mobile technology, learning, and achievement: Advances in understanding and measuring the role of mobile technology in education. *Contemporary Educational Psychology, 60,* 101827. doi:10.1016/j.cedpsych.2019.101827

Blankemeyer, S., Wiemann, R., Posniak, L., Pregizer, C., Raatz, A., Stief, P., Dantan, J., Etienne, A., & Siadat, A. (2018). ScienceDirect A new methodology to analyze the functional and physical architecture of Robot Programming Using Augmented Reality Nantes, France Reality Intuitive Robot Programming Using Augmented existing products for an assembly oriented product family. *Procedia CIRP, 76,* 155–160. doi:10.1016/j.procir.2018.02.028

Chiemeke, S., & Mike Imafidor, O. (2020). Web-based Learning In Periods of Crisis: Reflections on the Impact of Covid-19. *International Journal of Computer Science and Information Technologies, 12*(3), 33–46. doi:10.5121/ijcsit.2020.12303

Curcio, I. D. D., Dipace, A., & Norlund, A. (2017). Virtual realities and education. *Research on Education and Media, 8*(2), 60–68. doi:10.1515/rem-2016-0019

Dean, G. (2015). Digital Inclusion and Digital Literacy in the United States: A Portrait from PIAAC's Survey of Adult Skills. *Journal of Research and Practice for Adult Literacy, Secondary, and Basic Education, 4*(2), 58–62. http://search.ebscohost.com/login.aspx?direct=true&db=a9h&AN=108974345&site=ehost-live&scope=site

Dhawan, S. (2020). Online Learning: A Panacea in the Time of COVID-19 Crisis. *Journal of Educational Technology Systems, 49*(1), 5–22. doi:10.1177/0047239520934018

Gondchawar, N., & Kawitkar, R. S. (2016). IoT based smart agriculture. *International Journal of Advanced Research in Computer and Communication Engineering*, *5*(6), 838–842. doi:10.17148/IJARCCE.2016.56188

Huang, T. C., Chen, C. C., & Chou, Y. W. (2016). Animating eco-education: To see, feel, and discover in an augmented reality-based experiential learning environment. *Computers & Education*, *96*, 72–82. doi:10.1016/j.compedu.2016.02.008

Huang, T. K., Yang, C. H., Hsieh, Y. H., Wang, J. C., & Hung, C. C. (2018). Augmented reality (AR) and virtual reality (VR) applied in dentistry. *The Kaohsiung Journal of Medical Sciences*, *34*(4), 243–248. doi:10.1016/j.kjms.2018.01.009 PMID:29655414

Ji, C., Lu, H., Ji, C., & Yan, J. (2015). An IoT and Mobile Cloud based Architecture for Smart Planting. *Proceedings of the 2015 3rd International Conference on Machinery, Materials and Information Technology Applications*, *35*, 1001–1005. 10.2991/icmmita-15.2015.184

Kerthyayana Manuaba, I. B. (2021). Mobile based Augmented Reality Application Prototype for Remote Collaboration Scenario Using ARCore Cloud Anchor. *Procedia Computer Science*, *179*(2020), 289–296. doi:10.1016/j.procs.2021.01.008

Khan, T., Johnston, K., & Ophoff, J. (2019). The Impact of an Augmented Reality Application on Learning Motivation of Students. *Advances in Human-Computer Interaction*, *2019*, 1–14. Advance online publication. doi:10.1155/2019/7208494

Kljun, M., Geroimenko, V., & Čopič Pucihar, K. (2020). Augmented Reality in Education: Current Status and Advancement of the Field. Springer Series on Cultural Computing. doi:10.1007/978-3-030-42156-4_1

Krokos, E., Plaisant, C., & Varshney, A. (2019). Virtual memory palaces: Immersion aids recall. *Virtual Reality (Waltham Cross)*, *23*(1), 1–15. Advance online publication. doi:10.100710055-018-0346-3

Küçük, S., Kapakin, S., & Göktaş, Y. (2016). Learning anatomy via mobile augmented reality: Effects on achievement and cognitive load. *Anatomical Sciences Education*, *9*(5), 411–421. doi:10.1002/ase.1603 PMID:26950521

Lai, C. H., Wu, T. E., Huang, S. H., & Huang, Y. M. (2020). Developing a virtual learning tool for industrial high schools' welding course. *Procedia Computer Science*, *172*(2019), 696–700. doi:10.1016/j.procs.2020.05.091

Lindgren, R., Tscholl, M., Wang, S., & Johnson, E. (2016). Enhancing learning and engagement through embodied interaction within a mixed reality simulation. *Computers & Education*, *95*, 174–187. doi:10.1016/j.compedu.2016.01.001

Lotsaris, K., Fousekis, N., Koukas, S., Aivaliotis, S., Kousi, N., Michalos, G., & Makris, S. (2020). Augmented Reality (AR) based framework for supporting human workers in flexible manufacturing. *Procedia CIRP*, *96*, 301–306. doi:10.1016/j.procir.2021.01.091

Mahalakshmi, K., & Radha, R. (2020). Covid 19: A Massive Exposure Towards Web Based Learning. *Journal of Xidian University*, *14*(4). Advance online publication. doi:10.37896/jxu14.4/266

Mendez, K. J. W., Piasecki, R. J., Hudson, K., Renda, S., Mollenkopf, N., Nettles, B. S., & Han, H. R. (2020). Virtual and augmented reality: Implications for the future of nursing education. *Nurse Education Today*, *93*(June), 2019–2021. doi:10.1016/j.nedt.2020.104531 PMID:32711132

Moro, C., Smith, J., & Finch, E. (2021). Improving stroke education with augmented reality : A randomized control trial. *Computers and Education Open*, *2*(March), 100032. doi:10.1016/j.caeo.2021.100032

Mourtzis, D., Xanthi, F., & Zogopoulos, V. (2019). An adaptive framework for augmented reality instructions considering workforce skill. *Procedia CIRP*, *81*, 363–368. doi:10.1016/j.procir.2019.03.063

Murphy, M. P. A. (2020). COVID-19 and emergency eLearning: Consequences of the securitization of higher education for post-pandemic pedagogy. *Contemporary Security Policy*, *41*(3), 492–505. doi:10.1080/13523260.2020.1761749

Mylonas, G., Triantafyllis, C., & Amaxilatis, D. (2019). An Augmented Reality Prototype for supporting IoT-based Educational Activities for Energy-efficient School Buildings. *Electronic Notes in Theoretical Computer Science*, *343*, 89–101. doi:10.1016/j.entcs.2019.04.012

Osman, M. E. T. (2020). Global impact of COVID-19 on education systems: The emergency remote teaching at Sultan Qaboos University. *Journal of Education for Teaching*, *46*(4), 463–471. doi:10.1080/02607476.2020.1802583

Patil, G., & Vilasrao Bag, R. (2017). Smart Agriculture System based on IoT and its Social Impact. *International Journal of Computers and Applications*, *176*(1), 1–4. doi:10.5120/ijca2017915500

Popenici, S. A. D., & Kerr, S. (2017). Exploring the impact of artificial intelligence on teaching and learning in higher education. *Research and Practice in Technology Enhanced Learning*, *12*(1), 22. Advance online publication. doi:10.118641039-017-0062-8 PMID:30595727

Qian, J., Ma, Y., Pan, Z., & Yang, X. (2020). Effects of Virtual-real fusion on immersion, presence, and learning performance in laboratory education. *Virtual Reality & Intelligent Hardware*, *2*(6), 569–584. doi:10.1016/j.vrih.2020.07.010

Raja, R., & Nagasubramani, P. C. (2018). Impact of modern technology in education. *Journal of Applied and Advanced Research*, *3*(S1), 33. doi:10.21839/jaar.2018. v3iS1.165

Rashid, S., & Yadav, S. S. (2020). Impact of Covid-19 Pandemic on Higher Education and Research. *Indian Journal of Human Development*, *14*(2), 340–343. doi:10.1177/0973703020946700

Rauschnabel, P. A. (2021). International Journal of Information Management Augmented reality is eating the real-world ! The substitution of physical products by holograms. *International Journal of Information Management, 57*(December), 102279. doi:10.1016/j.ijinfomgt.2020.102279

Saab, M. M., Hegarty, J., Murphy, D., & Landers, M. (2021). Nurse Education Today Incorporating virtual reality in nurse education : A qualitative study of nursing students' perspectives. *Nurse Education Today, 105*(November), 105045. doi:10.1016/j.nedt.2021.105045

Sahu, H., Modala, P., Jiwankar, A., & Wagle, S. (2019). Multidisciplinary Model for Smart Agriculture using IoT. *Ijresm.Com, 3*, 245–247. https://www.ijresm.com/ Vol.2_2019/Vol2_Iss3_March19/IJRESM_V2_I3_63.pdf

Salsabila, U. H. (2019). A Preliminary Analysis: Digital Inclusion Domain in Islamic Education. *International Journal on E-Learning*, *1*(1), 12–18. doi:10.31763/ijele. v1i1.23

Scavarelli, A., Arya, A., & Teather, R. J. (2020). Virtual reality and augmented reality in social learning spaces: A literature review. *Virtual Reality (Waltham Cross)*. Advance online publication. doi:10.100710055-020-00444-8

Schleicher, A. (2020). The impact of COVID-19 on education: Insights from education at a glance 2020. *OECD Journal: Economic Studies*, 1–31. https://www. oecd.org/education/the-impact-of-covid-19-on-education-insights-education-at-a-glance-2020.pdf

Schumann, M., Fuchs, C., Kollatsch, C., & Klimant, P. (2020). Evaluation of augmented reality supported approaches for product design and production processes. *Procedia CIRP*, *97*, 160–165. doi:10.1016/j.procir.2020.05.219

Sharif, A., Anzum, F., Zavin, A., Suha, S. A., Ibnat, A., & Islam, M. N. (2018). Exploring the opportunities and challenges of adopting augmented reality in education in a developing country. *Proceedings - IEEE 18th International Conference on Advanced Learning Technologies, ICALT 2018*, 364–366. 10.1109/ICALT.2018.00091

Sonntag, D., Albuquerque, G., Magnor, M., & Bodensiek, O. (2019). Hybrid learning environments by data-driven augmented reality. *Procedia Manufacturing*, *31*, 32–37. doi:10.1016/j.promfg.2019.03.006

Spanaki, K., Sivarajah, U., Fakhimi, M., Despoudi, S., & Irani, Z. (2021). Disruptive technologies in agricultural operations: a systematic review of AI-driven AgriTech research. In Annals of Operations Research. Springer US. doi:10.100710479-020-03922-z

Toquero, C. M. (2020). Challenges and Opportunities for Higher Education amid the COVID-19 Pandemic: The Philippine Context. *Pedagogical Research*, *5*(4), em0063. Advance online publication. doi:10.29333/pr/7947

Trapero, H. A. (2018). Augmented reality in innovating pedagogy: Ethical issues on persuasive technologies. *ICCE 2018 - 26th International Conference on Computers in Education, Main Conference Proceedings*, 494–499.

Vargas, J. C. G., Fabregat, R., Carrillo-Ramos, A., & Jové, T. (2020). Survey: Using augmented reality to improve learning motivation in cultural heritage studies. *Applied Sciences (Switzerland)*, *10*(3), 897. Advance online publication. doi:10.3390/app10030897

Zhou, X., Tang, L., Lin, D., & Han, W. (2020). Virtual & augmented reality for biological microscope in experiment education. *Virtual Reality & Intelligent Hardware*, *2*(4), 316–329. doi:10.1016/j.vrih.2020.07.004

Zhu, Y., & Li, N. (2021). Journal of Safety Science and Resilience Virtual and augmented reality technologies for emergency management in the built environments : A state-of-the-art review. *Journal of Safety Science and Resilience*, *2*(1), 1–10. doi:10.1016/j.jnlssr.2020.11.004

## KEY TERMS AND DEFINITIONS

**Augmented Reality:** Integration of the physical environment with the virtual environment.

**AVR Technology:** Augmented and virtual reality technology enhances the teaching and learning process and bridges infrastructural costs.

**Cloud Computing:** Offering infrastructure, software, and platform as a service.

**Digital Inclusiveness:** Equal access to technology by students of all backgrounds.

**Digital Technologies:** Creation and use of Information Technology devices.

**Disruptive Technologies:** Advances in digital technologies.

**Inclusive Education:** Affording students of all backgrounds equal opportunities to learn and grow side by side.

**Marginalized Communities:** Populations that have limited access to digital technology.

**Virtual Reality:** A computer-simulated environment that is identical to the physical environment.

# Chapter 3
# Digitalization for Sustainable Agriculture Production in Marginalized and Remote Communities

**Njodzi Ranganai**
*Manicaland State University of Applied Sciences, Zimbabwe*

**Tendai Shelton Muwani**
*Manicaland State University of Applied Sciences, Zimbabwe*

**Nyasha Sakadzo**
*Manicaland State University of Applied Sciences, Zimbabwe*

**Andrew Tapiwa Kugedera**
 https://orcid.org/0000-0002-1700-6922
*Zimbabwe Open University, Zimbabwe*

**Florence Chimbwanda**
*Zimbabwe Open University, Zimbabwe*

**Lemias Zivanai**
*Midlands State University, Zimbabwe*

**Briget Munyoro**
*Midlands State University, Zimbabwe*

## ABSTRACT

*Digitalization is an important agriculture tool for achieving the Sustainable Development Goals (SDGs) in marginalized and remote communities. There is a scarcity of data linking digitalization, sustainable agriculture production, marginalized and remote communities in Sub-Saharan Africa. This study reviews digitalization for sustainable agriculture production in marginalized and remote communities of Sub-Saharan Africa. A total of 150 published papers from 2000-2022 were retrieved, and all those outside Africa were removed to leave a total of 125 papers. Results obtained indicate that digital technology transforms agriculture by promoting precision agriculture in marginalized rural communities in a more efficient approach by integrating different processes. Econet Wireless Zimbabwe is*

DOI: 10.4018/978-1-6684-3901-2.ch003

*offering various bundle options which come through small messages (SMS) and call centers such as Eco-Farmer. Governments should invest in and make policies to improve digitalization in marginalized communities as it ultimately solves challenges such as nutrition, food insecurity, and climate change.*

## INTRODUCTION

Digitalization is one of the recipes for sustainable agriculture in achieving sustainable development goals (SDGs) objectives in marginalized and remote communities. It is the only way of linking multinationals with a market of clients in remote and marginalized communities. Digitalization can involve the use of mobile phones as digital technologies and data for communicating platforms (OECD, 2018). Smallholder farmers can sell their agricultural products without the need for go-betweens as they are directly involved in the value chain locally or globally. Better involvement of various stakeholders along the value chain promotes global communication from the prevalent digitalization technologies (FAO, 2018). ITU and FAO (2020a) highlighted that United Nations coined a decade of action by considering the involvement of digital technology to ensure the attainment of the Sustainable development plan Agenda 2030.

Digital agriculture acts as a recovery plan in response to COVID-19 for most farmers in marginalized areas. These farmers are not well acquainted with market information during this pandemic. Haggag (2021) posits that digital technology encourages precision agriculture, promoting efficiency and improving farmers' productivity and quality. Wolfert et al. (2017), likewise postulated that digitalization in agriculture enhances improvement, productivity, and efficiency along the value chain.

## BACKGROUND

This chapter explores current digital innovation technologies for sustainable agricultural production for use in marginalized African communities. African communities' linkages with multinational companies unearth new markets. Technologies are documented so that recommendations are made to smallholder farmers to adopt technologies and electronic services for smart agriculture and farm productivity improvement hence marginalized and remote communities are put at the heart of digital technology research. Furthermore, this chapter will also discover the significance of electronic training of farmers and Agritex officers for extension-based technology transfer in remote areas. The elimination of technological gaps and digital illiteracy is a tool for auto-technical assistance.

Regardless of the benefits of digital technology, smallholder farmers in marginalized and remote areas experience many challenges in farming (FAO, 2014; Cheo and Tapiwa, 2021a). Various authors (Biles, 2006, Mupangwa et al., 2012, FAO, 2019) outlined various shocks of challenges that pertain to information such as (market, capital, climate change, and lack of modernized machinery). European Union (EU) (2017) notified the diversity of digital technologies that differ in terms of complexity and advance that can be accessed. Together, these technologies mentioned in the discussion promote a global village for better linkages of remote and marginalized farmers to participate in the value chain linkages, e-training, and advisory management.

Moreover, this chapter will also consider farmers' advisory management software through digitalization, such as climate forecasting (GIS and remote sensing), which encourages precision agriculture in marginalized rural areas. Farmers in remote areas where roads are bad will be exposed to various online advisory information from various sources. The use of farmers' advisory software through remote sensing and geographic information systems (GIS) in agriculture production in marginalized areas can improve production. For an agriculturally based country, reliable and timely information on the types of crops planted, their area, and predicted yield is critical. Shanmugapriya et al. (2019) postulated various benefits of remote sensing and modelling in creating graph-like linked markets.

Exploring digital market linkage value chain integration services for market transparency will be discussed for effective recommendations to farmers in remote communities. There will be a direct linkage of farmers with their consumers, eliminating overreliance on middlemen and maximizing profits. Marginalized farmers' involvement in the value chain will expose them to market information that links them to buyers and sellers. In addition, this chapter will explore opportunities and challenges for digital agriculture in remote and marginalized communities.

## MAIN FOCUS OF THE CHAPTER

The chapter focuses on sustainable agricultural production through digitalization. The major constructs discussed are digital innovation technologies for sustainable agricultural production in marginalized; benefits of digital innovation technologies for sustainable agriculture in marginalized communities; farmers advisory management software through digitalization that is Eco-farmer, climate forecasting (GIS and remote sensing); e-training of farmers and Agritex officers for extension-based technology transfer; and opportunities and challenges for digital agriculture in remote and marginalized communities. The study used a systematic literature research design in searching for published papers in Scopus, Web of Science, Google

Scholar, DHET, ISI, and Norwegian index. The study used papers published from 2000 to 2022 to show the changes done to meet sustainable agriculture. Literature was searched using the following keywords; Digitalisation*sustainable agriculture, digitalisation*marginalised areas, sustainable agriculture*marginalised areas, sustainable agriculture*sub-Saharan African areas, digitalisation*sustainable agriculture*marginalised areas (and/or) semi-arid/ arid areas and sustainable agriculture*Africa. A total of 150 published papers were retrieved, and all those outside Africa were removed to leave a total of 125 papers. The screening was done to remove all papers with grey information, conference papers, and papers published before 2000, leaving 35 published articles. All papers with duplicate information were removed, leaving one of the papers. The objective of this study was to explore digitalization for sustainable agriculture production in marginalized and remote communities of Sub-Saharan Africa.

## Digital Innovation Technologies for Sustainable Agricultural Production in Marginalized Communities

The digital innovation technologies in farming activities altered the way of doing farming business and are the latest evolution in agriculture (Fursteau et al., 2020). Agriculture 4.0 was initialized and strategized from the aspect of Industry, which refers to the utilization of digital innovation technologies to bring a chain that puts together the institutions, consumers, and other major stakeholders together (Sott, et al., 2020). The putting together, keeping, analyzing, and distribution of digital innovation technologies information from several sources with well-spelt objectives is characterized as digital agriculture (Oggioni et al., 2020). To add to this, digital farming includes deploying software and hardware infrastructure with digital innovation technology components. Digital farming supports the conversion of potential facts into intelligible information for sustainable farming production in marginalized remote communities (Bucci et al., 2019). Many authors believe digital innovation technologies offer a solution to the challenges faced by farmers in marginalized communities, and it works as part of a transition toward agriculture production.

The main innovative goal of digital innovation technologies in the agricultural sector vehemently is to speed up the making of decisions. These goals have significantly paid for sustainable agricultural activities in marginalized communities. Flak et al. (2020) argues that sustainability enables rethinking and focusing on implementing farming techniques supported by digital innovation technologies. These digital innovation technologies in agriculture aim to activate and improve supply chains and stimulate the management of natural resources to promote sustainability. To upgrade the knowledge of safety, sustainability-driven farming should be allowed for greater resilience and reactivity. More so, FAO postulated the utilization of digital innovation technologies to speed up productivity and include marginalized communities to address food safety risks (Lanucara et al., 2020).

Digital innovation technologies and the digital inclusion of sustainable agriculture are the centers of an attractive production process on the market. Sustainable digital farming creates emerging trends in technological agricultural enterprises. Furthermore, farming systems reduce the consequences of environmental sustainability failure. More so, digital technologies in agriculture enable social sustainability, which contributes to the development of marginalized remote communities. The shifting of farming into digital agriculture led the sector to integrate with other necessity industries. Therefore, such connections and activities will fight against barriers that hinder agricultural progress (Nikolidakis et al., 2015).

The concept of this digital innovation technology precisely updates farming activities in marginalized communities. Digital innovation technologies for sustainable farming are connected to five sustainable development objectives of the United Nations: smart cities, marginalized societies, competitive jobs, GDP growth, positive farming production, climate action, and infrastructure development (Quayson, 2020). Digital innovation technologies, on the other hand, have several undesirable or unknown implications which may be well-known and become open once these technologies are brought into action (Klerk et al., 2020). Some African countries are moving towards digitalization of agriculture in marginalized areas but the use of other methods such as the adoption of Agroforestry and rainwater harvesting techniques to improve crop production and meet sustainable agriculture, which is climate-smart is still scant (Wuta et al., 2018; Kimaru-Muchai et al., 2021; Kubiku et al., 2022). Countries that are adopting these techniques include Zimbabwe, Kenya, Burkina Faso, Mali, Niger, and Tanzania, although some like Zimbabwe also adopt digitalization.

## Benefits of Digital Innovation Technologies for Sustainable Agriculture in Marginalized Communities

Digital innovation technologies enhance the environmental, economic, and social contribution to sustainable agriculture production in marginalized communities through greater productivity.

### Access to Land by Marginalized Communities

Digital innovation technologies can improve access to geographical information systems for farming by modelling coordinates used for cadastral data, which provide a clear picture of access and utilization of land. Cadastral gathered data for farming help farmers to have the insight of impeding farming land market activities and farm acquisition. This will help smallholder farmers in marginalized communities to have some opportunity to access a piece of land for farming without hindrances since they are connected.

## Employment

Digital innovation technologies like machine learning create a range of jobs in sustainable farming production; proffers processes in land surveying, automation sowing of crops, livestock tracking and monitoring, weed control, and product delivery to the market. However, digital innovation technologies in agriculture may lead people in marginalized communities to be excluded during employment due to a lack of skills. Digital innovation farming enhances the efficiency of agricultural activities. It also reduces the cost of operating, and losses hence revenues are increased. Digital innovation technologies might create employment opportunities, and farmers in remote areas can now have equal recruitment platforms online with people in urban areas.

## Monitoring and Evaluation

The Data collection and analysis can achieve huge cost-effective evaluation and monitoring of farming programs in the country (remote communities) through innovative ICTs for sustainable farming production. Monitoring and evaluation include unbiased information on agricultural investment activities from the internet, which provides precise, timely, and consistent development projects which are sustainable and effective (Ahmed et al., 2016). Furthermore, digital innovation technology for sustainable agriculture enhances aerial imagery, allowing soil analyses, especially ground-level monitoring, drones, sensor plant, and water inspections in marginalized communities.

## Automation of Data Collection and Information Dissemination in Marginalized Communities

The bringing in of emerging trends in technologies to database systems led to data availability on a timely basis in agriculture operations which enables fast sharing of information. These trends in farming technology have been identified as the key opportunity in multiple African countries to achieve sustainable farming production. In remote areas, data gaps are large, and activities of collecting information are very poor. Therefore, if digital innovation technologies are well implemented, it offers dissemination of information in marginalized communities.

## Reduced Transaction Costs

ICT innovation technologies can upgrade farming supply chain production and management by electronic financial systems, even at home. Small-scale farmers can improve their transactions through digital innovation technologies through online payment systems. Farmers' cooperatives in marginalized communities can now connect online whilst they are at home and able to buy and sell their products. Farmers who can adopt digital innovation tools to improve gathering, movement, and quality services control will be able to reduce transaction operations in their business (Syaglova, 2016).

## Easy Market Access and Information

Digital innovation technologies in farming can expand farmers' access to international markets and reduce time in establishing markets and reduces food loss. ICT innovation technologies make it easy for farmers to access the market places. E-platforms for agricultural products allow farmers directly to directly link with customers thus shortening the agro-food value chains hence new business opportunities are established (European Commission, 2019; Syaglova, 2016).

## Access to Finance by Marginalized Farmers

Digital technologies solutions enable smallholder farmers to access information on finances acquisition from banks and other financial organizations in time (Moher et al., 2009). The internet platforms created opportunities for farmers to have access to online transactions. Furthermore, growers in remote areas have been promoted to online payment services, mobile phone-based financial activities such as Ecocash, and many insurance services products. Cost reduction benefits may be translated into affordable interest rates for farmers and they gain competitive advantages.

## Online Extension Services

Digital innovation technologies are key in improving the dissemination of up-to-date information to farmers in marginalized communities. Personnel in the extension services are currently very little in number to meet smallholder farmers' needs in remote areas their farm visits are meagre (Moher et al., 2009). Extension services personnel through digital technologies easily educate farmers in remote areas since information is readily available online. The challenges of reaching out to farmers are minimized as digital technology platforms are readily available. This is ideal for including digital technologies in marginalized farming as it fosters quick sending and receiving of information.

## Farmers Advisory Management Software Through Digitalization, Eco-Farmer, Climate Forecasting (GIS and Remote Sensing)

Farmers' decision-making is being aided by increasingly intelligent digital advice services that provide highly localized, detailed information. Throughout the agricultural cycle, digital solutions have evolved to address the issues encountered by marginalized and isolated populations and the value chain players with whom they engage. Funding remains a big barrier for AgriTech companies in Africa (GSMA AgriTech, 2020). The Digital Agriculture Maps (DAMs) created by the GSMA AgriTech in partnership with IDH Farmfit give an integrated approach to digital agriculture uses.

The Digital Advisory falls under the Access to Services area, according to the GSMA AgricTech categorization. Farmers in marginalized and rural areas lack key information, such as reliable meteorological and climate data, that may help plan their activities to enhance productivity and increase revenue. Governments, NGOs, and value chain actors provide agriculture extension services that are not adequate due to low farmer extension services.

### Digital Advisory

This is a form of artificial intelligence that promotes digital literacy in production, management, and marketing technologies. These come through machine learning which incorporates drones, satellite data, computer modeling, and meteorological services. Such data ensure higher yields when on-farm activities are carried out.

### Agricultural Value-added Services (Agri VAS)

Digital agriculture services are becoming more comprehensive, offering a variety of use cases that include agricultural advising as part of a package. Eco-Net Wireless in Zimbabwe is now offering various platforms that allow the use of bundles, SMS, and call center for farmers to utilize E-technical assistance services on crops and livestock. They now offer these services as part of the ZFU Eco-Farmer Combo service bundle, including advising suggestions, membership in the Zimbabwe Farmers Union, weather index insurance, and death coverage. Safaricom has supported the agriculture industry in Kenya with the DigiFarm platform, which provides agritech companies with a considerable chance to expand.

*Figure 1. Digital agriculture use cases and sub-use cases*
Source: GSMA-Agritech-Digital-Agriculture-Maps-2020-1

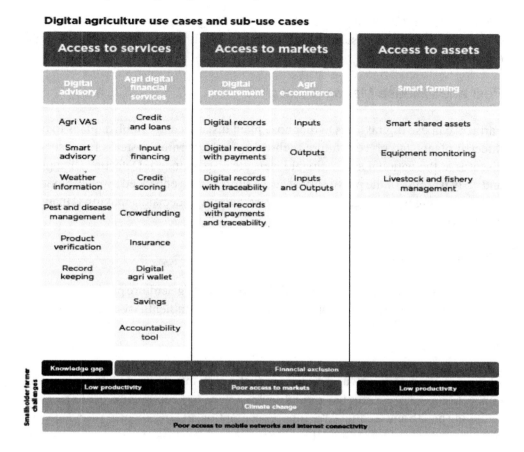

## Smart Advisory

Digital smart advice helps make better decisions, increase productivity, and save money. Marginalized farmers require information such as input cost, labor, and market price to make informed decisions. Profile SEE (2016) highlighted that remote sensing and GIS are important tools in carrying out crop surveys. These smart data advisory services are good for assessing crop status and forecasting yields since they provide a rapid, accurate, synoptic, and objective estimate of numerous agricultural metrics. For healthy growth and vitality, plants require water, sunlight, and sufficient nutrients (Mee et al., 2017). Detection of insufficient resources through remote sensing helps rectify and increase output (Shanmugapriya et al., 2019).

## Weather Information

Schumann et al. (2018) suggested that satellite images improve our understanding of weather information, such as predicting the likelihood of floods and drought occurrence.

## Pest and Disease Management

Farmers can use digital tools to diagnose plant diseases and establish plans to cure infected plants and prevent future outbreaks. Early warning systems for pests and diseases at the national and regional levels are also included. Detection, mapping, and early warning of the possibility of such outbreaks are enhanced by incorporating remote sensing technologies which are very helpful in decision-making (Huang et al., 2008).

## Product Verification

Farmers can use digital tools to verify the legitimacy of agriculture products. Product verification can incorporate digital barcoding for the authenticity of products.

## Record Keeping

These are used to assist in assisting reduction of infections and avoid missing conceptions. Farmers can use digital technologies to keep precise cattle records, including health and feeding data. Input consumption, procurement, cost and income records, and sales records are all kept using record-keeping software.

## E-Training of Farmers and Agritex Officers for Extension-Based Technology Transfer

Agricultural production has declined in most countries due to a lack of technology and poor extension service dissemination. This promoted low crop production for the past decades in Africa. The achievement of the Sustainable Development Goal 2 (SDG 2) of the United Nations for zero hunger has been a problem in many African and Asian countries (Cheo and Tapiwa, 2021a). Several countries in Africa are facing challenges in technologies to equip agricultural extension officers and train farmers to adopt new technologies and practices in Agriculture. Low crop production in marginalized areas in semi-arid regions is due to a lack of technical knowledge (Mupangwa et al., 2012). Several challenges faced by farmers like climate change, change in varieties, and pest and disease outbreaks can be easily solved through training extension officers and farmers using electronic training. Most countries are facing poor methods of disseminating information and training extension officers and farmers. Farmers are failing to get weather and climatic information in time, and they fail to prepare land in time. There is a need to digitalize agriculture and develop software friendly to farmers so that all age groups can operate and access information in all languages. Weather applications must be linked to global satellites, such as non-synchronous and geosynchronous, which provide weather updates. This will allow extension officers to update farmers in marginalized areas on crops to grow and livestock to keep in time. Digitalization of agriculture can be the way forward to achieve SDG 2, improve food security and reduce poverty. Digital agriculture can utilize technology to convert information into achievable knowledge for the best of farmers and countries.

Several European countries have adopted digital technologies to improve crop and livestock production through efficient information dissemination. The use of smartphones and computers were used to achieve better agricultural production and equip farmers with long-term information which will help them in future. According to Cheo and Tapiwa (2021b) agriculture production can be improved through technological advancements. This is the only way to move along with world agricultural advancement and achieve zero hunger (Cheo and Tapiwa, 2021a). Training of agriculture extension officers and farmers is a sustainable way to guarantee improved crop and livestock production. Electronic training of extension officers in the use of electronic devices such as Geographical Positioning Systems (GPS), operation of computerized irrigation, and use of modern-day equipment is critical. Effective training can only be achieved through the use of computers, smartphones, and Zoom meetings where training is mainly done online. This improves information dissemination timeously and allows farmers to adopt new farming technologies like herbicides, vermicompost, and computerized irrigation systems. The use of GPS in Hungary allows farmers to achieve precision farming (Kovacs and Husti, 2018). This improved agricultural production as farmers were able to install yield estimators on their equipment such as combine harvesters (John Deere, 2017). Companies such as tractor manufacturers like John Deere digitalized their equipment to allow farmers to digitalize agriculture (John Deere, 2017). The information gathered works effectively when information technology experts connect these machines to satellites for effective use.

There is a need for information technology experts to develop applications and software that are cheap for farmers, where information can be loaded and accessed easily by farmers through smartphones and mobile applications (Ministry of Agriculture, 2021). Electronic training can be the only way to reduce travel costs and allow information to reach marginalized areas where farmers are way behind in achieving production for human consumption. In Zimbabwe, the Ministry of

Agriculture has launched the training of Agritex extension officers online through smartphones with e-training and in-service training through zoom to allow all officers to be equipped with world-level information (Manyong, 2005; Cheo and Tapiwa, 2021a). The experience was witnessed in Nigeria and Libya where digitalization transforms agriculture to a certain level by adopting greenhouses and irrigation to transform deserts in the arable area (Federal Ministry of Agriculture and Rural Development (FMARD), 2012). Countries like Brazil achieved zero hunger through digitization (Slätmo et al., 2016; Cheo and Tapiwa, 2021b).

The Zimbabwean Ministry of Agriculture provided all its Agritex Officers with smartphones and trained them on how to access coordinates from farmers' plots as an easy way to monitor progress in the recently introduced conservation agriculture program (*Pfumvudza*). This created easy access to digitalization in marginalized areas since Agritex officers were also provided with motorbikes for easy movement. However, there is a need to bring information technology experts into training programs to facilitate the process of digitization in Agriculture, updating software and training extension officers on how to access online information. The government of Zimbabwe, through Agritex Officers, provided farmers with digital platforms, for example, an E-farming application in which farmers send questions and are quickly replied electronically. This platform also provides information about where farmers in their regions can get help and reputable suppliers of inputs such as seeds, herbicides, and fertilizers. This is also the case in some African countries like Ghana, Gambia, Zambia, and Tanzania (FAO, 2016, 2018, and 2020a; FAO, 2020b). These countries managed to introduce new digitalized irrigation equipment and allow easy management (FAO, 2008, 2014; EU, 2017).

Agriculture is not only centered on crop and livestock production but includes forestry, fishery, and wildlife management. The use of Geographical information systems (GIS) and remote sensing can improve forestry and wildlife management (Cheo and Tapiwa, 2021a). GIS and remote sensing can allow government departments, individuals, and researchers to have maps and pictures of forestry areas, which improves monitory and estimation of yield. This can also be used in wildlife, where counting animals becomes easy through airborne sensors and GIS. Remote sensing and GIS allow easy monitoring of agricultural production, estimating yield, and allowing policymakers in Agriculture to develop policies to improve yield (Kovacs and Husti, 2018).

## Digital Market Linkage and Value Chain Integration Services for Market Transparency

The agriculture value chains in Africa are characterized by high transaction costs resulting from searching for market information, searching for buyers and sellers, and negotiations between buyers and sellers. High transaction costs result in most smallholder farmers in marginalized areas failing to participate in agricultural markets. According to Tsan et al. (2019), digitalization can minimize these transaction costs, thus enabling marginal farmers' involvement in agricultural markets. Digitalization improves farmers' access to inputs, information, and other services across the value chain. Lake (2004) noted that digitalization enables virtual mobility, which also reduces transaction costs. The majority of smallholder farmers that participate in agriculture markets lack market information and have poor bargaining skills. Middlemen take advantage of this weakness and offer low prices to these farmers and charge exorbitant prices to processors or end-users of the commodity i.e., consumers. This has resulted in smallholder farmers getting low returns from selling their produce. This promotes access to markets by farmers and allows farmers to have full information about what is happening in both formal and informal economies (Bile, 2006; Clark et al., 2012; Chaddad, 2015). Digitalization has the capacity to allow local farmers to link with world markets, for example, horticulture and beef farmers.

The setup of value chains in developing countries results in many inefficiencies amongst the value chain actors (Louckos, 2020), and these can be reduced by the digitalization of agriculture value chains. Digital technologies improve farmers' participation in markets and engagement with buyers of their commodities, thus eliminating over-reliance on middlemen. Digital platforms provide farmers with information that they can use to make decisions. The information they receive helps decide what to produce, when, and the price at which they can sell their products and thus increase their profits. The notion is supported by Leonard et al. (2017), who noted that data collected through digital platforms helps in value chain decision-making.

Wolfert et al. (2017) noted that value chain and farm-level sustainability, productivity, and efficiency are enhanced with the introduction of digitalization in agriculture. If conducive environments are created for the smallholder farmers to participate in agriculture markets, they can contribute significantly to the national output and reduce poverty and food insecurity. The introduction of digital technology and its adoption and application by smallholder farmers' increases market participation and farm productivity and enhances business profitability (ITU, 2016). According to World Bank (2006), firms that use digital platforms get more profits than those that do not.

Digitalization provides new market opportunities and can be used to reach out to the poor and marginalized farmers outside the reach of multinationals. Increased digital platforms allow sustainable national growth and national development (Nyamadzawo, 2011). The digital platforms facilitate linkage amongst value chain actors (Trendov et al., 2019).

In particular, the adoption of digital technologies in Africa and Zimbabwe is slowly increasing. Agribusiness value chain actors included the use of phone applications and various digital platforms. Zimbabwe has quite a number of digital platforms that can be used in the agriculture value chains. These applications include the eMkambo, Kurima Mari, Agrishare, Zimbabwe farmers union, Eco-farmer program, and Turning Matabeleland Green. These applications give weather information, extension services, information on markets, and the hiring of farm equipment. In August 2021, three more platforms were introduced: the ZimAgric in-service training app, ZimHub, and ZimAgri Extension in-service training app. These complement agriculture training and research institutions. Agro-dealers can also use the platforms for advertising their products (Chikwati, 2021)

The benefits that can be accrued from digital technologies in agriculture value chains are immense. However, the successful adoption and use of these technologies are only possible if adequate government and private sector support in terms of policies and infrastructure. Government should introduce policies that support digital platforms and provide digital infrastructure and good internet connectivity. There is also a need for low call credit costs and training of farmers on how to use the digital platforms. The marginalized farmers are located in remote areas with poor network connectivity. Some farmers cannot purchase the devices required to access the digital platforms, and most are less tech-savvy.

## Opportunities and Challenges for Digital Agriculture in Remote and Marginalized Communities

Using digital technologies in agriculture has several contests and opportunities for farmers, especially those in marginalized communities. Fielke et al. (2019) noted that digitalization has several benefits, whilst (Ingram and Maye, 2020) suggested that there will be an overreliance on technical expertise rather than employing inferred knowledge. Haggag (2021) declared that digitalization improves rural development as an alternative to agricultural extension in the presence of COVID-19. This entails that digitalization can significantly alleviate the negative impacts of the COVID-19 pandemic. Digital technology allows food traceability and reduces the negative impacts on the environment (Wolfert et al., 2017; FAO, 2020c). Sustainable agriculture is ensured by digital knowledge as information on environmental conditions, crops, and soils ensure food security (Paul et al., 2019). (FAO, 2020c) highlighted that artificial intelligence helps in improving management by improving the accuracy of validation and monitoring of climate mitigation strategies.

Food and Agriculture Organisation (FAO, 2019) emphasized that smallholder farmers' access to digital technology exposes them to a lot of support services comprising the market, finance, and management. Digital support tools in data analytics ensure macro agricultural intelligence by integrating various data from smallholder farmers as a decision tool for government policymakers. There is the enhancement of farm productivity through weather forecasting and extension advice (Al-Hassan et al., 2013) and maximizing outputs from their lands. Advisory information will be personalized to diverse specific farmers around the globe. Dixie and Jayaraman (2011) noted that there is optimization in supply chain management and transportation, hence improving capacity utilization through digital technology. As highlighted by several authors, fast, secure, and efficient payments are made using mobile money (Grossman and Tarazi, 2014; Mbiti and Weil, 2015). Digital technologies ensure market transparency by increasing farmers' income in remote areas. Digital market linkages to agricultural inputs, access to markets, and mechanized machinery by marginalized farmers in remote areas expose them to high-quality low-cost inputs by lowering their production costs. This reduces overreliance on a go-between who can fix prices to their advantage at the expense of farmers. Farmers will be able to sell directly to consumers maximizing profitability. (UNCTAD, 2017) pointed out that solutions to global food challenges can be addressed by digitalization as new opportunities for agriculture entrepreneurs are accessed on global markets. The connectivity of major players in the agri-food system ensures sustainability as farmers can share information internationally, promoting resilience and improved productivity (Townsend et al., 2019).)

However, challenges such as network coverage in remote areas are limited by inadequate information technology (IT) infrastructure (McKinsey & Co, 2014) and network availability. Digital literacy due to lack of education attainment by some marginalized rural communities will reduce the adoption and use of digital technologies. Fakhoury (2018) posits that some developing countries do noprogramsicies and programs that enable digital agriculture. This reduces the adoption of such technologies resulting in limited success. CISA (2018) postulated that if cyber security is not implemented, there are associated cyber threats by third parties. This can destroy implements if cyber security shields software is not used on machines.

## CHAPTER SOLUTIONS AND RECOMMENDATIONS

Governments should invest and make policies to prioritize digitalization in marginalized remote communities to encounter challenges such as nutrition, food insecurity, climate change, and the current COVID-19 pandemic. There is a need for data standardization, digitalization policies, and connectivity to avoid disparities in agribusiness so that poor farmers in marginalized communities can afford it. It protects farmers from large international companies involved in digital technology, seeking opportunities to realize profits on poorly resourced farmers when they introduce their products on the market and offering promotional services to increase uptake as data costs are exorbitant in some sub-Sahara countries. This calls for major awareness campaigns/ information cascading to use these complex advisory services properly.

## FUTURE RESEARCH DIRECTIONS

Further studies examining the impact of agriculture activities on digital inclusiveness as a way to transform marginalized communities are needed. Artificial intelligence techniques can be a major key in driving digital inclusiveness in remote areas. Furthermore, an analysis of the role of government policy on agriculture activities that can digitally transform and include remote communities will be interesting to pursue.

## CONCLUSION

Digital technology transforms agriculture by promoting precision agriculture in marginalized rural communities in a more efficient approach by integrating information at once. Digital agriculture services through the introduction of bundles by Zimbabwe's EcoNet Wireless (EcoFarmer SMS Advisory Tips) provide technical advice in areas of livestock and crop production.

## REFERENCES

Ahmed, M., Ozaki, A., Ogata, K., Ito, S., Miyajima, I., Ahmed, A., Okayasu, T., Choudhury, D. K., & Al Amin, N. (2016). Poor farmer, entrepreneurs and ICT relation in production & marketing of quality vegetables in Bangladesh. *Journal of the Faculty of Agriculture, Kyushu University, 61*(1), 241–250. doi:10.5109/1564129

Al-Hassan, R., Egyir, I., & Abakah, J. (2013). Farm household level impacts of information communication technology (ICT)-based agricultural market information in Ghana. *Journal of Development and Agricultural Economics, 5*(4), 161–167. doi:10.5897/JDAE12.143

Biles, J. (2006). Globalization of food retailing and the consequences of Wal-Martization in Mexico. *Academia (Caracas), 24*, 343–355.

Bucci, G., Bentivoglio, D., Finco, A., Belletti, M., & Bentivoglio, D. (2019). Exploring the impact of innovation adoption in agriculture: How and where Precision Agriculture Technologies can be suitable for the Italian farm system? *IOP Conference Series. Earth and Environmental Science*, *275*(1), 012004. doi:10.1088/1755-1315/275/1/012004

Chaddad, F. (2015). *The economics and organization of Brazilian agriculture: Recent evolution and productivity gains.* Academic Press.

Cheo, A. E., & Tapiwa, K. A. (2021b). The Importance of SDG-2. In *SDG 2 – Zero Hunger: Food Security, Improved Nutrition and Sustainable Agriculture (Concise Guides to the United Nations Sustainable Development Goals)* (pp. 7–14). Emerald Publishing Limited. doi:10.1108/978-1-78973-803-220201005

Cheo, E. A., & Tapiwa, K. A. (2021a). *Sustainable Development Goal-2: End hunger, achieve food security and improved nutrition and promote sustainable agriculture.* Emerald Publishing Limited. doi:10.1108/9781789738032

Chikwati, E. (2021). (2021, August 19) Digital platforms change face of agriculture sector. *The Herald.*

CISA. (2018, October 3). *Cybersecurity Threats to Precision Agriculture.* Department of Homeland Security: CISA. https://www.us-cert.gov/ ncas/current-activity/2018/10/03/Cybersecurity-Threats-Precision-Agriculture

Clark, S., Hawkes, C., Murphy, S., Hansen-Kuhn, K. A., & Wallinga, D. (2012). Exporting Obesity: US Farm and Trade Policy and the Transformation of the Mexican Consumer Food Environment. *International Journal of Occupational and Environmental Health*, *18*(1), 53–65. doi:10.1179/1077352512Z.0000000007 PMID:22550697

Dixie, G., & Jayaraman, N. (2011). Strengthening agricultural marketing with ICT. The World Bank/InfoDev'ARD, ICT in agriculture: Connecting smallholders to knowledge, networks, and institutions. *Module*, *9*, 205–237.

EU. (2017). *Agriculture and rural development 2014-2020—The Netherlands fact sheet.* European Commission. Retrieved from https://ec.europa.eu/agriculture/rural-development-2014-2020/country-files/nl_en

European Commission. (2019). *The European Green Deal.* Available online: https://eur-lex.europa.eu/legal-content/EN/TXT/?qid=1588580774040&uri=CELEX:520 19DC0640

Fakhoury, R. (2018). *Digital government isn't working in the developing world. Here's why.* The Conversation. Available at: https://theconversation.com/digital-government-isnt-working-in-the-developing-world-heres-why-94737)

FAO. (2008). *An introduction to the basic concepts of food security. Food security information for action. Practical guides.* EC—FAO Food Security Programme.

FAO. (2014). Area equipped for irrigation. Infographic. In *AQUASTAT: FAO's information system on water and agriculture.* Food and Agriculture Organization of the United Nations (FAO). Retrieved from http://www.fao.org/nr/water/aquastat/infographics/Irrigation_eng.pdf

FAO. (2016). *Food and agriculture: Key to achieving the 2030 agenda for sustainable development.* Food and Agriculture Organization.

FAO. (2018). *The State of Food Security and Nutrition in the World: Building Resilience for Peace and Food Security.* Rome: FAO. Retrieved from http://www.fao.org/news/story/ en/item/1152031/icode/

FAO, ICRISAT, & CIAT. (2018). Climate-Smart Agriculture in the Gambia: CSA Country Profiles for Africa Series. International Center for Tropical Agriculture (CIAT); International Crops Research Institute for the Semi-Arid Tropics (ICRISAT); Food and Agriculture Organization of the United Nations (FAO).

FAO, IFAD, UNICEF, WFP, & WHO. (2019). *The State of Food Security and Nutrition in the World 2019. Safeguarding against economic slowdowns and downturns.* FAO.

FAO. (2019). *Digital technologies in agriculture and rural areas.* Briefing paper. https://www.fao.org/e-agriculture/

FAO. (2020a). *Ghana at a glance.* Retrieved from https://www.fao.org/ghana/fao-in-ghana/ghana-at-a-glance/en/

FAO. (2020b). *Gambia at a glance.* Retrieved from https://www.fao.org/gambia/gambia-at-a-glance/en/

FAO. (2020c). Realizing the potential of digitalization to improve the agri-food system: Proposing a new International Digital Council for Food and Agriculture. A concept note. FAO.

Federal Ministry of Agriculture and Rural Development (FMARD). (2012). *Agricultural Transformation Agenda.* FMARD.

Fielke, S. J., Garrard, R., Jakku, E., Fleming, A., Wiseman, L., & Taylor, B. M. (2019). Conceptualizing the DAIS. Implications of the 'Digitalisation of Agricultural Innovation Systems' on technology and policy at multiple levels. *NJAS-Wageningen of Life Sciences.*, *90*, 100296.

Flak, J. (2020). Technologies for Sustainable Biomass Supply—Overview of Market O_ering. *Agronomy (Basel)*, *10*(6), 798. doi:10.3390/agronomy10060798

Grossman, J., & Tarazi, M. (2014). Serving smallholder farmers: Recent developments in digital finance. Washington, DC: CGAP (Consultative Group to Assist the Poorest).

GSMA AgriTech. (2020). *Agritech in Nigeria: Investment Opportunities and Challenges.* Author.

Haggag, W. M. (2021). Agricultural digitalization and rural development in COVID-19 response plans: A review article. *Agricultural Technology (Thailand)*, *17*(1), 67–74.

Huang, Y., Lan, Y., & Hoffmann, W. C. (2008). Use of Airborne Multi-Spectral Imagery in Pest Management Systems. *Agricultural Engineering International: the CIGR Ejournal*, *X*, 1–14.

Ingram, J., & Maye, D. (2020). 'What are the implications of digitalization for agricultural knowledge? *Frontiers in Sustainable Food Systems*, *4*, 66. doi:10.3389/fsufs.2020.00066

International Telecommunications Unit. (2016). Impact of Agricultural Value Chains on Digital Liquidity. Focus Group Technical Report. ITU.

ITU & FAO. (2020). *Status of Digital Agriculture in 18 countries of Europe and Central Asia.* International Telecommunication Union Telecommunication Development Bureau Place des Nations CH-1211. Retrieved from https://www.itu.int/en/ITU-D/Regional Presence/Europe/Documents/Events/2020/

John Deere. (2017). *Agricultural Management Solutions.* AMS.

Kovacs, I., & Husti, I. (2018). *The role of digitalization in the Agricultural 4.0-How to connect the industry 4.0 to Agriculture?* Hungarian Agricultural Engineering. doi:10.17676/HAE.2018.33.38

Lake, A. (2004). *Time, mobility and economic growth.* http://www.flexibility.co.uk/issues/ transport/time-mobility.htm

Lanucara, S., Oggioni, A., Di Fazio, S., & Modica, G. A. (2020). Prototype of Service Oriented Architecture for Precision Agriculture. In A. Coppola, G. C. Di Renzo, G. Altieri, & P. D'Antonio (Eds.), *Book Innovative Biosystems Engineering for Sustainable Agriculture, Forestry and Food Production, Lecture Notes in Civil Engineering* (Vol. 67, pp. 765–774). Springer. doi:10.1007/978-3-030-39299-4_82

Leonard, E., Rainbow, R., Laurie, A., Lamb, D., Llewellyn, R., & Perrett, E. (2017). Accelerating *Precision Agriculture to Decision Agriculture: Enabling Frontiers in Sustainable Food Systems.* www.frontiersin.org

Loukos, P. (2020). *The GSMA AgriTech Toolkit for the Digitisation of Agricultural Value Chains.* GSMA.

Mazzetto, F., Gallo, R., Riedl, M., & Sacco, P. (2019). Proposal of an ontological approach to design and analyze farm information systems to support Precision Agriculture techniques. *IOP Conference Series. Earth and Environmental Science, 275*(1), 012008. doi:10.1088/1755-1315/275/1/012008

Mbiti, I., & Weil, D. (2015). Mobile Banking: The Impact of M-Pesa in Kenya, NBER Chapters, in: African Successes: Modernization and Development (vol. 3). National Bureau of Economic Research, Inc.

McKinsey & Co. (2014). *Offline and falling behind: Barriers to Internet adoption.* McKinsey and Company.

Mee, C. Y., Balasundram, S. K., & Hanif, A. H. M. (2017). Detecting and monitoring plant nutrient stress using remote sensing approaches: A review. *Asian Journal of Plant Sciences, 16*(1), 1–8.

Meinke, H. (2019). The role of modelling and systems thinking in contemporary agriculture. In R. Accorsi & R. Manzini (Eds.), *Book Sustainable Food Supply Chains: Planning, Design, and Control through Interdisciplinary Methodologies* (pp. 39–47). Elsevier. doi:10.1016/B978-0-12-813411-5.00003-X

Moher, D., Liberati, A., Tetzlaff, J., & Altman, D. G. (2009). Preferred Reporting Items for Systematic Reviews and Meta-Analyses: The PRISMA Statement. *BMJ (Clinical Research Ed.), 339*(1), 332–336. doi:10.1136/bmj.b2535 PMID:19622551

Mupangwa, W., Twomlow, S., & Walker, S. (2012). Dead level contours and infiltration pits for risk mitigation in smallholder cropping systems of southern Zimbabwe. *Physics and Chemistry of the Earth, 47-48*, 166–172. doi:10.1016/j.pce.2011.06.011

Nikolidakis, S. A., Kandris, D., Vergados, D. D., & Douligeris, C. (2015). Energy ecient automated control of irrigation in agriculture by using wireless sensor networks. *Computers and Electronics in Agriculture, 113*, 154–163. doi:10.1016/j. compag.2015.02.004

Nyamadzawo, J. (2011). *Digital opportunities for economic growth and development for Zimbabwe.* ZEPARU Working Paper Series (ZWPS 05/11). http://www.zeparu. co.zw/sites/default/files/201803/2011%20DIGITAL%20OPPORTUNITIES%20 FOR%20ECONOMIC%20GROWTH%20AND%20DEVELOPMENT%20FOR%20 ZIMBABWE.pdf

OECD. (2018). *Going Digital in a Multilateral World.* Report of the Meeting of the OECD Council at Ministerial Level, Paris, 30–31 May 2018. OECD. https://www. oecd.org/going-digital/C-MIN-2018-6-EN.pdf

Paul Antony, A., Sweeney, D., & Lu, J. (2019). *'Seeds of Silicon' Internet of Things for Smallholder Agriculture.* Academic Press.

Profile SEE. (2016). *Remote Sensing and GIS Applications in Agriculture.* Author.

Quayson, M., Bai, C., & Osei, V. (2020). Digital Inclusion for Resilient Post-COVID-19 Supply Chains: Smallholder Farmer Perspectives. *IEEE Engineering Management Review, 48*(3), 1. doi:10.1109/EMR.2020.3006259

Schumann, G. J., Brakenridge, G. R., Kettner, A. J., Kashif, R., & Niebuhr, E. (2018). Assisting Flood Disaster Response with Earth Observation Data and Products: A Critical Assessment. *Remote Sensing, 10*(8), 1–19. doi:10.3390/rs10081230

Shanmugapriya, P., Rathika, S., Ramesh, T., & Janaki, P. (2019). Applications of Remote Sensing in Agriculture - A Review. *International Journal of Current Microbiology and Applied Sciences, 8*(1), 2270–2283. doi:10.20546/ ijcmas.2019.801.238

Slätmo, E., Fischer, K., & Röös, E. (2016). The framing of sustainability in sustainability assessment frameworks for agriculture. *Sociologia Ruralis, 57*(3), 378–395. doi:10.1111oru.12156

Sott, M. K., Furstenau, L. B., Kipper, L. M., Giraldo, F. D., Lopez-Robles, J. R., Cobo, M. J., Zahid, A., Abbasi, Q. H., & Imran, M. A. (2020). Precision Techniques and Agriculture 4.0 Technologies to promote sustainability in the Co_ee Sector: State of the Art, Challenges and Future Trends. *IEEE Access: Practical Innovations, Open Solutions, 8*, 1. doi:10.1109/ACCESS.2020.3016325

Syaglova, Y. (2020). Digital transformation in food retailing. In *IOP Conference Series: Earth and Environmental Science*. IOP Publishing.

Trendov, N. M., Varas, S., & Zeng, M. (2019). *Digital Technologies in Agriculture and Rural Areas. Briefing Paper FAO*. FAO.

Tsan, M., Totapally, S., Hailu, M., & Addom, B. K. (2019). *The digitalization of African agriculture report, 2018–2019*. Wageningen: CTA. Retrieved from: www.cta.int/en/digitalisation-agriculture-africa

UNCTAD. (2017). *Information Economy Report 2017: Digitalization, Trade and Development*. Report UNCTAD/IER/2017/Corr. United Nations. https://unctad.org/en/ PublicationsLibrary/ier2017_en.pdf

Wolfert, S., Ge, L., Verdouw, C., & Bogaardt, M. J. (2017). 'Big data in smart farming'–A review. *Agricultural Systems*, *153*, 69–80. doi:10.1016/j.agsy.2017.01.023

World Bank. (2006). *2006 World Development Indicators*. World Bank.

## ADDITIONAL READING

Knierima, A., Kerneckerb, M., Erdlec, K., Krausb, K., Borgesb, F., & Wurbsb, A. (2019). Smart farming technology innovations—Insights and reflections from the German Smart-AKIS hub. *NJAS Wageningen Journal of Life Sciences*, *90–91*(1), 1–10. doi:10.1016/j.njas.2019.100314

Yahya, N. (2018). Agricultural 4.0: Its Implementation Toward Future Sustainability. In *Book Green Urea: Green Energy and Technology* (pp. 125–145). Springer. doi:10.1007/978-981-10-7578-0_5

## KEY TERMS AND DEFINITIONS

**Access:** The facility to receive and use.

**Agriculture:** The field of growing crops and keeping animals.

**Artificial Intelligence:** The field of making computers behave like humans without explicitly programmed.

**Digital Inclusiveness:** Supporting the use of Information Communication Technologies irrespective of individuals' backgrounds.

**Software:** A set of computer instructions to perform specific tasks.

**Sustainable:** Ability to support continuity whilst offering the expectations or needs.

**Value-Chain:** The network of synergizing processes.

Chapter 4

# Challenges and Opportunities for Digital Inclusion in Marginalised Communities

**Njodzi Ranganai**
*Manicaland State University of Applied Sciences, Zimbabwe*

**Briget Munyoro**
*Midlands State University, Zimbabwe*

**Tendai Shelton Muwani**
*Manicaland State University of Applied Sciences, Zimbabwe*

**Nyasha Sakadzo**
*Manicaland State University of Applied Sciences, Zimbabwe*

**Lemias Zivanai**
*Midlands State University, Zimbabwe*

## ABSTRACT

*The amalgamation of modern innovation, technological skills, and processes used to establish business models and satisfy customers in different societies is referred to as digital transformation. Digital transformation facilitates the development of economies, ways of doing business, and social constructs among marginalized communities. Digital inclusiveness has significantly been applied in a number of areas in communities and resource-constrained environments such as health, education, and agriculture. A systematic literature review was carried out. The authors find out that inclusiveness has great opportunities and challenges in digitally transforming marginalized communities. The implementation of interconnected digital innovation technologies provides new challenges and opportunities spanning the whole of Africa. This chapter explores the key drivers of digital technologies, the contribution of technology, gender imbalances, and challenges and opportunities for digital inclusiveness in remote areas.*

DOI: 10.4018/978-1-6684-3901-2.ch004

## INTRODUCTION

Apart from discussing the digital divide, scholars and practitioners now zero in on digital inclusion innovation infrastructure and how marginalized communities may be digitally transformed. The authors argue that digital inclusion is the process whereby marginalized communities acknowledge the importance of access to digital infrastructure, skills, and activities in their society. Digital transformation is pointed out as the process whereby digital technologies utilization, associated difficulties ranging from individual, a small organization to a large institution and their related impacts either positive or negative, have increased in the society (Vial, 2021).

The chapter postulates that the socioeconomic status of the inhabitants of the area would need to be considered so that it is easy to transform such a community if they have equitable and affordable infrastructure which can enable more connected devices and access to online content. However, it has been a question whether this digital inclusiveness gap will ever be closed with a universal government policy and bringing the provision of affordable internet connectivity to further reduce the divide without promising that the gap will ever be entirely eroded (Ohiagu, 2013). To add to this, it highlights the shortcomings of only focusing heavily on adoption and access to the internet. For the digital inclusion of communities to bring positive results, the focus should be much on implementing sustainable development policies as a way to close the subsequent knowledge gap. Furthermore, the government should find the right policy mix as digitalization becomes significant to reduce the use gap between urban dwellers and marginalized communities to empower everyone with the necessary skills for digital edge (Mulualem Walle, 2020). The government's mandate is to craft policies that will enhance digital technologies, and huge data flows in marginalized communities. It is a key to the living and working together of people who participate in producing a country's economy (Mulualem Walle, 2020). Through digitalization policies of marginalized communities, the government enhances the exploitation of opportunities offered by emerging technologies and is cross-cutting in any society. Focusing too much on digital innovation infrastructure and government policies may overlook other important societal barriers.

The objectives of this chapter are to; explore the digital transformation and inclusiveness for socioeconomic sustainability in marginalized communities, identify key drivers at the root of the digital innovation technologies, highlight the contribution of technological developments and open-source software to marginalized communities and identify challenges and opportunities for digital inclusiveness in marginalized communities. This chapter is structured as follows: background, the main focus of the chapter, solutions and recommendations, future study, and conclusion.

# BACKGROUND TO THE STUDY

Society considers digital inclusion as the solution to the challenges and opportunities that marginalized communities face in their business activities (Trendov et al., 2019; Group, 2019). However, contributions by researchers who are interested in the historical developments of technological revolutions suggest caution on this solution to marginalized communities (Bronson, 2019; Nettle & Rue, 2019). Technological innovation is given at a cost; it is not for free but normatively laden and driven by different people's views and visions. Currently, digital technologies may have a number of undesirable effects, which may hinder digital inclusion for possible transformation of marginalized communities, for example, problems that emanate once these technologies are put in place (Klerkx & Begemann, 2020; Pansera et al., 2019; Scholz et al., 2018). A number of authors argued that instead of digital transformation of marginalized communities and digital inclusiveness reinforces the available systems which are deemed unsustainable economically, socially, ecologically, and only conducive incumbent for large and financially stable players (Clapp & Ruder, 2020; Cowie et al., 2020; Miles, 2019; Prause et al., 2021). The potential of digital inclusivity and strategies for the digital transformation of marginalized communities put together with the socioeconomic conditions definitely will necessitate or influence digitalization processes if taken into account (Klerkx & Begemann, 2020).

However, for such elements to be workable, the government should have policies to enforce rules for digital innovation technologies. This directly led marginalized people to be submitted to a passive utilization of ICT infrastructure since they are guided by rules and regulations imposed on them. Bonilla and Pretto (2011) argued that the ICT policy hinders people's appropriation of technology. In this view, governmental policies can hamper the appropriation, especially when they cannot account for organizational and community structures. Dias (2011) argues that even though the government of these developing countries mobilizes a reasonable amount of resources geared to enable digital inclusiveness, the results and implications of these actions are poorly evaluated. The development of digital technologies for education about innovation and support to agricultural businesses in marginalized communities will be functional if the government policies are put in place to enhance the realization of innovations (Bucci et al., 2019).

Zimbabwe introduced the Innovation Hubs, which is taking a major role in raising awareness campaigning for digital inclusion in agriculture activities in marginalized communities. Through its extension workers, the government of Zimbabwe under command agriculture now can use GPS applications to monitor the usage of government inputs. Digital inclusion is there to bridge the gap between marginalized people who are working in the fields and consumers through cross-sectoral networking opportunities, which enable the marginalized communities to find suitable business partners through collaboration models, funding instruments, and legal aid (Flak, 2020). Digital inclusion for technological transformation to take place is strongly dependent on government policies and support from states (Sott et al., 2021); (Zhou et al., 2019). Agricultural innovation systems play a pivotal role as activities that can digitally include marginalized communities. However, more efforts should be on business activities that embrace economic sustainability and technology in marginalized communities. Governments of countries in Africa like Zimbabwe lack resources (power supply, high data cost, poor connectivity, and infrastructure) such that even if they put in place digital transformation policies in marginalized countries, they will always fail.

Digital inclusiveness is beyond physical networking, and access to ICT infrastructure and not access will promote inclusiveness but how these digital innovation technologies will achieve social sustainability of marginalized communities. If digital inclusion activities are properly implemented, the remote communities will automatically be empowered and be able to fight their own poverty, promote citizenship, compete with urban inhabitants, and improve education without any divide (Nemer & Reed, 2013). Some developing countries like Botswana and South Africa have since created technological spaces in their schools, these already foster opportunities to connect the digital culture and their way of teaching. Therefore, this space can better necessitate digital inclusion of students in marginalized communities at the school level, which will disseminate to society. If well implemented, such approaches can facilitate digital culture and a better understanding of digital innovation technologies through education. More so, including digital inclusiveness in the school curriculum will definitely improve digital inclusion in marginalized communities as students are part of the included communities and increase the chances of appropriation and conscious use of ICT infrastructures.

The social and educational needs of developing countries are concentrated in marginalized communities where the number of people is very high, and only the major aspect is fighting poverty whilst not digitally transforming the people. The fundamental of human rights in marginalized communities is to consider the right to access information and communication. Notably, government policies should simplify access to information and communication technology through digital inclusion activities on the agenda of human rights in contemporary society (Bonilla & Pretto, 2011). Digital inclusion can continue the human social sustainable economic development process of African countries. However, recently the pace of change in societies and digital innovation technologies has accelerated the implementation of digital infrastructure (Attrey, 2021). Dornberger et al. (2018) argue that the rapid change in recent years can trigger a massive digital transformation of marginalized communities since organizations now rethink their activities to suit the good change in societal, and technological values. Dahlman et al. (2016) supported that digital technology activities contribute to the digital transformation of developing countries and are not expected to slow down in the near future.

## MAIN FOCUS OF THE CHAPTER

The chapter mainly focuses on the challenges and opportunities of digital inclusion in a myriad of contexts.

### Digital Transformation and Inclusiveness of Gender Socioeconomic Sustainability in Marginalized and Remote Communities

Gender equality and strategic development are interconnected for a number of reasons. First and foremost, it is culturally and socially imperative: establishing gender socioeconomic sustainability and realizing women's ability, dignity, and varied group rights is the pivotal aspect of a sustainable country. Second, it is very important to address the imbalance among females of different ages on the effects of social, economic, and natural resources. Digital inclusiveness enables women and girls to exercise their human rights abilities and play critical roles in the welfare of their families. Thirdly, the most important aspect is digital innovation technologies to bridge the gender divide gap, which improve synergies between gender so that we can achieve gender digital transformation goals in marginalized areas. Digital transformation is essentially a transition brought about by the advancement of new technology. The term "sustainability" means the ability to achieve a decent optimal standard of living without harming the environment. Therefore, sustainability can be achieved by taking into account features like the well-being of people, justice, and ecological integrity. In other words, it can be seen as a goal of balance between humans and ecosystems. Socio-economic sustainability is the pillar of sustainability, and therefore, it is vital to understand them first. The improvement of current and future standards of living for generations to come is referred to as social sustainability. Furthermore, economic sustainability means the ability to withstand the forces of economic growth without damage to the environment of an economy; it fosters the efficient use of natural resources. Therefore, socioeconomic sustainability is described as the ability to secure economic growth in developing countries without compromising nature and meeting their needs (Mang et al., 2016).

Digital technology has expanded the amount of information available while also lowering costs and making it easier to access. This has led to information researching, downloading, sharing, and increased institutional interconnection and coordination among socioeconomic agents, altering the activities of the businesses, ICT platforms create opportunities, and citizens can directly contribute to their governments. Increased connection to ICT allows many individuals, including those in remote areas and marginalized areas, to access services and previously unavailable information. New connections, sensors, and applications generate data, offering a plethora of knowledge for future advances. This change affects economic transactions and women's participation in the workforce, understanding of the people in the surrounding area, and leisure activities. Digital technology can make development more integrated, efficient, and innovative by overcoming information barriers, expanding factors, and transforming products (Hartl & Hess, 2017).

Group (2016) claims that the areas with the marked potential digital dividends are: economic growth, digital innovation technologies, jobs, and the government's capacity to deliver better public services matters most. Around the African countries, many people, organizations, and governments are increasingly trying to get access to and adopt digital innovation technologies. Digital technology may make services and information more accessible at the micro and major levels, for example, to individuals in rural and marginalized communities. Although it is clear that ICTs are contributing to a faster and larger pace of marginalized communities' development, the influence is widely affected and uneven and hence goes unnoticed.

The objectives of digital inclusiveness are to make more flexible working conditions, network people in remote areas with urban, and create new opportunities such as e-commerce and gig economy, and all of these can bridge the gap between labor force participation. The internet boosts women's income and potential earnings. Females are expected to benefit from digital inclusion as there will be a shift in the working environment away from physical labor and into non-routine occupations. Musungwini et al. (2020) indicate that women's participation in ICT jobs is very low, although they make up the majority of the population.

Gender disparities play an important role in hindering the access and utilization of digital technologies in marginalized communities which are caused by difficulties in socio-economic and cultural barriers that adversely affect women. However, if a woman owns a mobile phone, in marginalized societies, usually it is the male counterpart who will be using it; there is a large gender gap in the use of the mobile phone. Women report that they use their phones less frequently and intensively than males on advanced services such as mobile internet (Zainudeen & Galpaya, 2015). To add to this, females who own and use mobile phones are at lower rates than men because of barriers that include network quality and coverage, cost, security and harassment, technical skills, and confidence (Zainudeen & Galpaya, 2015). Social norms affected females' access and utilization of digital technologies, which therefore contributed to more hindrances in possession and use of mobile phones than men did. Overall, costs continue to be the biggest stumbling block to mobile phone ownership and use, especially for females who are economically dependent on men. Safety and abuse have played a vital role in limiting the gender divide, and it also emerged as one of the top five barriers and a major factor affecting females (Jayachandran, 2021). Furthermore, in some African cultures, females are deprived of other education levels for male children to proceed to high levels. This play a pivotal role in widening the gender digital divide gap. Females also state that service delivery issues (connectivity, not included in technological training, ownership of infrastructure, and agent or operator trust) and expert knowledge are among major obstacles. Mobile technology helps empower women and provide access to services that improve their lives. Owning a mobile phone makes it easier for women to manage their mobile money and access different services. Women are often imbalanced in the impact of barriers, both in their connection to and their utilization of digital innovation technologies. Men in remote areas are treated as special in their families and believe that they have the privilege to own mobile phones first more than women. Even if females have mobile phones, they are unlikely to use them for transformative operations such as mobile money transactions, thereby widening the gap (Money, 2017).

Facilitating better connections and exploring alternative ways of life, norms, and values, digital technology also changes social norms and values. The conservative gender role can be more firmly rooted in individuals who do not have access to digital technology and do not use it. In undeveloped nations, Internet cafes are frequently owned by males; females are not confident to enter such businesses, especially in remote areas (Mumporeze & Prieler, 2017). A number of people have access to computers and Internet cafes as Internet connections improve in metropolitan places, but females are frequently openly or tacitly prohibited from stigmatized access. Males report having more money to afford to spend at cafes than females, who are expected to contribute more time and money to the family (Hartl & Hess, 2017).

Access to the Internet is very important but not enough to improve the integration of digital development in marginalized communities. The important complementary areas to work on are Digital innovation skills, access to the infrastructure, and analyses, creating, and communicating information using ICT models. This requires technical experts to train one's capability to adapt and use ICTs to develop marginalized females and properly participate fully in the digital environment. For females in marginalized communities, the general literacy level tends to be lower in education and digital skills. Therefore, to achieve digital transformation through inclusiveness, there is a need to upgrade digital literacy and self-confidence for both males and females. This means there is a need to understand the needs of males and females; marginalized racial groups invest in their education, development initiatives, development of skills and confidence, support for educators, and promotion of gender role models.

The rapid need for digital transformation and digital inclusiveness of society, necessitated by the ever-increasing pace of technological innovation and the impact on digital inclusion, particularly gender equity, is of paramount concern to the country at large. In order to harness digital inclusion in marginalized communities, the key drivers at the heart of digital innovation technologies must be clearly explained and understood. The preceding section defines and categorizes the issues to do with digital inclusion and its implications for traditionally marginalized groups which are of great importance to the digital transformation of society.

## Key Drivers at the Root of the Digital Innovation Technologies

Digital revolution is the use of the internet age to change socio-technical structures. Structures are systems made up of interconnected parts, such as a product, service, user experience, and process. The social, which include interactions, interrelations, culture, and technical aspects of the structure, is referred to as socio-technical structures. The socio-economic and cultural aspects of the constructs change as they are digitalized. Thus, digitalization is more than just a technical process of encoding analog data in a digital format (Yoo et al., 2010).

Drivers emanate from and affect both ends, explaining how communities are engaged in the digital economy. Shifting consumer attitudes and perceptions are frequently found to be the catalysts for digitalization. Haffke et al. (2017) illustrated that there is a need to keep up with digital shifts occurring in their industries and societies. The holy trinity of people, process, and technology remains the bedrock of transformational success. The possibility of digital inclusion for vulnerable communities is always present. Going digital is already at the forefront of 44 percent of organizations' decision-making processes, operations, and end-user engagement.

Primary motivators that drive businesses to undergo technology innovation include the need to survive in a competitive marketplace, an organizational culture that is supportive and adaptable, customer preferences, transformation activities that are well-managed, the need for speed, and the involvement of managers and employees.

### Survival

Companies must decide whether to sink or swim. Advances in digital technology mean more significant innovation, more opportunities, and increased business efficiency. However, these benefits will remain out of reach for many businesses without digital transformation - businesses must jump on board and ride the waves.

*Figure 1. Digital innovation technologies' key drivers*
Source: (Gupta, 2021)

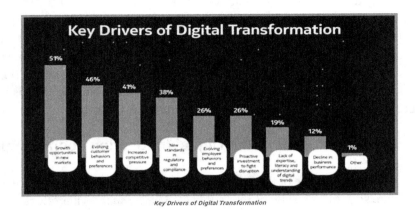

Key Drivers of Digital Transformation

## An Organizational Culture That Is Supportive and Adaptable

Acknowledging technology innovation is a process that is not easy; there is a lot to consider before and during the process. A change-oriented organization try to create a willingness to embrace, implement, promote, and put in place a change-oriented mindset of an institution (Hartl & Hess, 2017).

## Customer Preferences

With the click of a button, almost anything and everything is now accessible. Buying and selling is no longer an impediment for instance to someone from Asia who wants to order merchandise from North America. Furthermore, what used to take ages to deliver the item has been reduced to one or two weeks. This upsurge in accessibility provided an advantage to companies such as Amazon. Standards set by the global giants resulted in anyone expecting a shorter shipping period after purchase. Today no sector is growing as fast as e-commerce. It has changed the way of doing business because of technology. In business, the customer is king, which means business activities should consider the taste and preferences of consumers. As a customer, the use of credit cards and money transfers should be smooth and easy. It would be only possible if we digitally transform the marginalized communities to adapt to digital emerging trends.

## Transformation Activities That Are Well-managed

According to Berghaus and Back (2017), organizations typically engage in transformation activities prior to or during digital transformation. Although agility is a successful business model that embraces digital transformation, empirical evidence deduced that no "one size fits all" mechanisms for digital innovation transition; such scenario within an organization frequently determines the correct approach to adopt (Berghaus & Back, 2017). Furthermore, enterprises were discovered to engage in innovativeness and develop a digital strategy. These tasks were frequently put in place by appointed groups collaborating with third parties. However, not all the tasks identified by the authors are pertinent to institutions' digitization programs; organizations can establish them on the way to digital transformation by varying and combining their activities (Berghaus & Back, 2017).

## The Need for Speed

Eric Pearson, CIO of the InterContinental Hotel Group, stated that the industry has changed, and therefore, it's no longer about "big whacking the small" but about "fast beating the slow." Technological advances will continue to emerge; it is up to the company to change and adaptor to wait and possibly lose to those who were quick to act (Vibhavari, 2020). For example, Generative Pre-Trained Transformer-3) (GPT-3) is the third generation of Open AI's GPD, a linguistic process that uses machine learning techniques to write text and give answers, and translate text. It examines a data system, including text and words, and then expands on those samples to create original work, such as an image or an article.

## Managers and Employees Should Be Involved

Human capital in organizations undergoing technology innovation is critical to the process and outcome. Managers must consider their workers' concerns and involve them as active participants in the digital transformation. Partaking in the transformation process can reduce workers' dissatisfaction with the activities, improve goal attainment, and increase corporate loyalty (Mueller & Renken, 2017).

## Role of AI

An even more driving force driving businesses toward digital transformation is artificial intelligence. Beyond self-aware robots, artificial intelligence (AI) in the corporate world refers to real applications that automate tasks that humans previously governed. We have seen automation happening in manual habitats, but

AI has brought us a whole new world to figure out. Computers are slowly taking over manual tasks, and this has triggered fear in a tech giant you might be familiar with. Using artificial intelligence in marketing has now become a norm as it has transformed the marketing industry. There has been an increase in companies using AI for marketing and ad campaigns.

## The Emergence of Infrastructure Automation Software

Participating in the "digital revolution" has become an absolute necessity in manufacturing and other industries alike. You are probably behind the curve if you're running a modern business without embracing some digital transformation, and fortunately, more and more business owners seem to be realizing digital transformation. In addition, as the spotlight shone on the digital economy, a niche emerged, and companies that could provide a more seamless transition to digitalization emerged. These companies develop software tailored to the needs of a specific organization to streamline the entire process. Corporates use infrastructure automation software because time is of the essence for businesses, and the ability to adopt digitalization in the quickest time provides a competitive advantage. The path to digitalization is a tumultuous and fast-paced one. Certainly, for businesses, many tools are given to make the expedition more feasible and meaningful (Gupta, 2021).

## Contribution of Technological Developments and Open Source Software (OSS) to Marginalized Communities

The term 'open' refers to the source of software application that allows people free access, utilization, analysis, and sharing with others, whether in its initial form or in an upgraded form (Peirce et al., 2019). Open-source software is computer software that has a source available to the general public for use as it is or with modifications. It does not require a license fee (Baharuddin et al., 2018). In this case, to digitally transform the marginalized communities, they are supposed to have access to open-source software to compete well with people in urban centers. The idea behind free access to OSS in marginalized communities is to distribute the information across the society free of charge. This enables digital transformation and inclusiveness to be made upon what has been shared (Ciuriak & Ptashkina, 2018)

The developing countries have unequal aspects of digital inclusive innovation models and are gaining greater traction in education and government policy-making in marginalized areas (Paunov & Rollo, 2016). Digital technologies focus on how less privileged and remote areas can gain from being included in the access and utilization of technologies and transform their wellbeing in their societies. Mainstreams or traditional technologies often create and widen the digital inequality gap in developing countries. Digital inclusive innovation technologies reduce these inequalities in marginalized communities (Heeks et al., 2017). Digital technologies have been analyzed, modeled, and a comparison made to other similar aspects, such as innovative sustainable development, accountability, and bottom-of-pyramid innovation (Chataway et al., 2014).

Digital transformation to take place in marginalized communities, government policy should be put in place to facilitate free access to open-source software. In remote areas, technological infrastructures should be established that enable connectivity in such communities. Digital innovation technologies efficiently support and greatly contribute to the transformation of these communities, smart farming, flexible financial services, electronic transactions, and free education information from open sources. Digital technology models explain how these new technologies necessitate and help marginalized communities and upgrade them to be at par with urban inhabitants.

OSS contributes to shared prosperity in marginalized communities as it facilitates digital transformation. OSS and women's participation can contribute to prosperity in marginalized communities as it facilitates digital transformation. With digital technologies, through the use of OSS, women can now access software and work using computers in their daily activities rather than manual work. The implementation of digital technology reduces labor-intensive work, enabling the shareability of tasks between females and males. If put together properly, OSS brings positive economic opportunities and socio-economic activities to marginalized communities, ultimately contributing platforms for online job recruitment. Economically, OSS contributes to improvement in production and reduced operating costs since there is free access to digital resources. This allows new techniques like collaborations, which improve personnel's skills, flexibility, and efficiency in conducting their activities in marginalized communities. Access to OSS in marginalized communities contributes to the creation of new business ideas and setup, improving remote areas' welfare.

Through crowdfunding, an organization or government can put together equity-funding platforms; OSS also provides alternative financing sources. This will go a long way in helping remote people with digital transformation. Furthermore, technologies and OSS given a chance, can offer significant benefits that help access basic ICT services, including financial online services and academics. Digital technologies allow direct interaction between populations and governments through networked devices. Digital technologies enable the government to be present online, and increasing this will increase the efficient operation of public administration work. The internet critically plays key role in marginalized areas, it brings easy and new ways for citizens to safely contribute whilst at home their concerns in policy and decision-making processes by government. However, digital technologies and OSS enable government and people, regardless of remote or urban, to make the country's information at their fingertips and available online, which improves transparency, governance, and accountability, and marginalized communities may gain confidence to equally be heard in decision making.

More than a dozen possibilities for entrepreneurs to be created in developing countries specifically in Africa, which result from digital technologies and OSS. If marginalized areas were formerly excluded from economic opportunities and connected, they can access the internet for educational purposes and acquire vast knowledge, research, scholarships, and collaboration to start their own companies. They can also gain opportunities that would be unimaginable without access to the open Internet (Lin, 2017).

## ICT Infrastructure and Open Source Software In Marginalized Communities

Information Communication Technologies play a vital role in digital inclusion. Areas it supports include:

- Transforms the society by providing ICT platforms that enable people to find information for free charge and efficient data dissemination.
- Provides solutions to difficult questions, and these solutions can be accessed if only connected on a mouse click by organizations or individuals that may have not yet envisioned the needs of remote poor people without traveling and cost to town since they can access it on the internet.
- Creates employment opportunities, people get recruited for much-needed jobs online, and increases the GDP growth of developed countries (Okoye & Arimonu, 2016).

In conclusion, technologies and OSS can establish a more developed economy, which gives voice to the unheard and facilitates an equal share of public resources to less privileged societies. In support of this, government policies should make sure that their citizens in marginalized communities have the skills needed to participate and succeed in a digital innovation, technological-driven economy. The following section explores the challenges and opportunities for digital inclusiveness in marginalized communities through embracing digital innovation technologies.

## Challenges and Opportunities for Digital Inclusiveness in Marginalized Communities

Digital inclusiveness offers a variety of challenges and opportunities to marginalized communities. The challenges and opportunities were outlined future work that is technological-embedded to gain the less privileged communities were outlined. Digital technology tools enable marginalized community inhabitants to a range of online activities like employment, communication, service delivery, social changes and the societal global village. Digital transformation can be achieved by participants' total inclusiveness and by establishing an effort to support their daily routines (agriculture, schools, shopping and communication). Conversely, if remote areas' inhabitants do not afford or cannot possess the required skills to operate ICT infrastructure, they will be left behind in society.

Digital technologies are critically playing key roles in marginalized areas. Digital inclusiveness in remote areas creates a number of opportunities that contribute to society's welfare. If people in the marginalized society find it difficult to be included or have access to ICT tools, they continue to face problems in an attempt to digitally transform. If a number of digital technology tools remain inaccessible without the support of non-government organizations (NGO) and government policies in developing countries, remote people will face challenges in accessing ICT opportunities. In Zimbabwe, through Econet Wireless and NGOs like FACT, they extend their social responsibility through paying school fees and providing technological devices, such as mobile phones to students. Econet Wireless as a company provides connectivity of EDU-ZONE network in schools for free; this will go a long way in capacitating learners in marginalized communities, thereby digitally transforming the society.

As the advancement in digital innovation technologies, the environment is very dynamic if remote people are not included in the digital transformation era. Therefore, remote people are left behind by technological jobs, sustainable socioeconomic activities, and all opportunities that may be created through innovative technologies. The challenge of digitalization in a society demands digital skills for existing digital jobs that are constantly growing. For marginalized communities to benefit from innovative technologies, they should establish workshops, free digital training courses, and free ICT devices so that they can upgrade their abilities in ICT utilization. This is of paramount importance as it facilitates equal participation and opportunities that foster the digital employment of people in marginalized communities. Currently, marginalized communities frequently experience exclusion in digitalization activities as they encounter many challenges when it comes to accessibility, connectivity, and affordability of Information and Communications Technologies (ICTs) due to many factors. However, to promote the digital era, specifically when targeting marginalized communities, the challenges mentioned above are critical to paving the way for future inclusive digital work for everyone.

## Opportunities Realized by Digital Inclusion for People in Marginalized Communities Include

The government and NGOs serving marginalized communities in developing countries are working towards developing programs, systems, and technologies to mitigate existing challenges hindering digital transformation and proactively take steps to create a socio-sustainable economy. A positive implementation of digital inclusion in societies will further improve self-confidence, self-sufficiency, and economic empowerment, which are an integral part of building resilience and lowering the dangers of future exploitation now and in the future. Workers in marginalized communities can improve their skills-set through digital innovations, ultimately leading them to harness new talent and diverse labour markets associated with their potential. Here are a few examples of opportunities realized by digital inclusion for people in less-privileged areas.

- With the new creation of digital jobs, digitalization offers a number of employment opportunities, particularly interesting for marginalized communities. The jobs include IT data capture, systems analyst, technicians, programmers, and IT managers. People in remote areas can also start ICT businesses through selling accessories to their society.
- The online recruitment platforms and digital inclusion offer people in marginalized communities direct access and equal employment opportunities from organizations with people in urban areas.
- Digital inclusion tools can support marginalized communities to perform tasks such as agriculture activities like spraying weeds and irrigation mechanisms (pivot center irrigation).
- Digital inclusion equips marginalized communities on how to use technology to harness natural resources and keep them for future life.
- Digitalization expands marginalized communities' range of capabilities to access the market for their products and can advertise via WhatsApp platforms, Facebook, and other websites.
- Remote work is now applicable people can work in their comfort at home; therefore, digital inclusion can provide flexible work-life balance (Guo et al., 2017).
- Digital innovation technologies enhance the dissemination of information through internet platforms and e-mails. Digital technologies are the key to communication activities and bridge the gender divide in remote areas.
- Digital inclusiveness enables people in remote areas to be innovative in their activities which changes the cultural way of doing business and effective and efficient ways of operation due to technologies, online research of

information, and new forms of collaboration. Digital transformation is the potential for cultural development change that would help create more inclusive workplaces for persons in marginalized communities (Ahrendt & Patrini, 2020).

- Digital inclusion enhances better ways of farming sowing, irrigation, pest control, and weed control; this will go a long way in improving farm produce of marginalized communities.
- Digital inclusion will also create favorable communication and online financial transaction platforms same in urban areas. This will help search for new markets of produce, dissemination of crucial information, and electronic cash disbursement and employment opportunities through online interactions.
- Due to digital inclusion, Marginalized communities may upgrade their knowledge base through searching on the internet, which will help them make informed decisions.
- Better ways of learning at school and teaching learners through the use of projectors and e-learning resources.

## Challenges Posed by Digital Inclusion for People in Marginalized Communities

This section postulates the challenges and factors needed for the improvement of marginalized communities' global connection for digital transformation and inclusiveness. The study establishes the awareness of barriers to digital inclusion, mechanisms, and options to speed up digital transformation in these marginalized communities. African countries like Zimbabwe, Zambia, and Malawi are developing countries where technological illiteracy is the most prominent across rural areas and marginalized groups. The challenges include accessing infrastructure and internet content which is predominately text-based. The following section identifies the barriers to digital inclusion for the digital transformation of societies:

- Accessibility is a barrier to people in marginalized communities. They often find it challenging to have ownership or get connected to ICT devices may be due to affordability.
- Consequently, there is a lack of skills to operate digital technology devices, thus the challenge that people in marginalized communities lack the required skills that tally for new digital technological jobs.
- It's not all technological positions that are usually good jobs. They may be instances where over-qualified personnel in IT take low-level digital work.
- Marginalized communities cannot afford the electricity to power the digital innovation technologies. Usually, a poor power supply characterizes remote

areas, so it's very difficult to include remote people in digital transformation fully.

- No up-to-date statistics on marginalized communities on the level of eligibility, understanding, and usage of digital technologies currently working means can be ascertained.
- As mentioned before, marginalized communities may find it difficult to get jobs since they lack affordability and accessibility to the internet and infrastructure. However, companies these days embark on online recruitment processes, so marginalized communities are left out.
- Marginalized communities must acquire proper digital skills required of them to be able to navigate digital technology tools like remote working skills such as communication skills, partner collaboration, and time management; otherwise, they will be left behind again.
- Poor governments, marginalized communities need open-source software and ICT devices for free. The developing countries' government usually doesn't prioritize remote areas and cannot afford the demands of digital technologies.
- Affordability is a challenge in marginalized communities; people are not capable of purchasing technological infrastructure used during digital transformation. Digital inclusiveness is bizarre if there are no finances to fund remote areas, especially females, this will remain one of the key hurdles in digitally including marginalized communities.

## SOLUTIONS AND RECOMMENDATIONS

Agriculture is a sector in marginalized communities where more than 90% of the population depend on it for a living. Authors recommend that agricultural innovation systems through extension workers should be in the lead to capacitate farmers with digital skills and propose programs that embrace digital inclusivity for transformation. To add to this, the more the increase in digitalization systems, the more it becomes complex, digital transformation proceeds to stronger huge connected systems and a greater need for cyber security. Therefore, the authors recommend the implementation of strong security measures and increasing connectivity so that marginalized communities will have faith in emerging technologies.

Digital inclusiveness fosters different effects in different ways in society. Therefore, governments should invest and make policies so as to prioritize digital transformation through inclusion in marginalized communities. The developing countries' governments should put in place policies and standardizations that govern ICT innovation technologies, data usage, connectivity, and electricity and subsidize on acquiring ICT devices. This will go a long way in facilitating digital transformation in marginalized communities. Services providers in developing countries should also call for major awareness campaigns, workshops, training ICT skills, and information cascading for proper use of these digital technologies. In countries like Zimbabwe, authors recommend that government policies invite more telecommunication players to be socially responsible by implementing programs that promote digital transformation as Econet wireless company is performing by providing free internet EDU-ZONE in every learning institution. Furthermore, the government should establish sustainable gender balance policies on digital inclusiveness in marginalized communities for pure digital transformation by promoting female counterparts to proceed with their education at all levels. To add to this, the authors recommend that the needs of males and females, marginalized racial groups invest in their education, development initiatives, development of skills and confidence, support for educators, and promotion of gender role models through state promotions can positively digitally transform a community through inclusiveness.

## FUTURE RESEARCH DIRECTIONS

In this regard, future studies on digital transformation and inclusiveness of marginalized communities are a diverse and complex terrain. Therefore, the authors agree on future research on empirical analysis of digital technologies adoption in marginalized communities. Analyze the role of government policy on digital transformation and inclusiveness in remote communities. Security measures to guarantee safety in the use of digital technologies in marginalized communities.

## CONCLUSION

The chapter concludes that for digital transformation in marginalized communities to be achieved, total digital inclusiveness of marginalized communities' inhabitants is core. Full participation results from synergies from all stakeholders. If developing countries' policies positively support the activities of digital advances, remote areas will benefit from the use of new technologies, which will broaden their skills and be at the same level as urban setup. Developing countries that invest more in digital technologies in marginalized communities will positively affect the less privileged groups, achieving new opportunities associated with innovate technology and reducing barriers to achieving digital transformation. Using these technologies sensibly and putting key drivers of the digital tool as root for transformation factor in gender socioeconomic for the sustainability of digital transformation innovation which definitely widens the abilities of marginalized society and makes it more inclusive and socially just.

# REFERENCES

Ahrendt, D., & Patrini, V. (2020). *How to use the surge in teleworking as a real chance to include people with disabilities*. Academic Press.

Attrey, A. (2021). *Agile, comprehensive and principles-based: Policy making for a digital age*. Academic Press.

Baharuddin, M. F., Izhar, T. A. T., & Shoid, M. S. M. (2018). Adoption of Open Source Software (OSS) and Organization Performance in the Library. *International Journal of Academic Research in Business & Social Sciences, 8*(9), 285–297. doi:10.6007/IJARBSS/v8-i9/4591

Berghaus, S., & Back, A. (2017). *Disentangling the fuzzy front end of digital transformation: Activities and approaches*. Academic Press.

Bonilla, M. H. S., & Pretto, N. D. L. (2011). *Inclusão digital: polêmica contemporânea*. Edufba. doi:10.7476/9788523212063

Bronson, K. (2019). Looking through a responsible innovation lens at uneven engagements with digital farming. *NJAS Wageningen Journal of Life Sciences, 90*(1), 100294. doi:10.1016/j.njas.2019.03.001

Bucci, G., Bentivoglio, D., Finco, A., & Belletti, M. (2019). Exploring the impact of innovation adoption in agriculture: How and where Precision Agriculture Technologies can be suitable for the Italian farm system? *IOP Conference Series. Earth and Environmental Science, 275*(1), 12004. doi:10.1088/1755-1315/275/1/012004

Chataway, J., Hanlin, R., & Kaplinsky, R. (2014). Inclusive innovation: An architecture for policy development. *Innovation and Development, 4*(1), 33–54. doi:10.1080/2157930X.2013.876800

Ciuriak, D., & Ptashkina, M. (2018). The digital transformation and the transformation of international trade. RTA Exchange. Geneva: International Centre for Trade and Sustainable Development (ICTSD) and the Inter-American Development Bank (IDB).

Clapp, J., & Ruder, S.-L. (2020). Precision technologies for agriculture: Digital farming, gene-edited crops, and the politics of sustainability. *Global Environmental Politics, 20*(3), 49–69.

Cowie, P., Townsend, L., & Salemink, K. (2020). Smart rural futures: Will rural areas be left behind in the 4th industrial revolution? *Journal of Rural Studies*, *79*, 169–176. doi:10.1016/j.jrurstud.2020.08.042 PMID:32863561

Dahlman, C., Mealy, S., & Wermelinger, M. (2016). *Harnessing the digital economy for developing countries*. Academic Press.

Dias, L. R. (2011). *Inclusão digital como fator de inclusão social*. Inclusão Digital.

Dornberger, R., Inglese, T., Korkut, S., & Zhong, V. J. (2018). Digitalization: Yesterday, today and tomorrow. In Business Information Systems and Technology 4.0 (pp. 1–11). Springer.

Flak, J. (2020). Technologies for sustainable biomass supply—Overview of market offering. *Agronomy (Basel)*, *10*(6), 798. doi:10.3390/agronomy10060798

Group, W. B. (2016). *World development report 2016: digital dividends*. World Bank Publications. doi:10.1596/978-1-4648-0671-1

Group, W. B. (2019). *Future of food: Harnessing digital technologies to improve food system outcomes*. World Bank. doi:10.1596/31565

Guo, S., Ding, W., & Lanshina, T. (2017). Digital Economy for Sustainable Economic Growth. *International Organisations Research Journal*, *12*(4), 169–184.

Gupta, Y. (2021). *Key-Drivers-of-Digital-Transformation*. https://static.startuptalky. com/2021/09/Key-Drivers-of-Digital-Transformation-StartupTalky.jpg

Haffke, I., Kalgovas, B., & Benlian, A. (2017). *The transformative role of bimodal IT in an era of digital business*. Academic Press.

Hartl, E., & Hess, T. (2017). *The role of cultural values for digital transformation: Insights from a Delphi study*. Academic Press.

Heeks, R., Foster, C., & Nugroho, Y. (2017). *New models of inclusive innovation for development*. Routledge. doi:10.4324/9781315673479

Jayachandran, S. (2021). Social norms as a barrier to women's employment in developing countries. *IMF Economic Review*, *69*(3), 576–595. doi:10.105741308-021-00140-w

Klerkx, L., & Begemann, S. (2020). Supporting food systems transformation: The what, why, who, where and how of mission-oriented agricultural innovation systems. *Agricultural Systems*, *184*, 102901. doi:10.1016/j.agsy.2020.102901 PMID:32834403

Lin, N. (2017). Building a network theory of social capital. *Social Capital*, 3–28.

Mang, C. F., Piper, L. A., & Brown, N. R. (2016). The incidence of smartphone usage among tourists. *International Journal of Tourism Research, 18*(6), 591–601. doi:10.1002/jtr.2076

Miles, C. (2019). The combine will tell the truth: On precision agriculture and algorithmic rationality. *Big Data & Society, 6*(1), 2053951719849444. doi:10.1177/2053951719849444

Money, G. M. (2017). *State of the Industry Report on Mobile Money.* Retrieved from.

Mueller, B., & Renken, U. (2017). *Helping employees to be digital transformers–the olympus. connect case.* Academic Press.

Mulualem Walle, Y. (2020). The Impact of Digital Government on Whistleblowing and Whistle-blower Protection: Explanatory Study. *Journal of Information Technology Management, 12*(1), 1–26.

Mumporeze, N., & Prieler, M. (2017). Gender digital divide in Rwanda: A qualitative analysis of socioeconomic factors. *Telematics and Informatics, 34*(7), 1285–1293. doi:10.1016/j.tele.2017.05.014

Musungwini, S., Zhou, T. G., & Musungwini, L. (2020). Challenges facing women in ICT from a women perspective: A case study of the Zimbabwean Banking Sector and Telecommunications Industry. *Journal of Systems Integration, 11*(1).

Nemer, D., & Reed, P. (2013). Can a community technology center be for-profit? A case study of LAN houses in Brazil. *CIRN 2013 Community Informatics Conference,* 1–9.

Nettle, C. E. M. A. R., & Dela Rue, B. (2019). Making sense in the cloud: Farm advisory services in a smart farming future NJAS-Wageningen J. *Life Sciences.*

Ohiagu, O. P. (2013). Information and communication technologies: Widening or Bridging the Digital Divide. *Journal of Linguistics and Communication Studies, 3*(1), 87.

Okoye, R., & Arimonu, M. O. (2016). Technical and Vocational Education in Nigeria: Issues, Challenges and a Way Forward. *Journal of Education and Practice, 7*(3), 113–118.

Pansera, M., Ehlers, M.-H., & Kerschner, C. (2019). Unlocking wise digital techno-futures: Contributions from the Degrowth community. *Futures, 114,* 102474. doi:10.1016/j.futures.2019.102474

Paunov, C., & Rollo, V. (2016). Has the internet fostered inclusive innovation in the developing world? *World Development*, *78*, 587–609. doi:10.1016/j.worlddev.2015.10.029

Peirce, J., Gray, J. R., Simpson, S., MacAskill, M., Höchenberger, R., Sogo, H., Kastman, E., & Lindeløv, J. K. (2019). PsychoPy2: Experiments in behavior made easy. *Behavior Research Methods*, *51*(1), 195–203. doi:10.375813428-018-01193-y PMID:30734206

Prause, L., Hackfort, S., & Lindgren, M. (2021). Digitalization and the third food regime. *Agriculture and Human Values*, *38*(3), 641–655. doi:10.100710460-020-10161-2 PMID:33071450

Scholz, R. W., Bartelsman, E. J., Diefenbach, S., Franke, L., Grunwald, A., Helbing, D., Hill, R., Hilty, L., Höjer, M., Klauser, S., Montag, C., Parycek, P., Prote, J., Renn, O., Reichel, A., Schuh, G., Steiner, G., & Viale Pereira, G. (2018). Unintended side effects of the digital transition: European scientists' messages from a proposition-based expert round table. *Sustainability*, *10*(6), 2001. doi:10.3390ù10062001

Sott, M. K., Nascimento, L. da S., Foguesatto, C. R., Furstenau, L. B., Faccin, K., Zawislak, P. A., Mellado, B., Kong, J. D., & Bragazzi, N. L. (2021). A Bibliometric Network Analysis of Recent Publications on Digital Agriculture to Depict Strategic Themes and Evolution Structure. *Sensors (Basel)*, *21*(23), 7889. doi:10.339021237889 PMID:34883903

Trendov, M., Varas, S., & Zeng, M. (2019). Digital technologies in agriculture and rural areas: status report. *Digital Technologies in Agriculture and Rural Areas: Status Report.*

Vial, G. (2021). Understanding digital transformation: A review and a research agenda. *Managing Digital Transformation*, 13–66.

Vibhavari, M. (2020). *GPT3-revolution*. https://static.startuptalky.com/2020/08/GPT3-revolution_StartupTalky

Yoo, Y., Lyytinen, K., Boland, R., Berente, N., Gaskin, J., Schutz, D., & Srinivasan, N. (2010). The next wave of digital innovation: Opportunities and challenges. *Research Workshop: Digital Challenges in Innovation Research*, 1–37.

Zainudeen, A., & Galpaya, H. (2015). *Mobile phones, internet, and gender in Myanmar*. GSMA.

Zhou, Y., Xu, L., & Muhammad Shaikh, G. (2019). Evaluating and prioritizing the green supply chain management practices in pakistan: Based on delphi and fuzzy AHP approach. *Symmetry*, *11*(11), 1346. doi:10.3390ym11111346

## KEY TERMS AND DEFINITIONS

**Digital Divide:** The gap between demographics and regions that have access to modern information and communications technology (ICT), and those that don't or have restricted access.

**Digital Inclusion:** Digital inclusion involves the activities necessary to ensure equitable access to and use of information and communication technologies for participation in social and economic life including for education, social services, health, social and community participation.

**Digital Infrastructure:** The digital technologies that provide the foundation for an organization's information technology and operations.

**Digital Transformation:** The amalgamation of modern innovation, technological skills, and processes used to establish business models and satisfy customers in different societies.

**Information Communication and Technology:** Is the infrastructure and components that enable modern computing.

**Marginalized Communities:** Are groups and communities that experience discrimination and exclusion (social, political, and economic) because of unequal power relationships across economic, political, social and cultural dimensions.

**Remote Area:** Are areas away from cities and places where most people live, and are therefore difficult to get to.

**Technological Innovation:** Is an extended concept of innovation. While innovation is a rather well-defined concept, it has a broad meaning to many people, and especially numerous understanding in the academic and business world.

# Chapter 5
# Inclusive Digital Transformation for the Marginalized Communities in a Developing Context

**Samuel Musungwini**
 https://orcid.org/0000-0002-9315-6252
*Midlands State University, Zimbabwe*

**Petros Venganayi Gavai**
*Midlands State University, Zimbabwe*

**Samuel Simbarashe Furusa**
*Midlands State University, Zimbabwe*

**Raviro Gumbo**
*Midlands State University, Zimbabwe*

## ABSTRACT

*This chapter looks at Zimbabwe, a developing country in Sub-Saharan Africa that aspires to reach an upper-middle-income economy by 2030 through digital inclusiveness. Digital transformation (DT) and digital innovation (DI) may be the fundamental foundation to attain economic growth and productivity. To transit to Society 5.0, nations should develop robust technological systems, powerful, knowledgeable human resources, and a strategic direction policy by harnessing (DT) and (DI). A qualitative stance is applied using in-depth interviews and focus group discussions. Digital innovation identifies issues characterizing marginal communities in Zimbabwe that must be addressed to ensure that digital transformation targets rural areas, border posts, the informal sector, smallholder farmers, artisanal miners, vendors, and women (rural). The chapter then climaxes with a framework that if implemented may usher in Society 5.0, which may ensure that people, things, and technologies are all interconnected and intersect in the cyber and physical spaces.*

DOI: 10.4018/978-1-6684-3901-2.ch005

# INTRODUCTION

*...we live in a divided world: between rich and poor, healthy and sick, literate and ignorant, democratic and authoritarian, and between empowered and deprived. All the technologies that we developed in the past centuries and all the policies we enacted from enhancing human development have not wiped out these glaring disparities. (Tongia 2005, p 15).*

The above quotation appears to suggest that not all novel digital technologies will help the digital transformation (DT) agenda in any way. Neither will it close the gulf between the haves and have-nots, no those from marginalised communities who are excluded in the digitalisation processes. In simple terms, Tongia seems to contend that Information and Communication Technologies (ICTs) and associated digital tools are simple mirrors that reveal what is obtaining in the social strata and even exacerbate the naturally existing divides. However, chief proponents of Information and Communication for Development (ICT4D) concepts like (Avgerou, 2017; Heeks, 2014; Musungwini, 2016; Musungwini & Zyl, 2017; Pade-Khene & Lannon, 2017; Pfavai Natasha Nyajeka, 2018; Series, 2008) have circumvented such negative view of ICTs and are extensively ballyhooing these tools and wedging a promotional agenda to harness them to realize positive vistas of development. This promotion has been waged since the 1990s (Venkatraman, 1991), but became a focal point in the genesis of Millennium Development Goals (MDGs). The positives yielded by ICT in the MDGs era gave impetus to the ICT4D research agenda as the Sustainable Development Goals (SDG) framework 2016 to 2030 development framework was premised on the need to harness digital technologies for transformational processes to attain the world we want (inclusive development leaving no one behind). These authors also subscribe to this notion of ICTs for inclusivity and development agenda.

This is because ICTs have brought a multidimensional aura of possibilities to the modern-day era, this, coupled with the entrance of the Internet has amplified the ICTs' capabilities to significantly enrich people's lives in a short period across different economic and social strata. Empirical research has been carried out which shows that ICTs have been applied and are leaving an indelible mark on many socio-economic aspects including health (Zhou, Herselman, & Coleman, 2015), education (Mohamad, Idrus, & Ibrahim, 2018), mobile banking (Journal, 2020), e-commerce (Munyoka, 2022), smallholder agriculture (Musungwini, 2018), and vending (Musungwini & Zyl, 2017) among other areas. However, in tandem with the quotation in the introduction, there is also an increasing volume of empirical data of late, which is showing that they are also gaps that exist in the implementation of ICT programs, platforms, and tools and these have the potential to amplify the gap between the haves and have nots thereby damaging and controlling people especially the marginalised. This includes work by Musungwini, Zyl, and Kroeze,, (2022) which looked at mobile phone underutilization by smallholder farmers, Mahlangu and Ruhode, (2021) who looked at IT service gaps in e-government services, Tsokota, Musungwini, and Mutembedza, (2020) among others.

While ICTs afford access to vital state-of-the-art information and knowledge in real-time to all people, allowing for social and economic involvement by making vital services more prevalent, available, and accessible on digital platforms. In many developing contexts, ICTs have been found to exacerbate the problems in marginalised communities like smallholder agriculture, especially in developing countries including sub-Saharan Africa (Agyekumhene et al, 2018). This is mainly because the benefits of ICTs, as well as the Internet, cannot be guaranteed for all the citizens in a developing context especially those in marginalized rural and remote areas and the economically disadvantaged members of society. The currently existing socio-cultural and economic disparities are found to be illumined and aggravated by digital technologies. Authors like Mahlangu and Ruhode, (2021) and Steinke et al, (2020), argue that marginalised groups are not well represented or even considered in the design and application of digital technology.

As research has shown that in developing countries, generally men use the Internet more than women do and rural and indigenous populations all confront challenges that are akin when it comes to technology access, adoption, and effective uses (Krell et al, 2021; OECD, 2015; Sam, 2014). Yet the dominant narrative submits that technology can be "fixed" to address universal digitalisation marginalization issues that are prevalent in society today. However, the most emerging trend in literature posits that there is a need to give primacy to inclusive participation of these marginalised people at the epicenter of digital transformation programs in any country. This necessitates the creation of a framework to serve as a roadmap for the achievement of a digital transformation of marginalized communities in developing context.

To achieve that the chapter provides an overview of the current state of the DT literature. The researchers performed an analysis of co-occurrence centered on selected keywords mainly on the Google scholar database to achieve the objective of understanding the subject domain. A qualitative literature study evaluating DT in the context of digital business transformation was done to assess the most noteworthy articles to put the study into context. While technology is viewed as a driver of DT with social and institutional ramifications, in this chapter, the researchers gives preeminence to societal impact in a developing context. To situate DT in the inclusivity of marginalized people in a developing context, the chapter provides a rich background of marginalization in the context of Zimbabwe a developing country in SSA. This chapter is organized into several sections. The first section is the introduction followed by the background and context then the methodology. This will then be followed by a literature review and research results. The next section provides the background and contextualizes the research

## BACKGROUND AND CONTEXT

In the developed world, digital transformation is beginning to have a far-reaching spectral effect, with the capacity to create societal significant benefits that far outweigh the value earned by the industry (Ryll et al, 2020). Hence, this presents exciting times ahead, and society and technology may work together to create a dynamic economic society by increasing productivity and generating new markets. It is all about harnessing technologies like ICTs, IOTs, the Internet, Cloud computing, mobile technologies, social media, and big data for societal transformation while incorporating cyber insights into actual human existence, developing values for personal needs, and ultimately transforming society (Morze & Strutynska, 2021). However, in the developing world, this is not the case as country policymakers and planners including those from Sub-Saharan Africa (SSA) have been confronted with obstinate challenges for any sector, concerned with the potential use of digital technologies especially in remote and other marginalised areas as reported by Musungwini, (2016), Sam, (2014) and Siddiquee, (2016).

While some literature suggests that the bulk of digital products, their associated services, the expertise, and the complementary usage models and subsequent research on ICT uses across different sectors originated in high-developed contexts and environments. Some literature like Chepken et al., (2012) and Musungwini, (2018) point to the fact that research on the use of digital technologies in most parts of the developing world has been carried out by foreigners who are not resident in the countries in which they publish. Whatever the case is, literature is awash with suggestions that ICT usage in the developing world across different sectors is not useful for inclusivity and perhaps causes the differences between the haves and have-nots to be irradiated. A huge chunk of literature on digital transformation like Kokh and Kokh, (2020), Lichtenthaler, (2020), Morze and Strutynska, (2021), Putri, (2021), Saul and Gebauer, (2018) has continually focused on the digital disruption of organizations mainly job functions, operational processes, products and services, and customer services.

To realize extensive DT, which promotes inclusiveness of marginalized communities in a developing context there, is a need for empirically identifying the contemporary contextual existing inequalities in the adoption of digital technologies in a specific context and in this case Zimbabwe a SSA country. The main research question addressed by this research is stated as:

## How Can Inclusive Digital Transformation, Which Encompasses Marginal Communities in a Developing Context, Be Attained?

In line with the above stated question, this chapter intends to do the following: Identify and characterize marginal communities in Zimbabwe. Identify the most disruptive emerging technologies in Zimbabwe. Identify the existing inequalities in the adoption of digital technologies in marginalised communities in Zimbabwe. Identify the challenges to the digital transformation of marginalised communities in Zimbabwe. Develop a framework to enable the inclusive digital transformation of marginalized communities.

## METHODOLOGY

Qualitative research is distinguished by techniques that prioritize the research subject's point of view. This method likewise emphasizes extensive observation to provide a 'rich' and 'depth' description as suggested by Morrison, (2002). In qualitative research, careful thought should be given to the broader context in which the study problem is to be integrated. The basic concept is that the researchers can only make sense of obtained data if they grasp the data from the perspective of a greater contextual setting (Morrison, 2002). In this study, the researchers used a qualitative research method approach because the method was conceived in the social sciences as a result in enables researchers to explore social and cultural phenomena. According to Given, (2012), qualitative research enables a researcher to observe the research participants' feelings, thoughts as well as behaviors, and beliefs.

While qualitative research encompasses many variants like action research, case study research, and grounded theory among others this research will use case study. There are several qualitative data sources, and these include observation and participation observation (fieldwork), focus group discussion (FGD), interviews and open-ended questionnaires, documents, and texts as well as the researchers' impressions and reactions. However, this research employed in-depth interviews, a FGD, and a literature review. The literature review provides a basis for situating and grounding digital transformation in this chapter. The in-depth interviews with experts mainly in the ICT domain provided a way of gauging the level of awareness and insights into Zimbabwean issues regarding digital products and services. The interviewing of selected individuals is a very important method often used by qualitative researchers (Gubrium & Holstein, 2001). In-depth interviews enabled the researchers to find out what was on the participants' minds, their perceptions, and feelings about digital transformation for marginalized communities' inclusivity in

Zimbabwe. Twelve (12) FGD participants were a mixed bag with ten (10) representing digitally marginalized groups in Zimbabwe.

## LITERATURE REVIEW

With the approval of the 17 SDG 2016-2030 development framework and the 169 targets, by country governments, 193 countries throughout the world agreed to embark on a development framework anchored on the harnessing digital technologies to attain the world we want (Assembly, 2015). On that trajectory, the stance was to strive to reach those most vulnerable first, such that subsequently, no one would have been left behind (Bailey et al., 2019). However, in reality, country governments are frequently confronted with difficulties in reaching those who are most disadvantaged (Sam, 2014). This has been attributed to rudimentary and uncoordinated infrastructure, poor literacy rates, a lack of electricity and internet, and conventional socio-cultural expectations and prejudices can all hinder access to knowledge and opportunity for the most vulnerable groups. Despite this, mobile phones, the internet, and other novel digital technologies have offered tremendous opportunities to overcome present limits (Gavai, Musungwini and Mugoniwa, 2018; Van Dijk, 2017). The optimal use of technological innovations is a significant goal for the World Bank, which is the fore bearer, and chief custodian of the SDGs, and serving the most disadvantaged people has long been revealed in the body of literature. This section reviews the body of literature on digital transformation, characteristics, challenges and opportunities presented.

According to Westerman et al, (2011), pressures igniting digital transformation are akin for most business organizations, but the outcomes are a mixed bag and they attributed this to different digital transformation environments and the speeds characterizing the digital transformation. These researchers then illustrated that to shape digital transformation successfully there is a need to transform the business customer experience so that the customers can realize value from their association with the business organization. In addition, they asserted that there is a need to transform the business operational processes as well as the business models. Overall, the authors suggest that there is a need to transform the digital capabilities of the organization. This is very valuable extensive research, which, however, focuses on digitalisation from an organizational perspective.

Brunetti et al, (2020), explored digital transformation challenges and suggested strategies for realizing digital transformation. There, research findings highlight that the digital transformation process is an inescapable challenge in any circumstances. These writers proposed a slew of steps that would need to be implemented by policymakers to achieve successful transformational change digitally. In summary, this study demonstrates that stand-alone initiatives are unable to address digital transformation from a systemic standpoint. Another research carried out by Paramita, (2020), looked at the shifting technological trends characterizing digital transformation which has had an impact on several industries across the world. The study identified human resources processes in the recruiting and selection process as one interesting area. The author pointed out that different digital technological solutions provide distinct advantages for recruiting methods, particularly in terms of productivity, but it appears to disregard the interpersonal results. The research pointed out that there is a need to take a rational approach is determined by how a company considers its hiring processes. They argued for the need to embed Artificial Intelligence (AI) in recruitment, with both the interaction of many perspectives, particularly from human resources and systems integration in the organisation.

According to research by Gimpel and Röglinger, (2015), which focused on digital transformation challenges and opportunities argued that the people, organizations, and the society as a whole are all affected by digitalisation whether positively or negatively. The research asserted that the rapid proliferation of digital technologies, in particular, causes extensive cataclysm for the negatively affected. They contended that digital transformation presents enormous obstacles as well as exhilarating opportunities for businesses. Nevertheless, the authors argued that the successful harnessing of digitalisation opportunities compels the digital transformation of organizations. The research claimed that while businesses may not be interested in digitalisation, however, they cannot ignore joining the bandwagon of digital transformation, as ignoring it might spell doom for them. Another research carried out by (Mahlangu et al., 2018) identified ICT knowledge hubs as essential assets for a country to propagate towards a digital economy. The researchers argued that the development and growth of hubs is vital to a country's aspirations as they were identified as a springboard for techno-prenuership development and economic sustainability by many countries. Again, the research stance is digital transformation of organizations not inclusive to society and marginalised communities.

However, very little if any research has been conducted which focused on digitalization across society in general. Thus, outside of the business, the notion of digitalisation seeks to identify ways in which technology may assist all individuals in actively participating in socio-economic activities in society. Most of those innovations that are now affecting the industry will play a different but major role in shaping society because of digital metamorphosis, including social media, the internet of things, cybersecurity, GPS, artificial intelligence, data science, and robots. Digital transformation of marginalised communities is a means to this aspiration and the marginalised people must be put at the epicenter of that digital transformation. Historically, technological innovation has been responsible for social progress (e.g., mobile phones, social media, etc.), but the future requires a paradigm shift, concentrating on how to establish a society that makes all people happy and provides a feeling of value that is inclusive.

*Table 1. Interviewee profiles*

| Interviewee | Age | Position Profile | Interview Method | Date | Duration (Minutes) |
|---|---|---|---|---|---|
| INTER1 | 43 | ICT Lecturer at a local university | Google meet | | 37 |
| INTER2 | 52 | ICT Expert working for a Telecommunication company. | Telephone | | 25 |
| INTER3 | 35 | ICT Software developer with a local company. | Google meet | | 29 |
| INTER4 | 38 | Cybersecurity expert | Google meet | | 32 |
| INTER5 | 47 | ICT Lecturer at a local university | Google meet | | 35 |
| INTER6 | 39 | Agricultural extension services officer. | Face to face | | 27 |
| INTER7 | 45 | Mobile phone vendor. | Google meet | | 30 |
| INTER8 | 41 | Network engineer. | Google meet | | 31 |
| INTER9 | 37 | Rural district administrator. | Face to face | | 26 |
| INTER10 | 40 | Mining engineer | Face to face | | 25 |

## MAIN FOCUS OF THE CHAPTER

## Research Participants

*This section presents the research participants and their brief backgrounds.

The researchers developed the interview guide in line with the key tenets provided by Rowley, (2012). The interview guide was developed in a way meant to guarantee that the same main areas of evidence are acquired from each respondent. This places primacy on focus than the discursive technique while yet allowing for some flexibility and adaptation in gathering data from the participants while interviewing them. The researchers conducted ten (10) interviews with various experts with various backgrounds who met the criteria relevant to the research subject domain. The interviews were conducted using Google meet six (6), face-to-face two (2), and telephone two (2). Table 1 presents the interviewees' profiles and the interview method that was used to interview each participant and the duration of the interview.

The researchers conducted a focus group discussion with twelve (12) FGD participants. The FGD was conducted in line with the key tenets of conducting focus group discussions prescribed by Dzino-Silajdzic, (2018). The participants in the

FGD were a mixed bag with ten (10) representing digitally marginalized groups in Zimbabwe. The researchers facilitated the FGD meeting, and it lasted 63 minutes.

*Table 2. Focus group discussion participants' profiles*

| Participants | Age | Position Profile | Marginalization Knowledge and Experience | Digitalisation Knowledge and Experience |
|---|---|---|---|---|
| FGDP1 | 52 | Smallholder Farmer | Very high | Low |
| FGDP2 | 38 | Artisanal miner | Very high | Low |
| FGDP3 | 43 | Vendor | Very high | Low |
| FGDP4 | 49 | Rural housewife | Very high | Very low |
| FGDP5 | 45 | Rural school teacher | High | Moderate |
| FGDP6 | 39 | Rural health care nurse | High | Moderate |
| FGDP7 | 47 | Head of the Disability Resource Centre at a local university. | Very high | High |
| FGDP8 | 41 | Rural district administrator | Very high | Moderate |
| FGDP9 | 43 | Agricultural and extension services officer. | Very high | High |
| FGDP10 | 36 | Health Informatics Officer | High | High |
| FGDP11 | 42 | Agriculture Informatics Officer | High | High |
| FGDP12 | 39 | ICT expert | Moderate | Very High |
| FGDP13 | 41 | ICT Engineer | High | Very High |

# RESEARCH FINDINGS

## Characteristics of Marginalized Communities in Zimbabwe

Marginalised communities have been found to have two (2) dimensions, which are location and group, and these shall be presented separately in the following subsections

## Categorization by Location

### Rural Areas

According to research participants, the indicators for marginalization are geographical in scope, because other regions are persistently impoverished, deprived, and have limited access to basic services. While poverty and deprivation are synonymous with rural areas, with deprivation increasing in newly relocated communities following land reform, it has also been found to be prevalent even in urban areas in Zimbabwe. According to research participants, the majority of newly relocated regions have limited access to education, health, clean water supply, and sanitation services. Research participants lamented that in most cases children and women (pregnant) must travel considerable distances to schools and hospitals. Other areas lack hospitals and educational facilities, but some are under construction. Communities in the country's outskirts, along the borders, are often marginalized. Some of the locations are difficult to reach. In the urban areas, there is rampant unemployment, which is causing misery and strife among the bulk of the Zimbabwean populace.

The rural schools and health services are highly incapacitated digitally and the research participants cited these as vital centers, which should be considered and prioritized for digitalisation as they are very backward. Most of these facilities are not electrified and do not have digital equipment and services. Therefore, rural areas do not have the vital infrastructure, which is required for development to ride on. This includes poor road network, national electricity supply, telecommunication infrastructure, and digital equipment and services.

### Periphery or Border Communities

Such issues as radio, television, and mobile phone signals can easily exemplify the periphery areas particularly border areas are some of the most geographically marginalized areas and this requires a major transformation if the country is to realize inclusive transformative digitalisation for Society 5.0. Some people in these areas like Kanyemba, Malipati, and Chimanimani areas are receiving radio, television, and mobile signals from neighboring countries such that they are now using mobile phone services from those countries.

## Categorization by Group

### Smallholder Farmers

Smallholder farmers are generally some of the most marginalised communities in Zimbabwe and their situation is exacerbated by the fact that they are located in rudimentary and uncoordinated rural areas. According to research participants, a

*Figure 1. Ploughing a field-using ox drown plough*
Source: (Anita Anyango, 2022).

smallholder farmer is characterised as possessing a small-based plot of land where they practice their farming activities and they rely almost exclusively on family labour. These features are the size of land being farmed on, access to capital, the degree of exposure to risk and input technologies, and market orientation. The research participants indicated that the smallholder farmers face acute access challenges to things like cash, agriculture inputs, and markets for their agriculture output. These farmers rely primarily on agriculture for their living. This means that failing to be productive in agricultural operations spells disaster for smallholder farmers in many spheres of life. This frequently starts a cycle of poverty, and several studies have been conducted on smallholder farming in Sub-Saharan Africa. Agriculture is more directly linked to rural community development than anything else is. Smallholder farmers are critical players in the agricultural production and growth value chain. As a result, smallholder farmers' low productivity has a cascading effect on many aspects of their lives including affording to send their kids to school and acquiring and servicing digital technologies.

## Artisanal Miners

Artisanal miners are some of the most marginalized people in Zimbabwe as they solely depend on gold mining activities for their livelihood. This means that failure to be productive in mining activities spells out doom for many areas of life for the artisanal miners. Other areas of life affected for artisanal miners include education for the kids, health, procurement of household requirements, and most importantly

*Figure 2. A field with cotton and maize in the background*
Source: (World Bank, 2017)

the acquisition of food supplies for their next gold mining escapades and acquiring and using digital technologies. This often triggers a vicious cycle of poverty with a lock-in effect. Artisanal miners are critical players in the gold production and growth value chain as mining has been identified as one of the pillars of the country's vision 2030. As a result, Artisanal miners' low productivity has a cascading effect on many aspects of not only their lives but also the country at large.

However, these miners generate volumes of kilograms of gold each year running into tones. The research participants suggested that there is a need for the digitalization of artisanal mining activities as this might enable them to be tracked in terms of the extracted gold output. The government may as a result plug all the leakages that have seen so much gold being smuggled out of the country.

## Vending

Vending in Zimbabwe has become a source of livelihood for many people and yet some vendors solely depend on vending activities for their livelihood. This means that failure to be profitable in their vending activities spells out doom for many areas of life for these vendors. This automatically means that the education for the kids, health, and procurement of household requirements hence acquisition and sustenance of digital gadgets becomes very different for them. The digitalization of activities may result in vendors being able to procure their wares economically as they would be able to liaise with the suppliers of their wares and as a result, they would cut on unnecessary traveling costs expenses, as they would only travel to get their wares when they are certain about the commodities. On the selling front, digitalization

*Figure 3. Artisanal and small-scale miners at work*
Source: (Jack Dutton, 2021)

enables the vendors to get connected with customers and develop ties with some customers where they will get orders to frequently supply them on coordinated days.

*Figure 4. Fruit and vegetable vendors*
Source: (Tswangirai Mukwazhi, 2015)

## Women

Research participants revealed that there are gender divides across the social strata in Zimbabwe. This can be witnessed across many sections of society in the country which can be exemplified by a lack of education opportunities for women, especially in technical and digital labour markets which have seen low participation by women

*Figure 5. Clothes vendors*
Source: (Shamiso Dzingire, 2018)

in the digital labour market and in particular in high-quality jobs and top management positions. Research participants lamented the fact that women are the backbone of most informal economic activities spanning across the country, which are the bedrock of the Zimbabwean economy. These women need to be empowered with the right digital skills and supported by the enactment of a policy that can see them thriving on the digital front. A digital transformation is a tool through which gender equality and women's empowerment can be advanced as found by Musungwini et al., (2020). This can be accomplished by encouraging, educating, training, and capacitating the women, especially in marginalised communities to use digital tools effectively for social and economic empowerment and self-determination.

## CHALLENGES TO DIGITALISATION FACED BY MARGINAL COMMUNITIES IN ZIMBABWE

According to the interviews conducted with experts, Zimbabwe is faced with several challenges to digitalize its marginalized communities, and addressing these challenges is a precondition for digitalisation to take off. The interviewees identified the following challenges:

## The Country Lacks a Digital Infrastructure Presence in Marginalized Communities

The research participants believe that marginalised areas are held back by a lack of infrastructures like base stations, electricity, and other supportive infrastructure as in most rural areas where marginalised people lived. *There is only one telecommunications operator in Zimbabwe (Econet) whose operations are found across the country, all other operators' networks are very erratic and they do not have supporting agencies.* (INTER8).

## There Is a Lack of Digital Technology in the Hands of Many Marginalized People

The bulk of marginalised people was said to be lacking digital transformation gadgets. Research participants cited this lack of ownership of digital technology tools as a major drawback to the digital transformation aspirations of the country. *Marginalised people may feel that since they did they may not possess the necessary skills to operate digital transformation tools, they may be compelled to deliberately avoid them* (FGDP11). The farmers with smartphones lacked digital skills; hence they could not use the internet and mobile agricultural applications because of a lack of technical know-how.

## There Is a Lack of Digital Skills in the Informal Sector Where Most of the Economic Activities of Zimbabwe Are Happening

The research participants cited a lack of digital skills among the marginalised communities in Zimbabwe as some of these people were said to be lacking basic literacy skills. This coupled with a lack of financial power has resulted in most of the marginalised people failing to use digital transformation technologies available in Zimbabwe. The research participants asserted that there are those marginalised people who may own digitalisation transformation tools but are harm strung by lack of digital skills.

## There Is a Lack of Financial Resources to Power Economic Activities and Digitalization

The issue of a lack of financial resources was said to be double-barrelled as it was said to be both institutional and individual. The research respondents alluded to the privation of financial resources in the country, many business entities were said to be struggling for capitalisation funds to support business operations, and this was reported to be hurting digitalisation ambitions. On the people side, the marginalised people in Zimbabwe were said to be needy and struggling for survival let alone think of digital transformation technologies. *Digital transformation tools and their concomitant services are very expensive beyond the reach of many marginalised people in Zimbabwe* (FGDP9). The research participants argued digital tools and their associated services were very costly and beyond the reach of many marginalised people. This coupled with a lack of financial power has resulted in most of the marginalised people failing to use digital transformation technologies available in Zimbabwe.

## Exclusion of Minorities and Their Languages in Development Programs Including Digitalization

The research participants decried the exclusion of some minorities who are located in some of the marginalised communities in Zimbabwe. Participants claimed that there are those marginalised communities who are more marginalised than others and pose no hope for digitalisation because their level of marginalization requires decades of emancipation efforts before there can be visible signs on the horizon to talk about digitalisation transformation. *Come to think of places like Kanyemba where the Doma people come from [...] at the present moment some of those people still don't sleep in houses. How do you think such people can be a part of digital transformation when they have never been a part of the country's development programs?* (FGDP8).

## TECHNOLOGIES HAVING THE MOST DISRUPTING EFFECTS IN MARGINALIZED COMMUNITIES IN ZIMBABWE

This section presents the findings on technologies that have been found as having the most disrupting effects in marginalised communities in Zimbabwe.

### Social Media

The research participants indicated that the extensive use of social media due to the increase in the use of smartphones has resulted in rapid digital transformation amongst the youth. This has seen leaders of business firms turning to this technology to substantially improve their enterprises' operations or reach more clients. They suggest that it has the potential to fulfill the transformative ambition of many businesses in Zimbabwe today. This is in line with the increasingly competitive landscape, and consumer demand is requiring businesses to operate, advertise, and produce with greater agility and innovation than ever before. To stay competitive, executives across all sectors in Zimbabwe are embracing digital innovation. One effective approach their firms are expediting their digital transformation is with social media.

## FinTech's

The research participants indicated that financial technology is fast accelerating innovation in financial services. This was attributed to new emanating risks and increasing threats, as well as new emerging business models and technological use cases. This Fintech growth has been witnessed in a variety of fields' currency trading, money transfer, insurance, payments, and trade, as well as the cryptocurrency revolution. This is one area facing contestation and many Fintech products have sprouted.

*There is a battle for the digital financial market especially digital banking and money transfer (INTER2).*

*The need to move hard currency across the country from city to city has become a fertile ground for digital money transfer [...] traditional international hard currency movers like World remit, Mukuru and Western Union started offering the service but are very expensive and this attracted mobile telecommunication giants led by Econet. Since then banks like BancAbc joined the bandwagon and were followed by Insco brands and clothing retail giants led by Edgars. (INTER5).*

This has seen the Reserve Bank of Zimbabwe leading the creation of a National Fintech framework for managing the acceptance, deployment, and supervision of financial technology in the financial services industry, to reduce the cost of doing business and enable the inclusion of the bottom of the pyramid.

## Mobile Phones

Mobile phones especially smartphones and their associated applications are critical digital enablers that give a significant benefit to any organization across the strata. As respondents suggested that the high mobile penetration rate in Zimbabwe has seen the mobile phone in the hands of many including some of those in the marginalized areas. As per nuances from research participants' mobile phones are the only technology, which presents a realistic opportunity for marginalized people to be included in the digital transformation trajectory of developing countries like Zimbabwe. The significant role that mobile phones and associated applications can play in the digital transformation plan of countries in a developing context and how they assist businesses to improve productivity and growth is looking positive.

## Internet

Data is crucial to the digital transformation process and this data revolution rides on the superhighway (the Internet). Enabling access to the internet has been the most critical thing. This has been greatly facilitated by the mobile revolution, which was influenced by the plummeting prices of smartphones globally. This has seen the developing world benefit from that development. Access to the internet by many people and maintaining digital presents allows businesses to leverage consumer data instantly to drive their company. In practice, it allows businesses to become closer to their customers.

## GIS and Drone Technology

The research explored the general use of digital technologies by some marginalized communities in Zimbabwe to further our knowledge of digital transformation potential. The research engaged research participants, especially the marginalized ones, university lecturers, telecommunications experts, members of marginalized populations, community gatekeepers, and ICT specialists. These were engaged using semi-structured interviews and FGD. Drone technology is being used together with Global Positioning System and Remote Sensing (GPRS) systems for field and plant performance analysis. The drones collect data on the state of plant health and field nutrients, the presence of weeds, and diseases. The fusion of advanced crop aerial information, which is said to be acquired, using drones fused with data from other sources such as weather forecasts and soil maps, can help to refine the final information and enable the farmer to take full advantage of the farm and maximize the yields to their natural limits. The collection and analysis, as well as monitoring of plant health, enables farmers to make informed choices which can lead to high-quality products like high-quality tobacco which can then go on to fetch a higher price and enable the farmers to survive competition in the international market.

According to research participants, the advent of Internet technology has significantly given farmers greater access to web resources that help to make informed farming decisions. The Internet provides a plethora of production and planning tools to aid farmers in forecasting and planning for future cropsþ. Furthermore, the World Wide Web plays host to multiple agricultural platforms and forums aimed at enabling insightful discussions, and the exchange of ideas, tips, and advice among farmers. *"Technology is changing how we go about everyday work [...] although there is a slow uptake, but nonetheless it is a positive uptake"* INTER6. Based on these sentiments the uptake of available technologies for agricultural activities has given rise to new paradigms in the agricultural sector. Technology has brought about a big and positive change in agriculture and farmers in Zimbabwe ought to do more towards harnessing the available ICTs for greater productivity (Report, 2019). The chapter suggest that as marginalized communities, smallholder farmers need to keep up with trending technology for sustainable agricultural business. To avert the effects of climate change and meet food security requirements, farmers in Zimbabwe need to shift more towards smart agriculture.

## DISCUSSION

The results of this research posit that digital transformation is a ubiquitous technological phenomenon that shakes and involves various challenges for marginalized communities' innovation systems. Particularly, the research participants in this research underscored the major challenges as (1) the prerequisite to educating, training, capacitating and continuous updating the digital skills of marginalized communities in Zimbabwe. (2) The need to develop and establish infrastructures like good road networks, electricity supply, and digital telecommunication infrastructure as well as constantly adjusting to new digital technologies with cutting-edge infrastructures and services. (3) There is also a need to cultivate collaborations and synergies of different stakeholders from the public and private sectors among marginalized communities.

The interviewed experts suggested that if digitalization is to be a catalyst for progress for all people in Zimbabwe then it must be accessible to all people. Yet at the time of carrying out this research, just over half of the country's population was reported to be linked to the internet, and for the remaining segment of the population, especially the marginalized their digital access prospects are gloomy. As a result, people without internet connections cannot participate in digital socioeconomic platforms hence they cannot benefit from digital technology as well as access government services online. As stated here the marginalized people in Zimbabwe are made up of mainly smallholder farmers, vendors, artisanal miners, rural women, housewives, persons with lower levels of education, those involved in informal socio-economic activities and those living in poverty are more likely to lack digital access.

Therefore, to reach all citizens there is a need to think beyond the present digital transformation stance, which is anchored on organizational structures mainly commercial. To begin with, the business sector must design digitalization transformation blueprints for inclusion warranting that the poorest and most marginalized users are not left out of the loop. The private sector in Zimbabwe is very critical to the country's national digital transformation endeavor because a digitally transformed Zimbabwe may result in the generation of new socioeconomic opportunities while providing digital goods and infrastructure. Thus, developing countries cannot experience real digitalization transformation, which is inclusive of the marginalized communities without the coming together of the private sector and government. Marginalized communities' leadership has to be involved in developing a national digitalization framework. This is likely to see the development of tailor-made, low-cost digital products for those living in abject poverty, the smallholder farmers, rural housewives, and the disabled among others. The framework will be welcoming a disruptive competitive landscape, which ushers in inclusive new digital business models and the development of digital skills throughout the marginalized communities.

Technology, regardless of how inventive it is, will not ensure success. The social and economic milieu in which technology is employed is just as significant as new technology. Technology is virtually always a driver for progress, but it is not necessarily a force for inclusion. Without a concerted effort to involve everyone, digital technologies have the potential to perpetuate current inequity. That is why this chapter argues that the government, public society, and the commercial sector should collaborate to develop a common national vision that ensures that everyone is involved in massive economic transformation.

The research shows that the road to inclusive digital transformation is rather long, meandering, and littered with cavernous potholes for developing countries, especially SSA. The actual digitalization transformation processes of any country have been found to contain valleys of despair as shown in fig 6, which are attributed to the marginalized communities in developing countries mainly, encompasses smallholder farmers, artisanal miners, vendors, the disabled, and other informal socioeconomic activities. These present major hurdles to the inclusive digitalization transformation process for countries in a development context like Zimbabwe. The study advocates for human-centered multidimensional interventions involving the government and the private sector entrenched in the unique attributes within each marginalized community/informal socio-economic activity to improve the proficiency of each poor and marginalized framework in particular of experience and understanding, economic freedom, and sociocultural resources.

As a result, a digitalisation blueprint predicated on each marginalised group's technological and intellectual foundation, along with underlying resources and capabilities, could be developed to efficaciously harness the potential provided by digital transformation to enhance the business competitiveness of these underdeveloped sectors. These include the informal sectors, smallholder agriculture, artisanal mining, and vending. This may result in the boosting of productivity and promote the sustainable development of these territories. This may eventually create

*Figure 6. Showing the difference between the promise and the actual digitalisation transformation processes and valley of despair.*

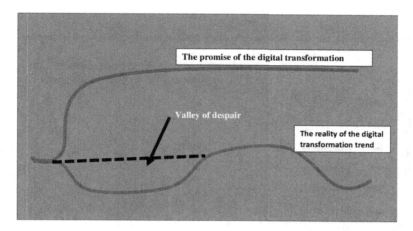

better quality jobs in these sectors and reshape the interactions between these sectors, the government, and the citizens at large.

## A FRAMEWORK FOR DIGITAL TRANSFORMATION FOR INCLUSIVITY OF MARGINALIZED COMMUNITIES IN ZIMBABWE A COUNTRY IN A DEVELOPING CONTEXT

This section presents the framework formulated in this chapter. Our book chapter specifically identifies a series of steps that must be taken for enabling inclusive digital transformation in a developing context. It is vital that existing marginalized communities are identified and characterized. This is bound to facilitate specific-marginalized community policy for inclusive digital transformation that is context-specific.

### Identify and Characterize Challenges to the Digital Transformation of Each Marginalized Community

The first step is to identify and classify marginalized communities and characterize specific salient needs and enabling factors in a given marginalized community. This will enable marginalized communities to digital transformation and subsequently develop digital culture and skills that are redolent to each specific marginalized setting.

*Figure 7. A framework for Digital transformation for inclusivity of marginalized communities in Zimbabwe a country in a developing context*
*Source: (Author)*

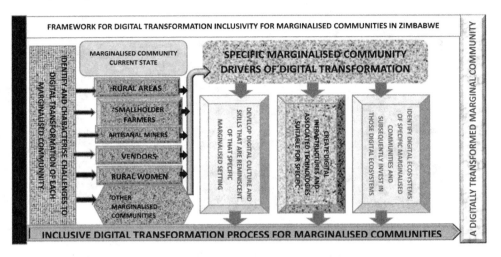

## Specific Marginalized Community Drivers of Digital Transformation

Secondly, the framework suggests that based on the established prominent features of specific marginalized communities and populations peculiar drivers of digital transformation can be found. This can assist in situating inclusive digital transformation roadmaps that are tailor-made to a specific situation. This will lead to three critical action points, or building blocks, which may lead to digital transformation diffusion inclusive to marginal communities.

- Develop digital culture and skills that are reminiscent of that specific marginalized setting.
- Create digital infrastructures and associated technologies suitable for specific.
- Identify digital ecosystems of specific marginalized communities and subsequently invest in those digital ecosystems

The authors believe that taking the prescribed steps provided by this framework can lead to context-specific targeted development and deployment of digital infrastructures and associated technologies that are apt for explicit marginalized communities. This may also result in the development, nurturing, and growth of digital ecosystems-specific marginalized communities and subsequently invest in those digital ecosystems. This may culminate in the inclusive digital transformation process for marginalized communities in Zimbabwe.

## CONCLUSION AND RECOMMENDATIONS

The major contribution of this book chapter refers to the framework that has been developed which entails the key pillars of digital transformation for inclusivity in marginalized communities. The chapter suggests that digital transformation can be undertaken using the framework to successfully identify and face the challenges of digital transformation by considering the ongoing subtleties contained within the context of marginalized communities. Our book chapter specifically argues that a specific-marginalized community policy for inclusive digital transformation should function in three (3) dimensions. There is a need to identify the deficiencies of a given marginalized community to digital transformation and subsequently develop digital culture and skills that are reminiscent of that specific marginalized setting. Secondly, based on the established digital and other infrastructure void found, there is a need for creating digital infrastructures and associated technologies suitable for specific marginalized communities. Lastly, there is a need to identify the digital ecosystems of specific marginalized communities and subsequently invest in those digital ecosystems. We believe that in doing, so inclusive digital transformation may take place in Zimbabwe and other countries in a developing context may also adapt our recommendations to their contexts and successfully implement inclusive digital transformations for their countries. We recommend that our framework may be applied as a model for digital transformation for the inclusivity of marginalized communities in SSA.

On the other hand, the numerous strategic tasks highlighted by this research show that understanding digitalization is tough because it is analogous to analyzing and understanding an ongoing revolution. In an ongoing revolution, numerous things do change, and many of these do change rapidly such that predicting what the next phases might be like is intricate. However, while predicting the outcome of such an occurrence is difficult, it should not stop the scholars to hypothesize, problematize, and researching as failing to do so may spell doom for the academic field. Therefore, with the ongoing evolution and revolution happening around digital technologies, low- and middle-income to which category Zimbabwe falls in, have the opportunity to promote inclusive digitalization processes targeted at the informal sector and hopeful marginalized communities. Digital transformation targeted at the informal sector and hopeful marginalized communities may enable these countries to diversify their economies, and alter the artisanal mining, smallholder agriculture, and vending and money transfers among other activities. This will generate new employment opportunities and augment the health and education systems of the country. Otherwise, if left alone, digital technologies have the potential to perpetuate ostracism as suggested by Tongia in the quotation provided in the introduction section and this may result in the disruption of people's lives. Grounded on one year of literature review research and analysis, ten 10 in-depth interviews, and a focus group discussion, this study is buttressed by comprehensive engagement with representatives of the marginalized communities, community gatekeepers, digital transformation experts, representatives of disadvantaged groups, and academia in Zimbabwe. The chapter is in sync with the key themes of the book.

## FUTURE RESEARCH DIRECTIONS

Research on how to create digital infrastructures and their associated technologies suitable for specific marginalized communities can be conducted. There is a need to identify digital ecosystems of specific marginalized communities and subsequently investing in those digital ecosystems.

## REFERENCES

Agyekumhene, C., de Vries, J. R., van Paassen, A., Macnaghten, P., Schut, M., & Bregt, A. (2018). Digital platforms for smallholder credit access: The mediation of trust for cooperation in maize value chain financing. *NJAS Wageningen Journal of Life Sciences*, *86–87*(1), 77–88. doi:10.1016/j.njas.2018.06.001

Assembly, G. (2015). Sustainable development goals. *SDGs, Transforming Our World: The, 2030*.

Avgerou, C. (2017). Theoretical framing of ICT4D research. *IFIP Advances in Information and Communication Technology*, *504*, 10–23. Advance online publication. doi:10.1007/978-3-319-59111-7_2

Bailey, A., Henry-Lee, A., Johnson-Coke, Y., Leach, R., Clayton, A., Gee, M., & Browne, O. (2019). ICT use in the context of electricity access in a developing country: A choice framework analysis. *IFIP Advances in Information and Communication Technology*, *551*, 27–38. doi:10.1007/978-3-030-18400-1_3

Brunetti, F., Matt, D. T., Bonfanti, A., De Longhi, A., Pedrini, G., & Orzes, G. (2020). Digital transformation challenges: Strategies emerging from a multi-stakeholder approach. *The TQM Journal*, *32*(4), 697–724. doi:10.1108/TQM-12-2019-0309

Chepken, C., Mugwanya, R., Blake, E., & Marsden, G. (2012). ICTD interventions: Trends Over the Last Decade. *Proceedings of the Fifth International Conference on Information and Communication Technologies and Development - ICTD '12*, 241. 10.1145/2160673.2160704

Dzino-Silajdzic, V. (2018). *Practical Guide; Focus group discussions.* https://www.crs.org/sites/default/files/tools-research/fgds_april_24_final_lo_res_.pdf

Gavai, P., Musungwini, S., & Mugoniwa, B. (2018). A Model for the Adoption and Effective Utilization of ICTs in Commercial Agriculture in Zimbabwe. *Journal of Systems Integration*, *9*(4), 40–58. doi:10.20470/jsi.v9i4.356

Gimpel, H., & Röglinger, M. (2015). Digital Transformation: Changes and Chances. Frauenhofer Institute for Applied Information Technology Fit.

Given, L. (2012). Grand Theory. In *The SAGE Encyclopedia of Qualitative Research Methods*. SAGE Publications, Inc. doi:10.4135/9781412963909.n188

Gubrium, J., & Holstein, J. (2001). *Handbook of Interview Research.* doi:10.4135/9781412973588

Heeks, R. (2014). *Future Priorities for Development Informatics Research from the Post-2015 Development Agenda: Development Informatics Working Paper no.57.* papers2://publication/uuid/E62B26A8-CEBC-4A60-A869-94B02AB6E969

Journal, U. G. C. C. (2020). *A Study of Mobile Banking in IDBI Bank Studies in Indian Place Names.* Author.

Kokh, L., & Kokh, Y. (2020). Banks and Fintech-companies: Who's Catching up with Whom. *Pervasive Health: Pervasive Computing Technologies for Healthcare.* doi:10.1145/3446434.3446533

Krell, N. T., Giroux, S. A., Guido, Z., Hannah, C., Lopus, S. E., Caylor, K. K., & Evans, T. P. (2021). Smallholder farmers' use of mobile phone services in central Kenya. *Climate and Development*, *13*(3), 215–227. doi:10.1080/17565529.2020.1748847

Lichtenthaler, U. (2020). Building Blocks of Successful Digital Transformation: Complementing Technology and Market Issues. *International Journal of Innovation and Technology Management*, *17*(1). Advance online publication. doi:10.1142/S0219877020500042

Mahlangu, G., Musungwini, S., & Sibanda, M. (2018). A framework for creating an ICT knowledge hub in Zimbabwe : A holistic approach in fostering economic growth. *Journal of Systems Integration*, *2004*(1), 32–41. doi:10.20470/jsi.v9i1.327

Mahlangu, G., & Ruhode, E. (2021). *Factors Enhancing E-Government Service Gaps in a Developing Country Context*. doi:10.48550/arxiv.2108.09803

Mohamad, A. G. M. M., Idrus, S. S., & Ibrahim, A. A. E. A. (2018). Model of behavioral attention towards using ICT in universities in libya. *Jurnal Komunikasi: Malaysian Journal of Communication, 34*(2), 89–104. doi:10.17576/JKMJC-2018-3402-06

Morze, N. V., & Strutynska, O. V. (2021). Digital transformation in society: Key aspects for model development. *Journal of Physics: Conference Series, 1946*(1). Advance online publication. doi:10.1088/1742-6596/1946/1/012021

Munyoka, W. (2022). *Inclusive Digital Innovation in South Africa : Perspectives from Disadvantaged and Marginalized Communities*. Academic Press.

Musungwini, S. (2016). A model for harnessing the power of the Mobile Phone Technology to improve Smallholder Agriculture in Zimbabwe. *Proceedings of the 5th International Conference on M4D Mobile Communication Technology for Development: M4D 2016, General Tracks, December*, 237–252.

Musungwini, S. (2018). Mobile Phone Use by Zimbabwean Smallholder Farmers : A Baseline Study. *The African Journal of Information and Communication, 22*(22), 29–52. doi:10.23962/10539/26171

Musungwini, S., & Van Zyl, I. (2017). ` Mobile Technology for Development ' Experiences from Zimbabwe Vending Markets a Naturalistic Enquiry. *International Journal of Business and Management Studies., 06*(01), 101–111.

Musungwini, S., Zhou, T. G., & Musungwini, L. (2020). Challenges facing women in ICT from a women perspective: A case study of the Zimbabwean Banking Sector and Telecommunications Industry. *Journal of Systems Integration, 11*(1), 21–33. doi:10.20470/JSI.V11I1.389

Musungwini, S., Zyl, I. van, & Kroeze, J. H. (2022). *The Perceptions of Smallholder Farmers on the Use of Mobile Technology: A Naturalistic Inquiry in Zimbabwe*. doi:10.1007/978-3-030-98015-3_37

OECD. (2015). Inequalities in Digital Proficiency: Bridging the Divide. *Pisa*, 123–143. https://www.oecd-ilibrary.org/education/students-computers-and-learning/inequalities-in-digital-proficiency-bridging-the-divide_9789264239555-8-en

Pade-Khene, C., & Lannon, J. (2017). Learning to be sustainable in ICT for development: A citizen engagement initiative in South Africa. *IFIP Advances in Information and Communication Technology, 504*, 475–486. Advance online publication. doi:10.1007/978-3-319-59111-7_39

Paramita, D. (2020). *Digitalization in Talent Acquisition: A Case Study of AI in Recruitment.* https://www.teknik.uu.se/student-en/

Pfavai Natasha Nyajeka. (2018). *How Whatsapp Strengthens Livelihoods of Women Farmers in Rural Zimbabwe | ICTs for Development.* https://ict4dblog.wordpress.com/2018/12/11/how-whatsapp-strengthens-livelihoods-of-women-farmers-in-rural-zimbabwe/

Putri, N. M. A. W. (2021). Digital Transformation: The Approach to Society 5.0 in Indonesia. *Proceeding - 2021 2nd International Conference on ICT for Rural Development, IC-ICTRuDev 2021.* 10.1109/IC-ICTRuDev50538.2021.9656528

Report, C. S. (2019). *Harnessing ICTs to Scale-up Agricultural Innovations (ICT4Scale) Case Study Report.* Academic Press.

Rowley, J. (2012). Conducting research interviews. *Management Research Review*, *35*(3–4), 260–271. doi:10.1108/01409171211210154

Ryll, L., Barton, M. E., Zhang, B. Z., McWaters, R. J., Schizas, E., Hao, R., Bear, K., Preziuso, M., Seger, E., Wardrop, R., Rau, P. R., Debata, P., Rowan, P., Adams, N., Gray, M., & Yerolemou, N. (2020). *Transforming Paradigms: A Global AI in Financial Services Survey. SSRN.* Electronic Journal., doi:10.2139/SSRN.3552038

Sam, S. (2014). Exploring Mobile Internet use among Marginalised Young People in Post-conflict Sierra Leone. *The Electronic Journal on Information Systems in Developing Countries*, *66*(5), 1–20. http://www.ejisdc.org/ojs2/index.php/ejisdc/article/view/1439

Saul, C. J., & Gebauer, H. (2018). Digital transformation as an enabler for advanced services in the sanitation sector. *Sustainability (Switzerland)*, *10*(3), 1–18. doi:10.3390u10030752

Series, W. P. (2008). Development Informatics. *Development*, *32*, 45. doi:10.1016/0736-5853(84)90003-0

Siddiquee, N. A. (2016). E-government and transformation of service delivery in developing countries: The Bangladesh experience and lessons. *Transforming Government: People, Process and Policy*, *10*(3), 368–390. doi:10.1108/TG-09-2015-0039

Steinke, J., Van Etten, J., Müller, A., Ortiz-Crespo, B., Van De Gevel, J., Silvestri, S., & Priebe, J. (2020). Tapping the full potential of the digital revolution for agricultural extension: an emerging innovation agenda Tapping the full potential of the digital revolution for agricultural extension: an emerging innovation agenda. *International Journal of Agricultural Sustainability.* doi:10.1080/14735903.2020.1738754

The Four Essential Pillars of Digital Transformation: a Practical Blueprint | Akorbi Digital RMP. (n.d.). Retrieved February 13, 2022, from https://www.runmyprocess. com/vision/white-papers/the-four-essential-pillars-of-digital-transformation/

Tsokota, T., Musungwini, S., & Mutembedza, A. (2020). A strategy to enhance consumer trust in the adoption of mobile banking applications. *African Journal of Science, Technology, Innovation and Development*, *0*(0), 1–16. doi:10.1080/2042 1338.2020.1829352

Van Dijk, J. A. G. M. (2017). Closing the Digital Divide The Role of Digital Technologies on Social Development, Well-Being of All and the Approach of the Covid-19 Pandemic. *Telematics and Informatics*, *34*, 1607–1624. doi:10.1016/j. tele.2017.07.007

Venkatraman, N. (1991). IT-Induced Business Reconfiguration. *The Corporation of the 1990s: Information Technology and Organizational Transformation*, 331.

Westerman, G., Calméjane, C., Bonnet, D., Ferraris, P., & McAfee, A. (2011). Digital transformation: a roadmap for billion-dollar organizations. MIT Center for Digital Business and Capgemini Consulting.

Zhou, M., Herselman, M., & Coleman, A. (2015). USSD technology a low cost asset in complementing public health workers' work processes. Lecture Notes in Computer Science, 9044, 57–64. doi:10.1007/978-3-319-16480-9_6

## KEY TERMS AND DEFINITIONS

**Developing Context:** A sovereign country that is less developed relative to other countries.

**Digital Transformation:** The integration of technology.

**Framework:** The structure that holds or support a theory.

**ICT4D:** Information and communications technology for development.

**SDGs:** Sustainable Development Goals.

**Zimbabwe:** A developing country in Sub-Saharan Africa.

# Chapter 6
# From Digital Divides to Digital Dividends:
## Embracing Basic Services in Zimbabwe's Digitalisation Agenda

**Fungai N. Mukora**
*University of Zimbabwe, Zimbabwe*

**Teurai Matekenya**
*University of Zimbabwe, Zimbabwe*

**Gilbert Mahlangu**
*Midlands State University, Zimbabwe*

**Innocent Chirisa**
*University of Zimbabwe, Zimbabwe*

**Caroline Hester Sarai Muparutsa**
*The Business Ark Training and Management Consultancy, Zimbabwe*

## ABSTRACT

*This chapter approached the national digital policy as a target for bridging the digital divide to gain digital dividends that will help in socio-economic development. The chapter argues that digital dividends are key to developing countries as they have helped break the digital divide that has been there for so long. Nevertheless, the findings reveal that some marginalized communities exist in developing countries like Zimbabwe, especially semi-urban and rural communities. Zimbabwe is yet to strengthen the pillars of digital transformation. The chapter recommends that the government and regulators consider taking the outside-in strategy to narrow the digital divide in the country.*

DOI: 10.4018/978-1-6684-3901-2.ch006

# INTRODUCTION

Digital technologies have become a prominent need in the lives of people more recently, with the use of the internet twisting to be one of the daily basic needs (Wiraniskalaa & Sujarwoto, 2020). United Nations strained more on the significance of the internet in resolving the current global socio-economic challenges (UN, 2015). The use of the internet is increasing day by day, slowly but steadily. According to Hootsuite and We Are Social 2019 annual report, the number of people using the internet in early 2019 was 4.388 billion, whilst 3.484 billion were active social media users globally (Kemp, 2019). The number of people using it is increasing daily from the young to the old ages as it increases choices and brings convenience in many aspects of life. The use of digital technologies continues to revolutionize people's lives and empower them. Access to the internet is turning people into entrepreneurs apart from transmitting information and entertaining them. It has created a virtual community using social media accelerated by the greater use of the internet worldwide (ibid). People have managed to cross social, political, and economic barriers, and the internet brings them together like never before. The World Summit on Information Society of 2003 held in Geneva, Switzerland projected the hope that the world would have universal access to the internet and be linked via Information Communication Technology (ICTs) by 2015 (Vidyasagar, 2006).

The wide gap between developed and developing countries has been a major concern on internet connectivity around the Globe. Vidyasagar, (2006) acknowledged the continued existence of the digital divide in developing countries and among the poor who live in developed countries. He termed the existence of this gap the digital divide. The concept materialized in the 1990s, describing the existence of inequalities in accessing Information Communication Technology (ICT) (Ragnedda, 2019). According to OECD (2018), the digital divide is weighed on a nation's ability to access ICTs and its citizens' capabilities to use the technologies due to variations in race, economic status, gender, and location. The 2nd meeting of the World Summit on Information Society held in 2005 in Tunis, the capital city of Tunisia concentrated on bridging the digital divide. Citizens of rich countries benefit from digital technologies through internet connectivity, while those in developing countries lag. Bukht and Heeks (2017) note a disparity in the digital economy between the global north and the global south countries. Ragnedda (2019, p.27) noted that the digital gap among citizens or countries is created by socio-demographic variables that influence ICT access, such as "…employment status, income, education level, geographic location, ethnicity, age, gender, and family structure." These factors have not been fully studied in Zimbabwe, thereby creating a gap in the literature on how to bridge the digital gap to yield digital dividends successfully.

## BACKGROUND

Like many other developing countries, Zimbabwe is currently focusing on ICT infrastructure deployment to foster digital transformation in public services. As part of the transformation and public sector reforms to improve service delivery among government agencies, departments, businesses, and citizens, Zimbabwe is implementing e-government projects/systems (Munyoka, 2019). Nevertheless, despite Zimbabwe's remarkable headway recorded to date in the development of digital tools for service delivery through the deployment of e-government flagship projects, the country's readiness to use technology to transform livelihoods still falls short compared to its regional peers. It records worse than other developing countries on other continents (Munyoka, 2019). Compared to some low-income countries (such as Mali, Burkina Faso, Gambia, Madagascar,) Zimbabwe, a country that aspires to be an upper-middle-income economy by 2030, compares worse. According to the Network Readiness Index (2020), which provides a global digital transformation glance, out of 134 economies, Zimbabwe is ranked 126 and is 24th in Africa. By 2018, the country was ranked 146 out of 193 in Electronic Government Development Index (EGDI) and last in SADC, while the Online Service Index (OSI) stood at the mean value of 0.3246 (Dias, 2020). Besides, it has been observed in Zimbabwe that citizens are required to travel a very long distance to access basic services at government offices physically, yet mobile applications or online platforms could be used to provide the same services remotely. In 2016 the World Bank sort to promote Digital dividends. The World Bank (2016) asserts that the digitization of the economy has proved to yield positive impacts on economic growth and welfare. It affects production, generates opportunities, and facilitates the exchange of information in a way that helps individuals and companies to collaborate efficiently.

Approximately 70% of the population lives in rural and marginalized areas that are located more than 100 km from urban areas. Rural areas are poorly covered in terms of digitization of services- making service provision digital by default significantly disadvantages the marginalized communities. Zimbabwe is yet to strengthen the pillars of digital transformation. There still exist some challenges associated with access to e-government services in Zimbabwe, such as technological marginalization, leading to the digital divide and poverty, thereby posing serious challenges in promoting digital inclusiveness or exploiting the full potential of digital transformation. Based on the foregoing, action should be taken to establish digital basic service interventions in Zimbabwe and explain why certain digital interventions do not reinforce inclusiveness in digital transformation and/or deliver an inclusive digital economy, digital society and digital government.

It is, therefore, the aim of this chapter to analyze the various factors that affect access to ICT in Zimbabwe that, in turn, bring digital inequalities. The study further assesses the necessary conditions for successful digital transformation in the country.

## OBJECTIVES

Against this background, this chapter seeks to highlight and discuss the following:

1.  The broader conditions necessary for successful digital transformation in Zimbabwe.
2.  The extent to which the broader conditions for successful transformation are being met and how complete these are for inclusive digital transformation in Zimbabwe.

This chapter argues that certain conditions must be met for Zimbabwe to move from digital divide to digital dividends.

## LITERATURE SURVEY

### Digital Divide

The term digital divide is relatively new in literature, but research in the field has managed to gain prominence in the academic field over the past few years (Wang et al., 2013). Bridging the divide may accelerate the benefits or dividends of digital transformation. An in-depth understanding of the theory behind the digital divide will help us understand how we can improve these dividends in the future. Coined in the 1990s, the term has no commonly accepted definition as it has different meanings depending on how it is used. Studies have shown that women, poor people, racial minorities and adults have a low rate of internet access and computer ownership, creating a digital divide across people and nations (Ragnedda, 2019).

DiMaggio et al. (2004) suggest that the digital divide went through two phases: the access divide from different access opportunities and the digital disparities resulting from different capabilities in the usage of the internet. This was supported by Ragnedda (2019), who came up with a three-level digital divide approach to explain differences in the digital divide. Taking the digital divide as a problem along technological lines and its adoption may result in ignoring other crucial variables such as the socio-cultural, political and educational context. Ragnedda (2017) came up with an approach to differentiate digital divide in terms of levels of its intensity, see Figure 1. The physical access to the internet that creates universal access to ICTs in every aspect of people's lives is the source of inequalities at the first level of the digital divide (Figure 1). This may include having the digital gadgets that are compatible with internet applications, access to internet connectivity, etc. Being marginalized from these creates a technological divide, hence the digital divide.

*Figure 1. levels of the digital divide*
*(Ragnedda, 2019)*

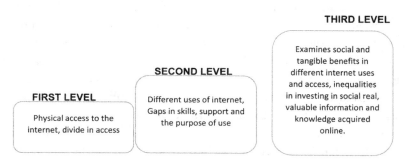

The second level of the digital divide is based on different uses of the internet, inequalities in skills, support to use the internet and the purpose for which the individual is using the internet. People may have physical access to the internet but may lack support to use the internet. A divide is also created because people go online for different reasons. Some are always active online. Others access it for research purposes, business (e-commerce), entertainment, etc. prestigious, educated, and people of high class may use the internet to augment their honoured positions. Prestigious people use the internet to exploit the opportunities offered by the internet (van Deursen et al, 2015). Building from this background, a gap is created in terms of the skills that are acquired in the use of internet-based on the purpose of use.

The third level of the digital divide relates to the ability to convert the digital benefits of using ICTs adequately into some social benefits that may advance the livelihoods of the users. This is also seen as the capacity to use or further invest the valued information and resources that would have been found on the internet into the social dominion. However, the access to the internet and the ability to use it do not just transform into social outcomes automatically. What people experience online impacts on the opportunities that they meet in the offline environment? Without the correct socio-cultural, economic or political environment to rely on countries will not be able to increase the benefits or exploit opportunities the internet comes with.

## Digital Dividends

Internet technology has played a big role in improving information access, health (telemedicine), education (e-learning), and hence the economy on a global scale. This is termed digital dividend. In 2016 the World Bank sort of promoted digital dividends. The World Bank (2016) asserts that the digitization of the economy has proved to yield positive impacts on economic growth and welfare. It affects production, generates opportunities and facilitates the exchange of information in a way that helps individuals and companies to collaborate efficiently. The different outcomes of internet usage are the socio-economic benefits that users gain through internet usage. This may come as the internet revenue that users get as connectivity dividends (Zeqi et al, 2019). The World Bank asserts that access to mobile broadband services is cheaper than fixed broadband services; hence, many people acquire it. Katz and Callorda (2015) also acknowledge broadband as a compliment and a substitute of fixed systems to bridge the divide and increase the dividends.

Digital dividends are key to developing countries as they have helped break the digital divide that has been there for so long. The size of digital dividends can be estimated (Krišelj & Copot, 2013), and this helps regulators estimate the benefits of transitioning to the use of digital methods for universal access to all. In Nigeria, regulators have forecasted how the transition to digital television broadcasting will help the economy (Gbenga-Ilori & Sanusi, 2020). Digital technology reduces expenses and costs and improves competence whilst protecting inclusion. In developing countries, it offers an avenue to deliver services in areas where old-fashioned rules of the game are weak. The potential to realize this is, however, far from being achieved. Graham and Avery (2013) acknowledge that the use of the internet has increased the interaction between the public and government agencies. The use of social media has also impacted human lives in many dimensions, including the world of business, changing the landscape of government agencies. Innovative technologies like social media applications are used to reach the innovative audience as they prefer to receive news through platforms such as WhatsApp, Facebook, Twitter etc. The public sector has taken advantage of these innovative technologies to increase transparency and improve citizens' engagement and participation in policy-making (Mergel, 2013). The use of digital technologies continues to revolutionize people's lives and empower them.

Grove et al. (2011) analyze why digital dividends will not close the digital divide in the near future. The study analyses the case of Europe to highlight the problem. It reveals that digital dividends discussions in Germany, the USA and Australia, were driven by a political goal. The study defines the digital divide as the widening gap between people with and without access to the internet. Being offline is also considered a digital divide, and lack of access to broadband was identified as one of the main reasons causing the wide gap. It widens social injustice not only for off liners but for the nation at large. Picot & Grove (2009) notes a lack of high-performance wired infrastructure in rural areas both in developed and developing countries. Political players quickly identified the digital dividend to yield a variety of things needed to provide internet access to rural communities. This would be supported by reduced infrastructure cost, convenience and rollout speed.

## Conditions Necessary for Successful Digital Transformation

Over the past few decades, the number of digital innovations has exploded, fundamentally changing how people engage with information and one another. A wide range of basic digital initiatives has been piloted in response to specific basic service challenges in low- and middle-income countries (LMICs) (Labrique et al., 2018). Although many small-scale digital interventions have been introduced to tackle basic service challenges, the use of digital devices for basic service delivery has not achieved the goal of digital transformation. Practical experience from real-life case studies of scaling and sustaining basic digital initiatives in LMICs has highlighted five critical focus areas: program characteristics, human factors and technical factors, and the features of the digital ecosystem and broader extrinsic ecosystem within which they operate (Labrique et al., 2018). These elements should be considered individually when planning for digital transformation intervention but must also form an interlinked system.

Findings by various authors revealed inequalities among men and women; developing countries and developed countries; the rich and the poor; the educated and the uneducated the young and the old, to mention but a few. These divides exist due to various factors:

### Political Will and Dedicated Leadership

The shift towards the fourth industrialization is a move that will help Africa to bridge the inequalities in the digital economy. The transition towards the fourth industrial revolution in Africa starts with the government's commitment, resource allocation, and dedicated leadership with dedicated strategy (Abersfelder, et al., 2016). Understanding the latest technology and its application to processes and process integration (Hofmann & Ruesch, 2017). Then the leaders and directors in organizations become more facilitators, with technology as an enabler (Longo, 2017). In September 2019, leaders and policymakers met in Cape Town, South Africa, to discuss strategies to realize Agenda 2063 in the fourth industrialization era. Whilst the fourth industrialization has been at the center of discussion on various international platforms, there is a dearth of orderly efforts to scrutinize this new revolution (Liao.et.al. 2017). Africa has previously been labelled a technological and digital desert (Wentrup et al., 2016). While African governments and policymakers have been choral about the promising benefits of the fourth industrialization, they are slowly implementing strategies to shift from their primary dependence on agrarian economies. It is the role of the leadership and policymakers to enforce the implementation of the strategies and to make sure that this comes to fruition. Without political will and strong leadership, the efforts fall in vain. Adeleye and Eboagu (2019) asserts that digitalization is a way forward to advance the continent through the stages of economic development (Ehigiamusoe & Lean, 2018; Pradhan et al., 2017; Nkikabahizi et al., 2018; Wamboye & Tochkov, 2018). Rich countries benefit more in the digital space than developing countries (Melhem et al., 2014).

## Socio-cultural Factors

Zeqi et al (2019) analyzed the divide dividend gap by reviewing the development of digital divided with the aim of bringing light to the hidden social facts that affect the transformation of various asset forms into online capital. The study revealed that the development of digital infrastructure that promotes internet growth had lessened the digital divide and improved dividend access in the world. The development of digital dividends has narrowed the access divide through enhancing connectivity enhanced and developing platforms. This has benefited people who previously invested assets into connectivity capital, with people turning to e-business, online stores, factories, and more sales revenue.

There are also inequalities between men and women in developing countries. Literature reveals that men are at an upper hand over women in the digital space within developing countries (Hilbert, 2011; Pande, 2012) due to a lack of access to education exacerbated by various factors, including cultural norms, household chores and lack of time to attend school, that gives a low priority to education (Pande, 2012; Chadwick et al., 2013). Hilbert (2011) associated this with the fact that the technology has not been designed to meet women's needs and that women are more technophobic than men. Traditional culture accelerates the rate of growth of inequalities at all levels. For example, in African countries and Southern India, there is a belief that women are a source of family support (Johnson, 2012). This brings a lot of disadvantages in upholding women's individual needs and their roles in society, and the technological space is not an exception. Findings in literature reveal that in some African countries like Ghana, a strong relationship lies between the environments one works in and his or her access to digital resources (Antonio and Tuffley, 2014). In Zimbabwe, poverty forced several citizens to join the informal sector. Zimbabwe ranks first in sub-Saharan Africa for having the largest informal economy and second-largest only to Bolivia in the world (Madina and Schneider,

2018). Such an environment is dominated by women and does not promote digital literacy (Antonio and Tuffley, 2014). The number of men using the internet is greater than that of men across all age groups in developing countries. However, a study in six West African countries on the digital gender gap in internet usage by young, educated women (Hafkin, 2007) revealed that education is more important in breaking the yoke, but women are given low priority to education.

## Technological Factors

The digital gap still exists between developed and developing countries. It seems rich countries benefit more in the digital space than poor countries (Melhem et al., 2014). More still needs to be done, especially in investing in ICT infrastructure. Most African governments lack technical skills and the ability to finance projects that make people aware of cyber security threats. That has been worsened by a dearth of computer skills which has seen 50% of schools in Africa (Zimbabwe included) adding modules on computer skills in their school curricula as compared to 85% globally (Kandri, 2019).

Zeqi et al (2019) analyzed the divide dividend gap by reviewing the development of digital divided to bring to light the hidden social facts that affect the transformation of various asset forms into online capital. The study revealed that the development of digital infrastructure that promotes internet growth had lessened the digital divide and improved dividend access in the world. The development of digital dividends has narrowed the access divide through enhancing connectivity enhanced and developing platforms. This has benefited people who previously invested assets into connectivity capital, with people turning to e-business, online stores, factories, and more sales revenue.

## Legal Frameworks, Policies and Law

The policy environment in developed countries promotes the development of skills in the digital economy that enhance efficiency in the digital field. Developing countries have a limited digital policy enabling policy environment that lacks privacy and security (Songwe, 2019). A lack of the same cyber legal framework, laws and policies in most developing countries hinders their efforts (Veiga et al., 2021). This is exacerbated by low levels of digital literacy, accompanied by feeble systems of cyber security (Calandro & Berglund, 2019). There are a lot of internet-related barriers in Africa (UN, 2014).

The African continent is set to accelerate the digital transformation by securing privacy and providing low-cost internet access using inexpensive gadgets made in Africa. Recent studies reveal that bridging the digital divide is complicated in Africa, a problem that is also present in West Asia. Korovkin (2019) carried out a study on 17 African countries to compare their national digital strategies. Like other studies in literature, the study acknowledged that the African continent still faces digital infrastructure challenges as the digital economy has lagged behind the rest of the world (Signé and Signé, 2021; Kabanda et al., 2018). Some nations like Algeria have taken up the process of national digital strategies but consequently abandoned them. The development of national strategies for the digital economy is not yet part of the majority of Africa's national digital strategy, with the majority of the African countries having no dedicated documents for digital strategy.

Specific objectives to drive digital transformation have been set in some African countries to bridge the digital gap. To facilitate extensive use of digital systems, Denis (2021) postulates that the continent aims to provide e-learning skills and knowledge to millions of Africans by the end of the year 2021. Nonetheless, it is also exciting to note that Gamreklidze (2014) still points to the fact that developing countries continue to be prey to cyber warfare regardless of how good or poorly digitalized their infrastructure is. The emergence of the COVID 19 pandemic accelerated internet usage, producing new challenges in cyber security, especially for Africa (Manalu et al., 2020; Gaffar et al., 2020). All this made countries to realize the omnipotence of cyber security to protect their cyberspace. Building on these foundations, an alarm has been blown to businesses and citizens to improve security measures in African countries like Nigeria, Tunisia, Kenya and Morocco inter alia. Zimbabwe recently signed a Cyber Bill in 2019.

## METHODOLOGY

The study is based on a document review. Documents were mined from Google Scholar, Ebsco, and websites with news, policies, statutes and other related material on digital transformation, the digital divide and digital dividends. The study used textual and discourse analysis that culminated in various themes

## RESULTS AND DISCUSSION

Zimbabwe's readiness to use technology to transform its livelihood still lags behind its regional peers. According to the Network Readiness Index (2020), which provides a global digital transformation glance, out of 134 economies, Zimbabwe is ranked 126 and is 24th in Africa. By 2018, the country was ranked 146 out of 193 in Electronic Government Development Index (EGDI), while the Online Service Index was at the mean value of 0.3246 and last in SADC. Approximately 70% of the population lives in rural and marginalized areas that are located more than 100 km from urban areas. Rural areas are not adequately covered in terms of digitization of services; making service provision digital by default significantly disadvantages the marginalized communities. Zimbabwe is yet to strengthen the pillars of digital transformation.

Bridging the digital divide and ensuring universal access to broadband for all is one of the major objectives of the Zimbabwe National policy on Information and Communication Technology of 2016 (Goz, 2016). In ensuring this achievement, the policy seeks to increase faster access to the internet and increase the usage of ICT in government, commerce, health, education, science, agriculture, and other spheres of life. The policy also seeks to achieve ICT leadership in the region and increase inclusivity in digital technologies. The policy will ensure sustainability by managing changes that come as a result of developments in the ICT industry. The regulators will seek to improve innovation and partnership to increase broadband coverage in the country.

In Zimbabwe, digital skills could be leveraged if training for both students and teachers is scaled up, and data flow and coordinated. The country boasts a high literacy rate (about 90 percent), one of the best basic education access and enrolment ratios in Africa with almost perfect gender parity, and the country's workforce is well educated by regional standards. However, the swift pace of innovation, coupled with a supply-side failure to supply the required digital skills, means that many service providers, businesses and organizations struggle to obtain employees with the right skills to harness technological opportunities.

The significance of the internet in resolving the current global socio-economic challenges has increased with the rapid increase in internet use. The number of people using it increases daily from the young to the old ages as it increases choices and brings convenience to many aspects of life. The internet has created a virtual community through social media accelerated by the greater use of the internet around the world. In Zimbabwe, the use of social media has also impacted human lives in many dimensions, including the world of business, changing the landscape of government agencies. The public sector has taken advantage of these innovative technologies to increase transparency and improve citizens' engagement and participation in policy making.

## CONCLUSION AND RECOMMENDATIONS

This chapter approached the national digital policy as a target for bridging the digital divide to gain digital dividends that will help in socio-economic development. The reviewed literature in the chapter shows that generally, there is continued existence of a digital divide in developing countries and among the poor who live in developed countries. The public sector has taken advantage of innovative technologies to increase transparency and improve citizens' engagement and participation in policy-making. The wide gap between rich and developing countries has been a major concern on internet connectivity around the globe. Citizens of rich countries benefit from digital technologies through internet connectivity, while those in developing countries lag. This chapter recommends the following pointer for accelerating the migration process from divide to dividends:

- Subsidizing network construction: Governments and regulators should consider taking the outside-in strategy to narrow the digital divide in the country. The digital divide arises when the internet network extends to other areas and marginalizes others. This is because demand rises as costs fall in densely populated areas, whereas demand falls as cost rises in sparsely populated areas. The government should prioritize subsidizing the least favoured poor areas. This involves introducing things like 4G mobile coverage in marginalized rural areas first before taking it to profitable areas. This will promote the areas, not at the cusp of becoming commercially viable.

- Regulators may also give out licences to mobile operators with their obligations. The obligation can be that the licensee should cover a specified population or area with mobile coverage by rolling out the network within the stipulated number of days without fail. This can be specific as in the case of Sweden, where the obligation was to provide at least 1 Megabit per one license to listed areas. The government should also consider entering into negotiations with independent providers where a coarse approach is required.

- Countries in Africa ought to find a niche in the global digital economy to fast-track inclusive economic and social development using technology. Africa should nurture some commendable solutions to help its nations to leapfrog into digital development. This can only be done by constructing modern digital systems and developing markets for the new digital enterprises.

- For the fourth industrial revolution to be developed, African governments and leaders should commit themselves to develop dedicated strategies and allocating resources more efficiently. The government must create a technology culture from grassroots to national levels, in which citizens are trained and are familiar with the modern technological systems.

- Governments should introduce, correctly implement and monitor cyber security policies and strategies. Sometimes national cyber-security strategies and policies are written, but are poorly implemented. There is no legislation requiring such protections from sectors considered critical to the economy such as the education sector. Sufficient financial resources to implement the cyber-security strategy and strengthen the country's cyber-resilience should be set aside to develop the culture from the national level.

- The transmitted data will remain encrypted and safe. The adoption and use of secure protocols should be the ICT sector's priority so as to allow institutions and end-users to protect their networks. The state should help by establishing the critical legal frameworks in regulating the use of cyberspace and sanctioning cybercrimes. The Zimbabwean government has made a promising step in this respect by introducing the Cyber bill.

- The fiscal policy should target the use of Information Communication and Technology through e-government and e-learning programs. The cost of transactions is still a major problem in this sector. The Zimbabwean government should put efforts into revising its data costs and keep them minimum for a technologically empowered Zimbabwe. Hence both the monetary and the fiscal policies should work on resolving this challenge. Furthermore, some rural areas are still having problems with mobile networks and internet connectivity. The fiscal policy should budget for investments in this sector to improve connectivity in marginalized areas.

- There is also a strong need to encourage public and private funding to support the digital economy. The government should engage academia, the private sector, and civil society in setting the digital development agenda, creating appropriate regulations, and implementing digital initiatives. Achieving a healthy and prosperous SME environment requires proper funding. There is a critical need for training to promote success in the digital economy, particularly for Business to Business e-commerce.

- Public-Private Partnership (PPP): Public-Private Collaboration is important, the private sector owns most of the internet infrastructure, and thus the private and public sectors should effectively cooperate to defend cyberspace. The strategies used in developed nations emphasize much on PPP where governments partner with ISPs to improve security of national cyberspace from external and internal cyber threats. Cooperating with Internet Service Providers is another way to go.

# REFERENCES

Abersfelder, S., Bogner, E., Heyder, A., & Franke, J. (2016). Application and validation of an existing Industry 4.0 guideline for the development of specific recommendations for implementation. *Advanced Materials Research, 1140*, 465–472. doi:10.4028/www.scientific.net/AMR.1140.465

Adeleye, N., & Eboagu, C. (2019). Evaluation of ICT development and economic growth in Africa. *NETNOMICS: Economic Research and Electronic Networking*, *20*(1), 31–53. doi:10.100711066-019-09131-6

Antonio, A., & Tuffley, D. (2014). The Gender Digital Divide in Developing Countries. *Future Internet*, *2014*(6), 673–687. doi:10.3390/fi6040673

Bukht, R. & Heeks, R. (2017). *Defining, Conceptualizing and Measuring the Digital Economy*. Centre for Development Informatics Global Development Institute.

Calandro, E., & Berglund, N. (2019). *Unpacking Cyber-Capacity Building in Shaping Cyberspace Governance: The SADC case*. Academic Press.

Dias, G. P. (2020). Global e-government development: besides the relative wealth of countries, do policies matter? *Transforming Government: People, Process and Policy*, 10–18. doi:10.1108/TG-12-2019-0125

DiMaggio, P., Hargittai, E., Celeste, C., & Shaferl, S. (2004). *From Unequal Access to Differentiated Use: A Literature Review and Agenda for Research on Digital Inequality*. Academic Press.

Ehigiamusoe, K. U., & Lean, H. H. (2018). Tripartite analysis of financial development, trade openness and economic growth: Evidence from Ghana, Nigeria and South Africa. *Contemporary Economics*, *12*(2), 189–206.

Gaffar, B., Alhumaid, J., Alhareky, M., Alonaizan, F., & Almas, K. (2020). Dental Facilities During the New Corona Outbreak: A SWOT Analysis. *Risk Management and Healthcare Policy*, *13*, 1343–1352. doi:10.2147/RMHP.S265998 PMID:32904653

Gamreklidze, E. (2014). Cyber security in developing countries, a digital divide issue. *Journal of International Communication*, *20*(2), 200–217. doi:10.1080/132 16597.2014.954593

Gbenga-Ilori, A. & Sanusi, O.I. (2020). Assessment of the Scope and Usage of Digital Dividend in Nigeria. *Journal of Science Technology and Education, 8*(2), 143-153.

Graham, M., & Avery, E. (2013). Government Public Relations and Social Media: An Analysis of the Perceptions and Trends of Social Media Use at the Local Government Level. *The Public Relations Journal*.

Hafkin, N. (2007). Women and gender in ICT statistics and indicators for development. *Information Technologies and International Development*, *2007*(4), 25–41.

Hilbert, M. (2011). Digital gender divide or technologically empowered women in developing countries? A typical case of lies, damned lies and statistics. *Women's Studies International Forum, 2011*(34), 479–489. doi:10.1016/j.wsif.2011.07.001

Hofmann, E., & Rüsch, M. (2017). Industry 4.0 and the current status as well as future prospects on logistics. *Computers in Industry, 89*, 23–34. doi:10.1016/j.compind.2017.04.002

Johnson, V. (2012). The gender divide: Attitudinal issues inhibiting access. In R. Pande & T. van der Weide (Eds.), *Globalization, Technology Diffusion, and Gender Disparity: Social Impacts of ICTs* (pp. 110–119). IGI Global. doi:10.4018/978-1-4666-0020-1.ch009

Kabanda, S., Tanner, M., & Kent, C. (2018). Exploring SME cyber security practices in developing countries. *Journal of Organizational Computing and Electronic Commerce, 28*(3), 269–282. doi:10.1080/10919392.2018.1484598

Kandri, S. E. (2019). *Africa's future is bright–and digital*. World Bank Blogs.

Kemp, S. (2019). *Digital 2019: Essential Insights into How People Around the World Use the Internet, Mobile Devices, Social Media, And ECommerce*. Kepios Pte. Ltd., We Are Social Ltd. and Hootsuite Inc. https://datareportal.com

Labrique, A. B., Wadhwani, C., Williams, K. A., Lamptey, P., Hesp, C., Luk, R., & Aerts, A. (2018). Best practices in scaling digital health in low and middle income countries. *Globalization and Health, 14*(1), 1–8. doi:10.118612992-018-0424-z PMID:30390686

Manalu, E. P., Muditomo, A., & Adriana, D. (2020) Role of Information Technology for Successful Responses to Covid-19 Pandemic. *2020 International Conference on Information Management and Technology (ICIMTech)*, 415–420. 10.1109/ICIMTech50083.2020.9211290

Melhem, S., Morrell, C., & Tandon, N. (2009). *Information Communication Technologies for women's Socioeconomic Empowerment*. World Bank Working Paper.

Mergel, I. (2013b). *Social Media in The Public Sector: A Guide to Participation, Collaboration, and Transparency in the Networked World*. John Wiley & Sons, Inc.

Munyoka, W. (2019). *Electronic government adoption in voluntary environments – a case study of Zimbabwe*. doi:10.1177/0266666919864713

Nielsen, M. M., Carvalho, J., Backhouse, J., & Makpor, M. (2019). *A global framework for digital inclusion*. Academic Press.

Nkikabahizi, F., Rizinde, T., & Karangwa, M. (2018). The Balance of Trade-Economic Growth Nexus in a Panel of Member Countries of the East African Community. In I. A. Heshmati (Ed.), *Macroeconomic determinants of economic growth in Africa.* Springer Nature, doi:10.1007/978-3-319-76493-1_11

Pande, R. (2012). Gender gaps and information communication technology: A case study of India. In R. Pande & T. van der Weide (Eds.), *Globalization, Technology Diffusion, and Gender Disparity: Social Impacts of ICTs* (pp. 277–291). IGI Global. doi:10.4018/978-1-4666-0020-1.ch022

Picot, A., & Grove, N. (2009). Flächendeckende Breitbandversorgung im internationalen Vergleich: Strategien für den Glasfaserausbau in ländlichen Gebieten. *Infrastrukturrecht, 6*(11), 315 – 326.

Pradhan, R. P., Arvin, M., Nair, M., Bennett, S., & Bahmani, S. (2017). ICT-finance-growth nexus: Empirical evidence from the Next-11 countries. *Cuadernos de Economía, 40*(113), 115–134.

Ragnedda, M. (2017). *The third Digital Divide: A weberian approach to digital inequalities.* Routledge. doi:10.4324/9781315606002

Ragnedda, M. (2019). Reconceptualising the digital divide. In Mapping the Digital Divide in Africa. A mediated Analysis. Amsterdam: Amsterdam University Press.

Signé & Signé. (2021). *How African states can improve their cyber-security.* Academic Press.

Tarka, P. (2018). An overview of structural equation modeling: Its beginnings, historical development, usefulness and controversies in the social sciences. *Quality & Quantity, 52*(1), 313–354. doi:10.100711135-017-0469-8 PMID:29416184

Veiga, A., Loock, M., & Renaud, K. (2021). Cyber4Dev-Q: Calibrating cyber awareness in the developing country context. *The Electronic Journal on Information Systems in Developing Countries*, 12198.

Vidyasaga, D. (2006). Digital divide and digital dividend in the age of information technology. *Journal of Perinatology, 2006*(26), 313–315. doi:10.1038j.jp.7211494 PMID:16598298

Wamboye, E. F., & Tochkov, K. (2018). Information and communication technologies' impact on growth and employment in Africa. In E. F. Wamboye & P. J. Nyaronga (Eds.), *The Service Sector and Economic Development in Africa.* doi:10.4324/9781315627373-12

Wentrup, R., Ström, P., & Nakamura, H. R. (2016). Digital oases and digital deserts in Sub-Saharan Africa. *Journal of Science & Technology Policy Management.*

Wiraniskala, B., & Sujarwoto, S. (2020). Reaping or Losing Digital Dividend? The Use of Social Media for Enhancing Public Participation: A Literature Review. *Journal of Public Administration Studies, 5*(2), 89–95. doi:10.21776/ub.jpas.2020.005.02.8

World Bank. (2016). *World Development Report 2016: Digital Dividends (Overview of Chinese Version).* Author.

Zeqi, Q., Shuqin, Z., & Shiding, L. (2019). From the Digital Divide to the Connectivity Dividend Difference: A Connectivity Capital Perspective. *Social Sciences in China, 40*(1), 63–81. doi:10.1080/02529203.2019.1556475

## KEY TERMS AND DEFINITIONS

**Developing Countries:** States that are less developed as compared to other countries.

**Digital Transformation:** Integration of technology.

**Inequalities:** Differences.

**Information and Communication Technology:** The infrastructure that promote computing.

**Internet:** A global network of computers.

**Marginalized Communities:** Communities considered to be on the lower end of society, faces discrimination and inequality.

**Rural Communities:** An open land that has few homes or other buildings.

**Socio-Demographic Variables:** Factors like age, sex, education, marital status, and income.

**Virtual Community:** A social computer network.

# Chapter 7
# Key Pillars for Digital Transformation of the Developing World

**Gibson Chengetanai**
*Botswana Accountancy College, Botswana*

**Ronald Chikati**
*Botswana Accountancy College, Botswana*

## ABSTRACT

*Digital transformation is happening at a considerable rate in the developing world; however, its adoption seems higher in the developed world. Therefore, this chapter aims to present the key drivers or pillars that make up digital transformation in developing countries. The chapter argued that strategy, technology, and innovation are the broad categories that influence digital transformation in any country, whether developing or developed. Also, the chapter articulates what has been happening in the developing world, focusing on Southern Africa to achieve digital transformation. A framework for digital transformation that consists of three broad pillars strategy, technology, and innovation was proposed. Lastly, the chapter proposed that future researchers on digital transformation can focus on the broad pillars of digital transformation.*

## INTRODUCTION

A lot of events have been happening in the technology space since the turn of the new millennium. Many services are now being driven by information technology (IT).

DOI: 10.4018/978-1-6684-3901-2.ch007

Digital transformation is happening at a tremendous pace, thanks to the enabling environment that many governments worldwide are advocating for to enable their respective citizens to utilize IT services from the comfort of their homes. The concept of global transformation hinges on the utilization of IT to generate new products and services and come up with better ways of delivering such products to the market. Authors (Pihir et al, 2018) presented digital transformation as "the profound transformation of business and organizational activities, processes, competencies and models to fully leverage the changes and opportunities of a mix of digital technologies and their accelerating impact across society in a strategic and prioritized way, with present and future shifts of mind". The development of better services and products has been happening at a better rate when comparing developed to developing countries.

However, more people are connected to the Internet in the developing world than before. The advent of the Covid-19 has awakened even those that have not been used to technology before. Digital transformation scope differs from one country to another and from people and sectors. The rest of this chapter is organized as follows; section 2 is focused on a literature review on digital transformation. Section 3 focuses on key pillars that make the digital transformation. Section 4 is on technologies and trends around digital transformation, while section 5 is on digital transformation scenarios. Section 6 is on privacy issues in digital transformation, and this will be followed by the strategies for reducing privacy issues during digital transformation. The chapter ends with a proposed digital transformation framework and a brief conclusion.

## LITERATURE REVIEW ON DIGITAL TRANSFORMATION

The digital transformation is affecting the way people are living nowadays. Digital transformation encompasses the adoption and integration of ICTs that will provide better services to society (Zhao, 2015; Kraus et al. 2021; Chen et al 2014). With digital transformation, society can enjoy efficient services that emanate from new business models due to embracing technology in people's way of life (Camarinha et al. 2019). The growth of the 4th industrial revolution is being pushed by digital transformation as many people are getting connected and interacting with others irrespective of geographical boundaries. Digital transformation can assist in modifying or creating new business services, and customer involvement can make it easy for the world to achieve accelerated digital transformation. Four significant domains that can accelerate digital transformation, vertical networking, horizontal networking, engineering, and acceleration manufacturing (Camarinha et al. 2019, Cha et al. 2015) have been identified as key drivers for improvement in business

*Figure 1. Drivers for digital transformation*
*(Camarinha et al., 2019)*

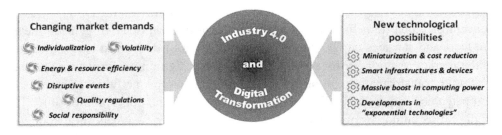

processes. Figure 1 shows the drivers for digital transformation in pushing the 4th industrial revolution. Improvements in technological possibilities and changes in mart demand are major factors that trigger digital transformation.

Collaboration between various industry players in using technology to improve business processes has been suggested by Ko et al. (2019). Figure 2 shows the collaborative framework that has been adopted by Ko et al. 2019. The framework shows that collaboration network organization, that is, long-term strategic networks and being goal-oriented networks are key drivers for digital transformation.

Another framework to represent the digital transformation has been presented by Vial (2019). This framework consists of several phases being disruption effects, i.e., both negative and positive, strategic responses, and changes in value whereby digital transformation is the key factor in causing rapid changes which ultimately influences the organization to change their strategic objectives. Both positive and negative impacts are felt in the short and long run; however, the benefits far outweigh the negative ones.

Identification of key drivers for digital transformation can greatly help the government of the developing world come up with the right e-governance strategies to help their citizens embrace information and communication technologies so that they will be better placed to match the developed world in the distant future. More value creation is realized when people fully embrace digital transformation (Ali et al, 2016; Chambers, 2018; Brunneti et al, 2020, Camodeca & Almici, 2020). There are, however, some disparities that are currently existing in the rate of digital transformation between the developed and developing world. Figure 3 shows the disparities existing between the rural and urban people as per data from Gallup in 2019.

From Figure 1, existing telecommunication in urban areas and the working population are the reasons for more users with internet access found in these areas. However, it is not the case with the rural area that lacks communication infrastructure, and many of the people found there are not working; hence the uptake on internet access remains low. There is a need to develop sound policies that will not leave anyone behind in the transition toward a digitized economy as a government.

*Figure 2. Collaborative digital transformation network*
*(Ko et al. 2019)*

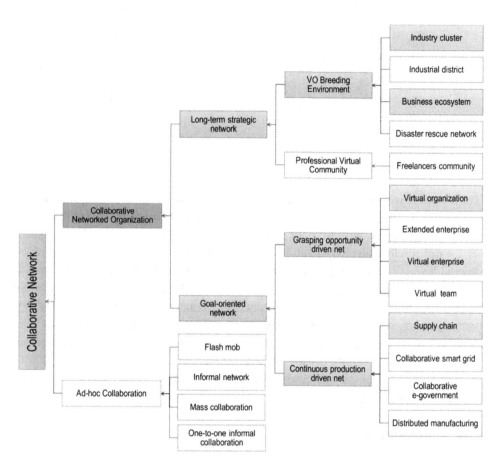

# KEY PILLARS OF DIGITAL TRANSFORMATION

## Customer-focused

There is a need to monitor what customers always want and adapt to their needs. During the Covid-19 pandemic, there has been a shift from traditional learning toward digital. For example, in Botswana, during the year 2017, the government launched

*Figure 3. Botswana, South Africa, Namibia, and Eswatini internet usage in 2018*

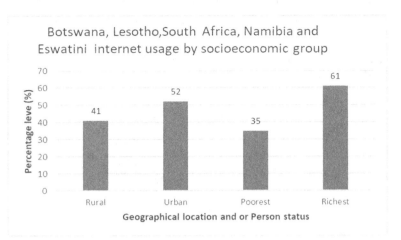

e-Thuto, which is interactive web-based learning that made it easier administratively for students and teachers to teach and share content with learners. In Zambia, there is a Let's Read project initiative for primary and secondary schools, which targeted over 1.4 million learners to read and understand the content that has been developed using the seven (7) local languages. Utilizing modern IT and updating the educational curriculum can result in greatly reducing educational mismatch where the content that students are being taught is different from what is expected in the industry. Currently, many industries in both the developing and developed world utilize IT in doing their work; hence, a graduate of this new millennium needs to be conversant with IT skills to execute their jobs perfectly (Garzoni et al, 2020; Ko et al, 2019). This points to the necessity of ensuring that the customer gets the right services to do their work efficiently.

## Organizational Culture

New skills are necessary in today's world to remain abreast with the ever-changing IT needs. Before the current new millennium, desktops and mainframe computers were mostly used, but nowadays it is laptops and other minute small handheld devices that enable work to be done even remotely. Wireless networking is now dominant and bringing your device (BYOD) at work is now common in the workplace (Pihir et al, 2018). All these entail that new skills must be adopted to match current trends in the IT space.

Organizational culture is a key ingredient in fostering the growth of the digital transformation adoption in developing communities (Che et al. 2014; Cha et al, 2015).

*Table 1. Initiatives adopted in Southern Africa to encourage digital transformation*

| Initiative Done | The Narration of the Initiative |
|---|---|
| Digital Southern African Development Community 2027 road map | This was adopted around 2012 for the block's regional infrastructure development masterplan, IT pillars which include harmonized broadband frequencies, fiber-optic infrastructure, and spectrum allocation |
| The Southern African Development Community Declaration of Information Communication Technologies (ICTs) | This is the Southern African Development Community policy adopted in 2001, pointing to ICT policy with particular emphasis on regulations and infrastructure |
| Conversion from analogue to digital transmission initiative | Support being technical for Southern African Development Community member states to convert from to digital transmission from analogue |

A culture of lifelong learning should be embraced in Africa so that graduates and youths can easily adapt to new skills required in the workplace. Several initiatives have been advocated in Southern Africa as a way of promoting digital transformation. Table 1 shows some of the initiatives that have been adopted in Southern Africa to encourage the growth of digital transformation.

## IT and Software Skills

IT is one of the fastest-changing areas in the world, new technologies emerge each time and there is a need to be compliant with the new software skills set that are required to interact with the new products and services. Continuous investment in software skills ensures that customers are up to date with the latest information. Improvement in soft skills requires a joint venture between the government and private industry. There is a high chance of skills mismatch when people are not involved in continuous professional development in IT. Many digital applications operate across different regulatory bodies and countries, especially in multinational companies (Koch & Corban, 2020). Laws pertaining to data protection in these different countries are different. Government support is needed to regulate responsibilities in government entities such as the central bank and telecommunication companies to regulate unfair competition practices. Table 2 shows some of the initiatives that have been done across Southern Africa to encourage innovation in ICT.

## Strategy and Vision

Strategy and vision are the directions the organization wants to achieve its long-term objectives. Electronic e-tax filing systems were introduced in South Africa in 2001

*Table 2. Innovation activities in the software industry across selected Southern African countries*

| Name of Initiative | The Narration of the Initiative |
|---|---|
| Southern Africa Innovation Support (SAIS) programme | Offers collaboration for innovative participants across Southern African Development countries and is based in Namibia |
| Western Cape Silicon initiative | Encourages IT entrepreneurship to generate software that meets the needs of the community, including business needs |
| Malawi mHub | Malawi's mHub trains and grooms' innovators who come up with IT entrepreneurial ideas to solve the societal problems |
| Harare's Impact Hub | Zimbabwe's Impact Hub trains and grooms' innovators who come up with IT entrepreneurial ideas to solve the societal problems |

and other countries such as Botswana started using electronic tax payment system in 2012. To embrace electronic commerce, some countries in the developing world some years back have also started collecting taxes using online systems (Koch & Corban, 2020; Pihir, et al., 2018). This efficient way assists the government in collecting more revenue in the form of taxes, but it also provides a database that provides for future planning purposes compared to the manual systems that have been done over ten years back. The South African government came up with the Health Patient Registration System project as part of their National e-Health strategy of 2012-2016 to improve standardized data collection as an e-governance approach to improve service delivery.

## Innovations Culture

Technological innovations can result in new products and services being offered. There is upward growth in the number of users utilizing digital money platforms. With the adoption of mobile money payments, even those that are in the informal business sector can benefit from such transactions (Koch & Corban, 2020; Ko et al., 2020). This platform helps those in the informal industry in the developing world as many are employed in this sector. Table 3 below shows the initiatives that have been developed in Southern Africa to develop digital skills.

*Table 3. Strategic initiatives that have been developed to improve digital skills in Southern Africa*

| Name of Initiative | The Narration of the Initiative |
|---|---|
| Africa Code Week | Coding workshops for youngsters in the age group between 8 and 24. Common in Botswana and Zimbabwe |
| IBM Digital Nation | An investment of over USD 70 million for cloud and digital skills targeting youth to ensure students have support to support the new millennium skill set requirements. Common in Botswana and South Africa |
| Malawi Digital Project | The project ensures the inclusion of components such as digital connectivity, digital platform, and project management in Malawi |
| Zambia's iSchool | iSchool provides devices as well as teacher training together with curriculum software to schools in Zambia |
| Malawi's mHub Digital Code Week | Teachers were trained across six selected districts in basic programming skills in Malawi |

## E-governance

E-governance involves using ICT to come up with better services to the customers. Governments across the Southern African Development Community are now encouraging their citizens to use ICT more, especially in this era of the Covid-19 pandemic (Koch & Corban, 2020). The cost of the Internet has been falling to enable more and more people to embrace technology as key driver to achieving growth in the developing world.

Figure 4 shows the cost of internet gigabytes for Southern African nations.

Having sound corporate governance in place can assist an organization to have better business processes by automating many of their processes. Figure 5 shows some data that was collected in 2018 and 2017, showing the relevance of IT departments in digital transformation (Ko et al. 2019).

## TECHNOLOGIES AND TRENDS AROUND DIGITAL TRANSFORMATION

Digital transformation is so pervasive that nearly every sphere of life is impacted. Companies and organizations that prove to be laggards in the uptake of this 4th Industrial Revolution-driven technology can count days before they are terminally rendered obsolete and most probably would cease to exist. Research has recently established various technologies and trends that define the frontiers of digital transformation. For example, Meenu (2021) maintained that although the pandemic

*Figure 4. Internet cost for Southern African Nations*
*(Sourced from htttp://*iresearch.worldbank.org/PovcalNet/home.aspx*).*

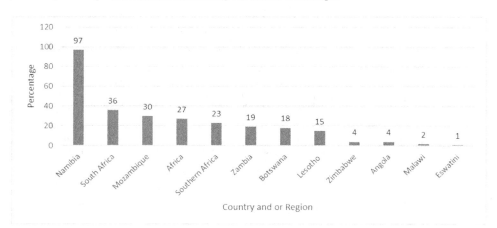

had hit the world hard and led many businesses to collapse, the crisis enabled rapid technology adoption and accelerated digital transformation across the industries. Hess et al. (2016) alluded to adopting innovative ways that use technology to "strategies that embrace the implications of digital transformation and drive better operational performance". Digital transformation is tied to disruptive technologies that help create value for organizations that choose a path for transformative change. However, it should be noted that digital transformation is limited to enterprises and includes the changes that take place in society and industries where digital technologies are embraced (Agarwal et al. 2010; Majchrzak et al. 2016).

Management operations of any entity must adapt to the new institutional thinking that is born out of digital transformation. Many innovations have been ushered into the market. For instance, the big technology companies have developed artificial intelligence-based question-answering assistants (chatbots): Google developed Javis,

*Figure 5. The role of IT departments in digital transformation*

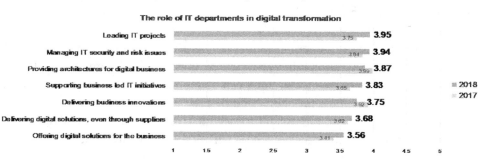

Amazon has Alexa, IBM's got Watson and Apple developed Siri. Some areas where digital transformation has been applied include the use of solar panels as a perfect substitute for the traditional roof tiles and the use of recycled glass to make new glass containers, among other examples have been successful areas where digital transformation has resulted in new business models that ultimately results in the provision of new goods (Ulas, 2019).

There is a need for the business to re-arrange the configuration of doing business. The business rules must change, the business processes are radically changed, and customer experiences are oriented to meet changing business and market requirements while new markets are quickly penetrated. Furthermore, digital transformation embraces a sudden need for reskilling and upskilling the organizational employees. If this transformation is not well planned for, the expected quick organizational gains may take long to realize. Digital transformation, therefore, demands business re-engineering, streamlining of processes, and strategic re-alignment. Businesses that adapt to the changing IT trends are likely to remain afloat in this rapid technological and globalization period (Ulas, 2019).

## Digital Technologies Application Scenarios

For many organizations, digital transformation is how they respond to spontaneous changes in their business ecosystem by using digital technologies. There are various technologies and digital platforms that are enablers for digital transformation. The Education and Training Department of Victoria state Government (2019) established that "digital technologies are electronic tools, systems, devices and resources that generate, store or process data and social media, online games, multimedia and mobile phones were the most well-known examples for digital learning".

Schwertner (2017) identified big data, cloud computing, mobile, and social technologies as critical digital technologies that must be part of the organization with which profitability and higher revenues are more guaranteed than is the case with competitors whose vision is not aligned with them. In addition to these digital technologies, Ulas (2019) extends to cover smartphones, Internet of Things (IoTs), 3D printing, virtualization, sensor technologies, cybersecurity, artificial intelligence (machine learning), robotics systems, automation etc. The technologies are intensely used in many fields of economic and social life. The proper deployment of the various digital technologies dictates a new business game. There is a need to combine digital transformation and business models in a structured manner to reimage old rule-based (algorithmic) processes. This hybridization breeds a data-oriented approach, which allows for the opportunity to gain new knowledge to assist in reimaging business models and operations. For example, Airbnb turned its attention from processes to data. Airbnb does not own its physical assets (e.g., hotels) (Bendor-Samuel, 2017).

*Figure 6. Four main enablers of digital transformation and related application domains*
Source: (Boueé and Schaible, 2015).

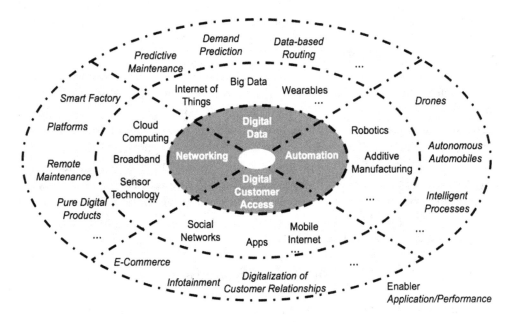

Figure 6 shows the four levers (enablers) that illustrate the extent of the digital transformation that is already underway: digital data, automation, digital customer access, and networking (connectivity). Each lever aids the business model with relevant information to build innovative services and applications.

## The Digital Data Lever

This category focuses on generating massive volumes of data that are received at different velocities, and the data comes from a variety of sources. Analyzing this data using suitable analytics tools and platforms will turn the bulk raw data into actionable insights. The insights provide the business with predictive, descriptive, diagnostic, and prescriptive information relevant for data-driven decision-making.

## The Automation Lever

Digital automation aims to execute business processes with human exception management autonomously. It helps ensure fewer error rates, increases speed, and reduces operating costs. Generally, this comprises involves using statistical and machine learning techniques that result in autonomous work and self-organizing systems.

## The Digital Customer Access Lever

Internet connectivity has ushered a combination of technologies that leverage the business with opinion mining (polarity) as numerous customers interact with the business via multimedia. The sentiment analysis data/information accrued will further assist businesses in bolstering their level of engagement with their clients. This may result in the building of online systems and other recommender systems for customer retention and value creation.

## The Networking Lever

The modern digital era demands that wireless and wired access technologies are enhanced. There is a need to connect the organization with its stakeholders using high-speed connection lines and ensure services and products can be exchanged 24/7. Thus, the digital radar provides the business with 360 degrees look at business processes, strategic initiatives and imperatives, and the key performance indicators (KPIs), all of which are catalytic to technological innovation.

The following section presents some selected examples of digital technology drivers that have stirred and are likely to continue pushing digital transformation. The explanation is abridged here, and the interested reader is referred to (Ulas, 2019; Meenu, 2021; Vial, 2019) for details on various technologies.

## Internet of Things (IoTs)

The Internet of things is a new technology that involves connecting everything to the Internet via sensors to smartphones, wearable devices, etc. IOT is currently used in farming where one can easily monitor their livestock and crops, and corrective action in case of some deviation, i.e. animal suffering from diseases, can be sent to the farmer, enabling remote operation. Utilizing IOT has the potential to uncover 3-11 trillion USD worth of economic value Manyika et al (2016).

## Artificial Intelligence and Machine Learning

Ulas (2019) maintains that Artificial Intelligence (AI) involves how a human brain thinks and how people learn and make choices as they try to solve a problem, and it imitates the results of this study with smart software. Machine learning, in turn, is a sub-field of AI that focuses on the task of enabling computational systems to learn from data about how to perform the desired task automatically. Machine learning (ML) has many applications, including "decision making, forecasting or predicting, and it is a key enabling technology in the deployment of data mining and big data techniques in the diverse fields of healthcare, science, engineering, business and finance" (Ali et al, 2016).

Machine learning combined with big data is currently used in the health fraternity to improve patient care and monitoring, early disease detection, and assist the doctor in diagnosing patient health-related issues. Robots do manufacturing with artificial intelligence and work without human intervention. Intelligent software systems that can perform mundane tasks and are in continual learning and improvement. The wide application of AI and ML and its increasing uptake define how companies manufacture, improve, and distribute their products and are the enabling digital technologies shaping the smart technology revolution.

## Cloud Computing

Information technology is a fast-changing industry. Cloud computing has been developing rapidly in recent years and has become the foundation of a wide range of major applications. According to the National Institute of Standards and Technology (NIST), "cloud computing is a model for enabling convenient, on-demand network access to a shared pool of configurable computing resources (e.g., networks, servers, storage, applications, and services) that can be rapidly provisioned and released with minimal management effort or service provider interaction". Adopting cloud computing means an organization will benefit through a pay-as-you-go opportunity, which means the organization no longer suffers from problem of bloatware and probably will cease to buy new hardware and software as the operational demands increase.

There are many advantages of infusing cloud computing technology in the business. For instance, the cloud model promotes availability and is composed of five essential characteristics (On-demand self-service, Broad network access, Resource pooling, Rapid elasticity, Measured Service); three service models (Cloud Software as a Service (SaaS), Cloud Platform as a Service (PaaS), Cloud Infrastructure as a Service (IaaS)); and with four (4) deployment models (Private cloud, Community cloud, Public cloud, Hybrid cloud) (Schwertner, 2017). With this new technology, services could be rendered from anywhere as long as one has an Internet connection and applications, and services can be run-on High-Performance Computing (HPC) infrastructure without having to incur extra costs since the organization only pays for what they use. This new digital transformation relies on virtualization infrastructure from cloud service providers' industry platforms like Amazon's Amazon Web Services (AWS), Microsoft's Azure and Google Cloud Platform (GCP). This initiative is bound to be a billion-dollar industry if the technology is well-aligned with the business strategy.

## Blockchain Technology

Blockchain technology started with the Bitcoin cryptocurrency initiative by Satoshi in which digital transactions cannot be copied and altered. Moreover, the transactions that are committed are not reversible. Basically, the technology is based on asymmetric cryptography where public and private keys are generated and mathematically paired for a successful end-to-end transaction to be successful. However, today blockchain technology is attracting its use in many other application areas. Vial (2019) has observed that Blockchain is a generic and extensible technology that uses distributed trust approaches in its design to keep track of transactions. These infrastructures can be applied to a variety of domains such as banking and contract management (Tilson et al.2010). Blockchain technology has the to replace the traditional, centralized institutions in conducting transactions because it allows easier secure exchange funds from peer to peer rather than through authoritative intermediaries that the traditional institutions do.

## Big Data (BD)

encompasses the retrieval of any large amount of structured, semi-structured or unstructured data that has the potential to be mined for decision making and ultimately allow an organization to make some strategic decisions. Big data is widely characterized by its volume, velocity, variety and value (4 Vs). However, the number of Vs keeps on growing to include veracity, variability, visualization, viscosity, volatility, validity, and etc. (Panimalar et al, 2017). The major dilemma with BD is to excavate actionable knowledge from collected huge datasets that are heterogeneous (could be of video, text, audio or image type). Big data help designers to derive decisive customer needs from the existing data to improve and develop designs. "Big Data and data analytics provide SMEs with a wide range of opportunities" (Gazoni et al., 2020). This will enable a better understanding of the processes within the organization, the needs of their clients and partners, and the overall business environment (Ulas,2019; Giri et al, 2014)). This could be extended to any organization nowadays; given that we are living in a deluge of data. Thus, organizations must handle their data as one of the mission-critical resources.

## Privacy/Security Issues in Digital Transformation

The 21$^{st}$ century has so far witnessed many technological developments, with many people getting more engrossed in the use of digital technology. Research has shown that many aspects of our lifestyle have been impacted by digital technology. For example, Minchev (2017), noted that "digital technologies have permeated a large majority of our lifestyle areas, to note: education, training, mass media, working environment, everyday life interactions, protesting, friends finding, shopping or even sports, health facilitation and entertainment". While on one side, digital transformation is bringing about a host of new opportunities to industry and commerce, the other side is witnessing a surge of cyber-attacks. The attack surface has grown wide in scope with many people connecting to the Internet. Attack vectors target various devices that shape the modern e-lifestyle of individuals, such as laptops, computers, tablets, phablets, smart watches, bands (wearables), IoT sensors, assistant avatars, and monitoring systems and so on.

Some of the attacks relate to denial-of-service attacks, phishing attacks, industrial espionage, malware, and multiple targeted attacks, with some unknown in the progressive new tech-social reality. Minchev (2016) asserts that web technologies generate numerous cyber opportunities and threats produced as a result of the evolving human-machine and machine-to-machine interactions.

The challenge with Cybersecurity attacks is to know where they are coming from and when and how the attack is going to be orchestrated. Sometimes AI can fail to detect an intrusion, and currently, many sophisticated tools that are difficult to detect are out there, probably in the wrong hands. There is roughly an inverse correlation between the amount of required knowledge of the attacker and the sophistication of the attacker tool used (Figure 4). As the attack tools have become more sophisticated, the knowledge needed to use them is becoming low because most of these attack software applications are more user-friendly than in the past.

Consequently, adequate securing of the new progressive tech-social reality inevitably produces a significant challenge to the modern cyber world. In the January 2022 policy paper, Julia Lopez (UK, MP) acknowledged that the "digital economy is growing, so too is the opportunity for malicious actors to exploit vulnerabilities in IT systems. High-profile cyber incidents where attackers have attacked organizations through vulnerabilities in their supply chains, such as SolarWinds and Microsoft Exchange, along with the notable increase in ransomware attacks on organizations and critical national infrastructure such as the Colonial Pipeline in the US, have demonstrated the disruptive potential of these threats and the real-world impacts they can realize" (UK Government, 2022).

*Figure 7. Increased sophistication of attack tools*
Source: (Mark Ciampa, 2009)

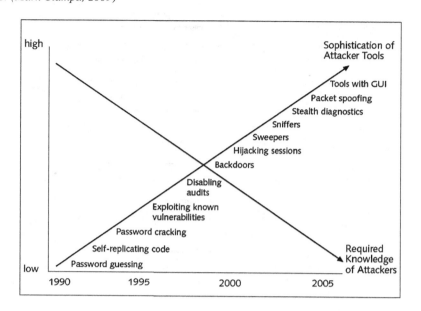

## Strategies for Reducing Privacy-Related Issues to Help Boost the Digital Transformation Process

The digital transformation revolution that the world has no choice but to adopt raises an urgent need to equip technology end-users with the right tools to remain safe. No one rule of thumb could be adopted to mitigate privacy-related violations. However, user training of cybersecurity warriors through reskilling and upskilling is one imperative that organizations may need to plan for. Information Technology (IT) teams must be in the forefront to be trained to become change agents for the organization. Communities of practice could be formulated that exchange idea on best practices. These experts may champion the design of organizational security policies that become road maps on how to use organizational digital infrastructure for cyber-resilience—a collaboration with other organizations on how to mitigate cybercrimes.

The UK National Cyber Security Strategy (NCSS) (2016) came up with three fundamental tenets to build a cyber-resilient digital world:

- Educating users on cyber threats
- Provide guidance, standards, and frameworks to be adopted in helping businesses to thrive

*Figure 8. Proposed digital transformation framework*

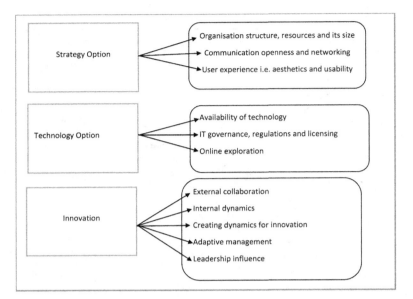

- Engagement activities

Although, circumstances may differ from country to country, from one organization to another or from one individual to the other, the articulated guidelines will go a long way in motivating the digital citizens to practice safe surfing.

## PROPOSED DIGITAL TRANSFORMATION FRAMEWORK

Following conducting a literature review on work published by the other researchers earlier on, we propose a framework that includes the pillars of strategy, technology, and innovation as the broad categories that influence digital transformation in any developing or developed country. Figure 8 shows our proposed digital transformation framework. Future researchers on a digital transformation can focus on the broad components of digital transformation as postulated in Figure 5.

## CONCLUSION

The government's involvement in enacting laws and regulations to promote digital transformation is critical to achieving digitalization. The Internet rate between rural and urban people came as a key that the government needs to come up with to realize the full potential of digital transformation. Privacy-related issues such as phishing attacks and eavesdropping are areas people need to be educated on to protect data. This is because, during digital transformation, sensitive information such as financial and health-related data can be shared, and if no secure channels are used, that can negatively hamper the success rate that digital transformation can have on the communities around the world. Key determinants for driving digital transformation such as customer focus, strategy, and innovation involve ensuring upgrade of the personnel so that everyone is up to date on new skill sets required at each time since IT is a dynamic field. More and more resources and education awareness need to be shaded globally for the achievement of digital transformation to be fully realized, especially in the developing world. A new proposed digital transformation framework has been presented that can significantly aid developing nations' organizations improve their business process.

## REFERENCES

Agarwal, R., Guodong, G., DesRoches, C., & Jha, A. K. (2010). The digital transformation of healthcare: Current status and the road ahead. *Information Systems Research*, *21*(4), 796–809. doi:10.1287/isre.1100.0327

Ali, A., Qadir, J., Rasool, R., Sathiaseelan, A., Zwitter, A., & Crowfot, J. (2016). Big data for development: Applications and techniques. *Big Data Analytics*, *1*(2), 1–24. doi:10.118641044-016-0002-4

Bendor-Samuel, P. (2017). *The power of digital transformation in a data-driven world*. Retrieved May 10, 2022, from https://www.forbes.com/sites/peterbendorsamuel/

Boueé, C., & Schaible, S. (2015). *Die Digitale Transformation der Industrie. In Studie: Roland Berger und BDI*. Predictive Maintenance.

Brunnetti, F., Matt, D. T., Bonfanti, A., De Longhi, A., Pedrini, G., & Orzes, G. (2020). Digital transformation challenges: Strategies emerging from multi-stakeholder approach. *The TQM Journal*, *32*(4), 697–724. doi:10.1108/TQM-12-2019-0309

Camarinha, L. M., Fornasiero, R., Ramexani, J., & Ferrada, F. (2019). Collaborative networks: A pillar of digital transformation. *Applied Sciences Journal*, *9*(24), 1–34. doi:10.3390/app9245431

Camodeca, R.; Almici, A. (2020). Digital Transformation and Convergence toward the 2030 Agenda's Sustainability Development Goals: Evidence from Italian Listed Firms. *Sustainability*, *13*(21), 11831. doi:10.3390/su132111831

Cha, K. J., Hwang, T., & Gregor, S. (2015). An integrative model of IT-enabled organizational transformation: A multiple case study. *Management Decision, 53*(8), 1755–1770. doi:10.1108/MD-09-2014-0550

Chambers, K. (2018, September/October). *Global megatrends driving manufacturing digital transformation. Latest software systems improve business performance.* Intech. www.isa.org

Chen, J. E., Pan, S. L., & Ouyang, T. H. (2014). Routine reconfiguration in traditional companies' e-commerce strategy implementation: A trajectory perspective. *Information & Management, 51*(2), 270–282. doi:10.1016/j.im.2013.11.008

Ciampa, D. M. (2009). *Information Security Security+ Guide to Network Security Fundamentals* (3rd ed.). Course Technology Cengage Learning.

Computations of internet use by socioeconomic group of Southern African Customs Union Countries. (2018). Retrieved April 20, 2022, from https://www.gallup.com/analytics

Garzoni, A., De Turi, I., Secundo, G., & De Vecchio, P. (2020). Fostering digital transformation of SMEs: A four level approach. *Management Decision, 58*(8), 1543–1562. doi:10.1108/MD-07-2019-0939

Giri, K. J., & Lone, A. T. (2014). Big Data - Overview and Challenges. *International Journal of Advanced Research in Computer Science and Software Engineering, 4*(6), 525–529.

Hess, T., Matt, C., Benlian, A., & Wiesboeck, F. (2016). Options for formulating a digital transformation strategy. *MIS Quarterly Executive, 15*(2), 123–139.

Ko, A., Feher, P., & Szabo, Z. (2019). Digital transformation – A Hungarian Overview. *Journal of Economic and Business Research, 21*(3), 371–392.

Koch, R., & Corban, T., (2020, September). Data governance in digital transformation. *Technology workbook on Strategic Finance,* 60-61.

Kraus, S., Schiavone, F., Pluzhnikova, A., & Invernizzi, A. C. (2021). Digital transformation in healthcare: Analysing the current state-of-research. *Journal of Business Research, 123,* 557–567. doi:10.1016/j.jbusres.2020.10.030

Majchrzak, A., Markus, M. L., & Wareham, J. (2016). Designing for digital transformation: Lessons for information systems research from the study of ICT and societal challenges. *Management Information Systems Quarterly, 40*(2), 267–277. doi:10.25300/MISQ/2016/40:2.03

Manyika, J., Chui, M., Bisson, P., Woetzel, J.R., Dobbs, R., Bughin, J., & Aharon, D. (2015). *The Internet of things: mapping the value beyond the hype.* Technical report, McKinsey Global Institute.

Meenu, E. G. (2021). *Digital Transformation.* Retrieved April 24, 2022, from https://www.analyticsinsight.net/author/meenu

Minchev, Z. (2017). *Security Challenges to Digital Ecosystems Dynamic Transformation.* The 9th International Conference on Business Information Security (BISEC-2017), Belgrade, Serbia.

Panimalar, A., Varnekha, S. S., & Veneshia, K. A. (2017). The 17 V's of Big Data. *International Research Journal of Engineering and Technology, 4*(9), 329–333.

Pihir, I., Tomicic-Pupek, K., & Furjan, M. T. (2018). Digital transformation insights and trends. *Proceedings from the 29th Central European Conference on Information Security and Intelligent Systems*, 141-149.

Schwertner, K. (2017). Digital Transformation of Business. *Trakia Journal of Sciences, 15*(1), 388–393. doi:10.15547/tjs.2017.s.01.065

Tilson, D., Lyytinen, K., & Sørensen, C. (2010). Research commentary - Digital infrastructures: The missing IS research agenda. *Information Systems Research, 21*(4), 748–759. doi:10.1287/isre.1100.0318

UK Government. (2022). *Cyber security incentives and regulation review.* Department for Digital, Culture, Media & Sport. Retrieved April 20, 2022, from https://www.gov.uk/government/publications/

Ulas, D. (2019). Digital Transformation Process and SMEs. 3rd World Conference on Technology, Innovation and Entrepreneurship (WOCTINE). *Procedia Computer Science, 158*, 662–671. doi:10.1016/j.procs.2019.09.101

Vial, G. (2019). Understanding digital transformation: A review and a research agenda. *Journal of Strategic Information Systems Review, 28*(2), 118–144. doi:10.1016/j.jsis.2019.01.003

Zhao, Z. (2015). "Internet Plus" cross-border management: The perspective of creative destruction. *China Industrial Economics, 10*(29), 146–160.

## KEY TERMS AND DEFINITIONS

**Digital Divide:** The digital divide is a term that refers to the gap between demographics and regions that have access to modern information and communications technology (ICT), and those that don't or have restricted access. This technology can include the telephone, television, personal computers, and internet connectivity.

**Digital Innovation:** Digital innovation refers to the application of digital technology to existing business problems to innovate new products or services.

**Digital Strategy:** In this context, the term refers to a plan that employs digital initiatives to achieve digital transformation in developing countries.

**prioritized way:** with present and future shifts of mind".

**Information and communication technologies:** This chapter defines ICTs as the combination of networks, hardware, and software, as well as the means of communication that enables digital transformation.

**Innovation:** Innovation can be defined as the creation of something new (product or services) or an improvement on an existing idea.

Chapter 8
# Technologies for Digital Transformation in Marginalized Communities

**Briget Munyoro**
*Midlands State University, Zimbabwe*

**Lemias Zivanai**
*Midlands State University, Zimbabwe*

**Ranganai Njodzi**
*Manicaland State University of Applied Sciences, Zimbabwe*

**Tendai Shelton Muwani**
*Manicaland State University of Applied Sciences, Zimbabwe*

## ABSTRACT

*Many technologies are referenced in the case of digital transformations, but internet technologies, emerging technologies, internet of things (IoT), analytical technologies, and mobile technologies are the most relevant in this chapter. Internet technologies, a collection of internet-based communication tools, can be used in the digital transformation of marginalized populations. Internet of things help marginalized communities seek opportunities, meet new targets, and minimize threats as people can have physical objects or self-reporting devices that improve productivity and rapidly bring vital information to the surface. When all this information has been collected, there is a need to identify the patterns and trends and produce meaningful insights using the analytical tools. Mobile technologies are technologies that go where a user goes, so communication, buying and selling, and making payments are possible with mobile phones. Governments and corporates should facilitate the adoption of digital technologies to promote digital inclusion in marginalized communities.*

DOI: 10.4018/978-1-6684-3901-2.ch008

## INTRODUCTION

Digital transformation is defined as the use of disruptive technology to increase production, create value, and society's welfare (Abad-Segura et al., 2020). The goals of digital transformation are to encourage the development of an advanced culture of collaboration in businesses and humanity. This aims to transform the didactic system, empower people with new skills and future-oriented people to achieve excellence in digital work and society, build and maintain digitalized communications infrastructure, and ensure data security. It further sets the foundations for democratic accountability, convenience, and improved services and accessibility. According to Deganis et al., (2021), rapid digitalization, which had begun before the COVID-19 outbreak and continued to accelerate during the epidemic, caused a greater possibility for digital inclusion. The expansion of e-rapid commerce has created job opportunities and increased levels of income, with the ability to improve livelihoods, alleviate poverty, and build the resilience of remote communities. By boosting market access for rural farmers, e-commerce contributes to the revival of rural villages. The Chilean Ministry of Agriculture has developed digital channels to help farmers promote their products (Deganis et al., 2021). Agrocenta, a Ghanaian B2B e-commerce platform, connects 10,000 producers with consumers, allowing them to earn a higher price for their produce.

Technology has played a critical role in governments' immediate response to COVID-19 and as part of national recovery measures and social protection services to benefit the most disadvantaged (Sevelius et al., 2020). Governments have embraced digital tools to expand social protection coverage and efficiently distribute funds (often in partnership with the corporate sector and civil society organizations). According to Deganis et al., (2021), the government of Luxembourg has created "Letzshop," an Internet-based and mobile phone sales platform that provides home delivery of over 40 basic commodities to the elderly with chronic diseases and those who are immunocompromised. By addressing inclusion and exclusion, improvements in database administration boosted openness in beneficiary lists of social security programs in Vietnam and the Philippines. People subscribe on their mobile devices, and those who meet the requirements receive bi-monthly cash transfers equalling 30-35 percent of the lowest wage, paid directly into their mobile money accounts. In April 2020, the government of Bangladeshi, in collaboration with the four primary national mobile money operators, launched a mobile-based cash support initiative for 5 million pandemic-affected households (Deganis et al., 2021).

In 2020, rapid digitalization hastened the transition to digital finance. Mobile money and electronic wallets, crowdsourcing, alternative credit sourcing score, and cross-border remittances are digital tools that help poor people and societies gain inclusion in monetary terms, reduce costs, and provide new business and economic prospects (Deganis et al., 2021). Deganis et al. (2021) cited mobile money such as M-Pesa used in Kenya and Alipay in China. In contrast, the COVID-19 epidemic has stimulated the development of digitalization, which is a dual-edged sword for initiatives to enhance community cohesion. While the crisis has increased awareness of the benefits of connectivity in preserving health of the public and livelihood, it is extending and worsening the technology gap in and between countries, promoting inequity and alienating everyone who is not available on the Internet. It will be vital to fully realize the capabilities of digital technology in furthering the implementation of the 2030 Agenda needed to guarantee that everybody has access to safe and low-cost access to the Internet. Given the underlying link between the digital gap and social economic inequity, increasing efforts to bridge the difference and promote digital inclusion is vital. The authors of this chapter have recognized internet technologies, the Internet of Things (IoT), analytical technologies, and mobile technologies as tools for digitally transforming marginalized populations (Ramakrishna et al., 2019; Tech-Student, 2016).

## BACKGROUND

Marginalized populations are groups or individuals who are alienated from dominant social, economic, academic, and/or cultural life (Sevelius et al., 2020). Marginalized groups include people who are excluded because of their race, gender identity, sexual orientation, maturity, physical abilities, dialect, and citizenship. Marginalization occurs as a result of power disparities among social groups. Due to long-standing political, financial, academic, and job marginalization, the majority of people in disadvantaged groups lack access to the technology and/or technology skills needed to engage in the digital transition. Economic marginalization complicates the constant access to smartphones and computers to marginalized people. As the name implies, digital transformation is essentially a transition brought about by the advancement of new technology. The digitization of businesses across industries is a developing trend, supported by emerging digital technologies such as the Internet of Things, big data analytics, artificial intelligence, and cloud computing. Digital transformation is likely the most ubiquitous managerial challenge for established businesses in the previous and future decades. It is defined as the evolution of a company's business strategy, product, or organizational structure because of technological advancements.

Disadvantaged and marginalized groups are overrepresented in the population that is not connected on the Internet, which is generally female, rural, impoverished, elderly, and/or with minimal education levels and low literacy (Calabrese Barton & Tan, 2018). ICT and Internet access are influenced by various characteristics, including area, economy, age, gender, ethnic, and disabilities. According to the most recent ITU data, 72 percent of households have home Internet access in metropolitan regions, while just 38 percent of families in rural areas have home Internet access. Deganis et al., (2021). In the U. S., 27% of adults aged 65 and older do not have internet connection. Disparities and other barriers to getting connected on the net, Information Communication Technologies, and people with disabilities have a variety of challenges, including limited access to ICT facilities, applications, and websites, as well as financial concerns (because of less earnings and expenses linked with their impairment). Indigenous people face unique challenges when it comes to digital inclusion; they face challenges such as a lack of digital information in their native language. 48% of the female population in 2019 were the only ones that could connect and use the Internet worldwide, compared to 58% of the male population. According to ITU, (2019), gender inequality spans from 3% in wealthy nations to 43% in the Least Developed Countries. Women and girls benefit from digital technologies and being online by increasing their confidence, financial power, freedom, and improvement in information access. The disparities in the digital gap in terms of gender suffocate chances for digital transformation and create risks for both males and females.

A good example is unequal access to online learning (Niţă & Pârvu, 2020). COVID-19 pandemic caused school closures, and this worsened inequity in attaining education. Students with inadequate digital abilities and exposure to the technology and Internet needed for distance learning are the most vulnerable. According to the United Nations Educational, Scientific, and Cultural Organization (UNESCO), 826 million pupils lack access to a home computer, 706 million lack home internet access, and another 56 million are not covered by mobile cellular technology networks (Montoya, 2020). Learners who do not have internet connectivity cannot learn digital skills that are relevant for a job, endangering their job prospects even more.

Coronavirus widened the digital gap in businesses (Banerjee, 2020). Although many high-skilled workers have moved to remote work, industries that require constant human interaction, such as medical services, public transportation, food, and household supplies, have not. The consequences of this misalignment may be seen not just in the latter's heightened exposure to health-related issues during the epidemic but also in the negative effects of government shutdowns on employment rates. Furthermore, limited exposure to digital technology skills harmed micro and small shops, which play an important role in conventional trade and food outlets. Many businesses have had to close permanently due to their inability to fulfil the unexpected spike in digital demand. Small-business and school closures are expected to stymie economic recovery in Latin America, Southeast Asia, and Africa, wreaking havoc on the livelihoods of the poor (UNESCO, 2021). Millions of disadvantaged households rely on small stores for financing, basic commodities, and services, making them an essential source of employment and economic support (Brito, 2020).

A robust digital foundation is critical to accomplishing the government's goal of smart governance, agriculture, health, trade, commerce, education, transportation, and cities. Rapid technological change without a systematic approach to development that is both inclusive and sustainable runs the risk of entrenching existing disparities while also producing new ones. Similarly, smallholder farmers in rural areas are at risk of falling behind in the digitalization process and missing out on new technology benefits. Developing a positive vision for future digital collaboration must take precedence. As a result, the book chapter aims to discover digital technologies that can help marginalized communities become more inclusive than the current level.

# MAIN FOCUS OF THE CHAPTER

## Technologies for Digital Transformation

Information technology has the potential to help people with impairments integrate more fully into society. Digital technology has been seen as a facilitator for social inclusion since it allows for the delivery of real-time services that allow individuals to learn, work, travel, socialize, shop, and interact with the community without being constrained by physical limits (Brunner et al., 2017; Vanderheiden, 2006). Digital technology has also been identified as one of the most important factors that can aid in the reduction of inequities by supporting and encouraging community cohesion and increasing people's quality of life (Manzoor & Vimarlund, 2017).

### Emerging Technologies

Following the COVID-19 outbreak, society has been forced to rely on technology for basic daily tasks such as procuring basic supplies, connecting with people, working from home, and completing schoolwork (Ra et al., 2019). On the other hand, completing these essential obligations is a huge issue for millions of people who either do not have access to or refuse to use high-speed Internet, putting them at a social, political, and economic disadvantage. A broadband Internet connection is a high-speed Internet connection is a necessary component of modern society's infrastructure (Rhinesmith, 2016). The digital divide affects those who do not have access to or the capacity to adopt the technology. The structural reality effectively leads to "digital redlining," which exacerbates socio-economic inequalities in society (Sanders & Scanlon, 2021). In marginalized populations, poor access to public services increases their vulnerability; technology can help make these services more accessible. Reducing the digital gap can assist communities in being more prepared for unforeseen threats. It is critical to adopt new and developing technologies to thrive in today's work and personal environments. Artificial intelligence solutions based on big data, deep learning, and robotics can have far financial., societal, and cultural implications. Opportunities are predicted to emerge because of artificial intelligence and robotics (AI/R).

Improving and stabilizing those that are marginalized exposure to services and marketplaces, such as economic, medical, and insurance services, as well as transfers of social status, is an important part of improving and stabilizing poor households' income and consumption prospects, as well as their overall well-being (Howard & Simmons, 2019). By eliminating entry barriers, AI/R may have an impact on several service industries and their operations. The impact of AI/R on government accountability and transparency for residents could be enormous, assuring better delivery of service and empowerment of local expansion players and policymakers (Howard & Simmons, 2019).

## Data and Information Systems Provide Opportunities for Poverty Research

A lack of trustworthy data hinders planning and investment in poor nations' sustainable development, food security, and disaster relief. Poverty data, for example, is often limited, sparsely covered, and time-consuming to gather. Data and new machine learning-based identification approaches are being developed to provide more current and well-defined information than traditional household surveys or indicator systems (Zurutuza, 2018). Night-time lights, for example, are strongly related to economic wealth. Furthermore, automated methods based on satellite photos could be used to determine the roofing material, light source, and access to water supplies, allowing for the assessment of a household's financial status. By providing real-time notifications to take proper action, such data may enable for prompt interventions.

Jean et al., (2016) demonstrate how artificial intelligence can be used to measure consumer spending and asset wealth using high-resolution satellite imagery. They demonstrate how a convolutional neural network can be trained to uncover visual components that can explain up to 75% of the diversity in local-level financial results using survey and satellite data from five African countries: Nigeria, Tanzania, Uganda, Malawi, and Rwanda. This can transform how developing countries measure and combat poverty (Jean et al., 2016). Furthermore, accurate population mapping can help with infrastructure development. Facebook, for example, recently set a goal to develop the most precise population density maps possible by combining satellite data, machine learning algorithms, and population data (Bonafilia et al., 2019).

## Links Between AI/R, Education, and Knowledge

AI/R could be extremely beneficial to the poor in improving their access to education and knowledge, upskilling their workforce, and increasing their revenue-earning capacities in small businesses and farming. However, education systems tend to exclude or marginalize the poor directly and indirectly through school fees or poor-quality education in developing nations and through children's lack of time and other parental limitations in poor civilizations, respectively. In addition to attending school, most child labourers face time constraints; when youngsters work too much, their schoolwork suffers, and their lifetime earnings are reduced., as shown by (Mussa, 2018) for associates of Ethiopian countryside child labourers. Education levels, such as secondary and university, tend to increase inequalities. According to du Boulay et al. (2018), AI can benefit both educators and children by providing personalized support for pupils, tools to help teachers become educational environment aware, and freeing up time to provide nuanced, individualized support. The "Kio Kit" (BRCK n.d.) is an intriguing Kenyan example. It is a complete integrated teaching system developed in Kenya that transforms a classroom into a virtual classroom by utilizing different types of handheld devices that are water-resistant and locked in a case. When AI-powered instruction systems are made available to the poor in rural areas, they have the potential to make a huge difference.

Speech recognition and translation aided by AI could help the underprivileged in overcoming language and literacy challenges. For instance, Google's speech-to-text service employs neural network models to translate voice to text in a range of languages, including Swahili, Zulu, Cantonese, Mandarin, and a number of Indian dialects. (Google Cloud 2019, 2019). The mentioned technologies can significantly improve access to services and information for marginalized societies.

## Poor People's Healthcare Services Powered by AI and Robotics

Poor people have a difficult time asserting their entitlement to government services. Given the continuous digitalization of all types of health data and information, the health sector is particularly potential for AI/R applications. When AI/R-assisted medical and public health decision-making saves money, the long-term potential for extending the field of digital health and precision and tailored treatment can be significant (Ciechanover, 2019). However, these advancements are still far from reaching the impoverished (Fernandez-Luque & Imran, 2018). While there are numerous examples of artificial intelligence in health care and humanitarian help, most of them are limited to outbreak detection, with their application in low-income countries or crises being understudied. In collaboration with the World Health Organization, the International Telecommunication Union (Von Braun, 2019) has formed a new Focus Group on "Artificial Intelligence for Health" (FG-AI4H, 2019). Even when private providers and health insurance systems supply health and care services, the government is often responsible for their control and delivery. (Khare et al., 2017) based on the available variables in the Indian Demographic and Health Survey (IDHS) dataset, a machine learning approach was employed to create a prediction model for malnutrition. Diagnostic technologies with artificial intelligence have the potential to improve health care in rural areas (Wood et al., 2019). Self-diagnosis or healthcare employees could benefit from these tools. Stanford University, for example, has developed a skin cancer detection system based on photographs (Kubota, 2017). Emerging epidemics like Ebola and Zika can also be discovered more quickly with AI (Wood et al., 2019). It will be necessary to make sure that AI technologies are tailored to the requirements and features of the poor.

## Artificial Intelligence-assisted Services and Social Transfers

Many low-income people cannot obtain traditional financial services such as banking, credit, or insurance. In 2017, only a third of people in rural Sub-Saharan Africa had a bank account, and only 5% had a formal financial institution loan (Demirguc-Kunt et al., 2018). In 2016, just a handful of smallholder farmers had crop insurance in the region (Hess 2016). Artificial intelligence (AI) may be able to aid the poor in acquiring credit and insurance. Banks are typically hesitant to lend to low-income households because they lack the ability to estimate the risk of default. Data from agronomy, the environment, economics, and satellites are combined with data from mobile phones, such as call detail records, social network analytics tools, and customer credit and debit account information. M-Pesa, is mobile money, a popular mobile phone financial software that began in 2007 in Kenya. AI could potentially help provide insurance to many scattered, low-income consumers by supplying high-quality data, eliminating uncovered basis risk, and reducing cost distribution routes. Weather services and weather risk insurances based on AI-enhanced weather observation and monitoring at the pixel level are relevant fields in light of climate change and the resulting increase in weather risks (Andersen, 2019). Index-based insurance, for example, has shown the potential to bring crop insurance products to previously unreached locations and customers (De Leeuw et al., 2014).

## AI/R Implications on Impoverished People's Jobs, Small Companies, and Small-scale Farming

When it comes to the distributional effects of these technologies, the impact of AI/R on employment is undoubtedly the most hotly debated topic (Von Braun, 2019). The biggest cause of concern is the loss of jobs for unskilled labour, which is especially important for the poor. Whether in the labour market, as a small business owner in the service sector, or as a small farmer, the ability to work is the poor's most valuable asset. Small enterprises can grow swiftly as a result of digital potential, expanding their borders and altering traditional production patterns. Technological effects are reaching more people faster than ever before because to the rise of digital platform companies. As a result of technology improvements, the skills that companies want are evolving. (Ernst et al., 2019) state that the drastically decreased capital costs demonstrated by some applications, as well as the prospects for increased production, particularly amongst low-skilled workers, can lead to prospects for higher productivity, including for developing countries. Small farms are home to a huge number of the impoverished, mainly in Africa, South and East Asia. Smallholder farmers can benefit from a variety of digital technologies, services, and tools that can help them make better decisions and boost productivity and income. Among the primary benefits of digitization are increased access to information and other services, such as financing, market connections, long-term production improvements, and better-informed policies (Von Braun, 2019). The following are some examples:

- **Certificate of land ownership:** Land rights are ambiguous and contentious in many developing countries. Smartphones, cameras, and drones capable of collecting geospatial and topographical data – such as via GPS and global navigation satellite systems – are thus useful tools for land mapping and tenure projects. If geolocation data and land transaction history are recorded using blockchain technology, land registries could become extremely trustworthy.
- Big data, satellite photos, sensors, robots, and drones are examples of precision technology. Aerobotics, a drone company based in South Africa, is employing AI and drone technology to assist farmers in optimizing yields, resulting in significant cost savings. In Kenya, AI and big data analytics provide important information on farming trends and production based on data acquired through soil analysis. Another AI-assisted application is image recognition, which uses images of plants taken with a smartphone to identify plant ailments, provide treatment suggestions, and track disease progress.
- **Farm machinery:** Sensor-equipped tractors connected to mobile platforms allow users to collect farm data such as soil, water, and crop conditions, calibrate input consumption, and track progress from afar. In developing countries, innovative ideas like "uberization" of tractors and farm machinery, which allows farmers to rent agricultural machinery and makes automation more effective and affordable, are gaining traction.
- **Innovations in irrigation and energy:** Farmers can save money on electricity while also profiting from surplus energy created when connected to the grid with solar-powered micro-irrigation equipment. Algorithms based on AI/R

complex systems can aid in the development of efficient water systems for communal irrigation, as well as the optimization of water resources, distribution, and infrastructure design.

- **ICT platforms that connect buyers and sellers:** A virtual market platform in India improves farmers' access to important weather, soil health, market pricing, and financial data. Farmers can utilize this data to manage their farming operations, anticipate possible yields, and bargain for better prices. Such platforms' data can be analyzed using AI approaches to help guide decisions such as which crops to grow based on demand or price trends, or government logistics infrastructure investments.

The issue is ensuring that these technologies effectively resolve field-level issues while remaining accessible to impoverished farmers. As a result, the focus should be on combining several of these programs into user-friendly platforms with built-in data interpretation and planned activities to provide users with end-to-end solutions.

## Empowerment and Voice

AI/R may have a negative impact on poor and marginalized people's rights and entitlements, as well as their ability to influence social and economic policy, to the extent that these technologies currently take over duties performed by persons who are impoverished and disadvantaged. However, marginalized and underprivileged people could gain more power if new AI/R functions could be used or even controlled by them. The latter direct effect will be more likely if poor people's collaborative actions make it easier for large groups of people to acquire access to AI/R applications, such as AI-facilitated land rights or R-facilitated drone technologies that reduce dangerous farm work.

Each of the five areas of impact identified in this section has a list of suggested actions. In the long run, AI/R-assisted precision medicine, for example, could set a precedent in medicine. A digital and robot tax may theoretically be introduced in the job market. (Bruun & Duka, 2018) propose introducing a basic income program in conjunction with curricular changes and retraining measures to avert future technological unemployment.

## Mobile Technologies

Contemporary world is technologically controlled and directed. All sectors of the economy are now technologically equipped such that almost all activities are being done or a technological gadget is aiding the human being. The use of mobiles technologies is benefiting a lot in the marginalized areas (Bernacki et al., 2020). The

*Figure 1. Pro-poor AI/R policy options*
Source: (Braun, 2019)

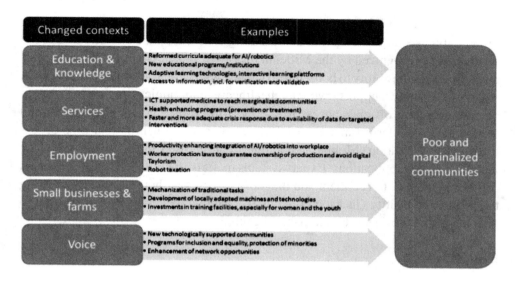

term "mobile technology" refers to technology that follows a user around wherever they go. It consists of two-way handheld communication devices as well as the network infrastructure that connects them. The technological uptake in marginalized areas has tremendously changed how the inhabitants of these marginalized areas live, do their business, learn, and communicate. A business that needed travelling to the urban areas can be done in the comfort of their homes, like communication, sending and receiving money. The technologies offer last-mile connectivity for those who do not have access to fixed network infrastructure. At the same time, the simplicity and affordability of mobile devices, as opposed to traditional communications devices, allow individuals to access digital services on their own time. Mobile networks cover a broad area, making them a more cost-effective option for connecting underserved areas than fixed-line technology, and rising smartphone adoption gives more people access to modern, feature-rich digital services.

The ability of digital technologies to assist marginalized societies was highlighted at the two World Summits on the Information Society (WSIS) held in Geneva in 2003 and Tunis in 2005, which acknowledged that ICTs are not only drivers of economic growth but also critical components in addressing development challenges (Nyamadzawo, 2011). In the age of mobile technology, the government has the opportunity to serve residents with better, faster services (Chang, 2020).

## E-health

The provision of health services is critical in a country's development and necessary in the public sector's attempts to achieve long-term economic stability and social wellbeing, as recognized by the Millennium Development Goals (MDGs). Mobile technology has the ability to boost the efficiency with which health care is delivered. ICTs increasingly support two-way healthcare communication, giving distant communities and officials access to the most up-to-date health information and treatment. Particularly fundamental ICTs applications, such as real-time access to patient information. Mobile technologies can be used in the health sector by installing health applications. Expert systems may also be installed, and the patients can be taught how to use them and diagnose diseases without necessarily visiting the healthcare facility (Jackson et al., 2016). Mobile technologies can be used to give tips on health issues like Maisha's health tips.

## E-commerce

The world has become a global village and many countries that have adopted mobile technologies are now benefiting from the technological gap between the developed and developing countries. On the global market their products are relatively cheaper because of the low cost of production compared to producers from the marginalized societies. This makes the products from marginalized areas very expensive and undesirable on the market. Mobile technologies have brought by ease of doing business and efficiency in doing business, payments are real-time, and aids to trade can be accessed electronically. Mobile technologies enable the marginalized societies to access what would have been nearly impossible to access. The marginalized societies have the problem of information access, mobile networks have expanded beyond the boarder of marginality, as (Naismith et al., 2004) there number of mobile phones is going to be five times the number of personal computer users by 2020. The marginalized can use mobile devices in the comfort of the house to make payments, advertise their products on the market, market research, and get information they might deem necessary for their dwelling.

## E-education

ICTs aid in the improvement of educational quality by facilitating access to massive amounts of information and facilitating multimedia presentation of materials, therefore improving the classroom experience (Dhawan, 2020). The government has made splendid effort to facilitate the learning and use of ICTs by investing in ICT education through some programmes as Presidential computer scheme Using the cybercafé model, create computer centres in libraries, district offices, and institutions. Distance learning can also be facilitated by mobile technologies, accessing materials, and making virtual classes from remote sites. Once education has can be accessed equally without boundaries and locations anybody interested can access including the marginalized societies.

## E-government

The invasion of mobile technologies has made a considerable impact on the demand and use of fixed line phones. Many governments service providers' office is characterized by long queues and corruption. The use of mobile phones will avoid contact between service providers and service applicants, reducing corruption and promoting e-government. E-government is the provision of government services electronically, through ICTs (Mahlangu, 2020). If government services are accessed remotely, the marginal societies can access the services they would have deemed expensive and very hard to access because of distance and the long queues that usually characterize the government, making the services rendered inaccessible. Most people from marginalized areas have no birth certificates and, consequently, national identification cards and therefore do not benefit from essential services, such as basic education and grade seven education, which the government says is compulsory.

The technologies provide last-mile connectivity for those without access to fixed network infrastructure, while the simplicity and affordability of mobile devices, as opposed to traditional communications devices, allows for personal access to digital services. Mobile networks are more cost-effective than fixed-line technology for connecting underserved areas, and rising smartphone adoption allows more people to access modern, feature-rich digital services.

## Internet of Things (IoT) for Digital Transformation in Marginalized Communities

The IEEE IoT Technical Community defines Internet of Things as a self-configuring technology, adaptable, sophisticated integrated network that connects 'things' to the Internet via optimized communication regulations (IEEE, 2020). The IoT-enabled digitalization of marginalized groups is a large, complex ecosystem with far more robust and effective systems than its separate components. Because the components interact and complement one another, they must be integrated. These technologies are now accessible, with some on the horizon, and they have the potential to improve marginalized groups' growth and well-being (OECD, 2017).

*Figure 2. An ecosystem of interdependent digital technologies*
*Source: (OECD, 2015)*

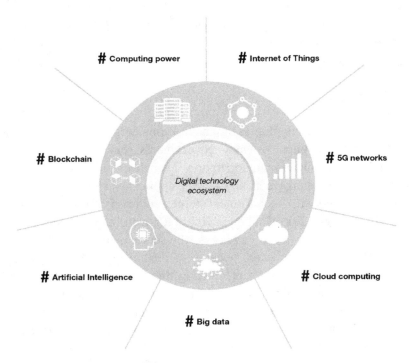

The dramatic increase in Internet and relatively decrease in related cost over the past 60 years contributed to rapid change in digital technologies, which can be attributed to the digital transformation of marginalized communities. Figure 2 depicts a network of interconnected digital tools that need transformational change to catalyze future economic and societal change.

IoT is about technology, data, process, hardware, and organizational change in the way of running business in communities (Malik & Singh, 2019). It is the digitization of the organization processes, data utilization and analytics for the improvement of user interactions which transform the activities of inhabitants in marginalized communities. These actions, carried out through the IoT platform, drive marginalized communities' digital transformation. Internet of Things plays a pivotal role in interconnecting devices like systems & smartphone cameras to work collaboratively in society. Therefore, IoT enables communities to make intelligent decisions, eventually acquiring innovations in their business that help to accomplish its business goals in the society thereby improving welfare (Ray, 2017).

In this competitive age, the Internet of Things (IoT) is one of the most important drivers of digital transformation in marginalized groups. As they compete with urbanization that is globally connected through modern IoT, marginalized groups are expected to explore possibilities, meet new targets, and minimize risks. Digital innovation technologies can enhance Digital transformation of marginalized communities' operations on many stages. These digital innovation technologies create synergies among marginalized communities' previously detached markets since not connected on the Internet. Collaboration became possible as a result of digital revolution, thanks to more advanced and diverse communication methods. Digital innovation technologies have also offered up new ways of obtaining, storing, and transforming data and a variety of other ways to disrupt traditional commercial practices in marginalized groups (Mohamad & Gombe, 2017). Organizations in marginalized communities that use IoT services can collect business data from sensors and take automatic actions without human interaction before service is impacted, allowing them to compete on an equal footing with businesses in urban settings. Organizations can use the data gathered to improve business processes and provide better services, giving them a competitive advantage (Keskin, T. & Kennedy, D. 2015).

Physical products are used in IoT-based digital transformation in marginalized populations. If it is linked with their culture, IoT-based digital transformation is both understandable and appealing enough to motivate individuals in remote regions to support it. Data collection is critical to both digital transformation and the Internet of Things. When used appropriately, IoT technology collects data from the actual world and transforms it into useful information for the community. The embedded system's software agent is in charge of transforming the data into a digital payload and wrapping it in protocols so it can be sent across the network. From the edge of the IoT network, the data payload is gathered and transported over the operational technology network to the IT network. The data is then transferred to the cloud and stored in a database, where it can be evaluated with analytics software or artificial intelligence (Spanaki et al., 2021). This processing develops models that generate data that is stored in marginalized groups, proving that IoT is a key technology for digital transformation and may be used to improve society's operability.

This process, which is carried out through the IoT platform, is what drives digital transformation. The Internet of Things platform, which allows physical things to be digitalized and data collected, also acts as a digital link between a company's products and its customers. Nowadays, the implementation of IoT as a technology for the digital transformation of marginalized communities benefited the society in several ways which include the following:

## Healthcare

IoT contributed to the improvement and technological innovation of hospitals' functionality in health and childcare services. If the marginalized communities positively adopt IoT for digital transformation, inhabitants will receive timely control drugs/medicines, increase automation in health services systems and individual health real-time management (AIOTI, 2018).

## Smart Cities and Communities

For the digital transformation of the marginalized communities IoT revealed that it is the pivotal technology to monitor communities and urbanization activities in city and optimization of resources and ultimately will improve the quality of life of citizens. IoT is a technology that proved to be as well important in engaging marginalized communities and increasing their awareness of their own community if digital transformation appreciated (Kempin Reuter, 2019).

## Industry 4.0

Technologies for digital transformation in marginalized communities through the adoption of IoT lead societies to enjoy the machine-to-machine communication across their activities in manufacturing plant, enabling real-time monitoring and control of the processes. In the agriculture sector in countries like Zimbabwe, Extension workers through the government programmes can now be able to monitor communities' farms through GPS applications. This ultimately allows the improvement in farming and quality production of products from farms and increase in levels of product customization (Bongomin et al., 2020).

## Retail

The buying and selling activities in society due to the utilization of IoT proved to be very important technology in increasing supply chain efficiencies and developing a new way of buying and selling services. This reshapes the customer experiences since they can purchase through credit cards and internet money transfers (Petar Popovski, 2018).

## Energy

Furthermore, through IoT, it is now possible to manage the behaviours of electricity suppliers and consumers in marginalized communities through the use of electricity meter billing, which improves energy efficiency (Samuel et al., 2020).

## Smart Food and Farming

Since IoT is becoming a big instrument in marginalized communities, the agriculture and farming industry is their key activity. These technologies can monitor and measure the real aspects of crops and animals that is can now automate watering, harvesting and feeding. IoT is a tool for transforming marginalized communities (Veena, 2018).

In this convergent market, the connection between innovation, competition, and investment is evolving, requiring policymakers to promote frameworks that encourage broadband network investment, protect consumers, promote competition, and provide opportunities for all (OECD, 2016). Broadband is the crucial general-purpose technology that allows a variety of traffic types, applications, and devices, including disruptive technologies like cloud computing, for IoT to transform marginalized communities. As markets evolve, policymakers must exercise prudence in ensuring that marginalized people are included in the digitalization of societies. OECD countries have found that countries with additional network lines, such as those expanding from three to four operators, are more likely to offer competitive and innovative services (OECD, 2014), albeit this varies per country.

Furthermore, IoT solutions should be evaluated in terms of whether they effectively promote competition among marginalized communities to transform a society digitally. IoT vehemently necessitates sharing network components, which also reduces connectivity costs in marginalized communities. Government policymakers should also encourage international cell phone roaming to be more competitive (Bourassa et al., 2016). Furthermore, crucial IoT decisions should be taken for each community such that there is a balance between end-to-end infrastructure competition and collaborative provisioning of facilities by rivals to support higher marginalized retail competition. IoT infrastructure sharing in a country can increase competition, especially where markets are dominated by a single operator, such as in urban regions, and can lower costs for network and service providers while allowing the creation of new and innovative services for end users (OECD, 2017).

## Analytical Technologies

Real-time business transformation is enabled by technology, and analytics technology makes firms more agile in terms of meeting changing customer demands and business trends in marginalized communities. Analytical techniques are used by today's big data pioneers for both high-level forecasting and real-time visualization. Businesses that use analytics technology provide new prospects for customers, products, revenue streams, and services and change their organizational structures. Analytics can help in every aspect of the business, from sourcing suppliers and forecasting demand to accounting and human resource tasks. Communities can make well-informed decisions using various analytical technologies that are easily accessible to them (Malik & Singh, 2019).

## SOLUTIONS AND RECOMMENDATIONS

Emerging technologies like Internet of things (IoT), analytical technologies, and mobile technologies bring an arsenal of advantages which marginalized communities can benefit from to promote their socio-economic status and promoting digital inclusion, as such these technologies should be adopted in these areas. The government and relevant stakeholders should promote the adoption of digital technologies to bridge the digital divide in marginalized communities.

## FUTURE RESEARCH DIRECTIONS

Future research can explore how these digital technologies can be embedded into the education, economic, social and political systems to improve the lives of people who reside in marginalized communities especially in the agricultural sector.

## CONCLUSION

We strongly recommend that governments, corporates, and individuals use some or all of the mentioned technologies to reduce marginalization in communities. Many social movements have been made feasible by technological advancements such as the Internet, which have allowed previously marginalized groups to express themselves and coordinate campaigns to effect change. Emerging technologies, IoT, analytical, and mobile technologies have been recognized as the most essential technologies that can be leveraged for digital transformation in marginalized groups in this chapter. Individuals who are socially marginalized, that is, those who are alienated from economic, political and societal systems worldwide, can use modern digital technology to make their views heard and be included in decision-making bodies if authorities can employ these technologies. In the chapter, digital technologies provide solutions for the marginalized through e-health, e-governance, poverty alleviation, and the inclusion of people with special needs. Future research opportunities within the third wave of digitization, which entails the adoption of a variety of technologies such as Big data analytics, 3D printing and Blockchain aimed at improving information processing and decision making while further automating routine tasks within businesses and governments, are still available to other researchers.

## REFERENCES

Abad-Segura, E., González-Zamar, M. D., Luque-de la Rosa, A., & Cevallos, M. B. M. (2020). Sustainability of educational technologies: An approach to augmented reality research. *Sustainability (Switzerland)*, *12*(10), 4091. Advance online publication. doi:10.3390u12104091

Andersen, L. (2019). Artificial Intelligence in International Development: Avoiding Ethical Pitfalls. *Journal of Public & International Affairs*.

Banerjee, D. A. K. (2020). *A Brief History of Pandemics*. Academic. https://medium. com/history-uncut/a-brief-history-of-pandemics-d9f372c89484

Bernacki, M. L., Greene, J. A., & Crompton, H. (2020). Mobile technology, learning, and achievement: Advances in understanding and measuring the role of mobile technology in education. *Contemporary Educational Psychology*, *60*, 101827. doi:10.1016/j.cedpsych.2019.101827

Bonafilia, D., Gill, J., Basu, S., & Yang, D. (2019). Building high resolution maps for humanitarian aid and development with weakly-and semi-supervised learning. *Proceedings of the IEEE/CVF Conference on Computer Vision and Pattern Recognition Workshops*, 1–9.

Bongomin, O., Gilibrays Ocen, G., Oyondi Nganyi, E., Musinguzi, A., & Omara, T. (2020). Exponential Disruptive Technologies and the Required Skills of Industry 4.0. *Journal of Engineering (United Kingdom)*, *2020*, 1–17. Advance online publication. doi:10.1155/2020/4280156

Brito, C. (2020). *Covid-19 has intensified the digital 2020., divide*. World Economic Forum.

Brunner, M., Hemsley, B., Togher, L., & Palmer, S. (2017). Technology and its role in rehabilitation for people with cognitive-communication disability following a traumatic brain injury (TBI). *Brain Injury: [BI]*, *31*(8), 1028–1043. doi:10.1080/0 2699052.2017.1292429 PMID:28471267

Bruun, E. P. G., & Duka, A. (2018). Artificial intelligence, jobs and the future of work: Racing with the machines. *Basic Income Studies, 13*(2).

Calabrese Barton, A., & Tan, E. (2018). A Longitudinal Study of Equity-Oriented STEM-Rich Making Among Youth From Historically Marginalized Communities. *American Educational Research Journal, 55*(4), 761–800. doi:10.3102/0002831218758668

Ciechanover, A. (2019). *The revolution of personalized medicine—Are we going to cure all diseases and at what price.* Concept Note of the Pontifical Academy of Sciences-Summit on the Revolution of Personalized Medicine.

De Leeuw, J., Vrieling, A., Shee, A., Atzberger, C., Hadgu, K. M., Biradar, C. M., Keah, H., & Turvey, C. (2014). The potential and uptake of remote sensing in insurance: A review. *Remote Sensing, 6*(11), 10888–10912. doi:10.3390/rs61110888

Deganis, I., Haghian, Pegah, Z., & Tagashira, M. (2021). *Leveraging digital technologies for social inclusion.* Department of Economic and Social Affairs Social Inclusion. https://www.un.org/development/desa/dspd/2021/02/digital-technologies-for-social-inclusion/

Demirguc-Kunt, A., Klapper, L., Singer, D., & Ansar, S. (2018). *The Global Findex Database 2017: Measuring financial inclusion and the fintech revolution.* World Bank Publications. doi:10.1596/978-1-4648-1259-0

Dhawan, S. (2020). Online Learning: A Panacea in the Time of COVID-19 Crisis. *Journal of Educational Technology Systems, 49*(1), 5–22. doi:10.1177/0047239520934018

du Boulay, B., Poulovasillis, A., Holmes, W., & Mavrikis, M. (2018). *Artificial Intelligence And Big Data Technologies To Close The Achievement Gap.* Academic Press.

Ernst, E., Merola, R., & Samaan, D. (2019). Economics of artificial intelligence: Implications for the future of work. *IZA Journal of Labor Policy, 9*(1), 20190004. doi:10.2478/izajolp-2019-0004

Fernandez-Luque, L., & Imran, M. (2018). Humanitarian health computing using artificial intelligence and social media: A narrative literature review. *International Journal of Medical Informatics, 114*, 136–142. doi:10.1016/j.ijmedinf.2018.01.015 PMID:29395987

Hess, U. (2016). *Innovations and Emerging Trends in Agricultural Insurance: How can we transfer natural risks out of rural livelihoods to empower and protect people?* Academic Press.

Howard, J., & Simmons, E. (2019). *Risk and resilience; advancing food and nutrition security in Nigeria through feed the future.* Center for Strategic and International Studies.

ITU. (2019). *Measuring Digital Development: Facts and Figures.* ITU.

Jackson, K., Lower, C. L., & Rudman, W. J. (2016). The Crossroads between Workforce and Education. *Perspectives in Health Information Management*, 13.

Jean, N., Burke, M., Xie, M., Davis, W. M., Lobell, D. B., & Ermon, S. (2016). Combining satellite imagery and machine learning to predict poverty. *Science*, *353*(6301), 790–794.

Kempin Reuter, T. (2019). Human rights and the city: Including marginalized communities in urban development and smart cities. *Journal of Human Rights*, *18*(4), 382–402. https://doi.org/10.1080/14754835.2019.1629887

Khare, S., Kavyashree, S., Gupta, D., & Jyotishi, A. (2017). Investigation of nutritional status of children based on machine learning techniques using Indian demographic and health survey data. *Procedia Computer Science*, *115*, 338–349.

Kubota, T. (2017). Artificial intelligence used to identify skin cancer. *A Research Review. International Journal of Communication*, *10*, 5032–5055.

Mahlangu, G. (2020). *A Multi-Dimensional Model for Assessing E-Government Service Gaps Gaps in the Context of a Developing Country : A Critical Realist.* Academic Press.

Malik, V., & Singh, S. (2019). Security risk management in IoT environment. *Journal of Discrete Mathematical Sciences and Cryptography*, *22*(4), 697–709. https://doi.org/10.1080/09720529.2019.1642628

Manzoor, M., & Vimarlund, V. (2017). E-services for the social inclusion of people with disabilities: A literature review. *Technology and Disability*, *29*(1–2), 15–33.

Mohamad, M., & Gombe, M. (2017). eAgriculture revisited : A systematic literature review of theories, concept, practices, methods, and future trends. *Usir*, 22.

Mussa, E. C. (2018). *Long-term effects of childhood work on human capital formation, migration decisions, and earnings in rural Ethiopia.* Academic Press.

Naismith, L., Vavoula, G. N., & Sharples, M. (2004). Mobile technologies and learning. *A Technology Update and M-Learning Project Summary*, 1–26.

Niță, A.-M., & Pârvu, M. C. (2020). Vulnerability and resilience in marginalized rural communities. Case study: projects for reduction of risk exclusion in Dolj County. *Revista de Stiinte Politice, 67*, 103–117. https://www.proquest.com/scholarly-journals/vulnerability-resilience-marginalized-rural/docview/2447285558/se-2?accountid=14166%0Ahttps://suny-alb.primo.exlibrisgroup.com/openurl/01SUNY_ALB/01SUNY_ALB:01SUNY_ALB?genre=article&atitle=Vulnerability+and+resi

Óskarsdóttir, M., Bravo, C., Sarraute, C., Vanthienen, J., & Baesens, B. (2019). The value of big data for credit scoring: Enhancing financial inclusion using mobile phone data and social network analytics. *Applied Soft Computing, 74*, 26–39.

Ra, S., Shrestha, U., Khatiwada, S., Yoon, S. W., & Kwon, K. (2019). The rise of technology and impact on skills. *International Journal of Training Research, 17*(sup1), 26–40. doi:10.1080/14480220.2019.1629727

Ramakrishna, C., Venkateshwarlu, B., Srinivas, J., & Srinivas, S. (2019). Iot based smart farming using cloud computing and machine learning. *International Journal of Innovative Technology and Exploring Engineering, 9*(1), 3455–3458. https://doi.org/10.35940/ijitee.A4853.119119

Ray, P. P. (2017). Internet of things for smart agriculture: Technologies, practices and future direction. *Journal of Ambient Intelligence and Smart Environments, 9*(4), 395–420. https://doi.org/10.3233/AIS-170440

Rhinesmith, C. (2016). *Digital Inclusion and Meaningful Broadband Adoption Initiatives Digital Inclusion and Meaningful Broadband Adoption Initiatives.* Academic Press.

Samuel, O., Almogren, A., Javaid, A., Zuair, M., Ullah, I., & Javaid, N. (2020). Leveraging blockchain technology for secure energy trading and least-cost evaluation of decentralized contributions to electrification in sub-Saharan Africa. *Entropy (Basel, Switzerland), 22*(2). https://doi.org/10.3390/e22020226

Sanders, C. K., & Scanlon, E. (2021). The digital divide is a human rights issue: Advancing social inclusion through social work advocacy. *Journal of Human Rights and Social Work, 6*(2), 130–143.

Sevelius, J. M., Gutierrez-Mock, L., Zamudio-Haas, S., McCree, B., Ngo, A., Jackson, A., Clynes, C., Venegas, L., Salinas, A., Herrera, C., Stein, E., Operario, D., & Gamarel, K. (2020). Research with Marginalized Communities: Challenges to Continuity During the COVID-19 Pandemic. *AIDS and Behavior, 24*(7), 2009–2012. https://doi.org/10.1007/s10461-020-02920-3

Spanaki, K., Sivarajah, U., Fakhimi, M., Despoudi, S., & Irani, Z. (2021). Disruptive technologies in agricultural operations: a systematic review of AI-driven AgriTech research. In *Annals of Operations Research*. Springer US. doi:10.1007/s10479-020-03922-z

Tech-Student, M. (2016). A Literature Study on Agricultural Production System Using IoT as Inclusive Technology. *Int. J. Innov. Technol. Res, 4*(1), 2727–2731.

UNESCO. (2021). *Adverse consequences of school closures.* https://en.unesco.org/covid19/educationresponse/consequences

Vanderheiden, G. (2006). *Over the Horizon: Potential Impact of Emerging Trends in Information and Communication Technology on Disability Policy and Practice.* National Council on Disability.

Veena, S. (2018). *The Survey on Smart Agriculture Using IoT.* Academic Press.

Von Braun, J. (2019). *Working Paper 188.* Academic Press.

Von Braun, J. (2019). *AI and robotics implications for the poor.* Available at SSRN 3497591.

Wood, C. S., Thomas, M. R., Budd, J., Mashamba-Thompson, T. P., Herbst, K., Pillay, D., Peeling, R. W., Johnson, A. M., McKendry, R. A., & Stevens, M. M. (2019). Taking connected mobile-health diagnostics of infectious diseases to the field. *Nature, 566*(7745), 467–474.

Zurutuza, N. (2018). *Information poverty and algorithmic equity: Bringing advances in AI to the most vulnerable.* Academic Press.

## KEY TERMS AND DEFINITIONS

**Analytical Technologies:** Techniques that are based on known data or models.
**COVID-19:** A contagious respiratory disease.
**Digital Divide:** The difference between people who have access to digital technologies and those that do not.
**Digital Inclusion:** Giving access to members of the community to use digital technologies.
**Digital Transformation:** The use of disruptive technology to increase production, create value, and society's welfare.
**Emerging Technologies:** New communication tools.
**Internet of Things:** The interconnection of computing devices via the internet.

**Internet Technologies:** A collection of internet-based communication tools.

**Marginalized Communities:** Groups of people that are excluded from social and economic activities.

**Marginalized Community:** Limited to the periphery of the society.

**Mobile Technologies:** Technology that goes where the user goes.

# Chapter 9
# Clusters for Transformation in Marginalized Areas

**Tendai Shelton Muwani**
*Manicaland State University of Applied Sciences, Zimbabwe*

**Lemias Zivanai**
*Midlands State University, Zimbabwe*

**Briget Munyoro**
*Midlands State University, Zimbabwe*

**Njodzi Ranganai**
*Manicaland State University of Applied Sciences, Zimbabwe*

**Nyasha Chipunza**
*Manicaland State University of Applied Sciences, Zimbabwe*

## ABSTRACT

*Most societies have been in abject poverty owing to a lack of proper education, gender alienation, and socio-economic and political factors. Localized external economies, particularly economies of scale and scope, as small firms specialize and engage in a division of labor, are among the benefits of clustering. Clusters are important because geographical agglomeration has the potential to help small businesses overcome size constraints, advance technologically, and improve competence in local and global markets. The adoption of technologies has the effect of replacing the old way of doing things with manual and mechanical methods. The study examined the potential of clustering to help marginalized communities to become integrated and improve their quality of life in a digital society and concluded that ICTs can, if adopted and used properly, shift and destroy social boundaries between the elite and the segregated. Future research can look at the adoption of digital technologies in marginalized areas.*

DOI: 10.4018/978-1-6684-3901-2.ch009

## INTRODUCTION

Digitalization has brought with it many changes to how people live in their societies and how they go about their day-to-day activities. The use of digital devices and other ubiquitous has taken over all other activities that were done manually and mechanically. Production has been boosted, and marketing has been made easier, with almost all markets reachable over the information superhighway. The growing population in developing countries like Zimbabwe is part of a larger trend of digitalization and inclusiveness that has already emerged across the African continent within the last ten years, creating geospatial apps, wind energy, electric vehicles, videogame, and, more notably, robotic prosthetics and ventilators for COVID-19 patients (Friederici et al., 2020; Mavhunga, 2017; Poggiali, 2016). Clusters are important because geographical agglomeration has the potential to help small businesses and communities overcome size constraints, advance technologically, and improve their competence both locally and globally.

## What Is Marginalization and Clustering?

The world has always been divided. There is a possibility that it will be further divided, and these divisions will bring inequality (Watkins, 2011; Danaher et al., 2013). This is a truism, yet a much more powerful and poignant statement. It provides the basis and the backdrop against which this book chapter has been written.

Marginalization is the process that pushes and uncontrollably places certain inhabitants and societies on the periphery of society's socio-economic, cultural, and political mainstreams, restricting them from enhancing their skills and gaining opportunities and services (Von Braun and Gatzweiler, 2014). Marginalization is a process and a condition that inhibits groups and individuals from fully engaging in the community, economic, and political life. "Marginalization is a ubiquitous social stratification tendency (Musthafa and Stephen, 2019). Marginalization assumes many forms; to which it has many causes and effects. These forms include age (Baril and Leblanc, 2015; Cramb et al., 2009; Gilleard and Higgs, 2011), addiction (Vera et al., 2009), disability (Grenier, 2010; Danaher et al., 2013; Wendelborg and Tøssebro, 2010), displacement (Price, 2009), gender (Bawa, 2012), and socio-economic status (Waldron, 2010).

The background of marginalization is based on socio-economic and political factors. Opportunities and benefits are denied to individuals living on the "margins," while prospects are encouraged for those living in the "center" of society (Chiru, n.d.). Clusters are geographically concentrated groups of intertwined producers, corporate entities, suppliers, and related institutions that generate direct and indirect collaborations, culminating in market integration (Spalevic et al., 2017).

The clusters will be based on these factors to bring inclusion and de-marginalize societies. Societies are backward because they have not cooperated in information and communication technologies (ICTs).

The adoption of technologies replaces the old manual and mechanical methods of doing things, lowering production costs and increasing output. In many societies, modern technologies have resulted in significant life changes (Sandu et al., 2019). Electronic government (e-government) has grown due to digital technologies, allowing citizens to access government services online (Mahlangu, 2020). It has also seen the birth of electronic commerce and, as a result, globalization. Many factors contribute to society's marginalization, but there are four main types of marginality: contingent, systematic, collateral, and leveraged. Every successful society's forerunner is digital inclusion. Many things can bring about the marginalization of societies, but generally, we have four types of marginality: contingent, systematic, collateral, and leveraged. Digital inclusion is the forerunner of every successful society (Haenssgen, 2018). The adoption of technologies has the impact of changing the old way of using manual and mechanical ways of doing things, thereby reducing the cost of production and increasing production. Modern technologies have brought tremendous change to life in many societies. Digital technologies have seen the growth of electronic government (e-government), where the citizenry can access government services online. It has also witnessed the emergence of electronic commerce and, consequently, globalization.

Due to a lack of adequate education and other factors, most societies have lived in abject poverty ever since independence (Niţă and Pârvu, 2020). Over time, these factors have widened the digital divide between societies in the global village. Digital technologies were adopted in every sector of the economy at the turn of the millennium. These factors have continued to widen the digital divide among global village societies. The turn of the millennium saw the adoption of digital technologies in every sector of the economy, and societies have come up with various initiatives to try and alleviate their societies from the poverty of the previous millennium using digital technologies. Technology adoption has the effect of displacing old manual and mechanical methods of doing things. Modern technologies have resulted in significant life changes in many societies. As a result of digital technologies, electronic government (e-government) has grown. Digital technologies have widened the digital divide between global village societies and their rural counterparts

In the context of this research, clusters of transformation will be based on three pillars: education, health, and agriculture. Besides being marginalized politically, socially, and economically, communities are also marginalized because of a lack of modern agriculture methods, which are less costly and more productive. There is still segregation amongst children in some societies, with the girl child either not getting a formal education or going up to a certain level. As has been perceived by

(Acharya, 2018), the cooperation of disempowered people's establishments with external funding agencies, particularly non-governmental organizations (NGOs), gave them the chance to access the resources available. Societies are marginalized because of different factors. Some are marginalized because of ethnicity, politics, climate, location, beliefs and customary beliefs, amongst other things.

## BACKGROUND

Every successful society begins with digital inclusion. The funding landscape underlying digital transformation for marginalized community clusters reflects larger transitions in the Global South's expansion and financing of health services, agriculture, education, and communication, toward a dominant approach of partnerships, philanthropic equity, and corporate investments providing "catalytic capital" to kick start digital transformation projects (Hunter and Murray, 2019).

Societies have evolved from the iron age to modern-day societies (Daalmans and Daalmans, 2012). Humankind has also evolved in many respects from how they have been producing their food, how they learn, and what they learn. Disease outbreaks have also been experienced during this evolution of humankind. Ethnic conflicts, floods, famines, and droughts have caused people to migrate from one society to another (Daalmans and Daalmans, 2012). As a result, some ethnic groups have become subjects to the other, paying taxes and providing free labor.

Similarly, the tools that humanity used in the previous millennium were mostly mechanical; the turn of the millennium has been characterized most by digital devices. Agriculture has also been adversely affected by the modern use of digital devices (Gondchawar and Kawitkar, 2016). The use of ox-drawn ploughs and holes seems to have affected production, thereby limiting surplus and production, which is in tandem with the labour put in the field. Knowledge has also been very little as some crops which were grown were not tolerant in that environment. In developing countries, because of their history and the political situation of pre-independence, black societies were treated as second-class citizens, such that healthcare facilities were unevenly distributed (Yannopoulos et al., 2020). Some societies might not have a single healthcare facility. It is against this background that these trends are still reflected. This goes with the education facilities. The number of educational facilities is unevenly distributed. The table below shows the distribution of tertiary institutions in Zimbabwe.

*Table 1. Distribution of tertiary institutions in Zimbabwe*

| Province | Harare | Bulawayo | Masvingo | Manicaland | Matebeleland North | Matebeleland South | Mashonaland West | Mashonaland East | Mashonaland Central |
|---|---|---|---|---|---|---|---|---|---|
| Universities | 4 | 1 | 2 | 1 | 1 | 1 | 1 | 1 | 1 |
| Teachers Colleges | 1 | 2 | 3 | 2 | 0 | 1 | 0 | 0 | 1 |
| Technical Colleges | 1 | 1 | 1 | 1 | 0 | 1 | 0 | 1 | 0 |

# MAIN FOCUS OF THE CHAPTER

## Clusters for Transformation in Marginalized Areas

### Agriculture

Agricultural exclusion can be defined as how certain areas of agriculture cease to be sustainable under existing land use and socio-economic structure due to the combined effects of social, economic, political, and environmental factors. It could be an amalgamation of intensification and accumulation of agricultural land. Marginalization manifests itself in various ways and at various scales, ranging from a single patch of land to large regions. It may eventually result in abandonment, limiting monitoring of semi-natural areas.

A marginal agricultural situation could be defined as one on the edge of financial viability. A marginal site, for example, could be defined as one where "the current agricultural use yields a factor income that cannot cover the costs of the element amounts of investment made in it or, given perpetual productivity and market prices, will fade away to cover them over the next few years" (Levers et al., 2018). Macroeconomic variables alone do not render a given agricultural situation marginal. Physical geography, agrarian structures, the sociocultural environment, and legislative factors must all be considered.

Marginalization can be defined as transforming farming fields from more lucrative businesses to less prosperous ones (Breman et al., 2010). This could include switching from cultivable cultivation to perpetual pastureland or from pastures to forest. Farmers may respond in various ways to the situation associated with agricultural marginalization in which farmland areas cease to be viable. It might try to enhance viability and combat exclusion, whereas others may reduce or abandon agriculture entirely. In certain instances, it may be feasible to amplify production and increase yield per hectare in certain instances, notably when substantial financial rewards are available as part of production-oriented fiscal incentives, as was the case with most EU Member States even during the 1960s and 1970s (de Boer and van Ittersum, 2018)

*Figure 1. Market access for African farmers*
Source: (Asia, 2021)

| Under-performing value chains | Limited coordination of research and development | Insufficient utilization of inputs and mechanization | Limited reach of extension to boost on-farm production | Poorly organized post-harvest aggregation and transport | Inconsistent capacity for effective value addition | Poorly developed market linkages and trade corridors |
|---|---|---|---|---|---|---|
| Insufficient infrastructure | Insufficient transport, energy, water, waste and other hard infrastructure, leading to uncompetitive cost structures | | | Undeveloped soft infrastructure including aging smallholder farmers and a lack of skills for commercial agriculture and agro-allied industries | | |
| Limited access to agricultural finance | Real and perceived risk limiting private sector investment | | High service cost due to small deal sizes, lack of credit data, and low capacity in agricultural lending | | Limited market attractiveness relative to perceived higher returns outside of the agricultural sector | |
| Adverse agri-business environment | Unfavorable market access and incentives limiting trade and capacity to produce high-quality products | | Ineffective sector regulation creating long lead times for new technologies and inconsistent trade policies | | Unsupportive business enabling environment restricting land tenure and general ease of doing business | |
| Limited inclusivity, sustainability and nutrition | Insufficient inclusivity of women and youth in agricultural development | | Limited incentives to ensure sustainability and climate-resilient practices | | Limited access and affordability of commodities with high nutrition levels | |

Marginalization involves various interconnected socio-economic disadvantages in diverse communities (at varying levels and qualifications) based on: an investment perspective associated with agricultural as well as non-agricultural events in remote regions (for instance, the extent of community, geographical, tribal, and globally competitiveness or economic dimension of these activities); an innovation perspective related to agricultural and non-agricultural events in rural areas. Governments can harness agriculture in underserved areas through global trade, monetary policies, industry, employment legislation, and a set of strategic policies. The above market regulations can always be tailored to provide monetary support, lending reimbursements, financial incentives for productivity gains, and infrastructure for curriculum and instruction (Harrison and Rodríguez-Clare, 2010).

Agribusiness continues to be an important part of the African economy and thus the daily livelihoods of millions of Africans, making up for slightly more than 60% of employment on the continent (Co, 2021). The "obstacles" confronting African agricultural production can be interpreted as a significant way to strengthen Africans' quality of life and boost economic growth if the sector is transformed.

Market access for African farmers, particularly women farmers, remains restricted at the community, national, regional, and global scales. Africa's involvement in the multilateral agricultural commodity and value-added markets remains very limited, at only 2% in an evolving global environment (Beddington et al., 2012)

## Education

Education is critical to achieving social justice, and educational institutions are responsible for preparing youth to the best of their abilities, ensuring they have a constructive status in society, and promoting an approach to developing an inclusive society. The troubling reality is that most learners are precluded from the school system and thus unable to participate meaningfully in their sections of the community's social, political, cultural, and economic aspects. These learners and communities are marginalized and vulnerable, and as a result, they are perceived as undesirable and lacking in any useful function in society. They exist beyond the current preservation and unification systems, limiting their prospects and way of life.

In its varying forms, education is unquestionably a tool for social transformation and the attainment of social equality (Musthafa and Stephen, 2019). In societies where education has been absorbed at early stages, as in post-independence Zimbabwe, strides of demarginalization have been witnessed. To achieve early education inclusion, Zimbabwe's legislature included provisions for access to quality education. To create an inclusive society, the education system can play a vital role in preparing children to maximize their skills and talents, thus ensuring a befitting status in society (Musthafa and Stephen, 2019).

Education is essential to a society's inclusive, peaceful, and long-term development. Article 26 of the Universal Declaration of the Human Rights considers education as essential for the sustainable development of a Nation and a fundamental human right (Lee Dr, 2013). If education is inclusive and of high quality, it can ensure the inclusion of disadvantaged people in the larger development phase, reducing inequities (Howard, 2019). The United Nations' sustainable development (SDG) agenda views equity as critical to achieving long-term advancement and demands for no one to be left behind. SDG 4 seeks to "ensure inclusive and equitable education for all and enhance skills" (SDG, 2019).

Societies that lack education have no opportunities exposed to them because they do not know what is prevailing. They cannot read the media, which is usually the mode of communication. Most of them cannot afford radios and lack power sources. Some societies are more based on their ethnic beliefs than others, to the point that they are ignorant of innovations. Education is the source of innovations and a way of spreading new knowledge. In that respect, not going to school means such societies are marginalized.

Digital devices in education can play a pivotal role and level the ground between the mainstream and the marginalized (Salsabila, 2019). The internet can be accessed anywhere provided there is network. Schools can use outsourced software for online teaching, for example, Google classes and Microsoft classes. The tutor can remotely give learning materials, and students can also access them remotely as long as they have access credentials (Dhawan, 2020). Debates and discussions can be done through digital devices, as well as the teacher can give feedback. Schools can have virtual seminars there, breaking the marginal barrier of distance and finance (Liu et al., n.d.). This makes the marginalized share ideas with the mainstream. Corporates can also help by developing websites that school children can access, irrespective of their background. Through its higher foundation, Econet has donated digital devices to schools and paid school fees for marginalized communities.

## Healthcare

Health and personal well-being disparities are significantly greater among socio-economically disadvantaged youths (Ramamoorthi et al., 2015). Many factors influence these inequalities. Healthcare access might also be a factor which causes marginality in society. In developing countries, healthcare facilities are far away, such that pregnant women might need to walk for about twenty kilometers to access the healthcare facility. Medical conditions such as mental and substance use disorders and recurring chronic conditions seem to be the dominant health concerns of the teenage population in some communities where drug abuse is prevalent. These are more prevalent in marginalized societies, where the school-going age is not occupied. To put it another way, according to (Chiru, n.d.), there seems to be a lack of health status information available for some marginalized groups, particularly the homeless, refugees, sex workers and/or gender diverse young people. In support of this (Dahrouge et al., 2018), marginalization can lead to the underutilization of the healthcare system because of inaccessibility. Another effect of a lack of health was identified by (Robards et al., 2020). Access to healthcare is a predictor of health, and yet many marginalized groups are renowned for facing barriers for sociocultural reasons.

Marginalized cultures are characterized as communities beyond the "mainstream society," implying an extremely susceptible population that is structurally ignored by regional or global policymaking conferences (Haenssgen, 2018). Homeless people, substance abusers, prostitutes, refugees, and racial minorities are all broadly categorized. Most of these populations suffer from substantial health disparities and face major obstacles to receiving high-quality care. Traditional approaches to health promotion sometimes neglect marginalized people. This could be attributed to a lack of confidence in those communicating or calling for change, a lack of resonance with the message's priority, culturally diverse expectations, awareness and expertise of critical issues, and, most importantly, a loss of self-esteem when it comes to the nation's indicators. As a result, the disempowered inhabitants have little agency in determining their own initiatives and the possible measures to deal with such difficulties (Roguski and McBride-Henry, 2020). As a result, individuals or groups often have poorer health status and have limited healthcare. This condition is similar to Tudor Hart's reciprocal care law, which states that people who need medical help the most are often the ones who are least likely to receive it (Baio et al., 2018).

For disadvantaged people, there are several barriers to healthcare. Concerns have been raised on how the health sector supports migrants, the homeless, substance abusers, and the poor. Patient factors such as suspicion of facilities and feeling unwelcome at healthcare facilities were reported for homeless people, travelers, drug users, and migrants. Two other barriers that have been identified are legal troubles for migrants and drug users. The homeless, travelers, addicts, and prostitutes compete for attention in the livelihoods of the marginalized, as do cultural barriers for migrants. It is frequently stated that these obstacles do not happen in isolation and reduce the likelihood of patients returning to the healthcare system. This would be in accordance with the idea of "candidacy," as well as the ever-changing relationship between the patient and the healthcare system. As a commonly associated access point into the larger health service, primary care can help reduce imbalances. Primary healthcare services that are easy to use and accepted by patients from all walks of life are required for this to occur. These groups are seldom invited to contribute to the development of primary care (O'Donnell et al., 2016).

Healthy lifestyles and wellbeing for all people of all ages are Goal 3 of the Sustainable Development Goals (SDGs) (SDG, 2019). It not only focuses on fundamental health but also recognizes that health entails a sense of wellbeing throughout one's life. It aspires to create a healthcare delivery system that is inclusive, with no obstacles to quality healthcare and wellbeing based on geography, income, race, or gender. To accomplish SDG 3, digital technology such as ICT tools can be leveraged to address all of the health concerns encountered by marginalized communities. Interconnectivity and reliable dissemination of information between varying parts of the health system, as illustrated by telemedicine and supply management linkages; improved efficiency of healthcare delivery for isolated places to create a "prevalent" healthcare delivery system; are all ways that ICT can help with the digitalization of health (Haenssgen, 2018). Health tips are posted on ubiquitous digital devices when ubiquitous health care systems are used. For example, Mashay's health tips are on cell phones. Awareness can be achieved through digital devices for relaying information on disease outbreaks and common diseases in the area. A further way ICTs can be used in health care is to improve data interaction and benchmarks in health care interventions. This facilitates learning for the communities where knowledge gained is shared across countries and regions. Thus, cost-effective healthcare systems are rolled out, where ICT-enable efficiencies at the national or regional level, allowing health budgets to be extended, equipping patients with basic general healthcare knowledge, and securing opportunities.

Emerging innovation areas such as data analytics and drones can assist in overcoming capacity constraints, increasing integration and coherence and removing barriers that have previously deterred medicinal products from reaching remote, vulnerable communities. A national healthcare technology strategy could also provide a realistic insight on how digital technology will optimize access to health care in any given country, as well as clear direction for stakeholders across the healthcare system, encouraging dependable operating conditions for solution providers. Involved parties must collaborate to create high-level policies to support digitalization investments.

## SOLUTIONS AND RECOMMENDATIONS

Digital tools are frequently viewed as a way to enable agriculture and industrial areas to have more sustainable futures. Since it affects so many facets of life, the digital transformation process is essential. The liable innovation approach necessitates a clear grasp and foresight of the often unforeseeable consequences. Education and internet access must be used for more than just acquiring knowledge online. They must inspire people by assisting them in developing the conscience and self-responsibility necessary to succeed in life. The subsequent COVID-19 epidemic has underscored the role of this. A government's health technology strategy should lay out a compelling view of how digitization would improve affordable healthcare in a given nation, including a strategic roadmap for stakeholders across the health system, and foster an encouraging, dependable investment climate for solution providers.

Our daily lives' digital transformation and datafication present new challenges and necessitate renewed commitments. Such commitments are especially important at the nexus of organizations and technologies and on pressing issues such as educational and cultural resources for skills and future jobs.

## FUTURE RESEARCH DIRECTIONS

Future research can examine the intersectionality of clusters in marginalized communities and how they can be integrated to bridge the digital divide and enhance societies.

## CONCLUSION

ICTs can, if adopted and used properly, shift and destroy social boundaries between the elite and the segregated. The gaps that the situation of yesteryear has socially created can be countered when digital devices are put to full use; educational information, agricultural information, and health information can be effectively shared. Agricultural marginalization refers to the loss of farmland that is no longer sustainable due to current land use and socio-economic structures. It may eventually lead to alienation, limiting semi-natural area management. Marginalization takes many forms and occurs on a variety of scales. Education is essential for a society's inclusive, peaceful, and long-term development. In post-independence Zimbabwe, strides of demarginalization have been witnessed. Digital devices in education can play a pivotal role and level the ground between the mainstream and the marginalized. Education is the source of innovations and a way of spreading new knowledge. For financially and socially disadvantaged adolescents, health and wellbeing disparities are higher. Traditional approaches to health promotion sometimes neglect marginalized people. Digital technology can be leveraged to address all of the health concerns encountered by marginalized communities. A governmental healthcare technology approach should define how digital technology improves access to healthcare.

## REFERENCES

Acharya, G. D. (2018). *Including the excluded: Marginalized poor communities and development practices in rural Nepal.* Academic Press.

Asia, D. (2021). *Funding Agricultural Innovation for the Global South: Does it Promote Sustainable Agricultural Intensification?* Academic Press.

Baio, J., Wiggins, L., Christensen, D. L., Maenner, M. J., Daniels, J., Warren, Z., Kurzius-Spencer, M., Zahorodny, W., Rosenberg, C. R., & White, T. (2018). Prevalence of autism spectrum disorder among children aged 8 years—Autism and developmental disabilities monitoring network, 11 sites, United States, 2014. *MMWR. Surveillance Summaries*, *67*(6), 1.

Baril, A., & Leblanc, C. (2015). Needing to acquire a physical impairment/disability:(re) thinking the connections between trans and disability studies through transability. *Hypatia*, *30*(1), 30–48. doi:10.1111/hypa.12113

Bawa, M. W. (2012). *Examination of leadership styles by gender: A case of Tamale Polytechnic.* Academic Press.

Beddington, J. R., Asaduzzaman, M., Bremauntz, F. A., Clark, M. E., Guillou, M., Jahn, M. M., Erda, L., Mamo, T., Van Bo, N., & Nobre, C. A. (2012). *Achieving food security in the face of climate change: Final report from the Commission on Sustainable Agriculture and Climate Change*. Academic Press.

Breman, B. A. S., Vihinen, H., Tapio-Biström, M.-L., & Pinto Correia, M. T. (2010). Meeting the challenge of marginalization processes at the periphery of Europe. *Public Administration*, *88*(2), 364–380. doi:10.1111/j.1467-9299.2010.01834.x

Cannarella, C. (2002). Processes of marginalization of agriculture: The role of non-agricultural sectors to support economic and social growth in rural areas. *Journal of Central European Agriculture*.

Chiru, S. S. (n.d.). Education and Development in India: Marginalizing the Margins. Editorial Board and Paper Review Committee, 6.

Co, N. O. (2021). *A Discourse on African Food Insecurity*. Academic Press.

Cramb, R. A., Colfer, C. J. P., Dressler, W., Laungaramsri, P., Le, Q. T., Mulyoutami, E., Peluso, N. L., & Wadley, R. L. (2009). Swidden transformations and rural livelihoods in Southeast Asia. *Human Ecology*, *37*(3), 323–346. doi:10.100710745-009-9241-6

Daalmans, J., & Daalmans, J. (2012). *Human behavior in hazardous situations: Best practice safety management in the chemical and process industries*. Butterworth-Heinemann.

Dahrouge, S., James, K., Gauthier, A., & Chiocchio, F. (2018). Engaging patients to improve equitable access to community resources. *Canadian Medical Association Journal*, *190*(Suppl), S46–S47. doi:10.1503/cmaj.180408 PMID:30404854

Danaher, M., Cook, J., Danaher, G., Coombes, P., & Danaher, P. A. (2013). Situating Education Research with Marginalized Communities. In *Researching Education with Marginalized Communities* (pp. 1–22). Springer.

de Boer, I. J. M., & van Ittersum, M. K. (2018). *Circularity in agricultural production*. Wageningen University and Research.

Dhawan, S. (2020). Online Learning: A Panacea in the Time of COVID-19 Crisis. *Journal of Educational Technology Systems*, *49*(1), 5–22. doi:10.1177/0047239520934018

Friederici, N., Wahome, M., & Graham, M. (2020). *Digital entrepreneurship in Africa: How a continent is escaping Silicon Valley's long shadow*. The MIT Press. doi:10.7551/mitpress/12453.001.0001

Gilleard, C., & Higgs, P. (2011). Frailty, disability and old age: A re-appraisal. *Health*, *15*(5), 475–490. doi:10.1177/1363459310383595 PMID:21169203

Gondchawar, N., & Kawitkar, R. S. (2016). IoT based smart agriculture. *International Journal of Advanced Research in Computer and Communication Engineering*, *5*(6), 838–842. doi:10.17148/IJARCCE.2016.56188

Grenier, M. (2010). Moving to inclusion: A socio-cultural analysis of practice. *International Journal of Inclusive Education*, *14*(4), 387–400. doi:10.1080/13603110802504598

Haenssgen, M. J. (2018). The struggle for digital inclusion : Phones, healthcare, and marginalisation in rural India. *World Development*, *104*, 358–374. doi:10.1016/j.worlddev.2017.12.023

Harrison, A., & Rodríguez-Clare, A. (2010). Trade, foreign investment, and industrial policy for developing countries. Handbook of Development Economics, 5, 4039–4214.

Howard, T. C. (2019). *Why race and culture matter in schools: Closing the achievement gap in America's classrooms*. Teachers College Press.

Hunter, B. M., & Murray, S. F. (2019). Deconstructing the financialization of healthcare. *Development and Change*, *50*(5), 1263–1287. doi:10.1111/dech.12517

Lee Dr, S. E. (2013). Education as a Human Right in the 21st Century. *Democracy & Education*, *21*(1), 1.

Levers, C., Schneider, M., Prishchepov, A. V., Estel, S., & Kuemmerle, T. (2018). Spatial variation in determinants of agricultural land abandonment in Europe. *The Science of the Total Environment*, *644*, 95–111. doi:10.1016/j.scitotenv.2018.06.326 PMID:29981521

Liu, D., Bhagat, K. K., Gao, Y., & Chang, T. (n.d.). *Virtual*. Augmented, and Mixed Realities in Education., doi:10.1007/978-981-10-5490-7

Mahlangu, G. (2020). *a Multi-Dimensional Model for Assessing E-Government Service Gaps Gaps in the Context of a Developing Country : A Critical Realist*. Academic Press.

Mavhunga, C. (2017). *What do science, technology, and innovation mean from Africa?* The MIT Press. doi:10.7551/mitpress/10769.001.0001

Musthafa, M. N., & Stephen, R. E. (2019). Education of the Marginalized; In the Context of Policy Initiatives for Universalization of Elementary Education. *International Journal of Research in Social Sciences*, *9*(7), 723–731.

Niță, A.-M., & Pârvu, M. C. (2020). Vulnerability and resilience in marginalized rural communities. Case study: projects for reduction of risk exclusion in Dolj County. *Revista de Stiinte Politice, 67*, 103–117. https://www.proquest.com/scholarly-journals/vulnerability-resilience-marginalized-rural/docview/2447285558/se-2?accountid=14166%0Ahttps://suny-alb.primo.exlibrisgroup.com/openurl/01SUNY_ALB/01SUNY_ALB:01SUNY_ALB?genre=articleandatitle=Vulnerability+and+resi

O'Donnell, P., Tierney, E., O'Carroll, A., Nurse, D., & MacFarlane, A. (2016). Exploring levers and barriers to accessing primary care for marginalized groups and identifying their priorities for primary care provision: A participatory learning and action research study. *International Journal for Equity in Health, 15*(1), 1–16. PMID:27912783

Poggiali, L. (2016). Seeing (from) digital peripheries: Technology and transparency in Kenya's silicon savannah. *Cultural Anthropology, 31*(3), 387–411. doi:10.14506/ca31.3.07

Price, S. (2009). Prologue: Victims or partners? The social perspective in development-induced displacement and resettlement. *The Asia Pacific Journal of Anthropology, 10*(4), 266–282. doi:10.1080/14442210903305821

Ramamoorthi, R., Jayaraj, R., Notaras, L., & Thomas, M. (2015). Epidemiology, etiology, and motivation of alcohol misuse among Australian Aboriginal and Torres Strait Islanders of the Northern Territory: A descriptive review. *Journal of Ethnicity in Substance Abuse, 14*(1), 1–11. doi:10.1080/15332640.2014.958642 PMID:25629929

Robards, F., Kang, M., Luscombe, G., Hawke, C., Sanci, L., Steinbeck, K., Zwi, K., Towns, S., & Usherwood, T. (2020). Intersectionality: Social marginalization and self-reported health status in young people. *International Journal of Environmental Research and Public Health, 17*(21), 8104. doi:10.3390/ijerph17218104 PMID:33153094

Roguski, M., & McBride-Henry, K. (2020). The failure of health promotion for marginalized populations. *Australian and New Zealand Journal of Public Health, 44*(6), 446–448. doi:10.1111/1753-6405.13048 PMID:33104285

Salsabila, U. H. (2019). A Preliminary Analysis: Digital Inclusion Domain in Islamic Education. *International Journal on E-Learning, 1*(1), 12–18. doi:10.31763/ijele.v1i1.23

Sandu, N., Gide, E., & Karim, S. (2019). Improving learning through cloud-based mobile technologies and virtual and augmented reality for australian higher education. *ACM International Conference Proceeding Series*, 1–5. 10.1145/3348400.3348413

SDG. (2019). Sustainable development goals. *The Energy Progress Report. Tracking SDG, 7.*

Spalevic, V., Lakicevic, M., Radanovic, D., Billi, P., Barovic, G., Vujacic, D., Sestras, P., & Khaledi Darvishan, A. (2017). Ecological-economic (Eco-Eco) modelling in the River Basins of Mountainous Regions: Impact of land cover changes on sediment yield in the Velicka Rijeka, Montenegro. *Notulae Botanicae Horti Agrobotanici Cluj-Napoca, 45*(2), 602–610. doi:10.15835/nbha45210695

Vera, E. M., Buhin, L., & Isacco, A. (2009). *The role of prevention in psychology's social justice agenda.* Academic Press.

von Braun, J., & Gatzweiler, F. W. (2014). Marginality—An overview and implications for policy. *Marginality,* 1.

Waldron, S. (2010). *Measuring subjective wellbeing in the UK.* Office for National Statistics.

Watkins, S. C. (2011). Digital divide: Navigating the digital edge. *International Journal of Learning and Media, 3*(2).

Wendelborg, C., & Tøssebro, J. (2010). Marginalization processes in inclusive education in Norway: A longitudinal study of classroom participation. *Disability & Society, 25*(6), 701–714. doi:10.1080/09687599.2010.505744

Yannopoulos, S. I., Grismer, M. E., Bali, K. M., & Angelakis, A. N. (2020). Evolution of the materials and methods used for subsurface drainage of agricultural lands from antiquity to the present. *Water (Basel), 12*(6), 1767. doi:10.3390/w12061767

## KEY TERMS AND DEFINITIONS

**Clusters:** Clusters are geographically concentrated societies.
**Digital Divide:** The gap between people with access to digital technologies and those that do not have.
**Digital Inclusion:** Gaining access to digital technologies.
**Digital Society:** A society that adopted Information technologies.
**Global Village:** A community that is linked by digital technology.
**Marginalization:** Areas that are excluded from social and economic activities.
**Modern Technologies:** Improvement of old technology.
**Societies:** A group of people.

# Chapter 10
# Opportunities, Challenges, and Digital Inclusion in Marginalized Societies

**Wilfreda Indira Chawarura**

https://orcid.org/0000-0003-0170-8003
*Midlands State University, Zimbabwe*

**Rukudzo Alyson Mawere**
*Midlands State University, Zimbabwe*

## ABSTRACT

*The developments in digital technology and information communication technology (ICT) have increased over the past 20 years and improved livelihoods, especially in developed countries with 97% access level to the internet and digital technology. However, those in African countries have had challenges accessing the internet, and the advent of the COVID-19 pandemic exacerbated the situation. The remote areas in Zimbabwe have not been spared as they experience challenges in the adoption of digital technology. Globally people are increasingly using information and communication technology (ICT) as a way of life to communicate, study, and access healthcare and entertainment, amongst other things. Investigating the causes of digital exclusion in general and also in the context of social exclusion in Zimbabwe is pertinent. This chapter seeks to fill a gap in the existing literature by exploring the opportunities and challenges that digital inclusion and exclusion bring to the marginalized societies in Zimbabwe.*

DOI: 10.4018/978-1-6684-3901-2.ch010

## INTRODUCTION

Digital transformation has become the apex of any society globally as all systems are progressively becoming digital; thus, more complex applications and technologies continue to be introduced to society and the economy (Galiardo, *et, al.* 2020; Gann, 2019). For the past thirty years, society and the economy have been characterized by digital knowledge, information and communication. (Alexio, *et, al.* 2012). However, though important and improving the livelihood of societies, the changes in technology had varying outcomes for different population subgroups (Gann., 2021). Technology has propelled the globe forward, but it has also revealed a divide and exclusion. (Alexio, *et, al.* 2012). The essence of digital inclusion is to leave no one behind as digital transformation soars in communities (Guenther, 2020).

Globally people are increasingly adopting Information and Communication Technology (ICT) as a way of life to communicate, study, access health care and entertainment, amongst other things. With the advent of Covid-19, the whole world went into lockdown to curb the spread of the novel virus. Life was restricted to digital means through ICT. The increased use of digital technology improved livelihoods, especially in developed countries with 97% internet access level. The adoption of electronic and digital devices such as smartphones, computers and laptops to share and store information increased significantly worldwide; however, some societies and ethnic groups were left behind, for example, in Africa, where internet access was below 45% on the advent of COVID-19 pandemic (Geodhart *et. al,* 2019; Rodriguez, *et. al,* 2022; Fang, *et. al,* 2019; Tsatsou,2020). Access to the internet and technology varies from country to country due to various factors, with the level of development in the country being a major determinant. Inability to have access and skill in technology use is termed the digital divide, and this digital divide affects who accesses and profits from digital inclusion (Fang et al., 2019, Van Dijk, 2017, Reddick et al 2020). Despite the prospect of enhancing everyday lives, the inaccessibility of ICTs has resulted in significant inequities with respect to who can access, use, and benefit from these interventions.

## BACKGROUND

Digital exclusion affects countries, societies, and gender differences; for example, in marginalized communities, access to the internet and digital devices such as smartphones and computers is still a challenge (Watts, 2020). Ali et al., (2020) found a significant relationship between social exclusion and digital exclusion, people who are socially excluded tend to be digitally excluded. Social exclusion includes lack of education, low income, unemployment, gender and age (Fang et al., 2018). People living in rural areas with little or no income and old people have challenges in accessing digital technologies (Ali et al., 2020; Gunnlaugsson et al., 2020; Helsper et al., 2008; Magis-Weinberg et al., 2021).). However, single young people and those with higher educational outcomes were digitally engaged regardless of being members of marginalized communities (Helsper et al., 2008).

The 21st-century digital revolution has changed how societies interact, learn and conduct business. Digital inclusion has become imperative to support the well-being and livelihood of all societies in this digital age. Digital inclusion ensures that all communities and societies have access to technology and are equipped with knowledge on how to use digital technologies for everyday use (Rodriguez, et. al, 2022). Ye & Yang (2020) defined digital inclusion as the appropriate and meaningful use of digital technologies by all stakeholders in society to improve social and economic relations. Featherstone, (2015), cited in (Guenther, 2020), comprehensively concludes that when societies are given the basic, affordable technology and are allowed to participate in economic and social development, their lives are changed for the better in totality, represents digital inclusion. Therefore, digital inclusion is an effort to involve everyone in every society in the digital developments to allow them to be updated with any global changes and to improve their quality of life. This concept has increasingly become the topic of debate in many countries such as Australia and China (Fang et. al, 2019; Ye & Yang, 2020).

Marginalized communities in Africa are faced with technology access and literacy challenges. Governments have tried to implement measures in such communities aimed at digital inclusion, but a greater population remains digitally excluded. During the COVID-19 pandemic, most countries, especially in Africa, implemented digital inclusion measures but these measures were mostly reactional to the global lockdowns. Marginalized communities, especially rural ones, were left out in digital inclusion measures and policies due to remoteness and economic marginalization that already affected such areas (Reddick et al 2020). Elderly people, people living with disability, farmers and school children in remote areas were left out of intervention measures implemented by Governments. Thus, they were unable to access digital technologies and the internet during the COVID-19 pandemic, thus further worsening the economic and social challenges they were already battling and creating or widening the digital divide. (Reddick et al, 2020).

Marginalized communities are mostly composed of women, unemployed, and racially and ethnically marginalized members of society. These people tend to be economically disadvantaged and cannot afford digital technologies. In developed countries such as the USA, there has been an increase in programes targeting marginalized communities and ethnicities to eradicate the digital divide. Such initiatives increased access to smartphone internet compared to home internet in disadvantaged communities. For example, in 2019, 19% of marginalized community members in the US had access to phone internet but lacked broadband. However, phone internet functional limitations are ineffective in solving inequality issues experienced in marginalized communities (Chen & Li, 2021).

## MAIN FOCUS OF THE CHAPTER

### Causes of Digital Exclusion

Most developing countries are in the first level of the digital divide, primarily about access to digital devices and the internet. In contrast, in developed countries, the digital divide is about skills, usage and general benefits (second and third-level digital divide) (Grun et al., 2020). However, the first-level digital divide remains a challenge in some of the technologically advanced societies in the world, Van Deursen & Van Dijk, (2019) observed that access to digital devices, remoteness of an area (Ali et al., 2020), ongoing maintenance expenses for hardware and software and subscription fees had an impact on existing inequalities related to internet skills, uses and outcomes. Technology deployment costs, profit-based discrimination, geographical disparities and socioeconomic factors play a significant role in digital inclusion. The digital divide is not limited to rural areas only but is prevalent within cities, as evidenced in low-income areas within cities, which are characterized by low broadband adoption rates (Reddick et al., 2020). Digital inequality emanates from lack of access and incompetence in most societies (Van Dijk, 2005). Certain people are excluded from access to the internet due to personal appearances, for example, blind people (Matthews et al., 2019). Digital inequalities are a reflection of the widening socioeconomic inequalities in societies. Most elderly people have been digitally excluded due to a lack of interest in technology, and other elderly people find the cost of internet installation outweighs the benefits of using it. However, some elderly people are keen on learning how to use technology and some even took some online courses to acquire technology skills (Matthews et al., 2019).

Greer, et. al (2019) have attributed the cause of the digital divide to a lack of knowledge. Their study found that most participants lacked knowledge of web-based services and how they could benefit from it. This lack of technology skills emanates from a lack of access to technological devices and the internet. The lack of expertise and knowledge made participants complacent on the use of technology; thus, community members remain in the dark without experiencing the full benefits of technology use. Lack of skills and technical capabilities disconnects the affected people and communities from the rest of the world and, resultantly, reduces professional growth, and access to necessary public systems and leaves children vulnerable.

The extent of digital exclusion varies from country to country, but marginalized communities and ethnicities are heavily affected, and their challenges are similar regardless of location. The urban and rural digital divide varies, with rural dwellers affected mostly by the first-level digital divide where they lack access to digital devices and the internet. In contrast, for people in cities, their main challenge is internet access and how to effectively utilize technology which is the second level of the digital divide (Gallardo et. al, 2020). Rural areas are characterized by poor internet and broadband infrastructure, and rural dwellers are often not equipped with ICT skills (Ye and Yang, 2020).

Digital redlining is the exclusion of broadband infrastructure in different communities, with the most common being rural communities and is prevalent in all countries regardless of economic status (Rodriguez, et. al, 2022). Nadaf (2021) revealed that controversial territories such as the area between India and Pakistan are deliberately left without internet access for political reasons. However, in Africa, redlining is due to lack of resources by Governments to fully put in place infrastructure in all parts of the country and are thus forced to only choose cities where there are more economic activities (Nedungadi et. al, 2018). Thus limited broadband infrastructure and steep prices for broadband accentuate the digital divide problem.

## Opportunities for Digital Inclusion

A digital economy enables access to digital services and technologies relevant to all sectors of the economy and society regardless of status. For example, creating relevant, useful, and friendly services to the two billion unbanked population (Hodgeson, 2017). An inclusive digital economy may boost the global economy by 6.7 trillion dollars and lift over 500 million people out of poverty (MIT solve, 2021).

A study by Tsatsou (2020) revealed that through digital inclusion, people living with disabilities could experience lower levels of stigma than they experience outside the use of digital technologies as they can connect with other people living with and without disabilities without any challenges. Such a connection increases a self-sense of belonging and improves their integration in society. People living with disabilities and the elderly have an opportunity to be included in mainstream development by being exposed to digital technology and being equipped with the relevant skills (Jolley et. al, 2017). Digital inclusion can impact how societies develop especially in the 4th Industrial Revolution (4IR). For instance, the integration of physical, biological and digital trends has given birth to cyber-physical systems, which have produced new economic and social realities. Big data, the internet of things, blockchain technology, and other digital platforms are at the forefront of the digital revolution creating new capabilities for manufacturers, consumers and suppliers to interact in novel ways (Gausi, 2021). Developing countries can improve their development trajectories by adopting 4IR technologies because these technologies offer new opportunities for both the economy and society. 4IR technologies positively affect economic growth in sub-Saharan Africa because the once excluded small to medium enterprises and informal traders can participate in e-commerce and social media adverting just like the multinational companies. However, rapid and excessive technological change can cause premature deindustrialization in low-income countries. Thus, the less developed countries should adopt appropriate technologies to achieve greater opportunities and tailor-make advancements and improvements (Myovella et al., 2020). The use of digital technology can improve the visibility and survival of small scale farmers and traders in times of economic crisis such as COVID-19. Digital inclusion help protect smallholder farmers from unscrupulous middlemen and shortens the supply chain (Quayson et al., 2020). However, digital inclusion for marginalized farmers depends on implementation strategy, collaborations and investment by both the farmer and other stakeholders (Quayson et al., 2020).

Digital inclusion in educational settings unifies diverse students from different backgrounds, thus levelling the playfield for every student. However, this is not an automatic process as a lot of intentional work needs to be cultivated to achieve the same (Juvonen, et. al, 2019). Online courses have opened a huge opportunity for marginalized students to participate in all the activities laid out for them and improve their future employment prospects. In higher education, the usage of Massive Open Online Courses has been noted to improve educational quality with the support of digital and face to face options (Lambert, 2020). Matthews et al. (2019) observed that digital inclusion in the elder population is beneficial, especially when their health starts to deteriorate. Internet usage reduced feelings of loneliness and isolation among elderly people, and it improved their mental well-being. During the COVID-19 pandemic, some governments lowered the broadband rates for senior citizens to ensure they could access online services such as online shopping, banking and communication because they were susceptible to the disease (Xie et. al, 2020). A study by Greer et. al, (2019) highlighted that mental health problems could be alleviated through the use of mental health management systems. These systems manage patient information, remind caregivers of medication times and necessary check-ups, etc. With the health systems going digital, marginalized communities must be included and partake in the changes that improve their livelihood.

Digital services have also increased in Finnish prisons, where their use has improved the quality of life of the incarcerated (Jarvelainen & Rantanen, 2021). Though confined to the prison and separated from the rest of the world, prisoners can receive health care, education, and social support. Prison services can be improved through digital therapies and peer support groups (Jarvelainen & Rantanen, 2021). The same could apply to those with substance abuse problems, a situation that has become rampant in most developing countries in Africa.

## Challenges of Digital Exclusion

Disparities in digital inclusion reflect economic disparities among individuals (Van Dijk, 2005). Half of the world's population does not have access to the internet, and the majority are in developing countries. Some of the digital technology developments have failed to yield both social and economic development. For example, a study by Brunat, 2020 showed that young people aged between 18 to 35 years used mobile money mostly for online gaming and television subscriptions.

Access to technology is a formidable challenge in marginalized communities, and a lack of skills is prevalent among members. Programmes aimed at eradicating digital exclusion have been polled in many countries. However, the expectations of participants of such programmes are mostly unknown. This uncertainty in expectations affects the outcomes of digital inclusion programmes (Chen & Li, 2021). In Australia, COVID-19 was a driver in digital transformation but failed to be a strong driver of digital inclusion, but the pandemic reinforced the use of digital technologies to already established users such as children and the urban population (Thomas et al., 2021). Residents in marginalized communities are concerned about their children's digital lives. However, children are not taking the initiative to train their elders on how the digital world operates. Digital inequality can be eradicated through basic digital training and educational advancement in disadvantaged communities (Chen & Li, 2021).

The differentials in access to computers and internet resources for education between students in urban and rural areas increases the digital divide and remains a challenge for Higher education in Africa. Individual economic challenges affected digital inclusion, Lembani et. al (2019) unearthed that most students in the urban areas had home access to education, whereas those in rural areas could not access education during COVID-19 lockdowns. Such challenges bring about other ripple effects, such as the inability to apply for online jobs, affecting future employment prospects (Geodhart et. al, 2019).

A study by Haensggen, (2018) revealed that the adoption of mobile phone usage in health care systems posed an opportunity for better access to health care in rural communities. However, the disadvantaged members of communities remained marginalized, without access to healthcare. Greer, et. al, (2019) revealed that many patients with mental health challenges are excluded from accessing digital technologies in the United Kingdom (UK) as they are prone to different conditions such as relapses, hallucinations and memory lapses.

## Role of Government and Other Stakeholders in Digital Inclusion

Government partnerships with other organizations such as enterprises and financiers have proven to eradicate or narrow the digital divide by establishing infrastructure that enables access to digital tools (Ye and Yang, 2020). These ICT enabled developments ensure successful digital inclusion because they incorporate supportive policy formulation and resources that facilitate infrastructure establishment. A study by Hanna, (2018) revealed that governments ameliorate the livelihood of the disadvantaged through developing and nurturing synergistic relationships amongst all digital service providers. The role of government is to align all partners in service provision to provide access and skills to the general populace to remove the digital divide.

Hanna, (2018) suggests the creation of legal frameworks that govern the use of the internet to protect users from cybercrimes such as bullying, fraud and identify theft, amongst other crimes. During the COVID-19 pandemic, there was an increase in cybercrimes, with children and the elderly being major victims.

Government policies should emphasize digital skills training, leading to greater proficiency in digital skills. Such measures can encourage community members to advance learning; for example, African countries such as Rwanda started a national coding academy aimed at expanding digital skills amongst its people (Chen & Li, 2021). There is a need to revamp and improve the educational systems in Africa to incorporate ICT education in the classroom; for example, in Zimbabwe ICT education is now starting from primary school.

In cases where financial costs have impeded digital technologies, the government could offer accessible sources of internet-enabled technology, for example, in libraries and public spaces Greer, et. al, (2019). Rural areas, if not offered the same options, may remain excluded. However, the government may extend the same initiatives to rural areas if it is paralleled with electricity access development initiatives. The synergistic partnerships between the government and private players may come in handy to eradicate these challenges. Greer, et. al, (2019) indicate that these free-internet spaces could be temporary or permanent depending on the country's financial position and the number of individuals requiring the support; hence it would be wise to assess the situation before any commitments are then made.

Policy formulation by governments in terms of digital inclusion should be done to improve the lives of the general populace. A study done by Rodriguez, et. al, (2022) reveals that policy formulation on technological infrastructure investment results in sustainable digital inclusion, which assures that everyone gets access and is equipped with the necessary skills to function in society. For example, the

Australian government implemented the healthcare homes programme to improve access to people with chronic health conditions.

Government policy should have a control function to ensure successful implementation. Standard evaluation and monitoring of policies that have been formulated and implemented should be done at national and regional levels to enforce the inclusion of digital technologies in marginalized societies (Jolley, 2017).

Digital inclusion improves the quality of life, and policymakers should include both supply-side strategies such as increased telecommunication infrastructure in socio-economically disadvantaged communities and demand-side strategies such as meeting the needs and requirements of the community to improve digital inclusion in marginalized communities (Ali et al., 2020).

Matthews et al., (2019) concluded that there was a relationship between age and socioeconomic circumstances. Poor elders in marginalized communities tend to be socially isolated. Elders with a disability could benefit from self-serving technology such as online banking and shopping. Such activities will improve their livelihoods and health; thus, the government must create digitally inclusive policies, especially for the poor elderly population. Such policies will improve the quality of life for both the elderly and the younger generations.

## RESEARCH METHODS

The researchers used both questionnaires and interviews in this study. The researchers conducted 200 interviews in marginalized and remote communities in Zimbabwe, and 100 questionnaires were sent out to poor neighborhoods in Harare and Gweru. Remote areas which the researchers targeted were Muzarabani and Binga. These communities were the best fit for the study because the researchers wanted to understand if the digital inclusion challenges and opportunities faced by city dwellers and remote area residents were the same.

## Research Findings

The causes of the digital divide varied slightly between city dwellers and remote area inhabitants. People living in marginalized communities in Zimbabwe faced the first level of the digital divide as they had challenges in accessing digital technologies due to poverty and illiteracy. Remote areas in Zimbabwe are characterized by poor to no telecommunication infrastructure and a lack of digital devices. People in remote rural areas had no access to the internet, and those areas had poor network reception due to poor telecommunication infrastructure coupled with illiteracy.

Individual economic situations significantly influenced the ability to access digital technology. Elderly respondents viewed technology devices as luxuries, whereas city dwellers could not afford digital technology, although they strongly desired access to technology. Poor communities were digitally excluded because they could not afford digital devices. Those with smartphones noted that these devices were poor receptors of poor networks; instead, the respondents pointed out that they preferred old phones, which at least enabled them to communicate with relatives and loved ones more than smartphones in remote areas.

Ninety percent of the research participants believed that their livelihoods would significantly improve once they had access to digital technology through digital inclusion. The respondents in rural areas believed that they would be able to buy and sell their products to other countries online. During the COVID-19 pandemic, 90% of rural farmers were unable to sell their produce profitably, and they ended up selling to middlemen who were ripping them off; hence they were keen on being digitally included so they could sell their produce on the internet or WhatsApp groups (Quayson et al., 2020). Most marginalized communities are hounded by middlemen who come to buy their goods at very low prices, but people can look for better markets for their products and develop their livelihoods through digital inclusion.

Young people in marginalized communities believed that access to digital technologies especially smartphones and the internet could assist them in learning new skills through YouTube and other free open-access learning platforms (Lambert, 2020). This access would improve their future employment prospect because 80% of the young respondents believed their education was inadequate to make them competitive in the employment market because they were not economically connected to important people in the industry (Juvonen, et. al, 2019). Other respondents, especially young people, believed that they would be able to learn new skills using technology through digital inclusion.

The major reason given by elderly marginalized members of the communities for accessing digital technology was the need to be able to keep in touch with loved ones in other parts of the country or the world. Some participants believed that having access to technologies would help herald their challenges, and plights and increased their chances to be heard as they would be able to effectively participate in social discussions, 75% of the respondents in rural areas believed the challenges they faced as communities were not being considered in the decision making process of the country.

Rural young people were eager and willing to have digital technologies because they felt isolated from what was happening to their peers in towns whereas the elderly members of the community especially in rural areas were not keen on accepting digital inclusion because they believed technology was eroding their values and core belief system as a society. Elderly members of the communities viewed digital technology as a threat to their belief systems for example a traditional leader in Muzarabani viewed technology as a tool being used to lure and trap the young people from their traditional ways of living. Regardless of poor network connectivity in most remote areas, 5% of the elderly population interviewed did not own any digital technologies voluntarily.

City dwelling respondents had better access to digital technologies; however, the quality of their gadgets was poor, primarily mostly because they bought their gadgets as second-hand products or received them as gifts from relatives. During the COVID-19 pandemic, 95% of school-going respondents were affected in their learning due to a lack of devices and lack of internet data, and learners in remote areas in Zimbabwe were the worst affected as they failed even to access radio lessons. Erratic electricity supply worsened the situation for all residents in marginalized communities in Zimbabwe.

Young people in marginalized communities believed that they lacked critical technology skills, which are mandatory in the 21st century; hence they were most unlikely to get employment in well-paying jobs. 90% of the young respondents in marginalized areas were not confident in their future employment prospects.

The researchers observed that digital inclusion posed a danger of laziness and addiction amongst young people. Some young people were now addicted to pornography, online gambling, drugs, and alcohol, and others got caught up trying to keep up with social media (Brunat, 2020). On the other hand, digital inclusion could be used as a weapon to eradicate poverty, especially in marginalized communities in Zimbabwe. With proper infrastructure in place, the government could train communities on how to utilize technology to their advantage. For example, effectively, people could learn new trades or enhance existing trades through technology and enhance their livelihoods (Lambert, 2020).

The government of Zimbabwe has introduced information communication and technology learning into the school curriculum from primary school. This initiative by the government aims to eradicate the existing digital divide in various communities. However, the researchers observed that participants were not happy with the initiative as a stand-alone because their children did not have the devices necessary for the successful implementation of the programme. The students in marginalized communities lacked practical knowledge of digital technologies. Hence they were not on the same footing as learners from the cities. This disparity was also evident during the COVID-19 pandemic, where learners in marginalized communities both in the city and rural areas had no access to education because they did not have access to digital technology. Digital disparity affected marginalized communities and made it difficult for them to get out of the vicious cycle of poverty. This digital inclusion could be the solution to eradicating poverty in marginalized communities because everyone is equal in the digital world.

Schools in remote areas did not have access to electricity, expert ICT teachers and computers for students and learners to use. This lack ensured that students from remote areas struggled academically and were illiterate in the 21st-century critical learning skills. However, donors and the government of Zimbabwe have donated computers to some schools in marginalized communities, but the resources are insufficient to cover all community members, and some of the computers are now old and obsolete.

## SOLUTIONS AND RECOMMENDATIONS

Government should engage in public-private initiatives to ensure all areas have access to telecommunication infrastructure and ensure that marginalized communities are digitally included. The government may also seek to form partnerships with other organizations with technological infrastructure and financiers. These synergistic partnerships can lead to the establishment of basic and relevant infrastructure to ensure affordable and robust broadband and access in rural communities and other communities that do not have access. The role of government is to align all partners in service provision to provide access and skills to the general populace to remove the digital divide.

There is a need for training both students, economic young people and parents on how to efficiently utilize technology for their economic benefits. This training will assist in ensuring that members of society will use technology productively to improve their livelihoods. Training will enable parents how to monitor their children's internet usage. Legal frameworks can also be formulated to ensure cyber security is enforced. Cyberbullying, which has been rampant across the globe will be reduced, and these marginalized communities may not be exposed to it.

All stakeholders in the community need to plough back into their communities. Community members need to pull resources into community development trusts to develop their areas economically. Legislators representing marginalized areas need to lobby and work tirelessly to attract investment into such areas.

Implementation of mobile digital libraries in remote areas, where community members can access computers and are taught how to use technology to benefit their day-to-day lives. Additionally, free-internet sources could be placed in the mobile digital libraries in areas with low incomes to allow everyone in those areas to access internet services fully. Such programs equip students with critical skills they will need for future employment and business.

## FUTURE RESEARCH DIRECTIONS

In Zimbabwe, digital inclusion is still a long way, especially in marginalized communities. Thus, it is imperative to constantly research the progress of the programs being implemented both in schools and communities to see if the gap in livelihoods between the economically abled members of society and marginalized members is being eradicated. Another area that needs to be looked at is analyzing the effects of digital inclusion on employment prospects for students from marginalized communities. The limitations of this study are the focus was mainly on rural dwellers as the marginalized community. Further studies may comparatively focus on high-income and low-income earners in the urban areas and how the digital divide can be reduced. Additionally, other marginalized communities such as the disabled, mentally challenged, incarcerated and children can be focused on.

## CONCLUSION

The researchers concluded that digital inclusion posed great benefits to all members of marginalized communities in Zimbabwe. The digital world levelled the playing field for marginalized and wealthy people; thus, policies should be put in place to ensure that marginalized communities are digitally included. Marginalized communities' livelihoods could significantly improve through trading directly with their markets, and the communities could showcase the uniqueness of their culture and habitat to the world through digital inclusion. Training in digital technologies could assist parents in disadvantaged communities track their children's activities online. Future employment prospects for school levers in marginalized communities improved through digital inclusion.

## REFERENCES

Aleixo, C., Nunes, M., & Isaias, P. (2012). Usability and Digital Inclusion: Standards and Guidelines. *International Journal of Public Administration*, *35*(3), 221–239. doi:10.1080/01900692.2011.646568

Ali, M. A., Alam, K., & Taylor, B. (2019). Do social exclusion and remoteness explain the digital divide in Australia? Evidence from a panel data estimation approach. *Economics of Innovation and New Technology*, 1–17. doi:10.1080/1043 8599.2019.1664708

Ali, M. A., Alam, K., Taylor, B., & Rafiq, S. (2020). Does digital inclusion affect quality of life? Evidence from Australian household panel data. *Telematics and Informatics*, *51*, 101405. doi:10.1016/j.tele.2020.101405

Chen, W., & Li, X. (2021). Digital inequalities in American disadvantaged urban communities: Access, skills, and expectations for digital inclusion programs. *Information Communication and Society*, 1–18. doi:10.1080/136911 8X.2021.1907434

Dijk, J. A. G. M. (2005). Digital Divide: Impact of Access. In P. Rössler, C. A. Hoffner, & L. Zoonen (Eds.), *The International Encyclopedia of Media Effects* (1st ed., pp. 1–11). Wiley., doi:10.1002/9781118783764.wbieme0043

Fang, M. L., Canham, S. L., Battersby, L., Sixsmith, J., Wada, M., & Sixsmith, A. (2019, February). Exploring privilege in the digital divide: Implications for theory, policy, and practice. *The Gerontologist*, *59*(1), e1–e15. doi:10.1093/geront/gny037 PMID:29750241

Gallardo, R., Bo Beaulieu, L., & Geideman, C. (2020). Digital inclusion and parity: Implications for community development. *Community Development (Columbus, Ohio)*. Advance online publication. doi:10.1080/15575330.2020.1830815

Gann, B. (2019). Digital Inclusion and Health in Wales. *Journal of Consumer Health on the Internet*, *23*(2), 146–160. doi:10.1080/15398285.2019.1608499

Goedhart, N. S., Broerse, J. E. W., Kattouw, R., & Dedding, C. (2019). *Just having a computer doesn't make sense': The digital divide from the perspective of mothers with a low socioeconomic position.* Academic Press.

Greer, B., Robotham, D., Simblett, S., Curtis, H., Griffiths, H., & Wykes, T. (2019). Digital Exclusion Among Mental Health Service Users: *Qualitative Investigation. Journal of Medical Internet Research*, *21*(1), e11696. doi:10.2196/11696 PMID:30626564

Guenther, J., Smede, B., & Young, M. (2020). Digital inclusion in central Australia: What is it and what makes it different? *Rural Society*, *29*(3), 154–170. Advance online publication. doi:10.1080/10371656.2020.1819524

Gunnlaugsson, G., Whitehead, T. A., Baboudóttir, F. N., Baldé, A., Jandi, Z., Boiro, H., & Einarsdóttir, J. (2020). Use of Digital Technology among Adolescents Attending Schools in Bissau, Guinea-Bissau. *International Journal of Environmental Research and Public.*

Helsper, E. J. (2008). *Digital inclusion: An analysis of social disadvantage and the information society*. Department for Communities and Local Government. http://www.communities.gov.uk/documents/communities/pdf/digitalinclusionanalysis

Hodgeson, C. (2017). *The world unbanked population*. https://www.businessinsider.com/the-worlds-unbanked-population-in-6-charts-2017-8

Jolley, E., Lynch, P., Virendrakumar, B., Rowe, S., & Schmidt, E. (2017). Education and social inclusion of people with disabilities in five countries in West Africa: A literature review. *Disability and Rehabilitation*, 1–9. doi:10.1080/09638288.2017.1353649 PMID:28705016

Juvonen, J., Lessard, L. M., Rastogi, R., Schacter, H. L., & Smith, D. S. (2019). Promoting Social Inclusion in Educational Settings: Challenges and Opportunities. *Educational Psychologist*, *54*(4), 250–270. doi:10.1080/00461520.2019.1655645

Lambert, S. R. (2020, February). Do MOOCs contribute to student equity and social inclusion? A systematic review 2014–18. *Computers & Education Volume*, *145*, 103693. doi:10.1016/j.compedu.2019.103693

Lembani, R., Gunter, A., Breines, M., & Dalu, M. T. B. (2019). The same course, different access: The digital divide between urban and rural distance education students in South Africa. *Journal of Geography in Higher Education*, 1–15. doi:10.1080/03098265.2019.1694876

Magis-Weinberg, L., Ballonoff Suleiman, A., & Dahl, R. E. (2021). Context, Development, and Digital Media: Implications for Very Young Adolescents in LMICs. *Frontiers in Psychology*, *12*, 632713. doi:10.3389/fpsyg.2021.632713 PMID:33967899

Matthews, K., Nazroo, J., & Marshall, A. (2019). Digital inclusion in later life: Cohort changes in internet use over a ten-year period in England. *Ageing and Society*, *39*(9), 1914–1932. doi:10.1017/S0144686X18000326

Myovella, G., Karacuka, M., & Haucap, J. (2020). Digitalization and economic growth: A comparative analysis of Sub-Saharan Africa and OECD economies. *Telecommunications Policy*, *44*(2), 101856. doi:10.1016/j.telpol.2019.101856

Nadaf, A. H. (2021, June). Lockdown Within a Lockdown: The "Digital Redlining" and paralyzed online teaching during COVID-19 in Kashmir, A Conflict Territory. *Communication, Culture & Critique*, *14*(2), 343–346. doi:10.1093/ccc/tcab019

Nedungadi, P. P., Menon, R., Gutjahr, G., Erickson, L., & Raman, R. (2018). Towards an inclusive digital literacy framework for digital India. *Education + Training*, *60*(6), 516–528. doi:10.1108/ET-03-2018-0061

Quayson, M., Bai, C., & Osei, V. (2020). Digital Inclusion for Resilient Post-COVID-19 Supply Chains: Smallholder Farmer Perspectives. *IEEE Engineering Management Review*, *48*(3), 104–110. doi:10.1109/EMR.2020.3006259

Rantanen, T., Järveläinen, E., & Leppälahti, T. (2021). Prisoners as Users of Digital Health Care and Social Welfare Services: A Finnish Attitude Survey. *International Journal of Environmental Research and Public Health, 18*(11), 5528. doi:10.3390/ijerph18115528

Reddick, C. G., Enriquez, R., Harris, R. J., & Sharma, B. (2020). Determinants of broadband access and affordability: An analysis of a community survey on the digital divide (Vol 106). doi:10.1016/j.cities.2020.102904

Reisdorf, B., & Rhinesmith, C., (2020). Digital Inclusion as a Core Component of Social Inclusion. In *Digital Inclusion Across the Globe: What Is Being Done to Tackle Digital Inequities*. Academic Press.

Rodriguez, J. A., Shachar, C., & Bates, D. W. (2022). Digital Inclusion as Health Care; Supporting Health Care Equity with Digital-Infrastructure Initiatives. *The New England Journal of Medicine*, *386*(12), 1101–1103. doi:10.1056/NEJMp2115646 PMID:35302722

Sharp, M. (2022). *Revisiting digital inclusion: A survey of theory, measurement and recent research*. https://www.bsg.ox.ac.uk/sites/default/files/202204/Revisiting%20digital%20inclusion-%20A%20survey%20of%20theory%2C%20measurement%20and%20recent%20research.pdf

Thomas, J., Barraket, J., & Parkinson, S. (2021). *Measuring Australia's digital divide: The Australian digital inclusion index 2021*. RMIT University. doi:10.25916/PHGW-B725ALI

Tsatsou, P. (2020). Is digital inclusion fighting disability stigma? Opportunities, barriers, and recommendations. *Disability & Society*. Advance online publication. doi:10.1080/09687599.2020.1749563

van Deursen, A. J., & van Dijk, J. A. (2019). The first-level digital divide shifts from inequalities in physical access to inequalities in material access. *New Media & Society*, *21*(2), 354–375. doi:10.1177/1461444818797082 PMID:30886536

Watts, G. (2020). COVID-19 and the digital divide in the UK. *The Lancet. Digital Health*, *2*(8), e395–e396. doi:10.1016/S2589-7500(20)30169-2 PMID:32835198

Xie, B., Charness, N., Fingerman,K., Kaye, J., Kim, M. T., & Khurshid, A. (n.d.). *When going digital becomes a necessity: Ensuring older adults' needs for information, services, and social inclusion during COVID-19*. doi:10.1080/08959420.2020.1771237

Ye, L., & Yang, H. (2020). From digital divide to social inclusion: A tale of mobile platform empowerment in rural areas. *Sustainability*, *12*(6), 2424. doi:10.3390u12062424

## KEY TERMS AND DEFINITIONS

**Digital Divide:** The gap that is created between those who can access digital technologies and those who cannot.

**Digital Exclusion:** Deprivation of digital technologies to some or selected communities.

**Digital Inclusion:** Engaging all communities and societies to have access and skills to use digital technologies.

**Digital Redlining:** Exclusion of broadband infrastructure in different communities with the most common being rural communities is prevalent in all countries regardless of economic status.

**Information Communication Technology:** The use of electronic and digital devices such as smartphones, computers and laptops to share and store information.

**Marginalized Communities:** Societies or groups that are deprived or excluded from social and economic activities.

Chapter 11

# The Global Digital Divide and Digital Transformation:
## The Benefits and Drawbacks of Living in a Digital Society

**Tendai Shelton Muwani**
*Manicaland State University of Applied Sciences, Zimbabwe*

**Njodzi Ranganai**
*Manicaland State University of Applied Sciences, Zimbabwe*

**Lemias Zivanai**
*Midlands State University, Zimbabwe*

**Briget Munyoro**
*Midlands State University, Zimbabwe*

## ABSTRACT

*The use of digital gadgets and services is pervasive. Digitalization in data, information, and technologies is driving the Fourth Industrial Revolution (also known as 4IR or Industry 4.0), resulting in a global digital divide. The chapter proposes a strategy in collaboration with a variety of service sector partners that would allow governments to capitalize on the possibility of closing the technology gap between nations in a manner that benefits inclusive and sustainable growth in middle and low countries. Emerging revolution and internet access can strengthen socio-economic development and improve people's way of living, but they also have the potential to widen political divides, undermine democracy, and increase inequality. In response to COVID-19, the chapter also proposes digital technologies as tools for achieving sustainable development goals and digitalization response measures in marginalized societies.*

DOI: 10.4018/978-1-6684-3901-2.ch011

## INTRODUCTION

The global digital divide describes global imbalances, typically among industrialized and developing economies, in access to information and communication technology and infrastructure resources such as Internet connectivity, as well as the advantages gained from such access (Van Deursen & Van Dijk, 2019). The concept "digital divide" refers to the gap between those who benefit from new technologies and those who do not (Van Dijk, 2017). The global digital divide can be caused by variances in revenue and academic achievement; others with low incomes and those with low educational attainment are less likely to use IT (Manstead, 2018). The global digital divide is characterized by the digital gap between developed and less developed countries this is often referred to as the urban-rural divide at the national level (Wang et al., 2021). Not just that, but this can also refer to the high frequency of information flow into major cities or urban areas in just about all emerging regions, as opposed to rural and local communities (Salemink et al., 2017). The use of digital gadgets and services is all-pervasive. Even though not fully appreciated, technology is reshaping nations worldwide in terms of government, industry, trade, culture, and how people live and interact daily. Technological progress surpasses policies and regulations' ability to create safeguards and increase the likelihood that it will be used for good rather than evil. Emerging revolution and internet access can strengthen socio-economic development and improve people's way of living, but they also have the potential to widen political divides, undermine democracy, and increase inequality (Cruz-Jesus et al., 2018). To digitally translate their marginalised groups, developing-country states must first ensure that the particular needs of disadvantaged people are comprehended and built through into design of new technology infrastructure (Viale Pereira et al., 2020). Infrastructure and applications must be built, and regulations must be established to ensure that underprivileged groups have access and digital literacy to avoid falling further behind Dawadi, S., et al (2020). The section presents the digital divide, how the digital revolution promotes sustainable development in marginalized societies and government policies that promote global technology adoption, and the benefits and challenges of living in a digital society.

## BACKGROUND

Digital innovation seems to have a significant impact on society that previous interventions could only dream of, thanks to its ease of implementation and scalability (Panori et al., 2021). Data solutions and millisecond data travel distances can serve local, national, and global populations at the same time. It allows hitherto inconceivable communication and collaboration between physically distant groups (the gap in society between individuals, including dimensions such as social class, religion or ethnicity, gender, or sexuality) (Ingram, 2021). Traditional modes of communication, corporate understanding, how people perform at home and at work, and possibly even governance are being impacted by digitalization. By broadening and deepening access to data and communication services, lowering operational expenditure, increasing productivity and efficiency, fostering economic growth, enabling financial intermediation, developing innovative or robust solutions, and lowering technology costs, it is improving openness and transparency, as well as citizen-government interaction. Covid-19 has proven its ability to provide factual information in charitable and stressful events (Commission, 2019).

On a personal and national level, as the Internet spreads worldwide, it creates a divide between those 0who have access to it and those who do not. This is known as the "**digital divide**," and it is a major concern for many people and nations worldwide (Ingram, 2021). The digital divide is defined as inequalities in access to and use of computer-based technology infrastructure. ICT access (Ilevbare, 2019) is defined as the affordability of hardware, software, applications, and connectivity and the usability of ICT devices and systems. Software and operating systems are examples, as are web-based information and applications such as remote learning, as well as telephones and other telecommunications equipment. The divide can span nations, regions, or even communities. This can be mitigated by a massive shift in business and organizational operations, procedures, proficiencies, and approaches to fully impact the opportunities available of a bunch of modern innovations and their advancing implications all over society in a tactical and given preference manner, taking into account both immediate and long-term shifts. This is known as digital transition and is critical to reducing the global digital divide. As a result of digital transformation, not only how businesses are perceived but also how they operate, the business world is changing.

When done correctly, digital transformation can also increase a company's efficiency and profitability. Digital transformation is creating unprecedented opportunities for innovation across all industries. Covid-19 sparked cultural shifts all over the entire globe when it was released. Industries decided to look into ways to continue their operations digitally due to the internet. Technology was seen as a significant instrument for interacting with clients, enabling some work flexibility and automating business procedures (Fernandez & Aman, 2018). People are at the center of products and services thanks to digital technology, which empowers them. It provides students with low-cost education and learning materials, real-time seasonal changes and market data for underserved subsistence farmers, teacher training, clinical issues and information for those living in remote areas, and investment management previously unavailable to underserved populations. Cross-border data transmission is expanding quickly and widely. This industry attracted more interest than traditional traded products in 2014, accounting for $2.8 trillion in national GDP. They are expected to be worth $11 trillion by 2025 (Sharpe, 2016). Digital platforms, including e-commerce, electronic content, and e-services, generated $3.8 trillion in revenue in 2019, with emerging markets accounting for $1 trillion of that total (Santarita, 2021).

The global digital divide refers to the disparities in access to technology and information internet resources, including the opportunities that come with such access, primarily between developed and developing economies (Cruz-Jesus et al., 2018). On a global scale, this gap, like a smaller level of analysis, describes an existing inequality. The global economy will continue to be disrupted and transformed by digital technologies (Schwertner, 2017). Countries of all economic levels will be affected by this.

Prior to actually quantifying the influence of digital connectivity on marginalized people in the developing world, it is crucial to know the precise level of acceptance and use of ICT tools (Kraus et al., 2021). Other next steps that must be recognized for digital connectivity to have a significant impact in these communities include training and usability (Radovanović et al., 2020). Closing the global digital divide and ensuring equitable access to technologies are unavoidable, as digitally enabled living has possible ramifications for alleviating poverty, education, health, social well-being, and general wellbeing (Aruleba & Jere, 2022). It is crucial to highlight that digital skills offer a good platform for poverty alleviation and act as catalysts (Urvashi et al., 2017). In the medium term, the effects of the global digital revolution will be felt across all industries. It will impact every aspect of life, including work, leisure, and connectivity.

## GLOBAL DIGITAL DIVIDE AND DIGITAL TRANSFORMATION

The global digital divide pertains to country-to-country inequality in access to technology and information (ICTs). ICT access disparity is the first-order digital divide, while ICT use inequality is the second-order digital divide (Ilevbare, 2019). The digital divide has geographical, social group, and socio-economic components. There are certain imbalances between ICT "haves" and "have-nots" in wealthy countries, just as in developing countries today. Half of the population still does not have access to the internet, and a billion population does not have access to power supply, posing a significant barrier to digitization (United Nations, 2019). Due to the general constant advancement of technology and the creation of new technological innovations, inequity is a fluid problem. Many of the access disparities are based on geography (**see figure 1**).

*Figure 1. The Internet is still unavailable or prohibitively expensive for the majority of the population. High-speed Internet (broadband) includes fixed-line broadband subscriptions as well as 4G/LTE mobile subscriptions*
Source: (Group, 2016)

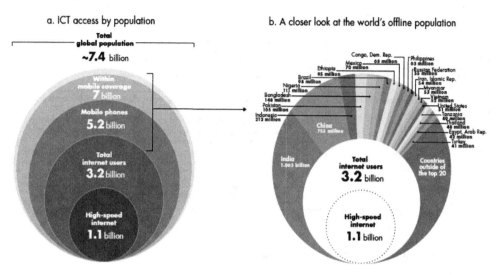

The digital transformation has been hailed as a panacea for raising living standards in economies with low and moderate-income, for instance, in developing countries. Inequalities are widening in the aftermath of the COVID-19 global epidemic, emphasizing the importance and urgency of this issue. As a result of technological transformation like meeting customers in digital channels, developing countries can now implement communications and banking solutions. Legislators should concentrate their efforts on ensuring universal hardware and software, which will necessitate investments in facilities and free software, such as smart grids, resulting in sustainable production and consumption. Education-related policies must be prioritized to make sure people, societies, and states stand to gain from digital transformation. Although the precepts of a digitalization that promotes sustainability were yet to be fully explored, some of the most likely priority areas and example measures can be seen in the Table 1. It highlights the principles for digital transformation as well key results areas for measurements for the performance.

While technological innovation is unavoidable, there is still uncertainty about where it will go, which aspects of technological advancement will thrive, for what specific purpose, and to whose greatest advantage. To gain a better understanding of technological systems, more research is required. It is possible to identify appealing alternatives and legislation that will accelerate society's transformation

*Table 1. Principles for digital transformation*

| Principles for digital transformation | Example measures |
|---|---|
| Enabling digital infrastructure, further expansion, and innovations | • Universal access to high-quality, low-cost mobile broadband |
| Online services | • Online governance to support public services and participation<br>• Online finance and payments to facilitate trade and business services<br>• Regulatory security for online identity and privacy<br>• Online national systems (or "platforms") for health care and education |
| Digital systems to increase efficiency of resource use | • Smart grids and Internet of Things for sustainable cities |
| Analytical packages for exploration and monitoring | • Income redistribution to address income inequalities arising from digital scale-up<br>• Tax and regulatory systems to avoid monopolization of Internet services<br>• Democratic oversight of cutting-edge technologies (biotech, nanotech, artificial intelligence, big data, autonomous systems)<br>• Universal access to high-quality, low-cost mobile broadband education to avoid new digital divides and to develop capacities for sustainable digitalization<br>• Aligning the emerging digital technologies and infrastructures with human norms and the paradigm of sustainable development |

toward a sustainable future by studying the trends, drivers, barriers, and impacts of technological progress (Figure 2).

Digital transformation can occur only if the technological advances approach those who are reportedly excluded. Prospect and more digitalization may exacerbate now existing divides if not managed properly. However, if properly managed, it has the potential to connect people and societies while also facilitating cross-border inclusion. The promise of social, political, and financial inclusion cannot be realized if we ignore existing inequalities. Digitalization is expected to have a significant impact on societies and economies, and it will be a prerequisite for the six major transformations required to meet the SDG targets by 2030: Human capital development; sustainable consumption and production; a carbon-free energy system; good health, reasonably priced food, and clean water; smart development and societies; and a digital government.

## ACHIEVING SUSTAINABLE DEVELOPMENT GOALS

Digital technologies are increasingly becoming a major driving force in marginalized communities' development (Craglia, 2018; Domingos, 2015). The transition to sustainable development must be coordinated with the Digital Revolution's challenges, opportunities, and dynamics. Innovative tools are being used to boost the performance of a given system in societal inequalities, and ecologic, viable, and environmental research applications. The world is entering the digitization age, for which cutting-

*Figure 2. By 2030, the majority of digital infrastructures and technologies will have passed the 50% diffusion mark, or equilibrium point, implying that the growth up to that point will have been exponential. This demonstrates the possibility of a rapid increase in global digitalization, as well as the emergence of new activities and behaviors.*
Source: (Saniee et al., 2017)

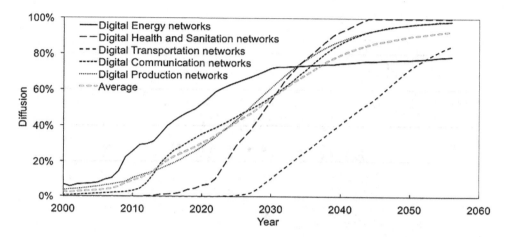

edge digital and computer technologies are highly dependent on most of our daily activities (Balogun et al., 2020; Ceipek et al., 2021). With a target date of 2030, the United Nations has established a blueprint for investments and long-term development (Nakicenovic et al., 2019). SDGs (Sustainable Development Goals) are 17 issues that must be addressed. These interconnected SDGs highlight our civilization's urgent need for a sustainable and competitive future. **Figure 3** summarizes which SDGs can be explained accurately and conceptually by the various sectors.

The effort of deploying new smart technologies to secure economic growth whilst still reflecting and incorporating the SDGs is called digital sustainability. Advanced analytics techniques, for example, have skyrocketed in value and are expected to contribute roughly 14% of global GDP through 2030 (George et al., 2020; Mondejar et al., 2021). In this section, we examine how the digital economy can aid in achieving the SDGs in various sectors, including the food-water-energy interlinkages, economy, community members' health, and wellbeing, climate variability, and ecosystem protection. The use of technological and digital tools to support the sector and achieve the SDGs is discussed.

The subcategories that comply clarify exciting possibilities made possible by internet technology and describe the relevant information and ramifications of online platforms for agro-based factors.

*Figure 3. Along with the food-water-energy nexus, manufacturers and citizen wellbeing, climate change, and biodiversity conservation, digital plays a significant role in addressing sustainability from a variety of perspectives. Most countries are harnessing the efficacy of artificial intelligence and digital transformation in achieving sustainable development goals.*
Source: (Mondejar et al., 2021)

*Figure 4. A synopsis of the features of digitization relevant to each of the development goals is discussed in this viewpoint.*
Source: (Mondejar et al., 2021)

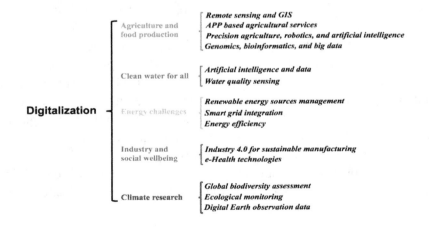

# DIGITALIZATION IN MARGINALIZED SOCIETIES

Traditionally discriminated against people appear to be the most vulnerable to increased marginalization in the COVID-19 context. Deprivation of essential human rights has exacerbated people's vulnerability. People have lived using whatever means were available, demonstrating greater resilience, tolerance, and perseverance. The use of ICTs and emerging cloud technologies can impact marginalized people's livelihoods in areas such as health, education, and socio-culture. During a pandemic, poor and marginalized individuals must be helped by relief programs, which is made possible by digitalization.

The government should spend more money and make better use of ICTs to put in place the right policies at the right time to achieve the total socio-economic transformation of marginalized groups. According to their paper, policymakers, new technology and innovation, and innovators have increasingly attempted to promote the progression of modernization as emerging revolutions play an increasingly important role all over the world (Jütting et al., 2021).

Even before the crisis, industrial production was undergoing extraordinary and rapid transformation. Artificial intelligence, advanced robotics, 3D printing, wearable technology, and the Internet of Things are all disrupting the manufacturing sector. The outbreak of Covid-19 provides an incentive to earn faster progress toward joint solutions to these global development concerns. In only a few months, the world has experienced more digital upheaval than it has in the previous decade. The crisis presents a once-in-a-generation chance to use the 4IR to future-proof productive sectors, enhance long-term resilience, and create a better future. Shifting to cyberspace, for example, allows us to lessen the psychosocial effects of social separation. The 4IR has resulted in a wide range of possibilities for combating COVID-19 and its social, economic, and ecosystem consequences.

During a pandemic, relief programs must assist the poor and marginalized, which is made possible by digitalization. The government should spend more money and use ICTs more effectively to implement the right policies at the right time in order to achieve the total socio-economic transformation of marginalized groups.

Zimbabwe's ICT infrastructure (ICT) history can be traced to 1972, when the Central Computing Services was established (CCS). CCS aimed to provide ICT services to the government. Zimbabwe has launched numerous programs over the years, indicating the government's readiness to take ICTs as drivers of the knowledge economy.

*Figure 5. In reaction to Covid-19, digital technologies are being used as an adaptive measure.*
*Source:(Nakicenovic et al., 2019)*

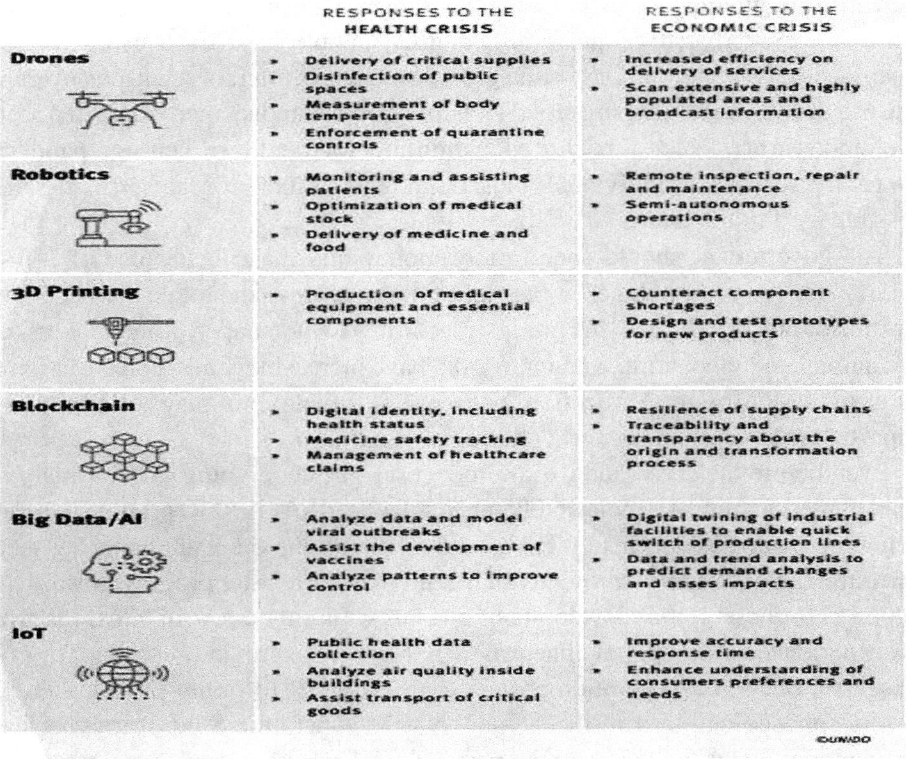

| | RESPONSES TO THE HEALTH CRISIS | RESPONSES TO THE ECONOMIC CRISIS |
|---|---|---|
| Drones | • Delivery of critical supplies<br>• Disinfection of public spaces<br>• Measurement of body temperatures<br>• Enforcement of quarantine controls | • Increased efficiency on delivery of services<br>• Scan extensive and highly populated areas and broadcast information |
| Robotics | • Monitoring and assisting patients<br>• Optimization of medical stock<br>• Delivery of medicine and food | • Remote inspection, repair and maintenance<br>• Semi-autonomous operations |
| 3D Printing | • Production of medical equipment and essential components | • Counteract component shortages<br>• Design and test prototypes for new products |
| Blockchain | • Digital identity, including health status<br>• Medicine safety tracking<br>• Management of healthcare claims | • Resilience of supply chains<br>• Traceability and transparency about the origin and transformation process |
| Big Data/AI | • Analyze data and model viral outbreaks<br>• Assist the development of vaccines<br>• Analyze patterns to improve control | • Digital twining of industrial facilities to enable quick switch of production lines<br>• Data and trend analysis to predict demand changes and asses impacts |
| IoT | • Public health data collection<br>• Analyze air quality inside buildings<br>• Assist transport of critical goods | • Improve accuracy and response time<br>• Enhance understanding of consumers preferences and needs |

©UNIDO

## State of Digital Transformation in Developing Countries

Despite the fact that the relevance of digitalization is widely recognized, businesses frequently struggle to comprehend its potential impact and benefits. In practice, there are numerous impediments to digital transformation. as stated by (Henriette et al., 2015), Instituting digital infrastructure that enables business model transformations affecting entire organizations, particularly operations and maintenance procedures, materials, local and global users, is the goal of a digital transformation project. This represents a significant shift in habits and working methods, which are premised on partnership and intensive interactions. The Global Executive Study and Research Project on Digital Business from (Kane et al., 2015) by MIT Sloan Management Review and Deloitte surveyed over 4800 business executives, managers, as well as experts from organizations across the globe in developing countries about how

*Table 2. The activities in which the Zimbabwean government has indeed been involved in the advancement of digital revolution are summarized below*

| ICT Initiative | Brief Description | Year Implemented |
|---|---|---|
| Science, technology and innovation | To make Science and Technology an integral part of both individual and national development. | 2012 |
| College IT Enhancement Programme (CITEP), | In ten Zimbabwean colleges, the Flemish Office for Development Cooperation and Technical Assistance (VVOB) is supporting a local capacity-building project. | 2010 |
| African Virtual University (AVU) Education Project | In collaboration with the African Development Bank (AfDB) and the NEPAD, a teacher education project involving ten African countries was established. | 2007 |
| National ICT framework | Guidelines for National ICT Implementation are provided. | 2006 |
| Web portal for the entire government | To consolidate government information and services into a single point of contact | 2005 |
| Survey of National e-Readiness | To evaluate the country's readiness for the transformation to a digital age. | 2005 |
| Millennium Development Goals for Zimbabwe (MDGs) | A report acknowledging ICT as a key player in having met the Millennium Development Goals of the United Nations. | 2005 |
| National Economic Recovery Strategy (NERP) | Science and Technology for Economic Recovery | 2004-2006 |
| Policy for Industrialization | Improving ICTs in the manufacturing sector in order to boost exports | 2004 |
| Nziramasanga Educational commission Report | It is recommended that ICTs be used in school teaching and learning. | 1999 |
| Central Computing Services CCS | For the provision of IT services to the public service | 1972 |

*Zimbabwe Government ICTs Initiatives; Source:* (Ruhode, 2016)

they perceived digitalization in their organizations. According to the findings of this survey, 76 percent of respondents believe that digital technology solutions are crucial to their own organizations, and 92 percent believe that digitalization would be vital in three years. Furthermore, 60 percent of respondents believed that digital technologies had the ability to dramatically revolutionize the way individuals in their entire organisation worked, and 76 percent believed that technological advances would significantly or moderately disrupt their industry in the near future. The study also asked participants how they saw their corporation progressing for the digital economy. According to the findings, 26 percent of the respondents were in the early stages of digitalization maturity, 45 percent deemed their corporation to be developing, and 29 percent assumed each other to be knowledgeable companies in aspects of digitalization. Mature firms generally had a clear strategy in place, as well as a teamwork culture and leadership that drove the evolution and inspired risk taking. However, failed enterprise resource planning implementation was common in many companies, often due to previous generations' knowledge management systems. The transformation failed because enterprises did not affect patterns of thinking and processes or create a culture conducive to change. According to the findings, 26 percent of the respondents were in the early stages of digitalization maturity, 45 percent deemed their corporation to be developing, and 29 percent assumed each other to be knowledgeable companies in aspects of digitalization. Mature firms generally had a clear strategy in place, as well as a teamwork culture and leadership that drove the evolution and inspired risk taking. However, failed enterprise resource planning implementation was common in many companies, often due to previous generations' knowledge management systems. The transformation failed because enterprises did not affect patterns of thinking and processes or create a culture conducive to change. The most common barriers to digitalization were a scarcity of a cumulative digitalization approach and competing priorities, as well as safety concerns and totally inadequate technical skills. The most common barriers to digitalization were a scarcity of a cumulative digitalization approach and competing priorities, as well as safety concerns and totally inadequate technical skills.

## Benefits of Living in a Digitized Society in Developing Countries

Digital transformation is acknowledged to cause a wide set of capabilities in all aspects of human society (Stolterman & Fors, 2004). Digitalization has been outlined as one of the key developments that will shape businesses and customers in the immediate and longer term (Parviainen et al., 2017). The impact of digital technology will be significant; numerous studies comparing it to the industrial revolution (Degryse, 2016) ;(Prince, 2014) ;(Fomunyam, 2019) ;(Tihinen et al., 2016). The improvements of digitalization are significant; simply digitizing knowledge processes can reduce costs by up to 90% and improve turnaround times by many orders of magnitude. Furthermore, substituting traditional paper - based processes with software enables businesses to obtain information that can be extracted to help comprehend performance of the process, cost drivers, and risk factors. Managers can tackle issues before they become critical by using real-time dashboards and reports on digital-process performance (Parviainen et al., 2017). According to Sabbagh et al. (Sabbagh et al., 2012) Digitalization promotes accumulative wealth creation; emerging economies at the most elevated level of digitalization benefit from 20 percent more net gains than those at the beginning. Digitalization has been shown to

*Table 3. The importance of internet innovations for businesses, individuals, as well as governments*

|  | **Efficiency** | **Incorporation in the Economy and Society** | **The Innovation Economy** |
|---|---|---|---|
| Business | Capital Effectiveness | Trade | Competition |
| People | In the workplace, profitability | Possibilities for Employment | Consumer wellbeing |
| Governments | Capability of the public sector | Participation | Voice |

Source: (Group, 2016)

reduce unemployment, improve quality of life, and increase civilian access to basic services. Finally, digitization enables governments to operate more transparently and efficiently. Because digitalization affects all aspects of life and society, People can be linked to and integrate into society based on their preferences thanks to digital technologies (Larsson et al., 2013); (Leist, 2013). Welfare and modern technology have both been identified as having the potential to improve the health and well-being of older adults (Fischl et al., 2020); (Organization, 2015).

The ultimate focus of closing the digital divide is to provide equal access to technological advancement for all members of society. According to the World Bank, the "full benefits" of digital development are as follows: Information sharing, transmission, and acquisition, as well as innovation (Group, 2016). Corporations and governments have replaced traditional factors including manual labour and non-ICT capital with ICT capital, along with automating some of their operations, as the role of technological innovations has waned. Non-substitutable factors are strengthened and increased in productivity by digital technologies. Information devices and all aspects of e-commerce help to reduce information barriers. Innovators must hire more people to manufacture, distribute, and service their products. Such offerings are transformed into low-cost, widely available products for a new audience by market-creating innovations (Mezue et al., 2015). Also, the "new economy" has emerged as a result of the rapid expansion of Internet technology, in which operations are highly automated and do not require human intervention.

## Technologies for Agricultural Development

Digital tools are being used to provide long-term solutions to various agrarian problems in various crop types grown worldwide. Everything from crop species identification to land-use and landform farming system sustainability management can benefit from remote sensing (RS) and geospatial data system (GIS) techniques (Basso & Antle, 2020). RS-GIS can map land-use trends, crop variety, planning, agronomic surveillance, and strategic planning. Food production must undergo significant technological innovation in trying to attain the always threat to food security and sustainability. Farming, scientific, and technical professionals are using phone apps to spread the news about climate-smart farming methods (Qiang et al., 2012). Despite the numerous benefits of CSA technological innovations, farmers' acceptance is currently low (Abegunde et al., 2020; Bu & Wang, 2019; Deressa et al., 2011).

In addition, precision agriculture makes use of robotics, intelligent systems, and deep learning. Modern unmanned drones (UAVs or drones) can help with various agricultural systems issues. Precision agriculture is growing faster than ever before, thanks to lower-cost sensors, improved control, and computer imaging systems. Seedbed sinking, watering, spraying, pruning, harvesting, real-time surveillance, and mapping are all successful uses of remotely operated vehicles, both semi-autonomous and automatic (Vasconez et al., 2019). Smart farming, made possible by technology, vastly improves efficiency and productivity. Navigation autonomous machinery can operate 24 hours a day, seven days a week, reducing labor and crop production costs. Smart objects, frequently used in tandem with aerial drones, can measure soil and plant characteristics, resulting in more effective fertilizer, pesticide, and water use (Kremen & Merenlender, 2018).

Also, technological advancements in agro-sciences, omics, and, predictive analysis are faring better in terms of agricultural production improvement. According to global forecasts, a single degree Celsius increase in global mean temperature reduces corn, cereals, grains, and soybean crop yields by 7.4, 6.8, 3.2, and 3.1 percent, respectively (Zhao et al., 2017). Batley and Edwards (2016) Agronomic qualities that genomics and bioinformatics can help improve include abiotic stresses, insect resistance, herbicide tolerance, and grain production. Varshney et al. (2020) The 5Gs agricultural spawning methodologies were presented for developing weather patterns and high-yielding, nutritionally crop varieties. Information and communication technology, in addition to genome sequencing and biostatistics, uses massive, diverse, and unstructured data via the internet and cloud computing. Using computational scripts, we can analyze such large amounts of data holistically to improve agricultural productivity and supply chain.

## Stimulate Consumer Protection in the Digital Age

Consumer choices are hampered in this information-rich environment by potential barriers to the unpredictability that are sometimes exacerbated by deceptive or outright fraud business practices. Platforms, including peer platforms, are expanding their reach, posing unique demands to consumer trust while also presenting new opportunities. Customized consumer protection laws and competitive forces are critical for establishing the trust required to further advance e-commerce markets for the financial advantage of consumers and businesses. Consumer rights must be implemented more effectively if e-commerce achieves its full potential. The OECD and UN regulations are excellent points, but governments must be more committed to implementing them. More work needs to be done in cross-border and cross-sectoral compliance cooperation. Approaches like data interoperability show promise in an increasing data model, but more research is needed to determine their effectiveness for both consumers and businesses.

As a result of digitalization's impact on all sectors of the economy and society, governments must reach across existing planning legacy systems and different levels of government to develop an all approach to policy development. This necessitates greater coordination between government departments and state institutions when setting policy and carrying out actions, as well as active participation in the policy development process by all relevant parties, including the corporate world, trade unions, society organizations, and the Internet technical community. To do so, detailed information on how the digital economy's rapid growth has influenced a wide range of legislative/regulatory frameworks and areas of government, including competitors in the market, fiscal policy, trade, cross-border data transmission, mass transit, financing, labor markets, and institutions, is required.

## Drawbacks of Living in a Digitized Society

Robots are increasingly common in everyday life, performing a variety of tasks in health care, hotels, food outlets, schools, and private homes. In each case, we must consider the criteria we use to qualify their use for decent life, both ethically and legally. Robotization could thus be viewed as a threat to human dignity, a value entrenched in the Universal Declaration of Human Rights (Capurro, 2017). Inside some ways, one such fear is a classic sign of how digitization is calling Western anthropocentrism into question.

The ethical application of new technologies and their data is a roadblock. Digital identities and information can be stolen and leaked, especially as 3D printing becomes more popular. Companies and government companies could intrude into people's private lives and regulate them against their own will. The ethical advancement of digital technologies and their data poses a major challenge. Particularly as 3D printing becomes popular, digital identities and information can be stolen and leaked. Governments and private companies can invade people's privacy and monitor them against their will. Individual energy use data that has been aggregated and anonymized can aid in the interpretation of energy technologies, such as load profiles, and assist consumers in saving money. Energy systems may become more vulnerable to cyberattacks as a result of digitalization. Consumers are also concerned about their privacy and data ownership.

## RECOMMENDATIONS

The digital transformation has been heralded as a panacea for raising living standards in low and middle-income economies, such as those in developing countries. Rising imbalances in the aftermath of the COVID-19 disease outbreak highlight the issue's importance and urgency. More research is required to understand technological systems better. By studying technological progress trends, drivers, barriers, and impacts, it is possible to identify appealing alternatives and legislation that will accelerate society's transitions toward a better economy. The transition to sustainable development must be coordinated with the Digital Revolution's challenges, prospects, and complexities. The use of ICTs and emerging cloud technologies can impact marginalized people's livelihoods in areas such as health, education, and socio-culture. Digitalization is expected to have far-reaching consequences for societies and economies. During a pandemic, relief programs must assist the poor and marginalized, made possible by digitalization. The Digital Revolution's repercussions on the resources, transportation, manufacturing, and utilization areas of the economy may benefit climate mitigation. Lowered emissions of greenhouse gases from a safer and more efficient energy sector will contribute significantly to a more carbon-free world. The government should spend more money and use ICTs more effectively to implement the right policies at the right time to achieve the total socio-economic transformation of marginalized groups. Given that high-quality digital infrastructure benefits all network users, the countries could agree to share ideas and best practices in recognizing concerns and guaranteeing a competitive market and investment. Furthermore, countries can define a set of joint, negotiated, and measurable targets to increase absorption and guarantee that critical technology success factors, including accessibility exchange points, spectrum, and IPv6 ado, are available.

## FUTURE RESEARCH DIRECTIONS

Digital technologies keep people, governments, and businesses connected during times of crisis. Thinking forwards, innovative trends like the Internet of Things (IoT) and technological innovations toward 5G digital technology are concreting the opportunities for better markets and industries, as well as further advances in big data. Countries will need to prioritize education and develop their workforce's digital skills to compete in the digital economy. Building capacity in cybersecurity and data protection areas is more important than ever.

## CONCLUSION

The global digital revolution propels the adoption of cutting-edge digital technologies such as ubiquitous computing, robotics, and artificial intelligence, resulting in a truly digitalized network society for all. Innovative tools are being used to improve the performance of a given system in applications such as societal inequalities, ecologic, viable, and environmental research. The world is entering the digitization era, in which cutting-edge digital and computer technologies heavily rely on our daily activities. Digitalization contributes to the sustainable development of marginalized societies hence improving wellbeing of people. However, it has introduced a slew of new complexities for businesses that must now comprehend rules and regulations, desires, and cultures from a variety of countries. The first phase toward closing connectivity and usage gaps and improving world economic performance and wellbeing is to advocate for strong national digital strategies that can adapt to changes in technology and social norms. This new internationalization has widened the digital divide. The moral application of digital technologies and their data poses a significant challenge. As 3D printing becomes more popular, digital identities and information can be stolen and leaked. Governments and private companies can intrude on people's privacy and monitor them against their will.

## REFERENCES

Aruleba, K., & Jere, N. (2022). Exploring Digital Transforming Challenges in Rural Areas of South Africa through a Systematic Review of Empirical Studies. *Scientific African*.

Capurro, R. (2017). Digitization as an ethical challenge. *AI & Society*, *32*(2), 277–283. doi:10.100700146-016-0686-z

Degryse, C. (2016). *Digitalisation of the economy and its impact on labour markets*. ETUI Research Paper-Working Paper.

Fernandez, D., & Aman, A. (2018). Impacts of robotic process automation on global accounting services. *Asian Journal of Accounting and Governance*, *9*(1), 127–140. doi:10.17576/AJAG-2018-09-11

Fischl, C., Lindelöf, N., Lindgren, H., & Nilsson, I. (2020). Older adults' perceptions of contexts surrounding their social participation in a digitalized society—An exploration in rural communities in Northern Sweden. *European Journal of Ageing*, *17*(3), 281–290. doi:10.100710433-020-00558-7 PMID:32904866

Fomunyam, K. G. (2019). Education and the fourth industrial revolution: Challenges and possibilities for engineering education. *International Journal of Mechanical Engineering and Technology*, *10*(8), 271–284.

Henriette, E., Feki, M., & Boughzala, I. (2015). *The shape of digital transformation: A systematic literature review*. Academic Press.

Kane, G. C., Palmer, D., Phillips, A. N., Kiron, D., & Buckley, N. (2015). Strategy, not technology, drives digital transformation. *MIT Sloan Management Review and Deloitte University Press*, *14*, 1–25.

Kraus, S., Schiavone, F., Pluzhnikova, A., & Invernizzi, A. C. (2021). Digital transformation in healthcare: Analyzing the current state-of-research. *Journal of Business Research*, *123*, 557–567. doi:10.1016/j.jbusres.2020.10.030

Larsson, E., Larsson-Lund, M., & Nilsson, I. (2013). Internet based activities (IBAs): Seniors' experiences of the conditions required for the performance of and the influence of these conditions on their own participation in society. *Educational Gerontology*, *39*(3), 155–167. doi:10.1080/03601277.2012.699833

Leist, A. K. (2013). Social media use of older adults: A mini-review. *Gerontology*, *59*(4), 378–384. doi:10.1159/000346818 PMID:23594915

Manstead, A. S. R. (2018). The psychology of social class: How socioeconomic status impacts thought, feelings, and behaviour. *British Journal of Social Psychology*, *57*(2), 267–291. doi:10.1111/bjso.12251 PMID:29492984

Organization, W. H. (2015). *World report on ageing and health*. World Health Organization.

Panori, A., Kakderi, C., Komninos, N., Fellnhofer, K., Reid, A., & Mora, L. (2021). Smart systems of innovation for smart places: Challenges in deploying digital platforms for co-creation and data-intelligence. *Land Use Policy*, *111*, 104631. doi:10.1016/j.landusepol.2020.104631

Parviainen, P., Tihinen, M., Kääriäinen, J., & Teppola, S. (2017). Tackling the digitalization challenge: How to benefit from digitalization in practice. *International Journal of Information Systems and Project Management*, *5*(1), 63–77. doi:10.12821/ijispm050104

Prince, J. D. (2014). 3D printing: An industrial revolution. *Journal of Electronic Resources in Medical Libraries, 11*(1), 39–45. doi:10.1080/15424065.2014.877247

Radovanović, D., Holst, C., Belur, S. B., Srivastava, R., Houngbonon, G. V., Le Quentrec, E., Miliza, J., Winkler, A. S., & Noll, J. (2020). Digital literacy key performance indicators for sustainable development. *Social Inclusion (Lisboa), 8*(2), 151–167. doi:10.17645i.v8i2.2587

Sabbagh, K., Friedrich, R., El-Darwiche, B., Singh, M., Ganediwalla, S., & Katz, R. (2012). Maximizing the impact of digitization. *The Global Information Technology Report, 2012*, 121–133.

Salemink, K., Strijker, D., & Bosworth, G. (2017). Rural development in the digital age: A systematic literature review on unequal ICT availability, adoption, and use in rural areas. *Journal of Rural Studies, 54*, 360–371. doi:10.1016/j.jrurstud.2015.09.001

Schwertner, K. (2017). Digital transformation of business. *Trakia Journal of Sciences, 15*(1, Suppl.1), 388–393. doi:10.15547/tjs.2017.s.01.065

Stolterman, E., & Fors, A. C. (2004). Information technology and the good life. In *Information systems research* (pp. 687–692). Springer. doi:10.1007/1-4020-8095-6_45

Tihinen, M., Iivari, M., Ailisto, H., Komi, M., Kääriäinen, J., & Peltomaa, I. (2016). An exploratory method to clarify business potential in the context of industrial internet–a case study. *Working Conference on Virtual Enterprises*, 469–478. 10.1007/978-3-319-45390-3_40

Urvashi, A., Chetty, K., Gcora, N., Josie, J., & Mishra, V. (2017). *Bridging the Digital Divide: Skills For The New Age.* Policy Brief, G20 Insights.

Van Deursen, A. J. A. M., & Van Dijk, J. A. G. M. (2019). The first-level digital divide shifts from inequalities in physical access to inequalities in material access. *New Media & Society, 21*(2), 354–375. doi:10.1177/1461444818797082 PMID:30886536

Van Dijk, J. A. G. M. (2017). Digital divide: Impact of access. The International Encyclopedia of Media Effects, 1–11.

Viale Pereira, G., Estevez, E., Cardona, D., Chesñevar, C., Collazzo-Yelpo, P., Cunha, M. A., Diniz, E. H., Ferraresi, A. A., Fischer, F. M., Cardinelle Oliveira Garcia, F., Joia, L. A., Luciano, E. M., de Albuquerque, J. P., Quandt, C. O., Sánchez Rios, R., Sánchez, A., Damião da Silva, E., Silva-Junior, J. S., & Scholz, R. W. (2020). South American expert roundtable: Increasing adaptive governance capacity for coping with unintended side effects of digital transformation. *Sustainability*, *12*(2), 718. doi:10.3390u12020718

Wang, D., Zhou, T., & Wang, M. (2021). Information and communication technology (ICT), digital divide and urbanization: Evidence from Chinese cities. *Technology in Society*, *64*, 101516. doi:10.1016/j.techsoc.2020.101516

## KEY TERMS AND DEFINITIONS

**Digital Age:** Is the time period starting in the 1970s with the introduction of the personal computer with subsequent technology introduced providing the ability to transfer information freely and quickly.

**Digital Transformation:** Is the process of using digital technologies to create new—or modify existing—business processes, culture, and customer experiences to meet changing business and market requirements.

**Global Digital Divide:** The global digital divide describes global disparities, primarily between developed and developing countries, in regards to access to computing and information resources such as the Internet and the opportunities derived from such access.

**Industrial Revolution:** Is the process of change from an agrarian and handicraft economy to one dominated by industry and machine manufacturing. These technological changes introduced novel ways of working and living and fundamentally transformed society.

**Internet:** A global computer network providing a variety of information and communication facilities, consisting of interconnected networks using standardized communication protocols.

**Sustainable Development Goals (SDGs):** Also known as the Global Goals, were adopted by the United Nations in 2015 as a universal call to action to end poverty, protect the planet, and ensure that by 2030 all people enjoy peace and prosperity.

**Technological Evolution:** Is a theory of radical transformation of society through technological development.

# Chapter 12
# A Strategy for the Digitalization of Marginalized Communities

**Samuel Simbarashe Furusa**
*Midlands State University, Zimbabwe*

**Samuel Musungwini**
iD https://orcid.org/0000-0002-9315-6252
*Midlands State University, Zimbabwe*

**Petros Venganayi Gavai**
*Midlands State University, Zimbabwe*

**Melody Maseko**
*Midlands State University, Zimbabwe*

## ABSTRACT

*The chapter explores the concept of digitalization and digital technology and its importance. The research is based on a systematic literature review, which analyzed articles on digitalization and digital technologies. However, primacy was given to articles on the digitalization of organizations in a marginalized context. The chapter identified the critical success factors and formulation of a digitalization strategy formulation for the transformation of marginalized communities in Zimbabwe. Therefore, the authors highlight the need to explore human-centered digital transformation capabilities and dynamic capabilities in developing countries. The chapter then formulated a strategy for the digitalization of marginalized communities in a developing context.*

DOI: 10.4018/978-1-6684-3901-2.ch012

# INTRODUCTION

Digital technology is persistently defining how society in the modern world should function including the marginalized communities and also the digitalization of organizations is being directed away from being innovative to becoming part of their central part functioning (Elers et al., 2022). Regardless of where people live, what they get as income, the language they speak, their skin color, their affiliation in political circles, their religion, their physical ability, their sexual orientation, or even gender people should be accorded unfettered access to digital technology such as the Internet (Hourcade et al., 2010a). The access to digital technologies across the globe and in developing economies to a large extent has not been convincing.

With the increase in the rise of digital technologies such as mobile gadgets, artificial intelligence, and social networks just to mention but a few, companies have embarked on conducting multiple initiatives as a way of exploring and exploiting the benefits that come with these technologies (Karimi & Walter, 2015; Reis et al., 2018). However, this has impacted the way key business operations are now being conducted thereby affecting end products and processes. Society has not been left unaffected as it is facing swift and drastic changes due to the maturation of these mentioned technologies and their universal penetration. Conversely, even though the assortment of technological innovations and procedures for putting them into practice, whether in business, governance or secretive life, actual digital transformation especially in marginalized communities is taking much longer and facing more challenges than what has been anticipated (Ghauri et al., 2022; Matt et al., 2015). This chapter looks at marginalization and all its different forms and how issues to do with access to digital technologies have affected the same communities the same way the other social issues have affected the same group of people. Thus the chapter seeks to propose a digital transformation strategy that would spur development in marginalized communities, especially in key sectors of the economy that include but are not limited to agriculture, education, health, and mining. This chapter seeks to achieve the following:

1.  To determine the critical success factors for digital transformation
2.  To identify the challenges of digital transformation in marginalized communities
3.  To identify strategies that have been employed by other countries in marginalized communities.
4.  To come up with components that could be included in formulating a strategy for digital transformation in marginalized communities.

## BACKGROUND

Digital transformation as postulated by Kraus et al., (2021) is using information and communication technology to capabilities that are produced in businesses, government, and in the lives of ordinary citizens and the society at large and at a high level, digital transformation takes in the insightful modification occurring in society and industries by bringing digital technologies. Rudder, (2019) defined digital transformation as the amalgamation of digital technology into all sections of a business consequential in fundamental changes in how businesses operate and how value is delivered to clients.

Marginalized communities refer to those areas that are disqualified or excluded from conventional social, economic, educational, technological, and/or cultural life (Sevelius et al., 2020). According to LibertiesEU, (2021) marginalization, also referred to as social exclusion, takes place when an individual or groups of individuals are less capable to perform things or have the right to use fundamental facilities or opportunities. The digital divide according to Lester, (2019) is the technological gap that exists between those who have and those who have not considering digital technologies. Aruleba & Jere, (2022) also referred a digital divide as a global disparity that occurs in accessing digital technologies that drive globalization by households, individuals, and business firms.

Because digital technologies are now a part of everyday life in many local settings resulting in changed societies, and have inspired some innovation, they are the solution to access gaps that exist globally. Despite the many advantages of these developments, technological advancements in all the three highlighted areas, this have made it simpler for monopolies or other types of concentrated ownership rights to emerge, mostly in the hands of people living in large urban centers. Therefore, an important part of the problem of reducing income gaps is the spreading of these technological advances to many marginalized communities and leaving ownership into the custody of a greater number of ordinary people.

The escalating digitalization of economies has been a testimony of how significant digital transformation has become and how it can aid firms to have an edge in the market. Nevertheless, disruptive transformations should not only happen at organizational height; they also have environmental and societal implications (Kraus et al., 2021). Digitalization according to Unho et al. (2015) impacts individuals, businesses, and society as a whole. In particular, the fast spread of digital technologies sets enormous changes in motion. This implies huge challenges and at the same time promising chances for companies and individuals. The issue of access to digital technologies should be considered in such a way that f societies, as well as institutions, are not left marginalized.

## MARGINALIZATION

Marginalization as discussed in the section above and asserted by Aanestad & Kankanhalli, (2022), entails distancing individuals or subpopulation from access to authority and possessions that grants them the capacity to have self-determination in settings such as economics, politics, education, health, social and nowadays technology. Access to technology seems to be guided by individual status in society. Although there are various broad types of marginalization or social injustices that can be identified which include but are not limited to social, economic, political, educational, and psychological marginalization, digital technologies have often been viewed as a way various subpopulations are made to access opportunities with the aim of promoting fairness and equal opportunities (Hourcade et al., 2010a). By mere looking, digital technologies have to some extent lived up to some expectations by according individuals that otherwise would have lacked access to social, political, educational, agricultural, and economic participation(Chib et al., 2019). Nevertheless, a closer look proposes a more difficult picture. While digital technologies have been used as a tool to expose inequalities, and advance social justice movements they have also been used negatively to expand inequalities through demonizing already marginalized sub-populations, and data is abused thus oppressing individuals in a way that broadens disproportions.

The past few decades have seen digital exclusion being associated with debates on access to digital technologies, adoption of these technologies, and conditions related to social and economic marginalization and historical forms of oppression (Gangadharan, 2021). Literature has revealed that global inequality continues to increase at alarming rates and that the digital divide, even based on gender, is widening, predominantly in developing countries(Ceia et al., 2021). Various studies (Aruleba & Jere, 2022; Banihashemi & Rejaei, 2015; Hourcade et al., 2010b; Kraus et al., 2021; Lester, 2019; Unho et al., 2015) coincide that the conception of the digital divide can be explained as an inequality that exists between individuals, living arrangements, companies and physical areas at various socioeconomic levels with reference to their chance of having access to digital technologies and the use of these technologies for a wide difference of activities. Other researchers like (Hourcade et al., 2010a)and (Salemink, 2016)) also pointed out that the increasing importance of digital technologies in general and the internet specifically as an alternative way of communicating has undoubtedly changed the shape of economies and societies. The two went on to consider digital technologies as equalizers, which are expected to lessen socioeconomic and geographical discrepancies, and have begun to be considered a stratification-inducing phenomenon. For all ranges of digital technologies to be enablers, people need to have enough material access to the technologies together with the associated knowledge and skills/capabilities so as to make valuable use of the technologies. Ample access to digital technologies is regarded as a key condition for social and economic development, and yet, nevertheless, it is often deficient in numerous rural regions even in highly developed societies (Karimi & Walter, 2015; Kraus et al., 2021) though according to (Aruleba & Jere, 2022), digital technologies have the possibility of impacting the livelihoods of people, especially in rural communities in a very significant way.

## MAIN FOCUS OF THE CHAPTER

### Critical Success Factors of Digital Transformation

Sahu et al. (2018) states that digital transformation focuses on changes that an organization experiences in its structure. It also considers how an organisation carries out its business, how it functions, and the business models it uses through the implementation of digital technologies for radically refining its performance. It is a disruptive way of bringing change and begins with embracing and using digital technologies, then developing into an embedded all-inclusive change of a firm in pursuance of value creation. Improvements in organizational processes, improved customer value propositions, better customer collaboration, better customer service quality, lower costs for goods and services, competitive advantages, and better customer experience are just a few advantages that come with the digital transformation. (Banihashemi & Rejaei, 2015; Sahu et al., 2018; Salemink, 2016).

### Challenges

Implementation of digitalization can provide positively impact on sustainability in the context of larger community prosperity and control of the environment. On the other hand, digitalization can have disruptive effects when actors involved are marginalized if they cannot cope with change. In light of this, Ferrari et al. (2022) emphasizes the importance for project teams to consider explicit socio-economic features of the area so as to gain positive effects while alleviating the negative impacts. A study was made by Ferrari et al. (2022) in order to compile a catalog of enablers, potential impacts, and barriers associated with the introduction of digitalization in rural communities which are part of the marginalized clusters. The barriers are listed in Fig 1 where the barriers were grouped in 4 clusters namely Socio-economic, technical, economic, and regulatory institutional.

Another study was conducted in Bangladesh to establish factors of digital inefficiency. The study had 326 participants who participated in a survey and the observed elements were educational, infrastructural, social, economic, and motivational challenges as shown in Figure 2.

*Figure 1. Challenges hindering digitization in marginalized areas*
*Source: (Ferrari et al., 2022)*

| Socio-cultural barriers | |
|---|---|
| Demographic | Age issues, social isolation, sparse population, seasonal work |
| Distrust | Distrust of funders, distrust of regulators, distrust of ICT supplier, distrust of technology |
| Fear | Fear of dependency from technology, fear of hidden costs, privacy concerns |
| Values | Attachment to tradition |
| Competence | Lack of education, lack of knowledge, lack of skills, digital debt |
| Complexity | Complexity of regulations, complexity of technology, paradox of choice |
| **Technical barriers** | |
| Connectivity | Absence of infrastructure, low quality of infrastructure |
| Dependability | Poor reliability, low efficiency |
| Usability | Poor ergonomic standards, poor usability in the field |
| Scalability | Limited data storage, limited computing capacity |
| **Economic barriers** | |
| Costs | Cost of technology, modernisation cost, maintenance cost, lack of evidence of cost-effectiveness, lack of funding |
| Scale | Small market size, small business size, atomised business structure |
| **Regulatory-institutional barriers** | |
| Data management | Unclear data ownership, unclear data governance |
| Regulations | Frequent change of regulations, legal restrictions on technology, inadequate grant schemes criteria |

*Figure 2. Determinants of digital inequality in Bangladesh*

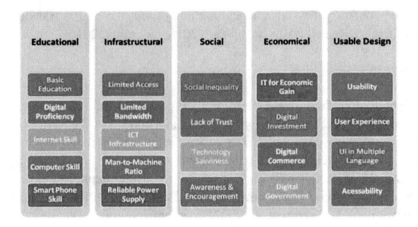

The educational element emphasizes on teaching or enhancing skill sets to use the information technologies. The cluster includes factors such as basic education, non-proficiency in the digital ecosphere, and lack of skills in using the internet, computers, and smartphones. Citizens who lack education will be reluctant to adopt digital technology in their personal and social lives. The infrastructural element takes into consideration enabling issues that help people have easy and effective access to digital technologies. It covers factors such as limited bandwidth, ICT infrastructure, high machine-to-machine ratio, and unreliable power supply. The Social element focuses on perspectives such as trust and awareness about digitization uses. This element includes social inequality constructs such as income, gender, special needs, etc., which vary with different people, and affects the adoption of digital services. In this cluster is the issue of lack of trust, which is common in the illiterate, semi-literate, and marginalized persons as an obstacle to digitization adoption. Marginalized communities fail to get support or mentorship about digital services for their economic development and as a result, they tend to be non-tech practical understanding and lack awareness. The economic element touches on the role of ICT use from an economic perspective. It is made up of a lack of digital investment, limited digital commerce opportunities for online business, digital government, and IT for Economic Gain. Marginalized communities are not willing to invest in e-commerce and as a result, will not be able to make use of the technology. Digital projects are normally initiated by governments but will benefit the less marginalized communities where the marginalized will not be able to access them owing to connection challenges. The last dimension is usable design, which emphasizes how easily citizens utilize ICT. It includes user experience (UX), usability, User Interface in multiple languages, and accessibility. If users face challenges in accessing and using the system, it becomes an obstacle to digitization. No matter how good the system is, if it does not have multiple languages may affect digital adoption. In this element, a poor user interface affects usability (Islam & Inan, 2021).

After combining the challenges of digital adoption in marginalized areas, Figure 3 illustrates the factors.

## THE THEORETICAL FOUNDATION OF THE STRATEGY

A strategy is an action taken by managers to attain one or multiple organizations' objectives. The research model underpinning this research was adapted from (Tsokota & van Greunen, 2017) as shown in Figure 4.

In the model, the major component of the strategy formulation process is setting of objectives. The model is guided by the research objectives of this research. The next component is Environmental assessment, which involves the analysis of both internal and external environments. The research formulation according to (Tsokota & van Greunen, 2017) is a kernel of strategy that affords the logical structure. The three components include guiding policy, diagnosis, and a set of coherent actions. Diagnosis represents the main component of the strategy by defining the nature

*Figure 3. Challenges faced in digital adoption of marginalized areas*
Source:(Authors)

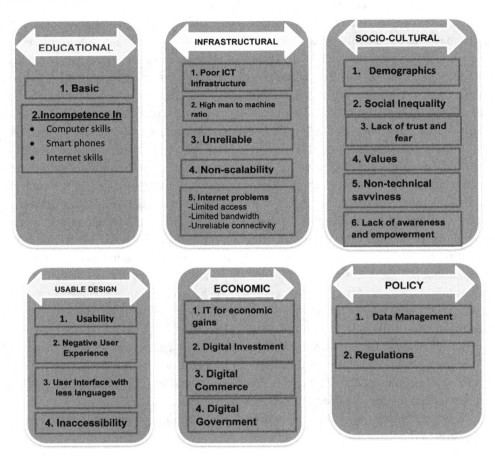

of challenges and examining the precarious aspects of the situations directly from environmental assessment. In other words, this component looks at obstacles to be overcome. The guiding policy outlines the whole approach to dealing with impediments identified during diagnosis without describing what needs to be done. Lastly, the set of coherent actions refers to steps and actions designed to actuate the guiding policy. Strategy implementation involves the execution of a set of coherent actions acknowledged in the strategy formulation process. Strategy control is a continual process that connects the kernel of strategy formulation together to evaluate its effectiveness as supported by (Marambi et al., 2018)

*Figure 4. Strategy formulation*
(*Tsokota and van Greunen, 2017*)

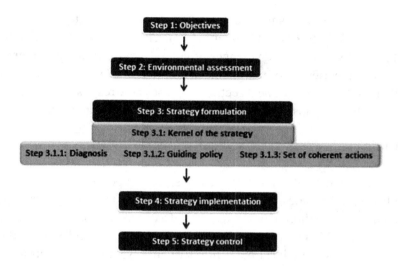

## SOLUTIONS AND RECOMMENDATIONS

In this section solutions and recommendations are discussed guided by issues and problems presented in the preceding section. Contextualization of the devised strategy formulation model will result in setting the strategy as the goal for this research. Specific details of the study are outlined in the context of the model depicted in Figure 4.

### Objectives

As outlined in Figure 4, objectives will form part of the strategy.

1.  To determine the critical success factors for digital transformation
2.  To identify the challenges of digital transformation in marginalized communities
3.  To identify strategies that have been employed by other countries in marginalized communities
4.  To come up with components that could be included in formulating a strategy for digital transformation in marginalized communities

Objectives stated will populate the first stage of the strategy. Environmental Analysis is the next section that will fulfill the objectives stated above.

## Environmental Assessment

The environmental assessment involves scanning both internal and external environments (Tsokota & van Greunen, 2017). This was done through a literature review to establish common challenges of Digital Transformation implementation to explore the experiences of marginalized communities on how they use ICT and the challenges they face. The next section discusses how results from literature were analyzed to identify gaps, weaknesses, and challenges in digital transformation.

## Diagnosis

Results of environmental assessment help in assessing possible challenges faced by marginalized communities and by the policy implementers who normally are the governments. After a thorough Environmental assessment, results were reported in the next section, which was synthesized into six diagnostics and explained in detail below. The themes are educational, infrastructure, socio-cultural, usable design, economic, and policy.

## Diagnostic 1: Educational D1

Lack of education is the first identified challenge in the form of non-proficiency and basic education in the digital world. Illiterate people are unable to utilize and adopt ICT-based services. As a result, a lack of basic education resists citizens from fully adopting digitization in their life. This implies that people will have proficiency deficiency in the use of computers, smartphones, the internet, and digital (Ferrari et al., 2022).

## Diagnostic 2: Infrastructural D2

Infrastructure is another factor, which is crucial for digital transformation. This element takes into consideration issues that facilitate citizens in having easy and effective access to information technologies. Factors identified include unreliable power, internet problems, scalability, poor ICT infrastructure, and a high ratio of man to machine. Lack of power results in inaccessibility to ICT systems which can hinder digitization. Poor bandwidth can cause disparities in accessing resources of digitization. Again, if there is a high ratio of man to machines it implies accessibility to digitization is hindered since a less percentage of the population will be able to access resources. Poor infrastructure is another factor to consider. This could be attributed to poor planning and cost barriers (Ferrari et al., 2022; Islam & Inan, 2021)

## Diagnostic 3: Socio-cultural D3

Socio-cultural considers people's perspectives on ICT uses together with issues of social/economic. This includes demographic, social inequality, lack of trust and fear, values, non-technical savviness, and lack of awareness and encouragement. On social inequality, there are variants that include gender, age, special needs, income, etc. Communities have varying incomes, which can be a hurdle in the adoption of digital services. As a result, low-income earners will not be interested in using the internet or a small percent will use the internet from a mobile phone with limited access. On trust and fear, the illiterate, semi-illiterate, and other marginalized will tend not to trust digital initiatives, ICT suppliers, regulators, and the internet. People tend to fear dependency on technology, hidden costs, and privacy concern (Ferrari et al., 2022; Islam & Inan, 2021). As a result, if people fear digitization they tend to be non-tech-savvy which means they will not be confident and technical to use it. If the initiators of digitization do not give adequate support, awareness, encouragement, and education on ICT use may result in the failure of a project or slow uptake (Islam & Inan, 2021). Communities have values that have been passed from generation to generation and as such tend to be attached to tradition. Consequently, some values may be parallel to digitization agendas which may affect initiatives.

## Diagnostic 4: Usable Design D4

Usable design mainly focuses on how the communities use ICT. Its dimensions include inaccessibility, experiences, multi-language support, and usability. Marginalized people lack adequate education to be able to use systems. They face difficulty in accessing and utilizing digital systems owing to the user interface and user-friendliness. Systems designed in mono languages such as English may hinder usage of ICT systems on the side of marginalized communities made up of illiterate and non-technical savvy. They would prefer systems written in their native language and with a more simplified user interface (Islam & Inan, 2021).

## Diagnostic 5: Economic D5

The economic element looks at the importance of using ICT from the economic perspective. It includes I.T for economic gain, digital commerce, digital governance, and digital investment. Digitization can be a tool for economic gain if implemented in the area of e-commerce. Organizations can market and sell their products online using ICT tools. Although cities have e-commerce sites in countries, marginalized communities are not keen to invest in the digitized business hence they are unable to utilize e-commerce sites. This implies that marginalized communities have limited opportunities for online businesses. On digital investment, governments invest in a number of digitization projects in cities in a bid to enhance digital government but neglect marginalized parts owing to less connectivity and poor networks (Islam & Inan, 2021).

## Diagnostic 6: Policy D6

The last dimension is policy. It is important to have policies that favor digitization. This element covers data management and regulations. Inadequate or unclear policies tend to hinder access to funds and technology. In data, management if ownership of data is unclear there are likely to be obstacles. If the policy on data ownership, and data governance is unclear there are likely to be challenges in the rate of uptake of digitization initiatives. The second aspect is regulations, which often affect marginalized areas. Inconsistent changes in the regulations such as the way grants will be awarded may favor large-size players at the expense of marginalized communities (Ferrari et al., 2022).

## Guiding Policy

In this section, we present the guiding policy which will direct towards solving the elements. Guiding policy is the first step in strategy formulation from Figure 4 as it specifies the approach to deal with challenges identifies in the diagnosis stage. Consequently, each diagnostic will be matched to a specific guiding policy.

## Guiding Policy 1: Provide Education and Training to the Population GP1

The suggested guiding policy for lack of education is training and educating the citizens. Education is important in ensuring growth in developing countries as the development of a varied labor force will make it possible to access and integrate knowledge into socio-economic activities. Access to knowledge and education addresses vulnerabilities and impediments which prevent marginalized persons from seeking opportunities that will improve their livelihoods. (Paden, 2006). Therefore, educating and empowering communities is a key driver to the digitization

## Guiding Policy 2: Provide Adequate Infrastructure GP2

Lack of infrastructure is countered by availing resources and the environment as the guiding policy. Infrastructure is crucial as it helps people have easy access to digitization(Islam & Inan, 2021). It is important to have adequate ICT tools such as computers, reliable broadband, and adequate power to ensure the success of ICT projects

The suggested guiding policy for socio-cultural factors is the empowerment of people is the empowerment of communities. It is important to consider the perspectives of citizens such as trust and awareness about ICT uses. Communities have various demographics and incomes vary from person to person, lack awareness, and as such there is a need to establish a system that empowers communities for successful digitization programs (Islam & Inan, 2021).

## Guiding Policy 3: Provide User-friendly Interfaces GP4

A user-friendly interface is selected as a guiding policy to the factor of usable design. It focuses on how communities find it easy to utilize ICTS. There is a need to consider both illiterate and literate people in designing the systems to avoid slow uptake. This may include having multiple languages to enhance the inclusion of everyone (Islam & Inan, 2021).

## Guiding Policy 4: Promoting a Digital Economy GP5

Promoting a digital economy is selected as a guiding policy for the diagnosis of economic factors. ICT uses need to be considered from an economical perspective as e-commerce and digital economies are key drivers nowadays. It is however of paramount importance to consider marginalized communities in digitization and not only consider cities only (Islam & Inan, 2021).

## Guiding Policy 5: Provision of Favorable Policies GP6

The provision of a favorable policy as a guiding policy to the diagnosis of policy has been chosen. Policy implementers are accountable for some challenges if unclear policies are there which can affect the uptake of digitization. Clear policies on aspects such as data management and regulations will ensure buy-in by all stakeholders (Ferrari et al., 2022)

## Set of Coherent Actions

This subsection outlines a set of coherent actions needed to carry out guiding policies. The set of coherent actions for diagnosis represents strategies for countering diagnosed elements.

*Table 1.*

| Diagnostics | Guiding Policy | Set of Coherent Actions |
|---|---|---|
| Educational D1 | Provide Education and Training to the Population GP1 | CA1 Developing an adult literacy program |
| | | CA2 Skills development programs |

## CA1: Developing an Adult Literacy Program

This solution responds to the basic education deficiency problem. Lack of education makes citizens resist the adoption of technologies in their day-to-day activities (Islam & Inan, 2021). Literacy is very crucial as it builds the foundation for further learning and enables human capital development, which will in turn create a knowledge economy (Fute et al., 2022). Education is viewed as the major instrument for development and equalizer (Akintolu et al., 2022). It is therefore important for governments to ensure that they offer literacy programs to all levels of the populace to support their initiatives to empower communities.

## CA2: Skills Development Programs

In marginalized communities, there is a need to set up Skill Development Centers, which work to empower and prepare them for the future. Such initiatives ensure that communities build awareness of the importance of education and training. This move will ensure that when digitalization takes place no one will be left out. Computer skills, smartphone usage, internet usage skills, and digital proficiency are some of the skills that communities must be capacitated for effective adoption of digitization projects.

*Table 2.*

| Diagnostics 2 D2 | Guiding Policy (GP) | Coherent Actions (CA) |
|---|---|---|
| Lack of interoperability for E-Health systems | GP2: Provide Infrastructure | CA3: Avail adequate computer equipment |
| | | CA4: Provide adequate power |
| | | CA5: Improve scalability |
| | | CA6: Avail reliable internet connectivity |

This coherent action considers facilitating issues that help communities have easy access to ICTS (Islam & Inan, 2021).

## CA3: Avail Adequate Computer Equipment

Providing adequate computers will ensure a favorable ratio between man and machines. Hence, there is a need to procure adequate computer equipment for communities. This will ensure that everyone will have access to digital resources.

*Table 3.*

| Diagnostic 3 D3 | Guiding Policy (GP) | Coherent Actions (CA) |
|---|---|---|
| Socio-cultural | **GP3: Empowerment of Communities** | **CA7**: Rreduction of social isolation |
| | | **CA8**: Improve Awareness of digitization |

## CA4: Provide Adequate Power

Electricity provision is crucial in digitization. Governments need to avail it or use backup alternatives such as generators and systems to ensure the viability of digitization projects as there is a need for 24/7 availability of services.

## CA5: Improve Scalability

Digitization presents data entry and capturing. This implies that there is a need for capacity to handle complexities and storage. It is important for governments to consider adopting cloud solutions so as to counter the need to have plenty of server machines that are subject to failure at any given time.

## CA6: Avail Reliable Internet Connectivity

For effective digitalization, there is a need for high-speed internet connectivity. It is therefore imperative that when internet connectivity is introduced in prioritized areas, there is also a need to consider marginalized areas. The connection must be fast and reliable for the effective adoption of digitization (Islam & Inan, 2021)

## CA7: Reduction of Social Isolation

Users tend to lose trust in technology owing to social inequality in the context of income, age, gender, and special needs to mention a few. Resultantly incomes vary from community to community and this social inequality can be an obstacle to adopt digitization. Hence, it is imperative for governments to include all social dimensions

*Table 4.*

| Diagnostic 4 D4 | Guiding Policy (GP) | Coherent Actions (CA) |
|---|---|---|
| Unusable | **GP4: Provide user friendly interfaces** | **CA9**: Provide a user-friendly interface |

in projects so that they do not feel left out. When projects are implemented, there will be participation from them and representatives will encourage their members to be part of digitization (Islam & Inan, 2021)

## CA8: Increased Awareness of Digitization

Social inequality can cause resistance from stakeholders. For example, low-income earners are most likely interested in using the internet, while a small fraction of the population uses the internet on mobile phones but has limited access. Resultantly there will be a lack of trust in the internet. Communities tend to resort to traditional values and methods of doing things. Governments need to therefore capacitate communities so that social inequality is removed. This also needs awareness programs for communities on the benefits of digitization and aspects of security and privacy (Ferrari et al., 2022; Islam & Inan, 2021).

## CA9: Provide a User-friendly Interface

The user interface is very crucial as it can also determine the acceptance or rejection of technology. Hence developers need to ensure that systems are usable, accessible, and support multiple languages for the inclusion of both illiterate and literate communities. For better experience and acceptance there is a need to provide a system that presents positive experiences so that users can recommend the next person to adopt a technology (Ferrari et al., 2022)

## CA10: Promoting a Digital Economy

Looking at ICT from a business perspective is very important. One of the challenges discovered was the lack of digital investment. It is important that governments engage with private companies and Non-Governmental Organizations to ensure that there is adequate infrastructure for digitization. It is also imperative for policy implementers to ensure that e-commerce is provided in all communities including the marginalized ones. It is important to ensure that communities realize the use of ICT for economic gains (Islam & Inan, 2021).

*Table 5.*

| Diagnostic 5 D5 | Guiding Policy (GP) | Coherent Actions (CA) |
|---|---|---|
| Economic | **GP5: Promoting a digital economy** | **CA10**: Promoting a digital economy |

*Table 6.*

| Diagnostic 6 D6 | Guiding Policy (GP) | Coherent Actions (CA) |
|---|---|---|
| Economic | **GP6: Provision of favorable policies** | **CA11**: Fair policy |

## CA11: Fair Policy

For community acceptance, there is a need to ensure that policies implemented favor all the communities. All communities including marginalized communities are part of the drafting process for easy implementation. There is needs to have the sense of ownership amongst communities and as such governments need to consider this (Islam & Inan, 2021)

A strategy was formulated in order to achieve the objectives of the study. The strategy needs to be implemented and guided by a set of actions. The phase encompasses carrying out some set of coherent actions.

## Strategy Evaluation

This section describes the evaluation procedure of the proposed strategy. It is crucial as it determines the value of the strategy within its context. This section provides a description of the evaluation procedure of the proposed strategic guideline framework. Evaluation is essential in determining the value of the strategic framework within its context. The process of evaluation consists of deciding the elements to be monitored and evaluated, and the basis of comparison.

The consolidated strategy is shown in Figure 5.

*Figure 5. Proposed strategy for digital transformation in marginalized communities*
*Source (Authors)*

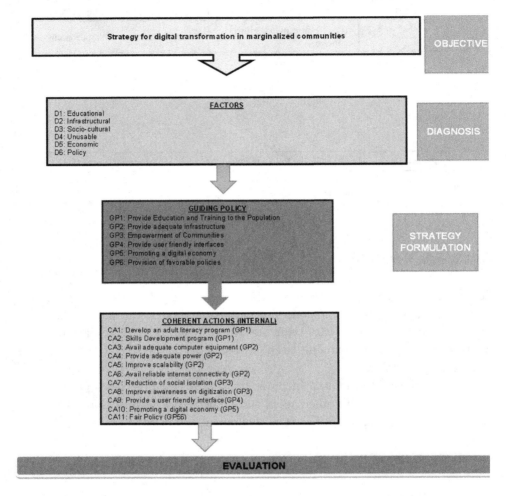

## FUTURE RESEARCH DIRECTIONS

This book chapter introduced the concept of digital transformation and digitization. In order to do that a systematic analysis of empirical research articles on digital transformation, digitization, and digital challenges in marginal communities was done. This enabled the chapter to ascertain the critical success factors of digital transformation. The chapter also identified and discussed issues, controversies, and challenges of digitalization in marginal communities. This enabled the contextualization of digitalization in marginal communities in line with the thematic areas of the book. The chapter culminated in the development of a digitalization strategy for marginalized communities in a developing context in sync with the theme of the book. This work contributes to the body of knowledge in two ways and to practice. Firstly, the chapter provides a systematic overview of the prevalent research in the field of digital transformation in general and marginalized communities in particular. The chapter establishes the critical success factors to the digital transformation of marginalized communities, issues, controversies, and negative effects of digitalization in marginal communities.

The chapter also contributes to practice as it proposed a strategy for digital transformation for marginalized communities in a developing context. We, therefore, believe that country governments and policy makers in developing contexts would benefit from this strategy if they intend to digitally transform their marginalized communities. Other scholars can also evaluate our strategy and empirically test its suitability in different circumstances and as result add any aspects, they may find in their empirical studies.

Future research can look at empirically evaluating the critical success factors for digital transformation in marginalized communities to shed more light on these factors and the implications of digital transformation in marginalized communities, which many countries in developing contexts are currently grappling with. The significance of a vibrant and supportive private sector especially the ICT, telecommunication industry, and a sound banking sector are vital to make inroads in the quest for the digital transformation of marginalized communities. This should be buttressed by a calm and enabling political climate, which exhumes stability and long-term planning.

In this book thematic emphasis was placed on digitalization transformation inclusivity in marginalized communities in a developing context. Hence, primacy was given to digitalization of marginalized communities, the critical success factors, and formulation of a digitalization strategy formulation for the transformation of marginalized communities in Zimbabwe. Therefore, firstly, there is need to explore human centered digital transformation capabilities and dynamic capabilities in developing countries. Secondly, there is a need for an exploration of the fundamental reasons for organizations that are undergoing digital transformation, the challenges they are facing and what it takes to achieve digital transformation in a developing context. This may afford further insight into both intrinsic and extrinsic factors affecting digitalization transformation of organizations in a developing context as well as positive and negative consequences of digital transformation if any. In addition to this, specific effects of digitalization on the workers and management is essential for academia and practice. Future research on digital transformation in a developing context could benefit from including such a perspective.

## CHAPTER SUMMARY

The book chapter explained the concept of digitalization in marginalized communities in the context of developing countries. The challenges hindering digitalization in marginalized communities were highlighted and a strategy was formulated for the transformation of marginalized communities in Zimbabwe. The critical success factors, which include a number of benefits that come with the digital transformation were, identified. An environmental assessment on the internal and external issues hindering digitalization in marginalized areas in developing countries was done so as to come up with solutions. Future research suggests the need to empirically evaluate the critical success factors for digital transformation in marginalized communities to shed more light on these factors. Implications of digital transformation in marginalized communities, which many countries in developing contexts are currently grappling with has been suggested as another interesting area for future research. Conclusively, this chapter investigated the digital transformation challenges faced by organization and the need to adapt to the rising need to digitally transform to meet the contemporary needs. The chapter place more thrust on marginalized communities in a developing context. The chapter concluded with the formulation of a strategy to assist in the digitalization process inclusively incorporating marginalized communities in the technological drive.

## REFERENCES

Aanestad, M., & Kankanhalli, A. (2022). Special Issue-Call for Papers-Digital Technologies and Social Justice-MIS Quarterly Call for Papers. *MISQ*.

Akintolu, M., Uleanya, C., & Letseka, M. (2022). Examining key challenges in adult community learning centres' programme of KwaZulu-Natal province of South Africa. *Journal of Adult and Continuing Education*. Advance online publication. doi:10.1177/14779714211070307

Aruleba, K., & Jere, N. (2022). Exploring Digital Transforming Challenges in Rural Areas of South Africa through a Systematic Review of Empirical Studies. *Scientific American*, *16*, e01190. doi:10.1016/j.sciaf.2022.e01190

Banihashemi, S. A., & Rejaei, Z. (2015). Analysis of the digital divide in Asia-Islamic countries: A topsis approach. *Journal of Asian Scientific Research.*, *5*(4), 165–176. doi:10.18488/journal.2/2015.5.4/2.4.165.176

Ceia, V., Nothwehr, B., & Wagner, L. (2021). *Gender and Technology: A rights-based and tntersectional analysis of key trends*. Oxfam.

Chib, A., Bentley, C., & Wardoyo, R. J. (2019). Distributed digital contexts and learning: Personal empowerment and social transformation in marginalized populations. *Comunicar*, *27*(58), 51–60. doi:10.3916/C58-2019-05

Elers, P., Dutta, J. M., & Elers, S. (2022). *Culturally centring digital inclusion and marginality: A case study in Aotearoa New Zealand*. Academic Press.

Ferrari, A., Bacco, M., Gaber, K., Jedlitschka, A., Hess, S., Kaipainen, J., Koltsida, P., Toli, E., & Brunori, G. (2022). Drivers, barriers and impacts of digitalization in rural areas from the viewpoint of experts. *Information and Software Technology*, *145*, 106816. doi:10.1016/j.infsof.2021.106816

Fute, A., Wan, X., Oubibi, M., & Bulugu, J. B. (2022). Adult Literacy Education and Reduction of Poverty in Tanzania: A Review of Policies and their Implementation. *Journal of Education*. Advance online publication. doi:10.1177/00220574221075204

Gangadharan, S. (2021). *Digital Exclusion: A Politics of Refusal*. University of Chicago Press.

Ghauri, P., Fu, X., & Minayora, A. (2022). Digital technology-based entrepreneurial pursuit of the marginalized communities. *Journal of International Management*, *28*(2), 100948. doi:10.1016/j.intman.2022.100948

Hourcade, J. P., Bullock-Rest, N. E., & Schelhowe, H. (2010a). Digital technologies and Marginalized Youth. *Proceedings of IDC2010: The 9th International Conference on Interaction Design and Children, May 2014*, 360–363. 10.1145/1810543.1810614

Hourcade, J. P., Bullock-Rest, N. E., & Schelhowe, H. (2010b). Digital technologies and Marginalized Youth. *Proceedings of IDC2010: The 9th International Conference on Interaction Design and Children*, 360–363. 10.1145/1810543.1810614

Islam, M. N., & Inan, T. T. (2021). Exploring the Fundamental Factors of Digital Inequality in Bangladesh. *SAGE Open*, *11*(2). Advance online publication. doi:10.1177/21582440211021407

Karimi, J., & Walter, Z. (2015). The role of dynamic capabilities in responding to digital disruption: A factor-based study of the newspaper industry. *Journal of Management Information Systems*, *32*(1), 39–81. doi:10.1080/07421222.2015.10 29380

Kraus, S., Jones, P., Kailer, N., Weinmann, A., Chaparro-Banegas, N., & Roig-Tierno, N. (2021). Digital Transformation: An Overview of the Current State of the Art of Research. *SAGE Open*, *11*(3). Advance online publication. doi:10.1177/21582440211047576

Lester, H. (2019). *Bridging the urban-rural digital divide and mobilizing technology for poverty eradication: challenges and gaps.* Department of Economics, University of the West Indies.

Liberties, E. U. (2021). *What Is Marginalization?* Definition and Coping Strategies.

Marambi, S., Musungwini, S., & Mzikamwi, T. (2018). Strategy for the adoption and effective utilization of mobile phone technologies in smallholder agriculture in Zimbabwe. In *Proceedings of 6th International Conference on M4D Mobile Communication for Development* (pp. 15–16). Universitetstryckeriet, Karlstad 2018. www.researchjournal.co.in

Matt, C., Hess, T., & Benlian, A. (2015). Digital Transformation Strategies. *Business & Information Systems Engineering, 57*(5), 339–343. doi:10.100712599-015-0401-5

Paden, C. I. (2006). *An Investigation of ICT Project Management Techniques for Sustainable ICT Projects in Rural Development.* Academic Press.

Reis, J., Amorim, M., Melão, N., & Matos, P. (2018). Digital transformation: A literature review and guidelines for future research. *Advances in Intelligent Systems and Computing, 745*(March), 411–421. doi:10.1007/978-3-319-77703-0_41

Rudder, C. (2019). What is digital transformation? Your top questions answered. *The Enterprisers Project*, 7.

Sahu, N., Deng, H., & Mollah, A. (2018). Investigating The Critical Success Factors of Digital Transformation for Improving Customer Experience. *Proceedings of the International Conference on Information Resources Management (Conf-IRM 2018)*, 1–13.

Salemink, K. (2016). How spatially and socially marginalized communities. Academic Press.

Sevelius, J. M., Gutierrez-Mock, L., Zamudio-Haas, S., McCree, B., Ngo, A., Jackson, A., Clynes, C., Venegas, L., Salinas, A., Herrera, C., Stein, E., Operario, D., & Gamarel, K. (2020). Research with Marginalized Communities: Challenges to Continuity During the COVID-19 Pandemic. *AIDS and Behavior, 24*(7), 2009–2012. doi:10.100710461-020-02920-3 PMID:32415617

van Dyk, R., & van Belle, J. P. (2019). Factors influencing the intended adoption of digital transformation: A South African case study. *Proceedings of the 2019 Federated Conference on Computer Science and Information Systems, FedCSIS 2019*, 519–528. 10.15439/2019F166

## KEY TERMS AND DEFINITIONS

**Digitization:** Changing from analog to digital.

**Digital Divide:** Lack of access to digital technology.

**Digital Technology:** Integration of computing systems.

**Information and Communication Technology:** Infrastructure that supports computing.

**Marginalized Communities:** Societies that are not part of the mainstream social, economic, educational, or cultural life.

**Strategy:** A plan of action.

# Conclusion

ICTs can if adopted and used properly, shift and destroy social boundaries between the elite and the segregated. The gaps that the situation of yesteryear has socially created can be countered when digital devices are put to full use. Digital technologies focus on how less privileged and remote areas can gain from being included in the access and utilization of technologies and transform their well-being in their societies. Although digital transformation has made some positive contributions to promoting digital inclusion in developing countries, there are still challenges, including access, affordability, digital skills, and usage. The use of digital devices for basic service delivery has not accomplished the goal of digital transformation. Currently, marginalized communities frequently experience exclusion in digitalization activities as they encounter many challenges regarding affordability or access to ICTs and connectivity due to a myriad of factors. Rural areas are poorly covered in terms of digitization of services—making service provision digital by default significantly disadvantages the marginalized communities. Most individuals in marginalized communities do not have access to the technology and/or technological skills required to participate in the digital transformation due to long-standing political, economic, educational, and employment marginalization. Access to the Internet is very important but not enough to improve the integration of digital development in marginalized communities. Digital inclusiveness is beyond physical networking and access to ICT infrastructure. Research on digital inclusion should be conceptualized beyond access and usage to provide actionable findings. The important complementary areas to work on are Digital innovation skills, access to the infrastructure, analyses, creation, and communication of information using ICT models.

The objectives of digital inclusiveness are to make more flexible working conditions, network people in remote areas with urban, and create new opportunities such as e-commerce and the digital economy, and all of these can bridge the gap between labour force participation. Based on the foregoing, action should be taken to establish digital basic service interventions in developing economies and explain why certain digital interventions do not reinforce inclusiveness in digital transformation and/or deliver an inclusive digital economy and digital society.

Marginalized communities must acquire the proper digital skills required to use digital technology tools, including remote working skills such as strong written communication, collaboration, time management, and adaptability; if they fail, they will once again be left behind. Furthermore, marginalized communities require a customized policy framework for digital inclusion, and the involvement of the government in enacting laws and regulations to promote digital transformation is a critical component of achieving digitalization. Thus, digital transformation can transpire if those who are apparently excluded become part of the larger economy.

Developing countries investing more in digital technologies in marginalized communities might positively impact other vulnerable groups, creating opportunities associated with innovative technology and reducing barriers to digital transformation. Bridging of the gap of the rate of internet penetration between the rural and urban people is key hence the government needs to come up with models to realize the full potential of digital transformation. Notably, government policies should simplify access to information and communication through digital inclusion activities. Thus, the significance of this book is to ensure that digital inclusion initiatives address the realities faced by those marginalized from the digital economy by moving away from a digital inclusive approach grounded on a technological perspective.

*Munyaradzi Zhou*
*Midlands State University, Zimbabwe*

*Gilbert Mahlangu*
*Midlands State University, Zimbabwe*

*Cyncia Matsika*
*Midlands State University, Zimbabwe*

# Compilation of References

Aanestad, M., & Kankanhalli, A. (2022). Special Issue-Call for Papers-Digital Technologies and Social Justice-MIS Quarterly Call for Papers. *MISQ*.

Abad-Segura, E., González-Zamar, M. D., Luque-de la Rosa, A., & Cevallos, M. B. M. (2020). Sustainability of educational technologies: An approach to augmented reality research. *Sustainability (Switzerland)*, *12*(10), 4091. Advance online publication. doi:10.3390u12104091

Abad-Segura, E., González-Zamar, M. D., Luque-de la Rosa, A., Cevallos, M. B. M., & Bao, W., Luz Yolanda Toro Suarez, Bloom, D. A., Reid, J. R., Cassady, C. I., Murphy, M. P. A., Osman, M. E. T., Papanastasiou, G., Drigas, A., Skianis, C., Lytras, M., Papanastasiou, E., Quintero, J., Baldiris, S., Rubira, R., … Jové, T. (2020). Global impact of COVID-19 on education systems: The emergency remote teaching at Sultan Qaboos University. *Contemporary Security Policy*, *10*(3), 425–436. doi:10.100700247-020-04728-8

Abersfelder, S., Bogner, E., Heyder, A., & Franke, J. (2016). Application and validation of an existing Industry 4.0 guideline for the development of specific recommendations for implementation. *Advanced Materials Research*, *1140*, 465–472. doi:10.4028/www.scientific.net/AMR.1140.465

Acharya, G. D. (2018). *Including the excluded: Marginalized poor communities and development practices in rural Nepal*. Academic Press.

Adam, I. O., & Dzang Alhassan, M. (2021). *Bridging the global digital divide through digital inclusion: the role of ICT access and ICT use. Transforming Government: People, Process and Policy*. doi:10.1108/TG-06-2020-0114

Adams, M., Klinsky, S., & Chhetri, N. (2020). Barriers to sustainability in poor marginalized communities in the United States: The criminal justice, the prison-industrial complex and foster care systems. *Sustainability (Switzerland)*, *12*(1), 220. Advance online publication. doi:10.3390u12010220

Adeleye, N., & Eboagu, C. (2019). Evaluation of ICT development and economic growth in Africa. *NETNOMICS: Economic Research and Electronic Networking*, *20*(1), 31–53. doi:10.100711066-019-09131-6

Agarwal, R., Guodong, G., DesRoches, C., & Jha, A. K. (2010). The digital transformation of healthcare: Current status and the road ahead. *Information Systems Research*, *21*(4), 796–809. doi:10.1287/isre.1100.0327

Agyekumhene, C., de Vries, J. R., van Paassen, A., Macnaghten, P., Schut, M., & Bregt, A. (2018). Digital platforms for smallholder credit access: The mediation of trust for cooperation in maize value chain financing. *NJAS Wageningen Journal of Life Sciences*, *86–87*(1), 77–88. doi:10.1016/j.njas.2018.06.001

Ahmed, M., Ozaki, A., Ogata, K., Ito, S., Miyajima, I., Ahmed, A., Okayasu, T., Choudhury, D. K., & Al Amin, N. (2016). Poor farmer, entrepreneurs and ICT relation in production & marketing of quality vegetables in Bangladesh. *Journal of the Faculty of Agriculture, Kyushu University*, *61*(1), 241–250. doi:10.5109/1564129

Ahrendt, D., & Patrini, V. (2020). *How to use the surge in teleworking as a real chance to include people with disabilities*. Academic Press.

Ajzen, I. (2014). *Attitude theory and the attitude-behavior relation*. Academic Press.

Akçayır, M., & Akçayır, G. (2017). Advantages and challenges associated with augmented reality for education: A systematic review of the literature. *Educational Research Review*, *20*, 1–11. doi:10.1016/j.edurev.2016.11.002

Akintolu, M., Uleanya, C., & Letseka, M. (2022). Examining key challenges in adult community learning centres' programme of KwaZulu-Natal province of South Africa. *Journal of Adult and Continuing Education*. Advance online publication. doi:10.1177/14779714211070307

Alamelu, K. (2013). Digital inclusion - a conceptual framework. *International Journal of Advanced Research in Management and Social Sciences*, *2*(12), 228–248.

Aleixo, C., Nunes, M., & Isaias, P. (2012). Usability and Digital Inclusion: Standards and Guidelines. *International Journal of Public Administration*, *35*(3), 221–239. doi:10.1080/0190 0692.2011.646568

Al-Hassan, R., Egyir, I., & Abakah, J. (2013). Farm household level impacts of information communication technology (ICT)-based agricultural market information in Ghana. *Journal of Development and Agricultural Economics*, *5*(4), 161–167. doi:10.5897/JDAE12.143

Ali, A., Qadir, J., Rasool, R., Sathiaseelan, A., Zwitter, A., & Crowfot, J. (2016). Big data for development: Applications and techniques. *Big Data Analytics*, *1*(2), 1–24. doi:10.118641044-016-0002-4

Ali, M. A., Alam, K., & Taylor, B. (2019). Do social exclusion and remoteness explain the digital divide in Australia? Evidence from a panel data estimation approach. *Economics of Innovation and New Technology*, 1–17. doi:10.1080/10438599.2019.1664708

Ali, M. A., Alam, K., Taylor, B., & Rafiq, S. (2020). Does digital inclusion affect quality of life? Evidence from Australian household panel data. *Telematics and Informatics*, *51*, 101405. doi:10.1016/j.tele.2020.101405

Al-Muwil, A., Weerakkody, V., El-haddadeh, R., & Dwivedi, Y. (2019). Balancing Digital-By-Default with Inclusion: A Study of the Factors Influencing E-Inclusion in the UK. *Information Systems Frontiers*, *21*(3), 635–659. doi:10.100710796-019-09914-0

Alotaibi, S. J., & Wald, M. (2012). Towards a UTAUT-based model for studying the integrating physical and virtual identity access management systems in e-government domain. *2012 International Conference for Internet Technology and Secured Transactions, ICITST 2012*, 453–458.

Alves Nascimento, L., Bouzada, M., Gonçalves, A., & Pitassi, C. (2016). *Factors that influence the adoption and implementation of public digital accounting according to the evaluation by managers of brazilian companies*. doi:10.4301/S1807-17752016000200003

Amelia, R. (2016). *Determinacy of actual usage through behavioral intention CIMB NIAGA*. Academic Press.

Andersen, L. (2019). Artificial Intelligence in International Development: Avoiding Ethical Pitfalls. *Journal of Public & International Affairs*.

Antonio, A., & Tuffley, D. (2014). The Gender Digital Divide in Developing Countries. *Future Internet*, *2014*(6), 673–687. doi:10.3390/fi6040673

Armenta, A., Serrano, A., & Cabrera, M. (2012). *Information Technology for Development The new digital divide : the confluence of broadband penetration, sustainable development, technology adoption and community participation*. doi:10.1080/02681102.2011.625925

Aruleba, K., & Jere, N. (2022). Exploring Digital Transforming Challenges in Rural Areas of South Africa through a Systematic Review of Empirical Studies. *Scientific African*.

Aruleba, K., & Jere, N. (2022). Exploring digital transforming challenges in rural areas of South Africa through a systematic review of empirical studies. *Scientific American*, *16*, e01190. doi:10.1016/j.sciaf.2022.e01190

Aryati, A. (2017). Mastering Digital Transformation Transforming Government. *The Electronic Library*, *34*(1), 1–5.

Asia, D. (2021). *Funding Agricultural Innovation for the Global South: Does it Promote Sustainable Agricultural Intensification?* Academic Press.

Assembly, G. (2015). Sustainable development goals. *SDGs, Transforming Our World: The, 2030*.

Attrey, A. (2021). *Agile, comprehensive and principles-based: Policy making for a digital age*. Academic Press.

Avgerou, C., & Madon, S. (2009). Information society and the digital divide problem in developing countries Book section. *Perspectives and Policies on ICT in Society*, 205–218.

Avgerou, C. (2017). Theoretical framing of ICT4D research. *IFIP Advances in Information and Communication Technology*, *504*, 10–23. Advance online publication. doi:10.1007/978-3-319-59111-7_2

Aziz, A., & Aziz, A. (2020). Digital inclusion challenges in Bangladesh : The case of the National ICT Policy ICT Policy. *Contemporary South Asia, 0*(0), 1–16. doi:10.1080/09584935.2020.1793912

Baharuddin, M. F., Izhar, T. A. T., & Shoid, M. S. M. (2018). Adoption of Open Source Software (OSS) and Organization Performance in the Library. *International Journal of Academic Research in Business & Social Sciences, 8*(9), 285–297. doi:10.6007/IJARBSS/v8-i9/4591

Bailey, A., Henry-Lee, A., Johnson-Coke, Y., Leach, R., Clayton, A., Gee, M., & Browne, O. (2019). ICT use in the context of electricity access in a developing country: A choice framework analysis. *IFIP Advances in Information and Communication Technology, 551*, 27–38. doi:10.1007/978-3-030-18400-1_3

Baio, J., Wiggins, L., Christensen, D. L., Maenner, M. J., Daniels, J., Warren, Z., Kurzius-Spencer, M., Zahorodny, W., Rosenberg, C. R., & White, T. (2018). Prevalence of autism spectrum disorder among children aged 8 years—Autism and developmental disabilities monitoring network, 11 sites, United States, 2014. *MMWR. Surveillance Summaries, 67*(6), 1.

Banerjee, D. A. K. (2020). *A Brief History of Pandemics.* Academic. https://medium.com/history-uncut/a-brief-history-of-pandemics-d9f372c89484

Banihashemi, S. A., & Rejaei, Z. (2015). Analysis of the digital divide in Asia-Islamic countries: A topsis approach. *Journal of Asian Scientific Research., 5*(4), 165–176. doi:10.18488/journal.2/2015.5.4/2.4.165.176

Bao, W. (2020). COVID -19 and online teaching in higher education: A case study of Peking University. *Human Behavior and Emerging Technologies, 2*(2), 113–115. doi:10.1002/hbe2.191 PMID:32510042

Baril, A., & Leblanc, C. (2015). Needing to acquire a physical impairment/disability:(re) thinking the connections between trans and disability studies through transability. *Hypatia, 30*(1), 30–48. doi:10.1111/hypa.12113

Bawa, M. W. (2012). *Examination of leadership styles by gender: A case of Tamale Polytechnic.* Academic Press.

Beddington, J. R., Asaduzzaman, M., Bremauntz, F. A., Clark, M. E., Guillou, M., Jahn, M. M., Erda, L., Mamo, T., Van Bo, N., & Nobre, C. A. (2012). *Achieving food security in the face of climate change: Final report from the Commission on Sustainable Agriculture and Climate Change.* Academic Press.

Bellalouna, F. (2021). The Augmented Reality Technology as Enabler for the Digitization of Industrial Business Processes: Case Studies. *Procedia CIRP, 98*, 400–405. doi:10.1016/j.procir.2021.01.124

Bendor-Samuel, P. (2017). *The power of digital transformation in a data-driven world.* Retrieved May 10, 2022, from https://www.forbes.com/sites/peterbendorsamuel/

Berghaus, S., & Back, A. (2017). *Disentangling the fuzzy front end of digital transformation: Activities and approaches.* Academic Press.

Bernacki, M. L., Greene, J. A., & Crompton, H. (2020). Mobile technology, learning, and achievement: Advances in understanding and measuring the role of mobile technology in education. *Contemporary Educational Psychology, 60*, 101827. doi:10.1016/j.cedpsych.2019.101827

Biles, J. (2006). Globalization of food retailing and the consequences of Wal-Martization in Mexico. *Academia (Caracas), 24*, 343–355.

Bonafilia, D., Gill, J., Basu, S., & Yang, D. (2019). Building high resolution maps for humanitarian aid and development with weakly-and semi-supervised learning. *Proceedings of the IEEE/CVF Conference on Computer Vision and Pattern Recognition Workshops*, 1–9.

Bongomin, O., Gilibrays Ocen, G., Oyondi Nganyi, E., Musinguzi, A., & Omara, T. (2020). Exponential Disruptive Technologies and the Required Skills of Industry 4.0. *Journal of Engineering (United Kingdom), 2020*, 1–17. Advance online publication. doi:10.1155/2020/4280156

Bonilla, M. H. S., & Pretto, N. D. L. (2011). *Inclusão digital: polêmica contemporânea*. Edufba. doi:10.7476/9788523212063

Boueé, C., & Schaible, S. (2015). *Die Digitale Transformation der Industrie. In Studie: Roland Berger und BDI*. Predictive Maintenance.

Bradley, E. H., Curry, L. A., & Devers, K. J. (2007). *Qualitative Data Analysis for Health Services Research : Developing Taxonomy, Themes, and Theory*. doi:10.1111/j.1475-6773.2006.00684.x

Breman, B. A. S., Vihinen, H., Tapio-Biström, M.-L., & Pinto Correia, M. T. (2010). Meeting the challenge of marginalization processes at the periphery of Europe. *Public Administration, 88*(2), 364–380. doi:10.1111/j.1467-9299.2010.01834.x

Brito, C. (2020). *Covid-19 has intensified the digital 2020., divide*. World Economic Forum.

Bronson, K. (2019). Looking through a responsible innovation lens at uneven engagements with digital farming. *NJAS Wageningen Journal of Life Sciences, 90*(1), 100294. doi:10.1016/j.njas.2019.03.001

Brunetti, F., Matt, D. T., Bonfanti, A., De Longhi, A., Pedrini, G., & Orzes, G. (2020). Digital transformation challenges: Strategies emerging from a multi-stakeholder approach. *The TQM Journal, 32*(4), 697–724. doi:10.1108/TQM-12-2019-0309

Brunner, M., Hemsley, B., Togher, L., & Palmer, S. (2017). Technology and its role in rehabilitation for people with cognitive-communication disability following a traumatic brain injury (TBI). *Brain Injury: [BI], 31*(8), 1028–1043. doi:10.1080/02699052.2017.1292429 PMID:28471267

Bruun, E. P. G., & Duka, A. (2018). Artificial intelligence, jobs and the future of work: Racing with the machines. *Basic Income Studies, 13*(2).

Bucci, G., Bentivoglio, D., Finco, A., Belletti, M., & Bentivoglio, D. (2019). Exploring the impact of innovation adoption in agriculture: How and where Precision Agriculture Technologies can be suitable for the Italian farm system? *IOP Conference Series. Earth and Environmental Science, 275*(1), 012004. doi:10.1088/1755-1315/275/1/012004

Bukht, R. & Heeks, R. (2017). *Defining, Conceptualizing and Measuring the Digital Economy.* Centre for Development Informatics Global Development Institute.

Cabero-Almenara, J., Fernández-Batanero, J. M., & Barroso-Osuna, J. (2019). Adoption of augmented reality technology by university students. *Heliyon*, *5*(5), e01597. Advance online publication. doi:10.1016/j.heliyon.2019.e01597 PMID:31193247

Calabrese Barton, A., & Tan, E. (2018). A Longitudinal Study of Equity-Oriented STEM-Rich Making Among Youth From Historically Marginalized Communities. *American Educational Research Journal*, *55*(4), 761–800. doi:10.3102/0002831218758668

Calandro, E., & Berglund, N. (2019). *Unpacking Cyber-Capacity Building in Shaping Cyberspace Governance: The SADC case.* Academic Press.

Camarinha, L. M., Fornasiero, R., Ramexani, J., & Ferrada, F. (2019). Collaborative networks: A pillar of digital transformation. *Applied Sciences Journal*, *9*(24), 1–34. doi:10.3390/app9245431

Camodeca, R.; Almici, A. (2020). Digital Transformation and Convergence toward the 2030 Agenda's Sustainability Development Goals: Evidence from Italian Listed Firms. *Sustainability*, *13*(21), 11831. doi:10.3390/su132111831

Campbell-meier, J., Sylvester, A., & Goulding, A. (2020). *Indigenous Digital Inclusion : Interconnections and Comparisons.* Academic Press.

Cannarella, C. (2002). Processes of marginalization of agriculture: The role of non-agricultural sectors to support economic and social growth in rural areas. *Journal of Central European Agriculture.*

Capurro, R. (2017). Digitization as an ethical challenge. *AI & Society*, *32*(2), 277–283. doi:10.100700146-016-0686-z

Carmi, E., & Yates, S. J. (2020). *What do digital inclusion and data literacy mean today?* doi:10.14763/2020.2.1474

Castillo, J. G. D., Cohenour, E. J. C., Escalante, M. A. S., & Del Socorro Vázquez Carrillo, I. (2019). Reducing the digital divide in vulnerable communities in southeastern Mexico. *Publicaciones de La Facultad de Educacion y Humanidades Del Campus de Melilla*, *49*(2), 133–149. doi:10.30827/publicaciones.v49i2.9305

Ceia, V., Nothwehr, B., & Wagner, L. (2021). *Gender and Technology: A rights-based and tntersectional analysis of key trends.* Oxfam.

Chaddad, F. (2015). *The economics and organization of Brazilian agriculture: Recent evolution and productivity gains.* Academic Press.

Chadwick, D., & Wesson, C. (2016). *Digital Inclusion and Disability.* Springer Science and Business Media LLC.

Cha, K. J., Hwang, T., & Gregor, S. (2015). An integrative model of IT-enabled organizational transformation: A multiple case study. *Management Decision, 53*(8), 1755–1770. doi:10.1108/MD-09-2014-0550

Chambers, K. (2018, September/October). *Global megatrends driving manufacturing digital transformation. Latest software systems improve business performance.* Intech. www.isa.org

Chataway, J., Hanlin, R., & Kaplinsky, R. (2014). Inclusive innovation: An architecture for policy development. *Innovation and Development, 4*(1), 33–54. doi:10.1080/2157930X.2013.876800

Chen, J. E., Pan, S. L., & Ouyang, T. H. (2014). Routine reconfiguration in traditional companies' e-commerce strategy implementation: A trajectory perspective. *Information & Management, 51*(2), 270–282. doi:10.1016/j.im.2013.11.008

Chen, T., Zhang, Y., Ding, C., Ting, K., Yoon, S., Sahak, H., Hope, A., McLachlin, S., Crawford, E., Hardisty, M., Larouche, J., & Finkelstein, J. (2021). Virtual reality as a learning tool in spinal anatomy and surgical techniques. *North American Spine Society Journal, 6*(January), 100063. doi:10.1016/j.xnsj.2021.100063 PMID:35141628

Chen, W., Li, X., & Chen, W. (2021). Digital inequalities in American disadvantaged urban communities : Access, skills, and expectations for digital inclusion programs inclusion programs. *Information Communication and Society, 0*(0), 1–18. doi:10.1080/1369118X.2021.1907434

Cheo, E. A., & Tapiwa, K. A. (2021a). *Sustainable Development Goal-2: End hunger, achieve food security and improved nutrition and promote sustainable agriculture.* Emerald Publishing Limited. doi:10.1108/9781789738032

Cheo, A. E., & Tapiwa, K. A. (2021b). The Importance of SDG-2. In *SDG 2 – Zero Hunger: Food Security, Improved Nutrition and Sustainable Agriculture (Concise Guides to the United Nations Sustainable Development Goals)* (pp. 7–14). Emerald Publishing Limited. doi:10.1108/978-1-78973-803-220201005

Chepken, C., Mugwanya, R., Blake, E., & Marsden, G. (2012). ICTD interventions: Trends Over the Last Decade. *Proceedings of the Fifth International Conference on Information and Communication Technologies and Development - ICTD '12*, 241. 10.1145/2160673.2160704

Chib, A., Bentley, C., & Wardoyo, R. J. (2019). Distributed digital contexts and learning: Personal empowerment and social transformation in marginalized populations. *Comunicar, 27*(58), 51–60. doi:10.3916/C58-2019-05

Chikwati, E. (2021). (2021, August 19) Digital platforms change face of agriculture sector. *The Herald.*

Chiru, S. S. (n.d.). Education and Development in India: Marginalizing the Margins. Editorial Board and Paper Review Committee, 6.

Chohan, S. R., & Hu, G. (2020). Strengthening digital inclusion through e-government: Cohesive ICT training programs to intensify digital competency. *Information Technology for Development, 0*(0), 1–23. doi:10.1080/02681102.2020.1841713

Ciampa, D. M. (2009). *Information Security Security+ Guide to Network Security Fundamentals* (3rd ed.). Course Technology Cengage Learning.

Ciechanover, A. (2019). *The revolution of personalized medicine—Are we going to cure all diseases and at what price*. Concept Note of the Pontifical Academy of Sciences-Summit on the Revolution of Personalized Medicine.

CISA. (2018, October 3). *Cybersecurity Threats to Precision Agriculture*. Department of Homeland Security: CISA. https://www.us-cert.gov/ncas/current-activity/2018/10/03/Cybersecurity-Threats-Precision-Agriculture

Ciuriak, D., & Ptashkina, M. (2018). The digital transformation and the transformation of international trade. RTA Exchange. Geneva: International Centre for Trade and Sustainable Development (ICTSD) and the Inter-American Development Bank (IDB).

Clapp, J., & Ruder, S.-L. (2020). Precision technologies for agriculture: Digital farming, gene-edited crops, and the politics of sustainability. *Global Environmental Politics, 20*(3), 49–69.

Clark, S., Hawkes, C., Murphy, S., Hansen-Kuhn, K. A., & Wallinga, D. (2012). Exporting Obesity: US Farm and Trade Policy and the Transformation of the Mexican Consumer Food Environment. *International Journal of Occupational and Environmental Health, 18*(1), 53–65. doi:10.1179/1077352512Z.0000000007 PMID:22550697

Co, N. O. (2021). *A Discourse on African Food Insecurity*. Academic Press.

Computations of internet use by socioeconomic group of Southern African Customs Union Countries. (2018). Retrieved April 20, 2022, from https://www.gallup.com/analytics

Correa, T. (2019). *Digital Inclusion in Rural Areas : A Qualitative Exploration of Challenges Faced by People From Isolated Communities Digital Inclusion in Rural Areas : A Qualitative Exploration of Challenges Faced by People*. doi:10.1111/jcc4.12154

Cowie, P., Townsend, L., & Salemink, K. (2020). Smart rural futures: Will rural areas be left behind in the 4th industrial revolution? *Journal of Rural Studies, 79*, 169–176. doi:10.1016/j.jrurstud.2020.08.042 PMID:32863561

Cramb, R. A., Colfer, C. J. P., Dressler, W., Laungaramsri, P., Le, Q. T., Mulyoutami, E., Peluso, N. L., & Wadley, R. L. (2009). Swidden transformations and rural livelihoods in Southeast Asia. *Human Ecology, 37*(3), 323–346. doi:10.100710745-009-9241-6

Daalmans, J., & Daalmans, J. (2012). *Human behavior in hazardous situations: Best practice safety management in the chemical and process industries*. Butterworth-Heinemann.

Dahlman, C., Mealy, S., & Wermelinger, M. (2016). *Harnessing the digital economy for developing countries*. Academic Press.

Dahrouge, S., James, K., Gauthier, A., & Chiocchio, F. (2018). Engaging patients to improve equitable access to community resources. *Canadian Medical Association Journal, 190*(Suppl), S46–S47. doi:10.1503/cmaj.180408 PMID:30404854

Dahunsi, F., & Owoseni, T. (2014). Cloud Computing in Nigeria: The Cloud Ecosystem Perspective. *Nigerian Journal of Technology*, *34*(1), 209. doi:10.4314/njt.v34i1.26

Danaher, M., Cook, J., Danaher, G., Coombes, P., & Danaher, P. A. (2013). Situating Education Research with Marginalized Communities. In *Researching Education with Marginalized Communities* (pp. 1–22). Springer.

Dash, N. S. (2014). *Context and Contextual Word Meaning*. Academic Press.

de Boer, I. J. M., & van Ittersum, M. K. (2018). *Circularity in agricultural production*. Wageningen University and Research.

De Leeuw, J., Vrieling, A., Shee, A., Atzberger, C., Hadgu, K. M., Biradar, C. M., Keah, H., & Turvey, C. (2014). The potential and uptake of remote sensing in insurance: A review. *Remote Sensing*, *6*(11), 10888–10912. doi:10.3390/rs61110888

Deganis, I., Haghian, Pegah, Z., & Tagashira, M. (2021). *Leveraging digital technologies for social inclusion*. Department of Economic and Social Affairs Social Inclusion. https://www.un.org/development/desa/dspd/2021/02/digital-technologies-for-social-inclusion/

Degryse, C. (2016). *Digitalisation of the economy and its impact on labour markets*. ETUI Research Paper-Working Paper.

Dehghani, M., Lee, S. H., & Mashatan, A. (2020). Touching holograms with windows mixed reality: Renovating the consumer retailing services. *Technology in Society*, *63*(August), 101394. doi:10.1016/j.techsoc.2020.101394

Demirguc-Kunt, A., Klapper, L., Singer, D., & Ansar, S. (2018). *The Global Findex Database 2017: Measuring financial inclusion and the fintech revolution*. World Bank Publications. doi:10.1596/978-1-4648-1259-0

Dhawan, S. (2020). Online Learning: A Panacea in the Time of COVID-19 Crisis. *Journal of Educational Technology Systems*, *49*(1), 5–22. doi:10.1177/0047239520934018

Dias, G. P. (2020). Global e-government development: besides the relative wealth of countries, do policies matter? *Transforming Government: People, Process and Policy*, 10–18. doi:10.1108/TG-12-2019-0125

Dias, L. R. (2011). *Inclusão digital como fator de inclusão social*. Inclusão Digital.

Dijk, J. Van. (2002). *A framework for digital divide The Pitfalls of a Metaphor*. Academic Press.

Dijk, J. A. G. M. (2005). Digital Divide: Impact of Access. In P. Rössler, C. A. Hoffner, & L. Zoonen (Eds.), *The International Encyclopedia of Media Effects* (1st ed., pp. 1–11). Wiley., doi:10.1002/9781118783764.wbieme0043

DiMaggio, P., Hargittai, E., Celeste, C., & Shaferl, S. (2004). *From Unequal Access to Differentiated Use: A Literature Review and Agenda for Research on Digital Inequality*. Academic Press.

Dixie, G., & Jayaraman, N. (2011). Strengthening agricultural marketing with ICT. The World Bank/InfoDev'ARD, ICT in agriculture: Connecting smallholders to knowledge, networks, and institutions. *Module, 9*, 205–237.

Dornberger, R., Inglese, T., Korkut, S., & Zhong, V. J. (2018). Digitalization: Yesterday, today and tomorrow. In Business Information Systems and Technology 4.0 (pp. 1–11). Springer.

du Boulay, B., Poulovasillis, A., Holmes, W., & Mavrikis, M. (2018). *Artificial Intelligence And Big Data Technologies To Close The Achievement Gap.* Academic Press.

Dzang, M., & Osman, I. (2021). Technology in society The effects of digital inclusion and ICT access on the quality of life : A global perspective. *Technology in Society, 64*(September). doi:10.1016/j.techsoc.2020.101511

Dzino-Silajdzic, V. (2018). *Practical Guide; Focus group discussions.* https://www.crs.org/sites/default/files/tools-research/fgds_april_24_final_lo_res_.pdf

Ehigiamusoe, K. U., & Lean, H. H. (2018). Tripartite analysis of financial development, trade openness and economic growth: Evidence from Ghana, Nigeria and South Africa. *Contemporary Economics, 12*(2), 189–206.

Ekbia, H. R. (2016). *Digital inclusion and social exclusion : The political economy of value in a networked world.* doi:10.1080/01972243.2016.1153009

Elers, P., Dutta, J. M., & Elers, S. (2022). *Culturally centring digital inclusion and marginality: A case study in Aotearoa New Zealand.* Academic Press.

Ernst, E., Merola, R., & Samaan, D. (2019). Economics of artificial intelligence: Implications for the future of work. *IZA Journal of Labor Policy, 9*(1), 20190004. doi:10.2478/izajolp-2019-0004

EU. (2017). *Agriculture and rural development 2014-2020—The Netherlands fact sheet.* European Commission. Retrieved from https://ec.europa.eu/agriculture/rural-development-2014-2020/country-files/nl_en

European Commission. (2019). *The European Green Deal.* Available online: https://eur-lex.europa.eu/legal-content/EN/TXT/?qid=1588580774040&uri=CELEX:52019DC0640

Fakhoury, R. (2018). *Digital government isn't working in the developing world. Here's why.* The Conversation. Available at: https://theconversation.com/digital-government-isnt-working-in-the-developing-world-heres-why-94737)

Fang, M. L., Canham, S. L., Battersby, L., Sixsmith, J., Wada, M., & Sixsmith, A. (2019, February). Exploring privilege in the digital divide: Implications for theory, policy, and practice. *The Gerontologist, 59*(1), e1–e15. doi:10.1093/geront/gny037 PMID:29750241

FAO, ICRISAT, & CIAT. (2018). Climate-Smart Agriculture in the Gambia: CSA Country Profiles for Africa Series. International Center for Tropical Agriculture (CIAT); International Crops Research Institute for the Semi-Arid Tropics (ICRISAT); Food and Agriculture Organization of the United Nations (FAO).

FAO, IFAD, UNICEF, WFP, & WHO. (2019). *The State of Food Security and Nutrition in the World 2019. Safeguarding against economic slowdowns and downturns*. FAO.

FAO. (2008). *An introduction to the basic concepts of food security. Food security information for action. Practical guides*. EC—FAO Food Security Programme.

FAO. (2014). Area equipped for irrigation. Infographic. In *AQUASTAT: FAO's information system on water and agriculture*. Food and Agriculture Organization of the United Nations (FAO). Retrieved from http://www.fao.org/nr/water/aquastat/ infographics/Irrigation_eng.pdf

FAO. (2016). *Food and agriculture: Key to achieving the 2030 agenda for sustainable development*. Food and Agriculture Organization.

FAO. (2018). *The State of Food Security and Nutrition in the World: Building Resilience for Peace and Food Security*. Rome: FAO. Retrieved from http://www.fao.org/news/story/ en/ item/1152031/icode/

FAO. (2019). *Digital technologies in agriculture and rural areas*. Briefing paper. https://www. fao.org/e-agriculture/

FAO. (2020a). *Ghana at a glance*. Retrieved from https://www.fao.org/ghana/fao-in-ghana/ ghana-at-a-glance/en/

FAO. (2020b). *Gambia at a glance*. Retrieved from https://www.fao.org/gambia/gambia-at-a-glance/en/

FAO. (2020c). Realizing the potential of digitalization to improve the agri-food system: Proposing a new International Digital Council for Food and Agriculture. A concept note. FAO.

Federal Ministry of Agriculture and Rural Development (FMARD). (2012). *Agricultural Transformation Agenda*. FMARD.

Fernandez, D., & Aman, A. (2018). Impacts of robotic process automation on global accounting services. *Asian Journal of Accounting and Governance*, *9*(1), 127–140. doi:10.17576/AJAG-2018-09-11

Fernandez-Luque, L., & Imran, M. (2018). Humanitarian health computing using artificial intelligence and social media: A narrative literature review. *International Journal of Medical Informatics*, *114*, 136–142. doi:10.1016/j.ijmedinf.2018.01.015 PMID:29395987

Ferrari, A., Bacco, M., Gaber, K., Jedlitschka, A., Hess, S., Kaipainen, J., Koltsida, P., Toli, E., & Brunori, G. (2022). Drivers, barriers and impacts of digitalization in rural areas from the viewpoint of experts. *Information and Software Technology*, *145*, 106816. doi:10.1016/j.infsof.2021.106816

Ferrati, F., Erkoyuncu, J. A., & Court, S. (2019). Developing an augmented reality based training demonstrator for manufacturing cherry pickers. *Procedia CIRP*, *81*, 803–808. doi:10.1016/j. procir.2019.03.203

Ferreira, S. M., Sayago, S., & Blat, J. (2016). Information Technology for Development Going Beyond Telecenters to Foster the Digital Inclusion of Older People in Brazil. *Lessons Learned from a Rapid Ethnographical Study.*, *1102*. Advance online publication. doi:10.1080/0268110 2.2015.1091974

Fielke, S. J., Garrard, R., Jakku, E., Fleming, A., Wiseman, L., & Taylor, B. M. (2019). Conceptualizing the DAIS. Implications of the 'Digitalisation of Agricultural Innovation Systems' on technology and policy at multiple levels. *NJAS-Wageningen of Life Sciences.*, *90*, 100296.

Fischl, C., Lindelöf, N., Lindgren, H., & Nilsson, I. (2020). Older adults' perceptions of contexts surrounding their social participation in a digitalized society—An exploration in rural communities in Northern Sweden. *European Journal of Ageing*, *17*(3), 281–290. doi:10.100710433-020-00558-7 PMID:32904866

Flak, J. (2020). Technologies for Sustainable Biomass Supply—Overview of Market O_ering. *Agronomy (Basel)*, *10*(6), 798. doi:10.3390/agronomy10060798

Flavián, C., Ibáñez-sánchez, S., & Orús, C. (2019). The impact of virtual, augmented and mixed reality technologies on the customer experience. *Journal of Business Research, 100*(November), 547–560. doi:10.1016/j.jbusres.2018.10.050

Fomunyam, K. G. (2019). Education and the fourth industrial revolution: Challenges and possibilities for engineering education. *International Journal of Mechanical Engineering and Technology*, *10*(8), 271–284.

Fonseca, D., Villagrasa, S., Martí, N., Redondo, E., & Sánchez, A. (2013). Visualization Methods in Architecture Education Using 3D Virtual Models and Augmented Reality in Mobile and Social Networks. *Procedia: Social and Behavioral Sciences*, *93*, 1337–1343. doi:10.1016/j.sbspro.2013.10.040

Friederici, N., Wahome, M., & Graham, M. (2020). *Digital entrepreneurship in Africa: How a continent is escaping Silicon Valley's long shadow*. The MIT Press. doi:10.7551/mitpress/12453.001.0001

Fute, A., Wan, X., Oubibi, M., & Bulugu, J. B. (2022). Adult Literacy Education and Reduction of Poverty in Tanzania: A Review of Policies and their Implementation. *Journal of Education*. Advance online publication. doi:10.1177/00220574221075204

Fuvattanasilp, V., Fujimoto, Y., Plopski, A., Taketomi, T., Sandor, C., Kanbara, M., & Kato, H. (2021). SlidAR+: Gravity-aware 3D object manipulation for handheld augmented reality. *Computers and Graphics (Pergamon)*, *95*, 23–35. doi:10.1016/j.cag.2021.01.005

Gaffar, B., Alhumaid, J., Alhareky, M., Alonaizan, F., & Almas, K. (2020). Dental Facilities During the New Corona Outbreak: A SWOT Analysis. *Risk Management and Healthcare Policy*, *13*, 1343–1352. doi:10.2147/RMHP.S265998 PMID:32904653

Gallardo, R., Bo Beaulieu, L., & Geideman, C. (2020). Digital inclusion and parity: Implications for community development. *Community Development (Columbus, Ohio)*. Advance online publication. doi:10.1080/15575330.2020.1830815

Gamreklidze, E. (2014). Cyber security in developing countries, a digital divide issue. *Journal of International Communication*, *20*(2), 200–217. doi:10.1080/13216597.2014.954593

Gangadharan, S. (2021). *Digital Exclusion: A Politics of Refusal*. University of Chicago Press.

Gann, B. (2019). Digital Inclusion and Health in Wales. *Journal of Consumer Health on the Internet*, *23*(2), 146–160. doi:10.1080/15398285.2019.1608499

Gargrish, S., Mantri, A., & Kaur, D. P. (2020). Augmented reality-based learning environment to enhance teaching-learning experience in geometry education. *Procedia Computer Science*, *172*(2019), 1039–1046. doi:10.1016/j.procs.2020.05.152

Garzoni, A., De Turi, I., Secundo, G., & De Vecchio, P. (2020). Fostering digital transformation of SMEs: A four level approach. *Management Decision*, *58*(8), 1543–1562. doi:10.1108/MD-07-2019-0939

Garzón, J., & Acevedo, J. (2019). Meta-analysis of the impact of Augmented Reality on students' learning gains. *Educational Research Review*, *27*(March), 244–260. doi:10.1016/j.edurev.2019.04.001

Gavai, P., Musungwini, S., & Mugoniwa, B. (2018). A Model for the Adoption and Effective Utilization of ICTs in Commercial Agriculture in Zimbabwe. *Journal of Systems Integration*, *9*(4), 40–58. doi:10.20470/jsi.v9i4.356

Gbenga-Ilori, A. & Sanusi, O.I. (2020). Assessment of the Scope and Usage of Digital Dividend in Nigeria. *Journal of Science Technology and Education, 8*(2), 143-153.

Georgiou, Y., & Kyza, E. A. (2020). Bridging narrative and locality in mobile-based augmented reality educational activities: Effects of semantic coupling on students' immersion and learning gains. *International Journal of Human-Computer Studies*, *102546*. Advance online publication. doi:10.1016/j.ijhcs.2020.102546

Ghauri, P., Fu, X., & Minayora, A. (2022). Digital technology-based entrepreneurial pursuit of the marginalized communities. *Journal of International Management*, *28*(2), 100948. doi:10.1016/j.intman.2022.100948

Gibreel, O., & Hong, A. (2017). *A Holistic Analysis Approach to Social*. Technical, and Socio-Technical Aspect of E-Government Development. doi:10.3390u9122181

Gilleard, C., & Higgs, P. (2011). Frailty, disability and old age: A re-appraisal. *Health*, *15*(5), 475–490. doi:10.1177/1363459310383595 PMID:21169203

Gimpel, H., & Röglinger, M. (2015). Digital Transformation: Changes and Chances. Frauenhofer Institute for Applied Information Technology Fit.

Giri, K. J., & Lone, A. T. (2014). Big Data - Overview and Challenges. *International Journal of Advanced Research in Computer Science and Software Engineering, 4*(6), 525–529.

Given, L. (2012). Grand Theory. In *The SAGE Encyclopedia of Qualitative Research Methods.* SAGE Publications, Inc. doi:10.4135/9781412963909.n188

Goedhart, N. S., Broerse, J. E. W., Kattouw, R., & Dedding, C. (2019). *Just having a computer doesn't make sense': The digital divide from the perspective of mothers with a low socioeconomic position.* Academic Press.

Gondchawar, N., & Kawitkar, R. S. (2016). IoT based smart agriculture. *International Journal of Advanced Research in Computer and Communication Engineering, 5*(6), 838–842. doi:10.17148/IJARCCE.2016.56188

Gounopoulos, E., Kontogiannis, S., Kazanidis, I., & Valsamidis, S. (2020). The Impact of the Digital Divide on the adoption of e-Government in Greece. *KnE Social Sciences, 2019*, 401–411. doi:10.18502/kss.v4i1.6002

Graham, M., & Avery, E. (2013). Government Public Relations and Social Media: An Analysis of the Perceptions and Trends of Social Media Use at the Local Government Level. *The Public Relations Journal.*

Greer, B., Robotham, D., Simblett, S., Curtis, H., Griffiths, H., & Wykes, T. (2019). Digital Exclusion Among Mental Health Service Users: Qualitative Investigation. *Journal of Medical Internet Research, 21*(1), e11696. doi:10.2196/11696 PMID:30626564

Grenier, M. (2010). Moving to inclusion: A socio-cultural analysis of practice. *International Journal of Inclusive Education, 14*(4), 387–400. doi:10.1080/13603110802504598

Grossman, J., & Tarazi, M. (2014). Serving smallholder farmers: Recent developments in digital finance. Washington, DC: CGAP (Consultative Group to Assist the Poorest).

Group, W. B. (2016). *World development report 2016: digital dividends.* World Bank Publications. doi:10.1596/978-1-4648-0671-1

Group, W. B. (2019). *Future of food: Harnessing digital technologies to improve food system outcomes.* World Bank. doi:10.1596/31565

GSMA AgriTech. (2020). *Agritech in Nigeria: Investment Opportunities and Challenges.* Author.

Gubrium, J., & Holstein, J. (2001). *Handbook of Interview Research.* doi:10.4135/9781412973588

Guenther, J., Smede, B., & Young, M. (2020). Digital inclusion in central Australia: What is it and what makes it different? *Rural Society, 29*(3), 154–170. Advance online publication. doi:10.1080/10371656.2020.1819524

Gunnlaugsson, G., Whitehead, T. A., Baboudóttir, F. N., Baldé, A., Jandi, Z., Boiro, H., & Einarsdóttir, J. (2020). Use of Digital Technology among Adolescents Attending Schools in Bissau, Guinea-Bissau. *International Journal of Environmental Research and Public.*

Guo, S., Ding, W., & Lanshina, T. (2017). Digital Economy for Sustainable Economic Growth. *International Organisations Research Journal, 12*(4), 169–184.

Gupta, Y. (2021). *Key-Drivers-of-Digital-Transformation.* https://static.startuptalky.com/2021/09/Key-Drivers-of-Digital-Transformation-StartupTalky.jpg

Haenssgen, M. J. (2018). The struggle for digital inclusion: Phones, healthcare, and marginalization in rural India. *World Development, 104*, 358–374. doi:10.1016/j.worlddev.2017.12.023

Haffke, I., Kalgovas, B., & Benlian, A. (2017). *The transformative role of bimodal IT in an era of digital business.* Academic Press.

Hafkin, N. (2007). Women and gender in ICT statistics and indicators for development. *Information Technologies and International Development, 2007*(4), 25–41.

Haggag, W. M. (2021). Agricultural digitalization and rural development in COVID-19 response plans: A review article. *Agricultural Technology (Thailand), 17*(1), 67–74.

Hansen, C., Wieferich, J., Ritter, F., Rieder, C., & Peitgen, H. O. (2010). Illustrative visualization of 3D planning models for augmented reality in liver surgery. *International Journal of Computer Assisted Radiology and Surgery, 5*(2), 133–141. doi:10.100711548-009-0365-3 PMID:20033519

Haque, M. F., & Haque, M. A. (2014). *Motivational Theories – A Critical Analysis Motivational Theories – A Critical Analysis.* Academic Press.

Harboe, G. (2020). *Real-World Affinity Diagramming Practices : Bridging the Paper – Digital Gap.* doi:10.1145/2702123.2702561

Harrison, A., & Rodríguez-Clare, A. (2010). Trade, foreign investment, and industrial policy for developing countries. Handbook of Development Economics, 5, 4039–4214.

Hartl, E., & Hess, T. (2017). *The role of cultural values for digital transformation: Insights from a Delphi study.* Academic Press.

Heeks, R. (2014). *Future Priorities for Development Informatics Research from the Post-2015 Development Agenda: Development Informatics Working Paper no.57.* papers2://publication/uuid/E62B26A8-CEBC-4A60-A869-94B02AB6E969

Heeks, R., Foster, C., & Nugroho, Y. (2017). *New models of inclusive innovation for development.* Routledge. doi:10.4324/9781315673479

Helsper, E. (2017). *The social relativity of digital exclusion : Applying relative deprivation theory to digital inequalities.* doi:10.1111/comt.12110

Helsper, E. J. (2008). *Digital inclusion: An analysis of social disadvantage and the information society.* Department for Communities and Local Government. http://www.communities.gov.uk/documents/communities/pdf/digitalinclusionanalysis

Helsper, E. J. (2013). *Digital inclusion : An analysis of social disadvantage and the information society.* Academic Press.

Henriette, E., Feki, M., & Boughzala, I. (2015). *The shape of digital transformation: A systematic literature review*. Academic Press.

Hernandez, K., & Roberts, T. (2018). Leaving No One Behind in a Digital World. *Ids K4D,* 1–34. https://assets.publishing.service.gov.uk/media/5c178371ed915d0b8a31a404/Emerging_Issues_LNOBDW_final.pdf%0Ahttps://www.ids.ac.uk/publications/leaving-no-one-behind-in-a-digital-world/

Herpich, F., Guarese, R. L. M., & Tarouco, L. M. R. (2017). A Comparative Analysis of Augmented Reality Frameworks Aimed at the Development of Educational Applications. *Creative Education, 08*(09), 1433–1451. doi:10.4236/ce.2017.89101

Hespanhol, L., & Farmer, J. (2018). *The Digital Fringe and Social Participation through Interaction Design*. Academic Press.

Hess, U. (2016). *Innovations and Emerging Trends in Agricultural Insurance: How can we transfer natural risks out of rural livelihoods to empower and protect people?* Academic Press.

Hess, T., Matt, C., Benlian, A., & Wiesboeck, F. (2016). Options for formulating a digital transformation strategy. *MIS Quarterly Executive, 15*(2), 123–139.

Hilbert, M. (2011). Digital gender divide or technologically empowered women in developing countries? A typical case of lies, damned lies and statistics. *Women's Studies International Forum, 2011*(34), 479–489. doi:10.1016/j.wsif.2011.07.001

Hodgeson, C. (2017). *The world unbanked population*. https://www.businessinsider.com/the-worlds-unbanked-population-in-6-charts-2017-8

Hofmann, E., & Rüsch, M. (2017). Industry 4.0 and the current status as well as future prospects on logistics. *Computers in Industry, 89*, 23–34. doi:10.1016/j.compind.2017.04.002

Hon, D. (2019). Medical reality and virtual reality. In Studies in Health Technology and Informatics (Vol. 29). doi:10.3233/978-1-60750-873-1-327

Hourcade, J. P., Bullock-Rest, N. E., & Schelhowe, H. (2010a). Digital technologies and Marginalized Youth. *Proceedings of IDC2010: The 9th International Conference on Interaction Design and Children, May 2014*, 360–363. 10.1145/1810543.1810614

Howard, J., & Simmons, E. (2019). *Risk and resilience; advancing food and nutrition security in Nigeria through feed the future*. Center for Strategic and International Studies.

Howard, T. C. (2019). *Why race and culture matter in schools: Closing the achievement gap in America's classrooms*. Teachers College Press.

Huang, Y., Lan, Y., & Hoffmann, W. C. (2008). Use of Airborne Multi-Spectral Imagery in Pest Management Systems. *Agricultural Engineering International: the CIGR Ejournal, X*, 1–14.

Hunter, B. M., & Murray, S. F. (2019). Deconstructing the financialization of healthcare. *Development and Change, 50*(5), 1263–1287. doi:10.1111/dech.12517

Huuskonen, J., & Oksanen, T. (2019). Augmented Reality for Supervising Multirobot System in Agricultural Field Operation. *IFAC-PapersOnLine*, *52*(30), 367–372. doi:10.1016/j.ifacol.2019.12.568

Ibrahim, M. (2012). *Thematic analysis : A critical review of its process and evaluation*. Academic Press.

Iji, C. O., & Abah, J. A. (2019). Internet Skills as a Measure of Digital Inclusion among Mathematics Education Students: Implications for Sustainable Human Capital Development in Nigeria. *International Journal of Education and Knowledge Management*. https://rpajournals.com/ijekm

Ingram, J., & Maye, D. (2020). 'What are the implications of digitalization for agricultural knowledge? *Frontiers in Sustainable Food Systems*, *4*, 66. doi:10.3389/fsufs.2020.00066

International Telecommunications Unit. (2016). Impact of Agricultural Value Chains on Digital Liquidity. Focus Group Technical Report. ITU.

Islam, M. N., & Inan, T. T. (2021). *Exploring the Fundamental Factors of Digital Inequality in Bangladesh*. doi:10.1177/21582440211021407

ITU & FAO. (2020). *Status of Digital Agriculture in 18 countries of Europe and Central Asia*. International Telecommunication Union Telecommunication Development Bureau Place des Nations CH-1211. Retrieved from https://www.itu.int/en/ITU-D/Regional Presence/Europe/Documents/Events/2020/

ITU. (2019). *Measuring Digital Development: Facts and Figures*. ITU.

Jackson, K., Lower, C. L., & Rudman, W. J. (2016). The Crossroads between Workforce and Education. *Perspectives in Health Information Management*, 13.

Jayachandran, S. (2021). Social norms as a barrier to women's employment in developing countries. *IMF Economic Review*, *69*(3), 576–595. doi:10.105741308-021-00140-w

Jean, N., Burke, M., Xie, M., Davis, W. M., Lobell, D. B., & Ermon, S. (2016). Combining satellite imagery and machine learning to predict poverty. *Science*, *353*(6301), 790–794.

John Deere. (2017). *Agricultural Management Solutions*. AMS.

Johnson, V. (2012). The gender divide: Attitudinal issues inhibiting access. In R. Pande & T. van der Weide (Eds.), *Globalization, Technology Diffusion, and Gender Disparity: Social Impacts of ICTs* (pp. 110–119). IGI Global. doi:10.4018/978-1-4666-0020-1.ch009

Jolley, E., Lynch, P., Virendrakumar, B., Rowe, S., & Schmidt, E. (2017). Education and social inclusion of people with disabilities in five countries in West Africa: A literature review. *Disability and Rehabilitation*, 1–9. doi:10.1080/09638288.2017.1353649 PMID:28705016

Journal, U. G. C. C. (2020). *A Study of Mobile Banking in IDBI Bank Studies in Indian Place Names*. Author.

Juvonen, J., Lessard, L. M., Rastogi, R., Schacter, H. L., & Smith, D. S. (2019). Promoting Social Inclusion in Educational Settings: Challenges and Opportunities. *Educational Psychologist, 54*(4), 250–270. doi:10.1080/00461520.2019.1655645

Kabanda, S., Tanner, M., & Kent, C. (2018). Exploring SME cyber security practices in developing countries. *Journal of Organizational Computing and Electronic Commerce, 28*(3), 269–282. doi:10.1080/10919392.2018.1484598

Kalenda, S., & Kowaliková, I. (2020). The digital exclusion of vulnerable children: Challenge for sustainability issues in czech social work practice. *Sustainability (Switzerland), 12*(23), 1–24. doi:10.3390u12239961

Kandri, S. E. (2019). *Africa's future is bright–and digital.* World Bank Blogs.

Kane, G. C., Palmer, D., Phillips, A. N., Kiron, D., & Buckley, N. (2015). Strategy, not technology, drives digital transformation. *MIT Sloan Management Review and Deloitte University Press, 14*, 1–25.

Karambakhsh, A., Kamel, A., Sheng, B., Li, P., Yang, P., & Feng, D. D. (2019). Deep gesture interaction for augmented anatomy learning. *International Journal of Information Management, 45*(October), 328–336. doi:10.1016/j.ijinfomgt.2018.03.004

Karimi, J., & Walter, Z. (2015). The role of dynamic capabilities in responding to digital disruption: A factor-based study of the newspaper industry. *Journal of Management Information Systems, 32*(1), 39–81. doi:10.1080/07421222.2015.1029380

Kemp, S. (2019). *Digital 2019: Essential Insights into How People Around the World Use the Internet, Mobile Devices, Social Media, And ECommerce.* Kepios Pte. Ltd., We Are Social Ltd. and Hootsuite Inc. https://datareportal.com

Kempin Reuter, T. (2019). Human rights and the city: Including marginalized communities in urban development and smart cities. *Journal of Human Rights, 18*(4), 382–402. doi:10.1080/14754835.2019.1629887

Khare, S., Kavyashree, S., Gupta, D., & Jyotishi, A. (2017). Investigation of nutritional status of children based on machine learning techniques using Indian demographic and health survey data. *Procedia Computer Science, 115*, 338–349.

Klerkx, L., & Begemann, S. (2020). Supporting food systems transformation: The what, why, who, where and how of mission-oriented agricultural innovation systems. *Agricultural Systems, 184*, 102901. doi:10.1016/j.agsy.2020.102901 PMID:32834403

Ko, A., Feher, P., & Szabo, Z. (2019). Digital transformation – A Hungarian Overview. *Journal of Economic and Business Research, 21*(3), 371–392.

Koch, R., & Corban, T., (2020, September). Data governance in digital transformation. *Technology workbook on Strategic Finance,* 60-61.

Koehler, M. J., Mishra, P., Akcaoglu, M., & Rosenberg, J. M. (2013). The Technological Pedagogical Content Knowledge Framework for Teachers and Teacher Educators. *ICT Integrated Teacher Mducation Models*, 1–8. http://cemca.org.in/ckfinder/userfiles/files/ICT teacher education Module 1 Final_May 20.pdf

Kokh, L., & Kokh, Y. (2020). Banks and Fintech-companies: Who's Catching up with Whom. *Pervasive Health: Pervasive Computing Technologies for Healthcare*. doi:10.1145/3446434.3446533

Kovacs, I., & Husti, I. (2018). *The role of digitalization in the Agricultural 4.0-How to connect the industry 4.0 to Agriculture?* Hungarian Agricultural Engineering. doi:10.17676/HAE.2018.33.38

Kraus, S., Jones, P., Kailer, N., Weinmann, A., Chaparro-Banegas, N., & Roig-Tierno, N. (2021). Digital Transformation: An Overview of the Current State of the Art of Research. *SAGE Open*, *11*(3). Advance online publication. doi:10.1177/21582440211047576

Kraus, S., Schiavone, F., Pluzhnikova, A., & Invernizzi, A. C. (2021). Digital transformation in healthcare: Analysing the current state-of-research. *Journal of Business Research*, *123*, 557–567. doi:10.1016/j.jbusres.2020.10.030

Krell, N. T., Giroux, S. A., Guido, Z., Hannah, C., Lopus, S. E., Caylor, K. K., & Evans, T. P. (2021). Smallholder farmers' use of mobile phone services in central Kenya. *Climate and Development*, *13*(3), 215–227. doi:10.1080/17565529.2020.1748847

Kubota, T. (2017). Artificial intelligence used to identify skin cancer. *A Research Review. International Journal of Communication*, *10*, 5032–5055.

Kumar, R., Subramaniam, C., & Zhao, K. (2021). Special issue on digital inclusion. *Information Systems and e-Business Management*, 1–4. doi:10.100710257-021-00531-6

Kurniawan, M. H., Suharjito, Diana, & Witjaksono, G. (2018). Human Anatomy Learning Systems Using Augmented Reality on Mobile Application. *Procedia Computer Science*, *135*, 80–88. doi:10.1016/j.procs.2018.08.152

Labrique, A. B., Wadhwani, C., Williams, K. A., Lamptey, P., Hesp, C., Luk, R., & Aerts, A. (2018). Best practices in scaling digital health in low and middle income countries. *Globalization and Health*, *14*(1), 1–8. doi:10.118612992-018-0424-z PMID:30390686

Lai, J., & Widmar, N. O. (2020). *Featured Article Revisiting the Digital Divide in the COVID-19 Era.* doi:10.1002/aepp.13104

Lake, A. (2004). *Time, mobility and economic growth.* http://www.flexibility.co.uk/ issues/transport/time-mobility.htm

Lambert, S. R. (2020, February). Do MOOCs contribute to student equity and social inclusion? A systematic review 2014–18. *Computers & Education Volume*, *145*, 103693. doi:10.1016/j.compedu.2019.103693

Lanucara, S., Oggioni, A., Di Fazio, S., & Modica, G. A. (2020). Prototype of Service Oriented Architecture for Precision Agriculture. In A. Coppola, G. C. Di Renzo, G. Altieri, & P. D'Antonio (Eds.), *Book Innovative Biosystems Engineering for Sustainable Agriculture, Forestry and Food Production, Lecture Notes in Civil Engineering* (Vol. 67, pp. 765–774). Springer. doi:10.1007/978-3-030-39299-4_82

Larsson, E., Larsson-Lund, M., & Nilsson, I. (2013). Internet based activities (IBAs): Seniors' experiences of the conditions required for the performance of and the influence of these conditions on their own participation in society. *Educational Gerontology*, *39*(3), 155–167. doi:10.1080/0 3601277.2012.699833

Laurillard, D. (2007a). *Laurillard's six learning types Inquiry / Investigation Practice Students work together to build on each other's learning through joint practice and*. http://eprints.ioe.ac.uk/627/1/Mobile_C6_Laurillard.pdf

Laurillard, D. (2007b). Pedagogical forms of mobile learning: framing research questions. *Mobile Learning: Towards a Research Agenda,* 153–175. http://eprints.ioe.ac.uk/627/1/Mobile_C6_Laurillard.pdf

Laurillard, D. (2008). The teacher as action researcher: Using technology to capture pedagogic form. *Studies in Higher Education*, *33*(2), 139–154. doi:10.1080/03075070801915908

Lee Dr, S. E. (2013). Education as a Human Right in the 21st Century. *Democracy & Education*, *21*(1), 1.

Leist, A. K. (2013). Social media use of older adults: A mini-review. *Gerontology*, *59*(4), 378–384. doi:10.1159/000346818 PMID:23594915

Lembani, R., Gunter, A., Breines, M., & Dalu, M. T. B. (2019). The same course, different access: The digital divide between urban and rural distance education students in South Africa. *Journal of Geography in Higher Education*, 1–15. doi:10.1080/03098265.2019.1694876

Leonard, E., Rainbow, R., Laurie, A., Lamb, D., Llewellyn, R., & Perrett, E. (2017). Accelerating *Precision Agriculture to Decision Agriculture: Enabling Frontiers in Sustainable Food Systems*. www.frontiersin.org

Lester, H. (2019). *Bridging the urban-rural digital divide and mobilizing technology for poverty eradication: challenges and gaps*. Department of Economics, University of the West Indies.

Levers, C., Schneider, M., Prishchepov, A. V., Estel, S., & Kuemmerle, T. (2018). Spatial variation in determinants of agricultural land abandonment in Europe. *The Science of the Total Environment*, *644*, 95–111. doi:10.1016/j.scitotenv.2018.06.326 PMID:29981521

Levy, Y., & Ellis, T. J. (2006). *A Systems Approach to Conduct an Effective Literature Review in Support of Information Systems Research*. Academic Press.

Liberties, E. U. (2021). *What Is Marginalization?* Definition and Coping Strategies.

Lichtenthaler, U. (2020). Building Blocks of Successful Digital Transformation: Complementing Technology and Market Issues. *International Journal of Innovation and Technology Management, 17*(1). Advance online publication. doi:10.1142/S0219877020500042

Lin, N. (2017). Building a network theory of social capital. *Social Capital*, 3–28.

Liu, D., Bhagat, K. K., Gao, Y., & Chang, T. (n.d.). *Virtual*. Augmented, and Mixed Realities in Education., doi:10.1007/978-981-10-5490-7

Lou, A. T. F., & Li, E. Y. (2017). *Integrating Innovation Diffusion Theory and the Technology Acceptance Model : The Adoption of blockchain technology from business managers' perspective (Work in Progress)*. Academic Press.

Loukos, P. (2020). *The GSMA AgriTech Toolkit for the Digitisation of Agricultural Value Chains*. GSMA.

Low, J., Dujacquier, D., & Kaur, S. (2021). *Bridging the digital divide, improving digital inclusion in Southeast Asia*. Academic Press.

Magis-Weinberg, L., Ballonoff Suleiman, A., & Dahl, R. E. (2021). Context, Development, and Digital Media: Implications for Very Young Adolescents in LMICs. *Frontiers in Psychology, 12*, 632713. doi:10.3389/fpsyg.2021.632713 PMID:33967899

Mahlangu, G. (2020). *a Multi-Dimensional Model for Assessing E-Government Service Gaps Gaps in the Context of a Developing Country : A Critical Realist*. Academic Press.

Mahlangu, G. (2020). *A Multi-Dimensional Model for Assessing E-Government Service Gaps Gaps in the Context of a Developing Country : A Critical Realist*. Academic Press.

Mahlangu, G., & Ruhode, E. (2021). *Factors Enhancing E-Government Service Gaps in a Developing Country Context*. doi:10.48550/arxiv.2108.09803

Mahlangu, G., Musungwini, S., & Sibanda, M. (2018). A framework for creating an ICT knowledge hub in Zimbabwe : A holistic approach in fostering economic growth. *Journal of Systems Integration, 2004*(1), 32–41. doi:10.20470/jsi.v9i1.327

Majchrzak, A., Markus, M. L., & Wareham, J. (2016). Designing for digital transformation: Lessons for information systems research from the study of ICT and societal challenges. *Management Information Systems Quarterly, 40*(2), 267–277. doi:10.25300/MISQ/2016/40:2.03

Malik, V., & Singh, S. (2019). Security risk management in IoT environment. *Journal of Discrete Mathematical Sciences and Cryptography, 22*(4), 697–709. https://doi.org/10.1080/09720529.2019.1642628

Malungu, C., & Moturi, C. (2015). ICT Infrastructure Sharing Framework for Developing Countries: Case of Mobile Operators in Kenya. *International Journal of Applied Information Systems, 9*(4), 17–24. doi:10.5120/ijais15-451392

Manalu, E. P., Muditomo, A., & Adriana, D. (2020) Role of Information Technology for Successful Responses to Covid-19 Pandemic. *2020 International Conference on Information Management and Technology (ICIMTech)*, 415–420. 10.1109/ICIMTech50083.2020.9211290

Mang, C. F., Piper, L. A., & Brown, N. R. (2016). The incidence of smartphone usage among tourists. *International Journal of Tourism Research*, *18*(6), 591–601. doi:10.1002/jtr.2076

Mangina, E. (2018). 3D learning objects for augmented/virtual reality educational ecosystems. *Proceedings of the 2017 23rd International Conference on Virtual Systems and Multimedia, VSMM 2017*, 1–6. 10.1109/VSMM.2017.8346266

Manstead, A. S. R. (2018). The psychology of social class: How socioeconomic status impacts thought, feelings, and behaviour. *British Journal of Social Psychology*, *57*(2), 267–291. doi:10.1111/bjso.12251 PMID:29492984

Manyika, J., Chui, M., Bisson, P., Woetzel, J.R., Dobbs, R., Bughin, J., & Aharon, D. (2015). *The Internet of things: mapping the value beyond the hype.* Technical report, McKinsey Global Institute.

Manzoor, M., & Vimarlund, V. (2017). E-services for the social inclusion of people with disabilities: A literature review. *Technology and Disability*, *29*(1–2), 15–33.

Marambi, S., Musungwini, S., & Mzikamwi, T. (2018). Strategy for the adoption and effective utilization of mobile phone technologies in smallholder agriculture in Zimbabwe. In *Proceedings of 6th International Conference on M4D Mobile Communication for Development* (pp. 15–16). Universitetstryckeriet, Karlstad 2018. www.researchjournal.co.in

Marcu, I. M., Suciu, G., Balaceanu, C. M., & Banaru, A. (2019). IoT based System for Smart Agriculture. *Proceedings of the 11th International Conference on Electronics, Computers and Artificial Intelligence, ECAI 2019.* 10.1109/ECAI46879.2019.9041952

Marshall, A., Dezuanni, M., Burgess, J., Thomas, J., & Wilson, C. K. (2020). Australian farmers left behind in the digital economy – Insights from the Australian Digital Inclusion Index. *Journal of Rural Studies*, *80*(September), 195–210. doi:10.1016/j.jrurstud.2020.09.001

Matsika, C., & Zhou, M. (2021). Factors affecting the adoption and use of AVR technology in higher and tertiary education. *Technology in Society*, *67*(July), 101694. doi:10.1016/j.techsoc.2021.101694

Matt, C., Hess, T., & Benlian, A. (2015). Digital Transformation Strategies. *Business & Information Systems Engineering*, *57*(5), 339–343. doi:10.100712599-015-0401-5

Matthews, K., Nazroo, J., & Marshall, A. (2019). Digital inclusion in later life: Cohort changes in internet use over a ten-year period in England. *Ageing and Society*, *39*(9), 1914–1932. doi:10.1017/S0144686X18000326

Mavhunga, C. (2017). *What do science, technology, and innovation mean from Africa?* The MIT Press. doi:10.7551/mitpress/10769.001.0001

Mazzetto, F., Gallo, R., Riedl, M., & Sacco, P. (2019). Proposal of an ontological approach to design and analyze farm information systems to support Precision Agriculture techniques. *IOP Conference Series. Earth and Environmental Science*, *275*(1), 012008. doi:10.1088/1755-1315/275/1/012008

Mbiti, I., & Weil, D. (2015). Mobile Banking: The Impact of M-Pesa in Kenya, NBER Chapters, in: African Successes: Modernization and Development (vol. 3). National Bureau of Economic Research, Inc.

McKinsey & Co. (2014). *Offline and falling behind: Barriers to Internet adoption*. McKinsey and Company.

Mee, C. Y., Balasundram, S. K., & Hanif, A. H. M. (2017). Detecting and monitoring plant nutrient stress using remote sensing approaches: A review. *Asian Journal of Plant Sciences*, *16*(1), 1–8.

Meenu, E. G. (2021). *Digital Transformation*. Retrieved April 24, 2022, from https://www.analyticsinsight.net/author/meenu

Meinke, H. (2019). The role of modelling and systems thinking in contemporary agriculture. In R. Accorsi & R. Manzini (Eds.), *Book Sustainable Food Supply Chains: Planning, Design, and Control through Interdisciplinary Methodologies* (pp. 39–47). Elsevier. doi:10.1016/B978-0-12-813411-5.00003-X

Melhem, S., Morrell, C., & Tandon, N. (2009). *Information Communication Technologies for women's Socioeconomic Empowerment*. World Bank Working Paper.

Mergel, I. (2013b). *Social Media in The Public Sector: A Guide to Participation, Collaboration, and Transparency in the Networked World*. John Wiley & Sons, Inc.

Michael, A., Ndaghu, A. A., & Mshelia, S. I. (2016). Assessment of Social Inclusiveness of Vulnerable and Marginalized Groups in Fadama Ii Project in Yola North Local Government Area of Adamawa State, Nigeria. *Scientific Papers. Series Management, Economic, Engineering in Agriculture and Rural Development*, *16*(April).

Miles, C. (2019). The combine will tell the truth: On precision agriculture and algorithmic rationality. *Big Data & Society*, *6*(1), 2053951719849444. doi:10.1177/2053951719849444

Minchev, Z. (2017). *Security Challenges to Digital Ecosystems Dynamic Transformation*. The 9th International Conference on Business Information Security (BISEC-2017), Belgrade, Serbia.

Mohamad, M., & Gombe, M. (2017). eAgriculture revisited : A systematic literature review of theories, concept, practices, methods, and future trends. *Usir*, 22.

Mohamad, A. G. M. M., Idrus, S. S., & Ibrahim, A. A. E. A. (2018). Model of behavioral attention towards using ICT in universities in libya. *Jurnal Komunikasi: Malaysian Journal of Communication*, *34*(2), 89–104. doi:10.17576/JKMJC-2018-3402-06

Moher, D., Liberati, A., Tetzlaff, J., & Altman, D. G. (2009). Preferred Reporting Items for Systematic Reviews and Meta-Analyses: The PRISMA Statement. *BMJ (Clinical Research Ed.)*, *339*(1), 332–336. doi:10.1136/bmj.b2535 PMID:19622551

Molala, T. S. (2021). *The connection between digital divide and social exclusion : Implications for social work*. Academic Press.

Money, G. M. (2017). *State of the Industry Report on Mobile Money*. Retrieved from.

Morze, N. V., & Strutynska, O. V. (2021). Digital transformation in society: Key aspects for model development. *Journal of Physics: Conference Series*, *1946*(1). Advance online publication. doi:10.1088/1742-6596/1946/1/012021

Mueller, B., & Renken, U. (2017). *Helping employees to be digital transformers–the olympus. connect case*. Academic Press.

Mulualem Walle, Y. (2020). The Impact of Digital Government on Whistleblowing and Whistle-blower Protection: Explanatory Study. *Journal of Information Technology Management*, *12*(1), 1–26.

Mumporeze, N., & Prieler, M. (2017). Gender digital divide in Rwanda: A qualitative analysis of socioeconomic factors. *Telematics and Informatics*, *34*(7), 1285–1293. doi:10.1016/j.tele.2017.05.014

Munyoka, W. (2019). *Electronic government adoption in voluntary environments – a case study of Zimbabwe*. doi:10.1177/0266666919864713

Munyoka, W. (2022). *Inclusive Digital Innovation in South Africa : Perspectives from Disadvantaged and Marginalized Communities*. Academic Press.

Mupangwa, W., Twomlow, S., & Walker, S. (2012). Dead level contours and infiltration pits for risk mitigation in smallholder cropping systems of southern Zimbabwe. *Physics and Chemistry of the Earth*, *47-48*, 166–172. doi:10.1016/j.pce.2011.06.011

Mussa, E. C. (2018). *Long-term effects of childhood work on human capital formation, migration decisions, and earnings in rural Ethiopia*. Academic Press.

Musthafa, M. N., & Stephen, R. E. (2019). Education of the Marginalized; In the Context of Policy Initiatives for Universalization of Elementary Education. *International Journal of Research in Social Sciences*, *9*(7), 723–731.

Musungwini, S., Zhou, T. G., & Musungwini, L. (2020). Challenges facing women in ICT from a women perspective: A case study of the Zimbabwean Banking Sector and Telecommunications Industry. *Journal of Systems Integration, 11*(1).

Musungwini, S., Zyl, I. van, & Kroeze, J. H. (2022). *The Perceptions of Smallholder Farmers on the Use of Mobile Technology: A Naturalistic Inquiry in Zimbabwe*. doi:10.1007/978-3-030-98015-3_37

Musungwini, S. (2016). A model for harnessing the power of the Mobile Phone Technology to improve Smallholder Agriculture in Zimbabwe. *Proceedings of the 5th International Conference on M4D Mobile Communication Technology for Development: M4D 2016, General Tracks, December*, 237–252.

Musungwini, S. (2018). Mobile Phone Use by Zimbabwean Smallholder Farmers : A Baseline Study. *The African Journal of Information and Communication*, 22(22), 29–52. doi:10.23962/10539/26171

Musungwini, S., & Van Zyl, I. (2017). ` Mobile Technology for Development ' Experiences from Zimbabwe Vending Markets a Naturalistic Enquiry. *International Journal of Business and Management Studies.*, 06(01), 101–111.

Musungwini, S., Zhou, T. G., & Musungwini, L. (2020). Challenges facing women in ICT from a women perspective: A case study of the Zimbabwean Banking Sector and Telecommunications Industry. *Journal of Systems Integration*, 11(1), 21–33. doi:10.20470/JSI.V11I1.389

Myovella, G., Karacuka, M., & Haucap, J. (2020). Digitalization and economic growth: A comparative analysis of Sub-Saharan Africa and OECD economies. *Telecommunications Policy*, 44(2), 101856. doi:10.1016/j.telpol.2019.101856

Nadaf, A. H. (2021, June). Lockdown Within a Lockdown: The "Digital Redlining" and paralyzed online teaching during COVID-19 in Kashmir, A Conflict Territory. *Communication, Culture & Critique*, 14(2), 343–346. doi:10.1093/ccc/tcab019

Naismith, L., Vavoula, G. N., & Sharples, M. (2004). Mobile technologies and learning. *A Technology Update and M-Learning Project Summary*, 1–26.

Namani, S., & Gonen, B. (2020). Smart agriculture based on IoT and cloud computing. *Proceedings - 3rd International Conference on Information and Computer Technologies, ICICT 2020*, 553–556. 10.1109/ICICT50521.2020.00094

Ndinde, S., & Kadodo, W. (2014). The Role of Community-Based Information Centers in Development: Lessons for Rural Zimbabwe. *International Journal of Learning, Teaching and Educational Research*, 2(1), 44–53.

Nedungadi, P. P., Menon, R., Gutjahr, G., Erickson, L., & Raman, R. (2018). Towards an inclusive digital literacy framework for digital India. *Education + Training*, 60(6), 516–528. doi:10.1108/ET-03-2018-0061

Nemer, D. (2016). *From Digital Divide to Digital Inclusion and Beyond : A Positional Review Is Access Enough ?* doi:10.15353/joci.v11i1.2857

Nemer, D., & Reed, P. (2013). Can a community technology center be for-profit? A case study of LAN houses in Brazil. *CIRN 2013 Community Informatics Conference*, 1–9.

Nettle, C. E. M. A. R., & Dela Rue, B. (2019). Making sense in the cloud: Farm advisory services in a smart farming future NJAS-Wageningen J. *Life Sciences*.

Nielsen, M. M., Carvalho, J., Backhouse, J., & Makpor, M. (2019). *A global framework for digital inclusion.* Academic Press.

Nikolidakis, S. A., Kandris, D., Vergados, D. D., & Douligeris, C. (2015). Energy ecient automated control of irrigation in agriculture by using wireless sensor networks. *Computers and Electronics in Agriculture, 113,* 154–163. doi:10.1016/j.compag.2015.02.004

Niţă, A.-M., & Pârvu, M. C. (2020). Vulnerability and resilience in marginalized rural communities. Case study: projects for reduction of risk exclusion in Dolj County. *Revista de Stiinte Politice, 67,* 103–117. https://www.proquest.com/scholarly-journals/vulnerability-resilience-marginalized-rural/docview/2447285558/se-2?accountid=14166%0Ahttps://suny-alb.primo.exlibrisgroup.com/openurl/01SUNY_ALB/01SUNY_ALB:01SUNY_ALB?genre=article&atitle=Vulnerability+and+resi

Niţă, A.-M., & Pârvu, M. C. (2020). Vulnerability and resilience in marginalized rural communities. Case study: projects for reduction of risk exclusion in Dolj County. *Revista de Stiinte Politice, 67,* 103–117. https://www.proquest.com/scholarly-journals/vulnerability-resilience-marginalized-rural/docview/2447285558/se-2?accountid=14166%0Ahttps://suny-alb.primo.exlibrisgroup.com/openurl/01SUNY_ALB/01SUNY_ALB:01SUNY_ALB?genre=articleandatitle=Vulnerability+and+resi

Nkikabahizi, F., Rizinde, T., & Karangwa, M. (2018). The Balance of Trade-Economic Growth Nexus in a Panel of Member Countries of the East African Community. In I. A. Heshmati (Ed.), *Macroeconomic determinants of economic growth in Africa.* Springer Nature, doi:10.1007/978-3-319-76493-1_11

Nyamadzawo, J. (2011). *Digital opportunities for economic growth and development for Zimbabwe.* ZEPARU Working Paper Series (ZWPS 05/11). http://www.zeparu.co.zw/sites/default/files/201803/2011%20DIGITAL%20OPPORTUNITIES%20FOR%20ECONOMIC%20GROWTH%20AND%20DEVELOPMENT%20FOR%20ZIMBABWE.pdf

Nyika, G. T. (2020). Use of ICTS for socio-economic development of marginalized communities in rural areas: Proposals for establishment of sectoral Rural Entrepreneurial Networks. *Journal of Development and Communication Studies, 7*(1–2), 71–91. doi:10.4314/jdcs.v7i1-2.5

O'Donnell, P., Tierney, E., O'Carroll, A., Nurse, D., & MacFarlane, A. (2016). Exploring levers and barriers to accessing primary care for marginalized groups and identifying their priorities for primary care provision: A participatory learning and action research study. *International Journal for Equity in Health, 15*(1), 1–16. PMID:27912783

OECD. (2015). Inequalities in Digital Proficiency: Bridging the Divide. *Pisa,* 123–143. https://www.oecd-ilibrary.org/education/students-computers-and-learning/inequalities-in-digital-proficiency-bridging-the-divide_9789264239555-8-en

OECD. (2018). *Going Digital in a Multilateral World.* Report of the Meeting of the OECD Council at Ministerial Level, Paris, 30–31 May 2018. OECD. https://www.oecd.org/going-digital/C-MIN-2018-6-EN.pdf

Ohiagu, O. P. (2013). Information and communication technologies: Widening or Bridging the Digital Divide. *Journal of Linguistics and Communication Studies*, *3*(1), 87.

Okoye, R., & Arimonu, M. O. (2016). Technical and Vocational Education in Nigeria: Issues, Challenges and a Way Forward. *Journal of Education and Practice*, *7*(3), 113–118.

Olumide, O. D. (2016). Technology Acceptance Model as a predictor of using information system' to acquire information literacy skills. *Library Philosophy and Practice (e-Journal)*, 1–27. doi:10.1016/j.ygyno.2014.12.020

Organization, W. H. (2015). *World report on ageing and health*. World Health Organization.

Ornstein, A. C., & Hunkins, F. P. (2018). Social Foundations of Curriculum. In *Curriculum* (7th ed.). Foundation, Principles and Issues.

Óskarsdóttir, M., Bravo, C., Sarraute, C., Vanthienen, J., & Baesens, B. (2019). The value of big data for credit scoring: Enhancing financial inclusion using mobile phone data and social network analytics. *Applied Soft Computing*, *74*, 26–39.

Pade-Khene, C., & Lannon, J. (2017). Learning to be sustainable in ICT for development: A citizen engagement initiative in South Africa. *IFIP Advances in Information and Communication Technology*, *504*, 475–486. Advance online publication. doi:10.1007/978-3-319-59111-7_39

Paden, C. I. (2006). *An Investigation of ICT Project Management Techniques for Sustainable ICT Projects in Rural Development*. Academic Press.

Pande, R. (2012). Gender gaps and information communication technology: A case study of India. In R. Pande & T. van der Weide (Eds.), *Globalization, Technology Diffusion, and Gender Disparity: Social Impacts of ICTs* (pp. 277–291). IGI Global. doi:10.4018/978-1-4666-0020-1. ch022

Panimalar, A., Varnekha, S. S., & Veneshia, K. A. (2017). The 17 V's of Big Data. *International Research Journal of Engineering and Technology*, *4*(9), 329–333.

Panori, A., Kakderi, C., Komninos, N., Fellnhofer, K., Reid, A., & Mora, L. (2021). Smart systems of innovation for smart places: Challenges in deploying digital platforms for co-creation and data-intelligence. *Land Use Policy*, *111*, 104631. doi:10.1016/j.landusepol.2020.104631

Pansera, M., Ehlers, M.-H., & Kerschner, C. (2019). Unlocking wise digital techno-futures: Contributions from the Degrowth community. *Futures*, *114*, 102474. doi:10.1016/j. futures.2019.102474

Paramita, D. (2020). *Digitalization in Talent Acquisition: A Case Study of AI in Recruitment*. https://www.teknik.uu.se/student-en/

Park, S., Freeman, J., & Middleton, C. (2019). Intersections between connectivity and digital inclusion in rural communities. *Communication Research and Practice*, *5*(2), 139–155. doi:10. 1080/22041451.2019.1601493

Parviainen, P., Tihinen, M., Kääriäinen, J., & Teppola, S. (2017). Tackling the digitalization challenge: How to benefit from digitalization in practice. *International Journal of Information Systems and Project Management, 5*(1), 63–77. doi:10.12821/ijispm050104

Paul Antony, A., Sweeney, D., & Lu, J. (2019). *'Seeds of Silicon' Internet of Things for Smallholder Agriculture.* Academic Press.

Paunov, C., & Rollo, V. (2016). Has the internet fostered inclusive innovation in the developing world? *World Development, 78*, 587–609. doi:10.1016/j.worlddev.2015.10.029

Pediatr, A., Dis, I., & Yazdani, S. (2021). *A Model for the Taxonomy of Research Studies : A Practical Guide to Knowledge Production and Knowledge Management.* doi:10.5812/pedinfect.112456.Review

Peirce, J., Gray, J. R., Simpson, S., MacAskill, M., Höchenberger, R., Sogo, H., Kastman, E., & Lindeløv, J. K. (2019). PsychoPy2: Experiments in behavior made easy. *Behavior Research Methods, 51*(1), 195–203. doi:10.375813428-018-01193-y PMID:30734206

Pfavai Natasha Nyajeka. (2018). *How Whatsapp Strengthens Livelihoods of Women Farmers in Rural Zimbabwe | ICTs for Development.* https://ict4dblog.wordpress.com/2018/12/11/how-whatsapp-strengthens-livelihoods-of-women-farmers-in-rural-zimbabwe/

Picot, A., & Grove, N. (2009). Flächendeckende Breitbandversorgung im internationalen Vergleich: Strategien für den Glasfaserausbau in ländlichen Gebieten. *Infrastrukturrecht, 6*(11), 315 – 326.

Pihir, I., Tomicic-Pupek, K., & Furjan, M. T. (2018). Digital transformation insights and trends. *Proceedings from the 29th Central European Conference on Information Security and Intelligent Systems*, 141-149.

Poggiali, L. (2016). Seeing (from) digital peripheries: Technology and transparency in Kenya's silicon savannah. *Cultural Anthropology, 31*(3), 387–411. doi:10.14506/ca31.3.07

Pradhan, R. P., Arvin, M., Nair, M., Bennett, S., & Bahmani, S. (2017). ICT-finance-growth nexus: Empirical evidence from the Next-11 countries. *Cuadernos de Economía, 40*(113), 115–134.

Pranoto, H., & Panggabean, F. M. (2019). ScienceDirect ScienceDirect. *Procedia Computer Science, 157*, 506–513. doi:10.1016/j.procs.2019.09.007

Prause, L., Hackfort, S., & Lindgren, M. (2021). Digitalization and the third food regime. *Agriculture and Human Values, 38*(3), 641–655. doi:10.100710460-020-10161-2 PMID:33071450

Price, S. (2009). Prologue: Victims or partners? The social perspective in development-induced displacement and resettlement. *The Asia Pacific Journal of Anthropology, 10*(4), 266–282. doi:10.1080/14442210903305821

Prince, J. D. (2014). 3D printing: An industrial revolution. *Journal of Electronic Resources in Medical Libraries, 11*(1), 39–45. doi:10.1080/15424065.2014.877247

Profile SEE. (2016). *Remote Sensing and GIS Applications in Agriculture.* Author.

Prosser, A., & Zajdela, N. (2018). *A multidimensional model of e-inclusion and its implications.* Academic Press.

Putri, N. M. A. W. (2021). Digital Transformation: The Approach to Society 5.0 in Indonesia. *Proceeding - 2021 2nd International Conference on ICT for Rural Development, IC-ICTRuDev 2021.* 10.1109/IC-ICTRuDev50538.2021.9656528

Quayson, M., Bai, C., & Osei, V. (2020). Digital Inclusion for Resilient Post-COVID-19 Supply Chains: Smallholder Farmer Perspectives. *IEEE Engineering Management Review, 48*(3), 1. doi:10.1109/EMR.2020.3006259

Quimba, F. M. A., Rosellon, M. A. D., Quimba, F. M. A., & Rosellon, M. A. D. (2020). *Digital Divide and the Platform Economy : Looking for the Connection from the Asian Experience.* Academic Press.

Quintero, J., Baldiris, S., Rubira, R., Cerón, J., & Velez, G. (2019). Augmented reality in educational inclusion. A systematic review on the last decade. *Frontiers in Psychology, 10*(AUG), 1–14. doi:10.3389/fpsyg.2019.01835 PMID:31456716

Ra, S., Shrestha, U., Khatiwada, S., Yoon, S. W., & Kwon, K. (2019). The rise of technology and impact on skills. *International Journal of Training Research, 17*(sup1), 26–40. doi:10.108 0/14480220.2019.1629727

Radovanović, D., Holst, C., Belur, S. B., Srivastava, R., Houngbonon, G. V., Le Quentrec, E., Miliza, J., Winkler, A. S., & Noll, J. (2020). Digital literacy key performance indicators for sustainable development. *Social Inclusion (Lisboa), 8*(2), 151–167. doi:10.17645i.v8i2.2587

Ragnedda, M. (2019). Reconceptualising the digital divide. In Mapping the Digital Divide in Africa. A mediated Analysis. Amsterdam: Amsterdam University Press.

Ragnedda, M. (2017). *The third Digital Divide: A weberian approach to digital inequalities.* Routledge. doi:10.4324/9781315606002

Ramakrishna, C., Venkateshwarlu, B., Srinivas, J., & Srinivas, S. (2019). Iot based smart farming using cloud computing and machine learning. *International Journal of Innovative Technology and Exploring Engineering, 9*(1), 3455–3458. https://doi.org/10.35940/ijitee.A4853.119119

Ramamoorthi, R., Jayaraj, R., Notaras, L., & Thomas, M. (2015). Epidemiology, etiology, and motivation of alcohol misuse among Australian Aboriginal and Torres Strait Islanders of the Northern Territory: A descriptive review. *Journal of Ethnicity in Substance Abuse, 14*(1), 1–11. doi:10.1080/15332640.2014.958642 PMID:25629929

Rangaswamy, N. (2008). Telecenters and Internet cafe's: The case of ICTs in small businesses. *Asian Journal of Communication, 18*(4), 365–378. doi:10.1080/01292980802344208

Rantanen, T., Järveläinen, E., & Leppälahti, T. (2021). Prisoners as Users of Digital Health Care and Social Welfare Services: A Finnish Attitude Survey. *International Journal of Environmental Research and Public Health, 18*(11), 5528. doi:10.3390/ijerph18115528

Rashid, A. T. (2016). Digital Inclusion and Social Inequality: Gender Differences in ICT Access and Use in Five Developing Countries. *Gender, Technology and Development, 20*(3), 306–332. doi:10.1177/0971852416660651

Ray, P. P. (2017). Internet of things for smart agriculture: Technologies, practices and future direction. *Journal of Ambient Intelligence and Smart Environments, 9*(4), 395–420. doi:10.3233/AIS-170440

Reddick, C. G., Enriquez, R., Harris, R. J., & Sharma, B. (2020). Determinants of broadband access and affordability: An analysis of a community survey on the digital divide (Vol 106). doi:10.1016/j.cities.2020.102904

Reisdorf, B., & Rhinesmith, C. (2020). *Digital Inclusion as a Core Component of Social Inclusion.* doi:10.17645/si.v8i2.3184

Reisdorf, B., & Rhinesmith, C., (2020). Digital Inclusion as a Core Component of Social Inclusion. In *Digital Inclusion Across the Globe: What Is Being Done to Tackle Digital Inequities.* Academic Press.

Reis, J., Amorim, M., Melão, N., & Matos, P. (2018). Digital transformation: A literature review and guidelines for future research. *Advances in Intelligent Systems and Computing, 745*(March), 411–421. doi:10.1007/978-3-319-77703-0_41

Report, C. S. (2019). *Harnessing ICTs to Scale-up Agricultural Innovations (ICT4Scale) Case Study Report.* Academic Press.

Rhinesmith, C. (2016). *Digital Inclusion and Meaningful Broadband Adoption Initiatives Digital Inclusion and Meaningful Broadband Adoption Initiatives.* Academic Press.

Rice, R. E. (2017). *Divide and diffuse : Comparing digital divide and diffusion of innovations perspectives on mobile phone adoption.* doi:10.1177/2050157915590469

Robards, F., Kang, M., Luscombe, G., Hawke, C., Sanci, L., Steinbeck, K., Zwi, K., Towns, S., & Usherwood, T. (2020). Intersectionality: Social marginalization and self-reported health status in young people. *International Journal of Environmental Research and Public Health, 17*(21), 8104. doi:10.3390/ijerph17218104 PMID:33153094

Robinson, L., Schulz, J., Dodel, M., Correa, T., Villanueva-mansilla, E., Leal, S., Magallanes-blanco, C., Rodriguez-medina, L., Dunn, H. S., Levine, L., McMahon, R., & Khilnani, A. (2020). Digital Inclusion Across the Americas and Caribbean. *Digital Inclusion Across the Americas and the Caribbean., 8*(2), 244–259. doi:10.17645i.v8i2.2632

Rodgers, S., Thorson, E., & Rodgers, S. (2018). Special Issue Introduction. *Digital Engagement with Advertising, 3367*(1), 1–3. Advance online publication. doi:10.1080/00913367.2017.1414003

Rodriguez, J. A., Shachar, C., & Bates, D. W. (2022). Digital Inclusion as Health Care; Supporting Health Care Equity with Digital-Infrastructure Initiatives. *The New England Journal of Medicine, 386*(12), 1101–1103. doi:10.1056/NEJMp2115646 PMID:35302722

Rogers, E. M. (2003). Elements of diffusion. *Diffusion of Innovations*, *5*, 1–38.

Roguski, M., & McBride-Henry, K. (2020). The failure of health promotion for marginalized populations. *Australian and New Zealand Journal of Public Health*, *44*(6), 446–448. doi:10.1111/1753-6405.13048 PMID:33104285

Rowley, J. (2012). Conducting research interviews. *Management Research Review*, *35*(3–4), 260–271. doi:10.1108/01409171211210154

Rudder, C. (2019). What is digital transformation? Your top questions answered. *The Enterprisers Project*, 7.

Ruzevicius, J. (2016). *Quality of Life and of Working Life : Conceptions and Research*. Academic Press.

Ryll, L., Barton, M. E., Zhang, B. Z., McWaters, R. J., Schizas, E., Hao, R., Bear, K., Preziuso, M., Seger, E., Wardrop, R., Rau, P. R., Debata, P., Rowan, P., Adams, N., Gray, M., & Yerolemou, N. (2020). *Transforming Paradigms: A Global AI in Financial Services Survey. SSRN*. Electronic Journal., doi:10.2139/SSRN.3532038

Sabbagh, K., Friedrich, R., El-Darwiche, B., Singh, M., Ganediwalla, S., & Katz, R. (2012). Maximizing the impact of digitization. *The Global Information Technology Report*, *2012*, 121–133.

Sahu, N., Deng, H., & Mollah, A. (2018). Investigating The Critical Success Factors of Digital Transformation for Improving Customer Experience. *Proceedings of the International Conference on Information Resources Management (Conf-IRM 2018)*, 1–13.

Salemink, K. (2016). How spatially and socially marginalized communities. Academic Press.

Salemink, K., Strijker, D., & Bosworth, G. (2017). Rural development in the digital age: A systematic literature review on unequal ICT availability, adoption, and use in rural areas. *Journal of Rural Studies*, *54*, 360–371. doi:10.1016/j.jrurstud.2015.09.001

Salsabila, U. H. (2019). A Preliminary Analysis: Digital Inclusion Domain in Islamic Education. *International Journal on E-Learning*, *1*(1), 12–18. doi:10.31763/ijele.v1i1.23

Sam, S. (2014). Exploring Mobile Internet use among Marginalised Young People in Post-conflict Sierra Leone. *The Electronic Journal on Information Systems in Developing Countries*, *66*(5), 1–20. http://www.ejisdc.org/ojs2/index.php/ejisdc/article/view/1439

Samuel, M., Doctor, G., Christian, P., & Baradi, M. (2020). Drivers and barriers to e-government adoption in Indian cities. *Journal of Urban Management*, *9*(4), 408–417. doi:10.1016/j.jum.2020.05.002

Samuel, O., Almogren, A., Javaid, A., Zuair, M., Ullah, I., & Javaid, N. (2020). Leveraging blockchain technology for secure energy trading and least-cost evaluation of decentralized contributions to electrification in sub-Saharan Africa. *Entropy (Basel, Switzerland)*, *22*(2). https://doi.org/10.3390/e22020226

Sanders, C. K., & Scanlon, E. (2021). The digital divide is a human rights issue: Advancing social inclusion through social work advocacy. *Journal of Human Rights and Social Work, 6*(2), 130–143.

Sandu, N., Gide, E., & Karim, S. (2019). Improving learning through cloud-based mobile technologies and virtual and augmented reality for australian higher education. *ACM International Conference Proceeding Series*, 1–5. 10.1145/3348400.3348413

Sannikov, S., Zhdanov, F., Chebotarev, P., & Rabinovich, P. (2015). Interactive Educational Content Based on Augmented Reality and 3D Visualization. In Procedia Computer Science (Vol. 66). Elsevier Masson SAS. doi:10.1016/j.procs.2015.11.082

Sarantou, M., & Akimenko, D. (2018). Margin to Margin. *Arts-Based Research for Digital Outreach to Marginalized Communities., 14*, 139–159.

Saul, C. J., & Gebauer, H. (2018). Digital transformation as an enabler for advanced services in the sanitation sector. *Sustainability (Switzerland), 10*(3), 1–18. doi:10.3390u10030752

Scholz, R. W., Bartelsman, E. J., Diefenbach, S., Franke, L., Grunwald, A., Helbing, D., Hill, R., Hilty, L., Höjer, M., Klauser, S., Montag, C., Parycek, P., Prote, J., Renn, O., Reichel, A., Schuh, G., Steiner, G., & Viale Pereira, G. (2018). Unintended side effects of the digital transition: European scientists' messages from a proposition-based expert round table. *Sustainability, 10*(6), 2001. doi:10.3390u10062001

Schumann, G. J., Brakenridge, G. R., Kettner, A. J., Kashif, R., & Niebuhr, E. (2018). Assisting Flood Disaster Response with Earth Observation Data and Products: A Critical Assessment. *Remote Sensing, 10*(8), 1–19. doi:10.3390/rs10081230

Schwertner, K. (2017). Digital Transformation of Business. *Trakia Journal of Sciences, 15*(1), 388–393. doi:10.15547/tjs.2017.s.01.065

Scott, S., & Mcguire, J. (2017). *Using Diffusion of Innovation Theory to Promote Universally Designed College Instruction.* Academic Press.

SDG. (2019). Sustainable development goals. *The Energy Progress Report. Tracking SDG, 7.*

Seale, J. (2009). *Digital Inclusion.* Academic Press.

Series, W. P. (2008). Development Informatics. *Development, 32*, 45. doi:10.1016/0736-5853(84)90003-0

Servaes, J. (2015). *The tools of social change : A critique of techno-centric development and activism.* doi:10.1177/1461444815604419

Sevelius, J. M., Gutierrez, L., Sophia, M., Haas, Z., Mccree, B., Ngo, A., Jackson, A., Clynes, C., Venegas, L., Salinas, A., Herrera, C., Stein, E., Operario, D., & Gamarel, K. (2020). Research with Marginalized Communities : Challenges to Continuity During the COVID - 19 Pandemic. *AIDS and Behavior*, (7), 1–4. doi:10.100710461-020-02920-3 PMID:32415617

Sevelius, J. M., Gutierrez-Mock, L., Zamudio-Haas, S., McCree, B., Ngo, A., Jackson, A., Clynes, C., Venegas, L., Salinas, A., Herrera, C., Stein, E., Operario, D., & Gamarel, K. (2020). Research with Marginalized Communities: Challenges to Continuity During the COVID-19 Pandemic. *AIDS and Behavior*, *24*(7), 2009–2012. https://doi.org/10.1007/s10461-020-02920-3

Shanmugapriya, P., Rathika, S., Ramesh, T., & Janaki, P. (2019). Applications of Remote Sensing in Agriculture - A Review. *International Journal of Current Microbiology and Applied Sciences*, *8*(1), 2270–2283. doi:10.20546/ijcmas.2019.801.238

Sharp, M. (2022). *Revisiting digital inclusion: A survey of theory, measurement and recent research*. https://www.bsg.ox.ac.uk/sites/default/files/202204/Revisiting%20digital%20inclusion-%20A%20survey%20of%20theory%2C%20measurement%20and%20recent%20research.pdf

Siddiquee, N. A. (2016). E-government and transformation of service delivery in developing countries: The Bangladesh experience and lessons. *Transforming Government: People, Process and Policy*, *10*(3), 368–390. doi:10.1108/TG-09-2015-0039

Signé & Signé. (2021). *How African states can improve their cyber-security*. Academic Press.

Sipior, J. C., & Ward, B. T. (2005). Bridging the Digital Divide for e-Government inclusion: A United States Case Study. *Electronic Journal of E-Government*, *3*(3), 137–146. doi:10.1108/02640470510631308

Slätmo, E., Fischer, K., & Röös, E. (2016). The framing of sustainability in sustainability assessment frameworks for agriculture. *Sociologia Ruralis*, *57*(3), 378–395. doi:10.1111oru.12156

Smidt, H. J., & Jokonya, O. (2021). Information Technology for Development Factors affecting digital technology adoption by small-scale farmers in agriculture value chains (AVCs) in South Africa. *Information Technology for Development*, *0*(0), 1–27. doi:10.1080/02681102.2021.1975256

Sorko, S. R., & Brunnhofer, M. (2019). Potentials of Augmented Reality in Training. *Procedia Manufacturing*, *31*, 85–90. doi:10.1016/j.promfg.2019.03.014

Sott, M. K., Furstenau, L. B., Kipper, L. M., Giraldo, F. D., Lopez-Robles, J. R., Cobo, M. J., Zahid, A., Abbasi, Q. H., & Imran, M. A. (2020). Precision Techniques and Agriculture 4.0 Technologies to promote sustainability in the Co_ee Sector: State of the Art, Challenges and Future Trends. *IEEE Access: Practical Innovations, Open Solutions*, *8*, 1. doi:10.1109/ACCESS.2020.3016325

Sott, M. K., Nascimento, L. da S., Foguesatto, C. R., Furstenau, L. B., Faccin, K., Zawislak, P. A., Mellado, B., Kong, J. D., & Bragazzi, N. L. (2021). A Bibliometric Network Analysis of Recent Publications on Digital Agriculture to Depict Strategic Themes and Evolution Structure. *Sensors (Basel)*, *21*(23), 7889. doi:10.339021237889 PMID:34883903

Spalevic, V., Lakicevic, M., Radanovic, D., Billi, P., Barovic, G., Vujacic, D., Sestras, P., & Khaledi Darvishan, A. (2017). Ecological-economic (Eco-Eco) modelling in the River Basins of Mountainous Regions: Impact of land cover changes on sediment yield in the Velicka Rijeka, Montenegro. *Notulae Botanicae Horti Agrobotanici Cluj-Napoca*, *45*(2), 602–610. doi:10.15835/nbha45210695

Spanaki, K., Sivarajah, U., Fakhimi, M., Despoudi, S., & Irani, Z. (2021). Disruptive technologies in agricultural operations: a systematic review of AI-driven AgriTech research. In *Annals of Operations Research*. Springer US. doi:10.1007/s10479-020-03922-z

Steinke, J., Van Etten, J., Müller, A., Ortiz-Crespo, B., Van De Gevel, J., Silvestri, S., & Priebe, J. (2020). Tapping the full potential of the digital revolution for agricultural extension: an emerging innovation agenda Tapping the full potential of the digital revolution for agricultural extension: an emerging innovation agenda. *International Journal of Agricultural Sustainability.* doi:10.10 80/14735903.2020.1738754

Stolterman, E., & Fors, A. C. (2004). Information technology and the good life. In *Information systems research* (pp. 687–692). Springer. doi:10.1287/1-4020-8095-6_45

Study, C., Countries, F., & Republic, D. (2019). ICT for Learning and Inclusion in Latin America and Europe Case Study From Countries: Bolivia, Brazil, Cuba, Dominican Republic, Ecuador, Finland, Poland, Turkey, Uruguay. doi:10.24917/9788395373732

Sun, Y., Fang, Y., & Lim, K. H. (2012). *User Satisfaction with Information Technology Service Delivery : A Social Capital Perspective.* doi:10.1287/isre.1120.0421

Syaglova, Y. (2020). Digital transformation in food retailing. In *IOP Conference Series: Earth and Environmental Science.* IOP Publishing.

Tan, K. L., & Lim, C. K. (2018). Development of traditional musical instruments using augmented reality (AR) through mobile learning. *AIP Conference Proceedings*, *2016*(September), 1–7. doi:10.1063/1.5055542

Tarka, P. (2018). An overview of structural equation modeling: Its beginnings, historical development, usefulness and controversies in the social sciences. *Quality & Quantity*, *52*(1), 313–354. doi:10.100711135-017-0469-8 PMID:29416184

Tech-Student, M. (2016). A Literature Study on Agricultural Production System Using IoT as Inclusive Technology. *Int. J. Innov. Technol. Res*, *4*(1), 2727–2731.

The Four Essential Pillars of Digital Transformation: a Practical Blueprint I Akorbi Digital RMP. (n.d.). Retrieved February 13, 2022, from https://www.runmyprocess.com/vision/white-papers/the-four-essential-pillars-of-digital-transformation/

Thomas, J., Barraket, J., & Parkinson, S. (2021). *Measuring Australia's digital divide: The Australian digital inclusion index 2021.* RMIT University. doi:10.25916/PHGW-B725ALI

Tie, Y. C., Birks, M., & Francis, K. (2019). *Grounded theory research : A design framework for novice researchers.* doi:10.1177/2050312118822927

Tihinen, M., Iivari, M., Ailisto, H., Komi, M., Kääriäinen, J., & Peltomaa, I. (2016). An exploratory method to clarify business potential in the context of industrial internet–a case study. *Working Conference on Virtual Enterprises*, 469–478. 10.1007/978-3-319-45390-3_40

Tilson, D., Lyytinen, K., & Sørensen, C. (2010). Research commentary - Digital infrastructures: The missing IS research agenda. *Information Systems Research*, *21*(4), 748–759. doi:10.1287/isre.1100.0318

Trendov, M., Varas, S., & Zeng, M. (2019). Digital technologies in agriculture and rural areas: status report. *Digital Technologies in Agriculture and Rural Areas: Status Report.*

Trendov, N. M., Varas, S., & Zeng, M. (2019). *Digital Technologies in Agriculture and Rural Areas. Briefing Paper FAO.* FAO.

Tsan, M., Totapally, S., Hailu, M., & Addom, B. K. (2019). *The digitalization of African agriculture report, 2018–2019.* Wageningen: CTA. Retrieved from: www.cta.int/en/digitalisation-agriculture-africa

Tsatsou, P. (2020). Is digital inclusion fighting disability stigma? Opportunities, barriers, and recommendations. *Disability & Society.* Advance online publication. doi:10.1080/09687599.2020.1749563

Tsokota, T., Musungwini, S., & Mutembedza, A. (2020). A strategy to enhance consumer trust in the adoption of mobile banking applications. *African Journal of Science, Technology, Innovation and Development*, *0*(0), 1–16. doi:10.1080/20421338.2020.1829352

Turkan, Y., Radkowski, R., Karabulut-Ilgu, A., Behzadan, A. H., & Chen, A. (2017). Mobile augmented reality for teaching structural analysis. *Advanced Engineering Informatics, 34*(October), 90–100. doi:10.1016/j.aei.2017.09.005

UK Government. (2022). *Cyber security incentives and regulation review.* Department for Digital, Culture, Media & Sport. Retrieved April 20, 2022, from https://www.gov.uk/government/publications/

Ulas, D. (2019). Digital Transformation Process and SMEs. 3rd World Conference on Technology, Innovation and Entrepreneurship (WOCTINE). *Procedia Computer Science*, *158*, 662–671. doi:10.1016/j.procs.2019.09.101

UNCTAD. (2017). *Information Economy Report 2017: Digitalization, Trade and Development.* Report UNCTAD/IER/2017/Corr. United Nations. https://unctad.org/en/ PublicationsLibrary/ier2017_en.pdf

UNESCO. (2021). *Adverse consequences of school closures.* https://en.unesco.org/covid19/educationresponse/consequences

Urvashi, A., Chetty, K., Gcora, N., Josie, J., & Mishra, V. (2017). *Bridging the Digital Divide: Skills For The New Age.* Policy Brief, G20 Insights.

Uy-Tioco, C. S. (2019). 'Good enough' access: Digital inclusion, social stratification, and the reinforcement of class in the Philippines. *Communication Research and Practice*, *5*(2), 156–171. doi:10.1080/22041451.2019.1601492

Valverde-Berrocoso, J., del Carmen Garrido-Arroyo, M., Burgos-Videla, C., & Morales-Cevallos, M. B. (2020). Trends in educational research about e-Learning: A systematic literature review (2009-2018). *Sustainability (Switzerland)*, *12*(12), 5153. Advance online publication. doi:10.3390u12125153

van Deursen, A. J., & van Dijk, J. A. (2019). The first-level digital divide shifts from inequalities in physical access to inequalities in material access. *New Media & Society*, *21*(2), 354–375. doi:10.1177/1461444818797082 PMID:30886536

Van Dijk, J. A. G. M. (2017). Digital divide: Impact of access. The International Encyclopedia of Media Effects, 1–11.

Van Dijk, J. A. G. M. (2017). Closing the Digital Divide The Role of Digital Technologies on Social Development, Well-Being of All and the Approach of the Covid-19 Pandemic. *Telematics and Informatics*, *34*, 1607–1624. doi:10.1016/j.tele.2017.07.007

van Dyk, R., & van Belle, J. P. (2019). Factors influencing the intended adoption of digital transformation: A South African case study. *Proceedings of the 2019 Federated Conference on Computer Science and Information Systems, FedCSIS 2019*, 519–528. 10.15439/2019F166

Vanderheiden, G. (2006). *Over the Horizon: Potential Impact of Emerging Trends in Information and Communication Technology on Disability Policy and Practice*. National Council on Disability.

Veena, S. (2018). *The Survey on Smart Agriculture Using IoT.* Academic Press.

Veiga, A., Loock, M., & Renaud, K. (2021). Cyber4Dev-Q: Calibrating cyber awareness in the developing country context. *The Electronic Journal on Information Systems in Developing Countries*, 12198.

Venkatraman, N. (1991). IT-Induced Business Reconfiguration. *The Corporation of the 1990s: Information Technology and Organizational Transformation*, 331.

Vera, E. M., Buhin, L., & Isacco, A. (2009). *The role of prevention in psychology's social justice agenda*. Academic Press.

Verdegem, P., & Verhoest. (2008). The 'relative utility' approach for stimulating ICT acceptance : profiling the non-user. *European Journal of EPractice,* 1–11.

Vial, G. (2021). Understanding digital transformation: A review and a research agenda. *Managing Digital Transformation*, 13–66.

Viale Pereira, G., Estevez, E., Cardona, D., Chesñevar, C., Collazzo-Yelpo, P., Cunha, M. A., Diniz, E. H., Ferraresi, A. A., Fischer, F. M., Cardinelle Oliveira Garcia, F., Joia, L. A., Luciano, E. M., de Albuquerque, J. P., Quandt, C. O., Sánchez Rios, R., Sánchez, A., Damião da Silva, E., Silva-Junior, J. S., & Scholz, R. W. (2020). South American expert roundtable: Increasing adaptive governance capacity for coping with unintended side effects of digital transformation. *Sustainability*, *12*(2), 718. doi:10.3390u12020718

Vial, G. (2019). Understanding digital transformation: A review and a research agenda. *Journal of Strategic Information Systems Review, 28*(2), 118–144. doi:10.1016/j.jsis.2019.01.003

Vibhavari, M. (2020). *GPT3-revolution.* https://static.startuptalky.com/2020/08/GPT3-revolution_ StartupTalky

Vidyasaga, D. (2006). Digital divide and digital dividend in the age of information technology. *Journal of Perinatology, 2006*(26), 313–315. doi:10.1038j.jp.7211494 PMID:16598298

Von Braun, J. (2019). *AI and robotics implications for the poor.* Available at SSRN 3497591.

Von Braun, J. (2019). *Working Paper 188.* Academic Press.

von Braun, J., & Gatzweiler, F. W. (2014). Marginality—An overview and implications for policy. *Marginality*, 1.

Waldron, S. (2010). *Measuring subjective wellbeing in the UK.* Office for National Statistics.

Wamboye, E. F., & Tochkov, K. (2018). Information and communication technologies' impact on growth and employment in Africa. In E. F. Wamboye & P. J. Nyaronga (Eds.), *The Service Sector and Economic Development in Africa.* doi:10.4324/9781315627373-12

Wang, D., Zhou, T., & Wang, M. (2021). Information and communication technology (ICT), digital divide and urbanization: Evidence from Chinese cities. *Technology in Society, 64*, 101516. doi:10.1016/j.techsoc.2020.101516

Watkins, S. C. (2011). Digital divide: Navigating the digital edge. *International Journal of Learning and Media, 3*(2).

Watts, G. (2020). COVID-19 and the digital divide in the UK. *The Lancet. Digital Health, 2*(8), e395–e396. doi:10.1016/S2589-7500(20)30169-2 PMID:32835198

Wendelborg, C., & Tøssebro, J. (2010). Marginalization processes in inclusive education in Norway: A longitudinal study of classroom participation. *Disability & Society, 25*(6), 701–714. doi:10.1080/09687599.2010.505744

Wentrup, R., Ström, P., & Nakamura, H. R. (2016). Digital oases and digital deserts in Sub-Saharan Africa. *Journal of Science & Technology Policy Management.*

Westerman, G., Calméjane, C., Bonnet, D., Ferraris, P., & McAfee, A. (2011). Digital transformation: a roadmap for billion-dollar organizations. MIT Center for Digital Business and Capgemini Consulting.

Williams, M. (2017). John Dewey in the 21st century. *Journal of Inquiry and Action in Education, 9*(1), 91–102.

Willis, K. S. (2019). *Making a 'Place' for ICTs in Rural Communities.* Academic Press.

Wiraniskala, B., & Sujarwoto, S. (2020). Reaping or Losing Digital Dividend? The Use of Social Media for Enhancing Public Participation: A Literature Review. *Journal of Public Administration Studies*, *5*(2), 89–95. doi:10.21776/ub.jpas.2020.005.02.8

Witarsyah, D., Sjafrizal, T., Fudzee, M. F. M., & Salamat, M. A. (2017). The critical factors affecting e-government adoption in indonesia: A conceptual framework. *International Journal on Advanced Science, Engineering and Information Technology*, *7*(1), 160–167. doi:10.18517/ijaseit.7.1.1614

Wolfert, S., Ge, L., Verdouw, C., & Bogaardt, M. J. (2017). 'Big data in smart farming'–A review. *Agricultural Systems*, *153*, 69–80. doi:10.1016/j.agsy.2017.01.023

Wood, C. S., Thomas, M. R., Budd, J., Mashamba-Thompson, T. P., Herbst, K., Pillay, D., Peeling, R. W., Johnson, A. M., McKendry, R. A., & Stevens, M. M. (2019). Taking connected mobile-health diagnostics of infectious diseases to the field. *Nature*, *566*(7745), 467–474.

World Bank. (2006). *2006 World Development Indicators*. World Bank.

World Bank. (2016). *World Development Report 2016: Digital Dividends (Overview of Chinese Version)*. Author.

Xie, B., Charness, N., Fingerman,K., Kaye, J., Kim, M. T., & Khurshid, A. (n.d.). *When going digital becomes a necessity: Ensuring older adults' needs for information, services, and social inclusion during COVID-19*. doi:10.1080/08959420.2020.1771237

Yannopoulos, S. I., Grismer, M. E., Bali, K. M., & Angelakis, A. N. (2020). Evolution of the materials and methods used for subsurface drainage of agricultural lands from antiquity to the present. *Water (Basel)*, *12*(6), 1767. doi:10.3390/w12061767

Ye, L., & Yang, H. (2020). From digital divide to social inclusion: A tale of mobile platform empowerment in rural areas. *Sustainability (Switzerland)*, *12*(6), 2424. Advance online publication. doi:10.3390u12062424

Yilmaz, Z. A., & Batdi, V. (2016). A meta-analytic and thematic comparative analysis of the integration of augmented reality applications into education. *Egitim ve Bilim*, *41*(188), 273–289. doi:10.15390/EB.2016.6707

Yoo, Y., Lyytinen, K., Boland, R., Berente, N., Gaskin, J., Schutz, D., & Srinivasan, N. (2010). The next wave of digital innovation: Opportunities and challenges. *Research Workshop: Digital Challenges in Innovation Research*, 1–37.

Yu, B., Ndumu, A., Mon, L. M., Fan, Z., Yu, B., Ndumu, A., & Mon, L. M. (2018). *E-inclusion or digital divide : An integrated model of digital inequality digital divide*. doi:10.1108/JD-10-2017-0148

Zabadi, A. M. (2016). Adoption of Information Systems (IS): The Factors that Influencing IS Usage and Its Effect on Employee in Jordan Telecom Sector (JTS): A Conceptual Integrated Model. *International Journal of Business and Management*, *11*(3), 25. doi:10.5539/ijbm.v11n3p25

Zainudeen, A., & Galpaya, H. (2015). *Mobile phones, internet, and gender in Myanmar*. GSMA.

Zeqi, Q., Shuqin, Z., & Shiding, L. (2019). From the Digital Divide to the Connectivity Dividend Difference: A Connectivity Capital Perspective. *Social Sciences in China*, *40*(1), 63–81. doi:10 .1080/02529203.2019.1556475

Zhao, Z. (2015). "Internet Plus" cross-border management: The perspective of creative destruction. *China Industrial Economics*, *10*(29), 146–160.

Zhou, M., Herselman, M., & Coleman, A. (2015). USSD technology a low cost asset in complementing public health workers' work processes. Lecture Notes in Computer Science, 9044, 57–64. doi:10.1007/978-3-319-16480-9_6

Zhou, Y., Xu, L., & Muhammad Shaikh, G. (2019). Evaluating and prioritizing the green supply chain management practices in pakistan: Based on delphi and fuzzy AHP approach. *Symmetry*, *11*(11), 1346. doi:10.3390ym11111346

Zurutuza, N. (2018). *Information poverty and algorithmic equity: Bringing advances in AI to the most vulnerable*. Academic Press.

# About the Contributors

**Munyaradzi Zhou** received his Ph.D. degree in Information Systems from the University of South Africa, South Africa, in 2018. He is currently a Senior Lecturer of the Department of Information Systems at the Midlands State University, Zimbabwe. He instructs Data Science modules, namely, Foundations of Data Science, Business Intelligence, and Data Structures and Algorithms. His current research area is Artificial Intelligence and Machine Learning in Education, Agriculture, and different sectors to support sustainability and inclusiveness. He participates in different boards in the application of ICTs and is the Board Member for the Institute of Sustainable Project Planning, Monitoring, and Evaluation.

**Gilbert Mahlangu** is a holder of Doctor of Information Communication Technolgy from Cape Peninsula University of Technology (CPUT), South Africa. He is currently a Lecturer in the Department of Information and Marketing Sciences at the Midlands State University, Zimbabwe. He teaches Informatics and Business modules. These include but are not limited to, Introduction to Informatics, Strategic Information Management and E-business, Innovation and design thinking, Applied Research Methods. His current research area is Digital inclusion, the Digital divide, and electronic government in developing countries. He participates in policy development for ICT in Agriculture and different presentations supporting ICTs at university and national level.

**Cyncia Matsika** is an experienced database administrator who lectures in the department of Information and Marketing Science. She instructs Data Science modules like Principles of programming for Data Science and Informatics. She possesses an arsenal of extensive current Information Technology knowledge and holds 38 International Business Machines Corporation (IBM) certifications and 1 certification from Cisco Networking Academy in various fields that include Artificial Intelligence, Data Science & Analytics, Blockchain, Machine Learning, Internet of Things, Computer Vision, Cloud and Natural Language Processing. She also holds a Master of Science in Information Systems Management and a Bachelor of

Technology Honors Degree in Information Technology plus a Post Graduate Diploma in Tertiary education. She has a passion for Augmented and Virtual Reality in Education, Digital inclusion in marginalized communities and is a member of the Organization for Women in Science for the Developing World (OWSD).

\* \* \*

**Wilfreda Indira Chawarura** is a holder of a Master of Science degree in Finance and Investments from National University of Science and Technology, Zimbabwe. She is currently a lecturer in the department of Accounting Sciences at the Midlands State University, Zimbabwe. She teaches finance and banking modules which includes but not limited to Banking law, International Banking, Corporate Finance, Marketing of Financial services. Her current research interests are in digital inclusion and divide in Africa, financial inclusion, personal finance management, developmental economics, and environmental economics. She participates in environmental policy formulation and awareness campaigns in Zimbabwe and Southern African Development Community (SADC) region.

**Gibson Chengetanai** is a holder of a PhD in Computer Science, M.Sc. in Computer Science and a B.Sc. (Hons) Information Systems degrees. He is currently a lecturer at Botswana Accountancy College (BAC), in the School of Computing and Information Systems in Botswana. He has been lecturing at tertiary institutions for over 16 years. He has accredited publications and practical research interests in ICT for development in marginalised communities, Wireless Networks, Information Systems Auditing, Databases, Digital forensics and Cyber security. He is a member of ISACA and is a qualified Certified Information Systems Auditor (CISA) and Certified Ethical Hacker (CEH) certified among other industry qualifications.

**Ronald Chikati** received his BSc (Hons) in Computer Science with education from the University of Zimbabwe, an MSc in Computer Science from National University of Science and Technology (Zimbabwe) and another MSc in Strategic Management from Derby (UK). He is a PhD candidate. He has industry certifications in Routing and Switching, Cloud Computing, Machine Learning & Data Science and Big data Analytics. His research interests are in ICT4D, Artificial Intelligence (Computational Intelligence, Machine Learning and Data Science), Business Intelligence and Data Mining. A Zimbabwean native and a Botswana resident, Ronald likes Chess playing, travelling, gardening and reading novels.

**Florence Chimbwanda** holds an M.Sc. in Agricultural and Applied Economics and BSc in Agriculture, both from the University of Zimbabwe (UZ). She is currently doing her Ph.D. in Agriculture at the University of South Africa (UNISA), in South Africa. She is a Senior Lecturer in the Department of Agriculture Management in the Faculty of Agriculture at Zimbabwe Open University (ZOU). She teaches Agricultural and food marketing, introduction to agricultural management, and farm business management. Her research areas are natural resource management and economics, animal nutrition, agribusiness management, rural development, soil and water conservation, farm resources management, agricultural and food marketing, agricultural policy analysis, new institutional economics, and extension. Florence is a member of the Zimbabwe Association of University Women (ZAUW) and the Organization for Women in Science for the Developing World (OWSD).

**Nyasha Chipunza** is an Academic, Researcher and Acting Chairperson in the Department of Agricultural Economics and Development at Manicaland State University of Applied Sciences in Zimbabwe. His research and teaching interest include Agricultural policy Analysis; International; Markets and Price Analysis; Production Economics; Econometrics and Quantitative Analysis.

**Innocent Chirisa** is a Full Professor of Urban and Regional Planning in the Department of Demography Settlement and Development at the University of Zimbabwe. He is also a Research Fellow in the Department of Urban and Regional Planning, University of the Free State, South Africa. Currently, Prof Chirisa is serving as the Dean of the Faculty of Social and Behavioural Sciences at the University of Zimbabwe. His research interests are human settlement planning and resilience. He has written so far 25 books, 100 book chapters, and over 150 journal articles in peer-reviewed journals.

**Samuel Simbarashe Furusa** is a lecturer at the Midlands State University, in the Department of Information and Marketing Sciences. He is a member of the ZIMCHE physical assessment for facilities and resources checklist for the academic program. The program included an assessment of the curriculum of the academic program for accreditation by ZIMCHE. This included the review of the degree programs at the University of Zimbabwe and the National University of Science and Technology in the domain of Computer Science, Information Systems and Informatics. He is a published author who has published research articles in Scopus indexed journals and non-Scopus indexed journals. He has also attended and presented at a number of international conferences (ICT4D, Springer link organized and Elsevier organised). He holds a Post Graduate Diploma in Tertiary education from Midlands State University, a Bachelor of Science Honours Degree in Information Systems from Midlands State University, a Master Science Degree in Information Systems

Management from Midlands State University, and a Ph.D. in Information Systems from the University of South Africa (UNISA).

**Petros Venganayi Gavai** is a lecturer at the Midlands State University, in the Department of Information and Marketing Sciences. He is a published author who has published research articles in Scopus indexed journals and non-Scopus indexed journals. He has also attended and presented at a number of international conferences. He holds a Post Graduate Diploma in Tertiary education from Midlands State University, a Bachelor of Science Honours Degree in Information Technology from Harare Institute of Technology, and a Master Science Degree in Information Systems Management from Midlands State University.

**Raviro Gumbo** is a lecturer at the Midlands State University, in the Department of Information and Marketing Sciences. He holds a Post Graduate Diploma in Tertiary education from Midlands State University, a Bachelor of Science Honours Degree in Information Systems from Midlands State University, a Master Science Degree in Information Systems Management from Midlands State University, a Higher Diploma in Computer Science from Higher Education Examination Council, Research Interests: Digital Transformation Mobile and web technologies Cloud computing Information Security Computer Graphics Data Science and Business Intelligence.

**Andrew Tapiwa Kugedera** is a holder of Bsc Honours in Agriculture from UZ, MSc Agroforestry from BUSE, and Post Graduate Diploma in Education from ZOU. Andrew is a Ph.D. candidate in Land Management and Conservation at BUSE. Andrew is a renowned researcher in Agriculture with interests in Agroforestry, Forestry, Sustainable Agriculture, soil fertility management, animal Nutrition in Agroforestry, and soil and water conservation. He published 60 articles, 10 book chapters, and 1 book. His current research on soil fertility management strategies can be used to improve crop production in smallholder farming systems in semi-arid areas. He is also researching orphaned crops that need attention in marginalized areas of Zimbabwe. He published extensively on rainwater harvesting techniques and integrated nutrient management.

**Samuel M.** is a lecturer at the Midlands State University, in the Department of Information and Marketing Sciences. He is a member of the ZIMCHE physical assessment for facilities and resources checklist for academic programs. The program included an assessment of the curriculum of academic programs for accreditation by ZIMCHE. This included the review of the degree programs at the University of Zimbabwe and the National University of Science and Technology in the domain of Computer Science, Information Systems, and Informatics. He has contributed to the

2019 Technology Transfer Workshop (Intellectual property (IP)) at Gweru Polytechnic. He is a published author who has published research articles in Scopus indexed journals and non-Scopus indexed journals. He has also attended and presented at a number of international conferences (ICT4D, Springer link organized and Elsevier organised) He holds a Post Graduate Diploma in Tertiary education from Midlands State University, a Bachelor of Science Honours Degree in Information Systems from Midlands State University, a Master Science Degree in Information Systems Management from Midlands State University. He is currently studying for PhD in Information Systems at the University of South Africa (UNISA).

**Melody Maseko** is a lecturer at the Midlands State University, in the Department of Information and Marketing Sciences. She is a published author who has published research articles in Scopus indexed journals and non-Scopus indexed journals. She has also attended and presented at a number of international conferences. She holds a Post Graduate Diploma in Tertiary education from Midlands State University, a Bachelor of Science Honours Degree in Information Systems from Midlands State University, a Master of Business Administration from University of Zimbabwe and a Master Science Degree in Information Systems Management from Midlands State University.

**Teurai Matekenya** is a technologist, statistician, researcher and author. Teurai is best known for her passion in carrying out organisation and industry specific researches as well as national surveys. As a technologist, Teurai focuses on how Data Science is changing the business landscape as well as the disaster management landscape. She has written a number of book chapters on IT application in business as well as IT application in disaster management. Teurai is a holder of a bachelor's degree in Computer Science and Statistics, MBA, MIT and currently a PhD student working on: "A Knowledge Management Framework for improving crisis response." Teurai likes travelling and learning about different cultures.

**Rukudzo Alyson Mawere** is a holder of Master of Commerce in Marketing Strategy from Midlands State University(MSU). She is currently a Lecturer in the Department of Information and Marketing Sciences at the Midlands State University, Zimbabwe. She teaches Principles of Marketing, Consumer Decision Sciences, Digital Marketing, Services Marketing and Business modules. Her current research area is Digital inclusion, the Digital divide, Digital Technologies for Higher Education and Sustainable Marketing.

**Fungai Mukora** is a Lecturer in the Department of Computer Engineering at the University of Zimbabwe. She has over 12 years experience teaching Hardware

Engineering modules that includes Logic Design and Circuits, Number Systems and Digital Computer Fundamentals. She holds a Master of Science Degree in Computer Science and currently a candidate for the PhD Engineering. Her research interests include 4IR, ICT4D and ICT Adoption with emphasis on marginalized groups and communities.

**Briget Munyoro** is a lecturer at Midlands State University (MSU) in the department of Information and Marketing Sciences. She holds a Master of Science Degree in Information Systems with National University of Science and Technology (NUST) and a Bachelor of Technology Honours Degree with Harare Institute of Technology (HIT). She teaches Mobile computing, Operating systems, Software Project Management, Web technologies, Introduction to Informatics, Foundation of Information Systems and Information Informatics. Briget has been in the academic industry as an instructor for 8 years and has earned IBM badges in Data Science and Analytics, Artificial Intelligence, Cybersecurity, Building a chatbot and Cloud computing in order to enhance her skills in the field of Computing. Her research interests are in the ICT application areas, Business Intelligence and Distributed Databases.

**Caroline Muparutsa** is an Organization Development specialist who is passionate about leadership development focusing more on coaching and mentoring. As a professional business consultant, she has worked with different industries and has tackled different challenges in organizations with success. She has a unique approach to tackling organizations challenges resulting in significant transformation for her clients. Currently she has her focus on helping organisations achieve agility as a strategy to tackle this volatile and dynamic environment. Caroline is a holder of bachelor's degree and two master's degrees, an MBA and a master's degree in leadership development. Her career has progressed leaning towards Organisation behaviour and developed extensive knowledge in this field. She has a diverse work experience, she has worked in different countries in Africa, the UK, and the USA. In her spare time, she loves to travel and learning about different cultures.

**Tendai Shelton Muwani** has a Masters of Commerce in Information Systems from Great Zimbabwe University, a Bachelor of Technology Honours Degree from Harare Institute of Technology (HIT), a Higher National Diploma in Information Technology, and a Diploma in Technical and Vocational Education from Kushinga Phikelela Polytechnic. He is a lecturer in Computer Science and Information Systems at Manicaland State University of Applied Sciences in Zimbabwe. He is the student Innovation Project Coordinator in the department. He teaches programming and object oriented modules. His current research interests include the Digital Divide, Tourism and big data, machine learning, and cyber security. He recently published

"Particle Swarm Optimization-based Empirical Mode Decomposition Predictive Technique for Nonstationary Data" in the Journal of Supercomputing and an article "Assessing an online marketing application tool for curios and crafts roadside vendors' business in the Vumba Mountains, Zimbabwe" in the African Journal of Hospitality, Tourism and Leisure.

**Njodzi Ranganai** has a post graduate diploma in education (ZOU), BSc Honors degree in Information systems (2010) Midlands State University and Master of Commerce degree in Information Systems, Great Zimbabwe University (2014). He has been working since 2012 in higher education. Research topics include machine learning (its applications) and Data communication and computer networks. His expertise covers applications of machine and deep learning in business. He teaches several courses on Computer Science & Information Systems, data communication, software engineering, MIS and Business Intelligence & analytics.

**Nyasha Sakadzo** is a holder of an MSc Crop Protection degree, a BSc Agronomy Honours degree, and a Post Graduate Diploma in Education. He is a Lecturer in the Department of Agriculture Economics and Development at Manicaland State University of Applied Sciences. He is teaching modules that fall under crop production. Currently a Dphil in Agriculture (Crop Science) candidate with Great Zimbabwe University. His study interests are in the use of biopesticides for weed, pest, and disease control in crops which he has published in refereed journals.

**Lemias Zivanai** was born in Masvingo province, Zimbabwe. He obtained his bachelor of science in Information Systems, MSU. He did his Master of science in Computer Science. Currently is lecturing at the Midlands State University in department of information Science and marketing.

# Index

# Ensure Quality Research is Introduced to the Academic Community

# Become an Evaluator for IGI Global Authored Book Projects

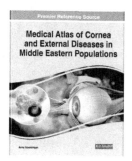

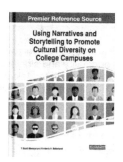

## The overall success of an authored book project is dependent on quality and timely manuscript evaluations.

## Applications and Inquiries may be sent to:
### development@igi-global.com

Applicants must have a doctorate (or equivalent degree) as well as publishing, research, and reviewing experience. Authored Book Evaluators are appointed for one-year terms and are expected to complete at least three evaluations per term. Upon successful completion of this term, evaluators can be considered for an additional term.

If you have a colleague that may be interested in this opportunity, we encourage you to share this information with them.

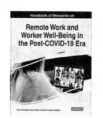

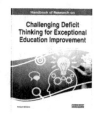

Printed in the United States
by Baker & Taylor Publisher Services